Reading Subaltern Studies

Critical History,
Contested Meaning and the
Globalization of South Asia

Reading Subaltern Studies

Critical History,
Contested Meaning and the
Globalization of South Asia

DAVID LUDDEN

Anthem Press

Anthem Press is an imprint of
Wimbledon Publishing Company
PO Box 9779
London
SW19 7QA

This edition first published by
Wimbledon Publishing Company 2002
Reprinted by arrangement with Permanent Black (© 2001)
and only available for sale outside South Asia.

British Library Cataloguing in Publication Data
Data available

Library of Congress in Publication Data
A catalogue record has been applied for

ISBN   (Hb) 1 84331 058 9
       (Pb) 1 84331 059 7

1 3 5 7 9 10 8 6 4 2

Printed by Bell & Bain Ltd, Glasgow

This book is dedicated
in grateful remembrance to
ASHOK RUDRA AND BURTON STEIN

Contents

III. Later Critiques in India

Acknowledgements

Full details of all sources for the articles reproduced in this book appear on the part-title fly-leaf which prefaces each of the three parts. Grateful acknowledgements are due to the authors, journals, and publishers who, singly or collectively, gave the permissions that made this book possible.

A Brief History of Subalternity

DAVID LUDDEN

SUBALTERN STUDIES[1] began its impressive career in England at the end of the 1970s, when conversations on subaltern themes among a small group of English and Indian historians led to a proposal to launch a new journal in India. Oxford University Press in New Delhi agreed instead to publish three volumes of essays called *Subaltern Studies: Writings on South Asian History and Society*. These appeared annually from 1982 and their success stimulated three more volumes in the next five years, all edited by Ranajit Guha. When he retired as editor in 1989, Ranajit Guha and eight collaborators[2] had written thirty-four of forty-seven essays in six *Subaltern Studies* volumes, as well as fifteen related books.[3] By 1993, the group he remembers as originally being 'an assortment of marginalised academics'[4] had sufficient international prestige for a Latin America Subaltern Studies Group to be inspired 'by this interdisciplinary organisation of South Asian scholars led by Ranajit Guha.'[5] Today, eleven (and counting) *Subaltern Studies* volumes have appeared. They include essays by forty-four authors whose allied publications approach two hundred, including translations in several languages,[6] yet the core group still includes eight founders[7] and Ranajit Guha's 'intellectual driving force'[8] is still visible.

Readings of *Subaltern Studies* began in India, where writing about Subaltern Studies began in book reviews. At first, each volume in the series was reviewed separately as a collection of essays, but by 1986 an accumulation of writing inside and outside the project had established a distinctive school of research whose adherents came to be called 'subalternists' or simply, 'subalterns.' Their seminal essays appeared in paperback in 1988, when *Selected Subaltern Studies* was published by Oxford University Press in New York and Oxford, edited by Ranajit Guha and Gayatri Chakravorty Spivak, with a foreword by Edward Said. By 1990 the historian Burton Stein could cite the growing interest in Subaltern Studies as one sign that the 1980s were 'a decade of historical efflorescence' in South Asian studies.[9] In the 1990s Subaltern Studies became a hot topic in academic circles on several continents; a weapon, magnet, target, lightning rod, hitching post, icon, gold mine, and fortress for scholars ranging across disciplines from history to political science, anthropology, sociology, literary criticism, and cultural studies.

I have compiled *Reading Subaltern Studies* to provide a non-subalternist introduction to Subaltern Studies.[10] The book brings together a dozen essays published in South Asia, Australia, Europe, and North America, from 1983 to 1997. Authors of these essays have all made their mark on the intellectual history of subalternity, each in their own way, in their own place and time, outside Subaltern Studies. Each interprets subalternity contextually. In the introduction, my main task is to outline a history of contextuality at the intersection of Subaltern Studies and its readership, and in doing this I also indicate how the subject of subalternity has changed over the years. My goal is not to formulate a critique, to assess the merits, or to measure the contribution of Subaltern Studies—let alone to unravel the inner history of the project—but rather to inform reading and discussion.

Subaltern Studies does not mean today what it meant in 1982, 1985, 1989, or 1993. How did this change occur? Intellectual environments have changed too much to allow us to measure cause-and-effect in particular acts of writing and reading. Change has occurred inside the Subaltern Studies project, but ambiguously, as we will see, and how much internal change is cause or effect of external change is unknowable, because inside and outside, subaltern subjects have been reinvented disparately. When approaching the intellectual history of subalternity, it will not do to imagine that *Subaltern Studies* dropped a weighty stone into a quiet pond, or to trace the influence of teachers and students, or to speculate that cutting-edge ideas have dispersed globally like news on the internet. This book proposes instead that a compact but complex history of reading and writing has constituted the subject of subalternity in a widening world of scholarship, where some readers accept and others reject the claim that Subaltern Studies represents the real substance of subalternity, even in India. The intellectual history of subalternity has emerged outside and in opposition to Subaltern Studies as much as inside it.

Academic work on subaltern themes quickly detached subalternity from its various inventors. Migrations of reading dispersed research on subaltern themes connected by circulating terminologies, arguments, and texts. As we will see, outside forces moulded the project itself, and its own institutional boundaries have always been permeable. Its internal coherence has been less intellectual than personal and more formal than substantive, being composed primarily by group loyalties and by invitations to join Subaltern Studies activities. Intellectual cohesiveness has never been a project priority, as the leaders often say, and it has appeared primarily in solidarity against critics. Outsiders have built outer walls for Subaltern Studies and landscaped its environment to dramatise its distinctiveness. Respondents, interlocutors, interpreters and translators have worked with Subaltern Studies material and redefined it by writing about it differently. Insiders have become outsiders. Outsiders have become insiders. Outsiders doing independent work on subaltern themes have embraced Subaltern Studies as a kindred project—for example, in a 1994 collection of essays in the *American Historical Review*.[11]

This book provides a reference guide for reading Subaltern Studies in a world context, and most of that context is outside India, though *Subaltern Studies* and essays reprinted here primarily concern India. Subaltern Studies occupies a subject position inside India, but is written for readers everywhere. Outside India, it is often the only brand of Indian history that readers know by name, but other brands are more powerful. National narratives, orientalist images, ethnic stereotypes, and Hindu majoritarianism are vastly more influential.[12] In opposition to these, subalterns have made little headway. Readings of

the Indian history contained in Subaltern Studies are inflected variously by national contexts in the world of globalisation. Peter Gran
argues, for instance, that in India, Subaltern Studies is *read against*
liberalism, Marxism, and 'religious fascism,' whereas in the US, its
'principal novelty' is its ability to represent India by being *read into*
ideologies of difference and otherness.[13] Though globalisation circu-
lates texts and ideas around the world, it nonetheless divides reading
environments. In the US, readers are generally encouraged to think
about cultures in essentialist terms, in the ethnographic present; to
see colonialism and nationalism as cultural phenomena; to disdain
Marxism; and to distance academic work from partisan politics, a
separation that bolsters academic credibility. But in South Asia, cultural change preoccupies scholars and activists, colonialism includes
capitalist imperialism (which is still at work in the world of globalisation), Marxism is alive, and most scholars embrace politics in one
form or another as a professional responsibility of citizenship. Such
contextual differences differentiate readings of subalternity. To map
the whole world of contested meanings lies far beyond the scope of
this book, which endeavours, more modestly, to locate Subaltern Studies in the context of relevant English language scholarship.

Historical Origins: Insurgency, Nationalism, and Social Theory

In the last forty years, scholars have produced countless studies of societies, histories, and cultures 'from below' which have dispersed
terms, methods, and bits of theory used in Subaltern Studies among
countless academic sites. Reflecting this trend, the 1993 edition of
The new shorter Oxford English dictionary included 'history' for the
first time as a context for defining 'subaltern.' The word has a long
past. In late-medieval English, it applied to vassals and peasants. By
1700, it denoted lower ranks in the military, suggesting peasant origins. By 1800, authors writing 'from a subaltern perspective' published novels and histories about military campaigns in India and
America; and G.R. Gleig (1796–1888), who wrote biographies of
Robert Clive, Warren Hastings, and Thomas Munro, mastered this
genre. The Great War provoked popular accounts of subaltern life

in published memoirs and diaries; and soon after the Russian Revolution, Antonio Gramsci (1891–1937) began to weave ideas about subaltern identity into theories of class struggle. Gramsci was not influential in the English-reading world, however, until Raymond Williams promoted his theory in 1977, well after translations of *The modern prince* (1957) and *Prison notebooks* (1966) had appeared.[14] By 1982, Gramsci's ideas were in wide circulation.[15] Ironically, though Gramsci himself was a communist activist whose prison notes were smuggled to Moscow for publication and translation, scholars outside or opposed to communist parties (and to Marxism) have most ardently embraced his English books (as well as those of the Frankfurt School).

Subaltern Studies deployed some of Gramsci's ideas[16] at a critical juncture in historical studies. By the late 1970s, a rapid decline in state-centred historical research had already occurred and social history 'from below' was flourishing. E.P. Thompson's 1963 book, *The making of the English working class,*[17] is often cited as an inspiration for the growing number of 'bottom up' studies of people whose history had been previously ignored.[18] By 1979, women's history was popular enough in the US to merit source books and guides to research.[19] In 1982, Eric Wolf published what can be called the first global history from below.[20] In South Asia, the history of subaltern groups was thriving, though they were not called that then.[21] In the 1970s, two new journals featuring studies of South Asian peasants had begun publishing in the US and UK.[22] Hundreds of titles on rural history had appeared.[23] In 1976, Eric Stokes announced the 'return of the peasant' to colonial history.[24] Guides to sources promoted more local research.[25]

Insurgency attracted special attention. In India, the 1857 centenary had stimulated new histories of rebellion, some directly inspired by rebels like Kattabomman Nayakkar,[26] whose epic of resistance to British rule had been reproduced in many popular media, including cinema.[27] Romantic heroism attached to old rebel histories, but in addition, the 1960s and 1970s raised concern about revolution in the present. Even the Indian Home Ministry feared revolution.[28] In this context, more scholars took up studies of insurrection. N.G. Ranga and L. Natarajan pioneered this field, decades before,[29] and elements of its intellectual history go back to the 1920s, when early Indian studies of Indian rebels sought to recuperate insurgent mentalities.[30] Indigenous Indian theories of peasant revolt had emerged in the 1930s, among communists and in the Kisan Sabha,[31] but in the 1960s, the academic study of insurrection came into its own, when Hamza Alavi theorised peasant revolution,[32] Stephen Fuchs explored tribal messianism,[33] J.C. Jha studied Kol rebellions,[34] and Muin-ud-din Ahmad Khan studied early Fara'Idi rebels in Bengal.[35] In the 1970s, the upward trend in research on popular insurgency accelerated: highlights include work by K.K. Sengupta, B.B. Chaudhuri, and S.K. Sen on rebels in Bengal;[36] V. Raghavaiah's work on tribal revolts (published by the Andhra Rastra Adimajati Sevak Sangh);[37] Ghanshyam Shah's early studies of Gujarat;[38] a flurry of work on Mappillai revolts in Malabar;[39] Kathleen Gough and Hari Sharma's path-breaking *Imperialism and revolution in South Asia*;[40] and A.R. Desai's masterful collection, *Peasant struggles in India.*[41]

When the founders of Subaltern Studies first met in England at the end of the 1970s, they were surrounded by decades of research on history from below and on insurgency in colonial India. Sumit Sarkar used it to write a new kind of national history text with popular movements at centre stage; and his landmark 1983 book, *Modern India, 1885–1947,*[42] also conveys the intensity of debates at the time by starting off with a thumping critique of historians (mostly at Cambridge University) who comprised the so-called Cambridge School of South Asian history. Following the appearance of Anil Seal's *The emergence of Indian nationalism: Competition and collaboration in the later nineteenth century,*[43] they had been hard at work unpacking the politics of Indian nationalism at the local, regional, and national levels.[44] In 1979, Tapan Raychaudhuri captured his critique of their work in the phrase, 'animal politics,'[45] but we can now appreciate that Cambridge scholars had opened the historical study of political institutions in South Asia by exploring the agency of individuals, formation of cliques, and power of specific class interests inside political parties and factions.[46] They had also begun to integrate studies of politics *before and after* 1947. Their timing was critical, for a Cambridge 'school' developed around the study of Indian national politics just when disillusionment with India's national government was deepening. A major transition in political culture was under way, which entailed new interpretations of the national past; and not only in India, as we will see. At the same time, the international expansion of historical studies fostered new schools of specialisation that defined themselves by opposition to one another.[47] Its critics actually named the Cambridge School and made it seem more a 'school' than it was. Provocation became its legacy. Nationality had become a pivotal subject of contention and Cambridge had sparked controversy about two questions that stood out above others: What is the role of culture in nationalism? and: What is the relationship between states and popular politics? On both questions, debates raged in the early days of the Iranian revolution, when Mujahedin fought Soviets in Afghanistan and Antonio Gramsci, Jurgen Habermas, and Michel Foucault were beginning to influence English writers. American historians castigated Cambridge inattention to Indian culture at a time when a 'cultural school' of Indian history was developing around Bernard S. Cohn at the University of Chicago.[48] Indian historians castigated Cambridge inattention to national ideals and popular forces. Cambridge had drained radicalism and national resurgence from Indian political history just when they were attracting more attention from scholars who were concerned to chart new national trajectories.

Similar academic oppositions occurred elsewhere. One telling debate concerned Southeast Asia, where James C. Scott argued that anticolonial revolutions expressed an insurgent peasantry's moral economy and Samuel Popkin countered that rational calculations motivated competing rebel groups.[49] Scott's approach—adapted from E.P. Thompson and George Rude[50] and drawing liberally from theories of peasant struggles against global capitalism[51]—supported the idea that popular insurgency in British India emerged from enraged indigenous moral sensibilities. Sumit Sarkar argued on these lines to show that autonomous popular movements shaped Indian nationalism by provoking dialogue and tension with national leaders that produced various contingent outcomes. By contrast, Cambridge historians echoed Popkin and political anthropologist F.G. Bailey,[52] who insisted that politics operate inside institutions that organise competition for power. From this theoretical perspective, class and other interest groups fought for power under the banner of nationalism at every level of the colonial system, and after 1947, they continued to struggle from above and below inside national regimes.

Historians were dividing along schisms in social theory into opposing schools that separated society and culture from state institutions and political economy. *Subaltern Studies* dramatised this division. So did Benedict Anderson's book, first published in 1983, *Imagined communities: Reflections on the origin and spread of nationalism*,[53] which abandoned class analysis, ignored state politics, and argued that cultural forces produced national identity and passion. By 1983, scholars were writing two kinds of national history: one, a people's history filled with native culture and popular insurgency; the other, an official history filled with élites and political parties. Nations and states were separating like oil and water. So were culture and political economy. A new kind of nationality was coalescing in a separate domain of popular experience, which was becoming increasingly isolated from state institutions and national élites.

But even so, when Ranajit Guha announced, in 1982, that 'the politics of the people . . . [form] . . . an autonomous domain,'[54] even those who agreed with him—like Sumit Sarkar, who soon joined the project—still assumed that diverging domains of nationality were connected. After all, this connection sustained the possibility of radical change, even revolution. In the 1970s, this *possibility* had become a serious problem, because state institutions had remained substantially *unchanged* despite many decades of popular insurgency, nationalist agitation, and tumultuous independence not only in 1947 (India and Pakistan) and 1948 (Sri Lanka) but also in the 1971 Bangladesh liberation war. Modern states did not prevent rebellion, but insurgency had not become revolution. Why did nationalism provoke revolution in China and Vietnam, but not India? How do oppressed people take over governments? How do nations redesign states? Why not revolution in South Asia? These were pressing questions.

Opposing theories served opposing schools. In 1966, Barrington Moore had explained the lack of revolution in British India by accepting the wisdom of Indology and social theory that India's caste culture and self-contained village societies made revolution impossible.[55] Traditionally localised social hierarchies formed a fragmented political base, impervious to class mobilisation, which the modern urban bourgeoisie had incorporated into a national system of electoral representation.[56] Bolstering this argument, Louis Dumont's influential *Homo hierarchicus: The caste system and its implications* (published in English in 1966) presented a comprehensive model of Indian civilisation based on the logic of caste.[57] In this perspective, India's indigenous culture can sustain a diverse, fragmented, electoral democracy, but all insurgency is self-limiting. Class conflict could never engender revolutionary class solidarity. In fierce opposition to this line of argument, Hamza Alavi, A.R. Desai, Kathleen Gough and others asserted that theories of caste are ruling class ideology. High-caste élites had always needed coercive power to keep low castes, peasants, workers, and tribal groups in place. Élites needed states to suppress revolution. National politics had always included both popular insurgency and élite conservatism, struggling against one another, producing conflict-ridden political movements and state regimes. Despite the lack of revolution, significant social change, opposition to caste oppression, and class struggles by low-caste and untouchable (Dalit) workers did occur, and in places like Tanjavur district, Tamil Nadu, local struggles led by communists were potentially revolutionary.[58]

Shifting Ground: Nations, Politics, and Globalisation

Subaltern Studies joined debates about insurgency and nationality[59] at the breach between popular unrest and state power. The breach was widening at the time, in part because, despite rampant crises, dominant state institutions had managed to survive as though secure inside a mountain fortress high above the plains.[60] Looking back from 1980 into the decades before 1947, historians were busy exploring *dis*connections between official nationalism and popular movements. Muslims had acquired a separate political history[61] that became more prominent in the context of Hindu majoritarianism.[62] Regional movements became prominent—and most thoroughly studied by Cambridge historians[63]—after the 1956 reorganisation of Indian states along linguistic lines.[64] But communalism and regionalism did not attract Subaltern Studies,[65] which instead focused on the separation of political strata. D.N. Dhanagare, Majid Siddiqi, and Gyanendra

Pandey had already published books on splits between the Indian National Congress and peasant movements.[66] Sumit Sarkar's *Modern India* gave workers' and peasants' movements more autonomous political space than any history text had ever done before. Ranajit Guha's *Elementary aspects of peasant insurgency* depicted tribal revolts as completely separate from nationalism, inside a subaltern space, below. *Subaltern Studies* entered the academic scene by asserting the complete autonomy of lower class insurgency.

The breach between popular and national history then expanded to vast proportions in the 1980s and 1990s. This changing intellectual climate has yet to be adequately historicised and can only be outlined here in the sketchiest manner. One key feature stands out when we recall that histories 'from below' had originally emerged inside an intellectual fusion of historical research and national politics. Books like A.R. Desai's *Peasant struggles in India* (1979) and *Agrarian struggles in India after independence* (1986) not only promoted the study of agrarian upheavals in the past, they also opposed the technocratic developmentalism of the Green Revolution and the *status quo* politics of cultural traditionalism.[67] In South Asia, this kind of scholarship goes back to the 1870s, when a nationalist *academic* critique of empire inspired national *politics and history* at the same time. It is easy to forget how radical the intellectual work of the early Indian nationalists was in its day.[68] A third generation of nationalists, including Jawaharlal Nehru and Mahatma Gandhi, built upon a long legacy of critical scholarship. Nehru used history to inform his politics, the way Gandhi used philosophy, and in 1930, when he became President of the All-India Congress Committee, Nehru announced an enduring theme in historical research by saying, 'the great poverty and misery of the Indian People are due not only to foreign exploitation in India but also to the economic structure of society, which the alien rulers support so that their exploitation may continue.'[69] Such pronouncements at the apex of nationalism stimulated many histories from below, which engaged the past to inform national debates about land reform, planning, local democracy, farm finance, industrialisation, and other topics of hot dispute.[70] In this intellectual environment, history 'below' embraced history 'above.' Gaps and failures separating levels and types of national activity seemed to be conjunctural problems to be overcome within a unified national history.

After 1980, an expanding gulf between the histories of peoples and states ripped many old bonds between academics and politics. Scholars who claimed to speak for people who had been left out of nationalism marched away from scholars who continued to fuse popular history with national politics. Ranajit Guha accounts for his own alienation from nationalism by citing the early seventies' 'drama of Naxalite clashes with the organs of the state and the violence of counterinsurgency measures.'[71] But more importantly for many others, Indira Gandhi's Emergency in 1975 made the Indian state blatantly dictatorial.[72] As new popular movements arose from many quarters in India—communal,[73] regional,[74] and expressing radical aspirations among women, peasants, workers, and tribal groups[75]—old nationalism lost legitimacy and the Left and the Right fought for its legacy. Popular resistance to state power became a prominent academic theme in the 1980s. In 1986, James C. Scott's *Weapons of the weak: Everyday forms of peasant resistance*[76] announced a broad move away from studies of revolution into the analysis of localised, personal resistance to the power of élites and states. Foucault's influence was spreading. By the 1990s, an array of scholars inside and outside Subaltern Studies had made everyday resistance a basic feature of life in South Asia.[77]

As the Cold War came to an end, critical attacks on the public sector widened what many scholars began to see as a permanent rift between people and states. Ronald Reagan and Margaret Thatcher fought to 'get the state off our backs.' The World Bank and IMF forced structural adjustment on poor countries to open their markets. Global capitalism fought states for power over national resources.[78] Development theory sidelined governments and valorised non-governmental organisations. Socialist regimes died from various causes; what became known as their 'failure' came to symbolise state failure generally. In India, a new derogatory phrase entered political discourse, 'Nehruvian socialism.' Critics of state-led development stood up for the interests and cultures of the poor and marginalised.[79] Constraints exerted by state power—theorised most trenchantly by

Foucault—were discovered in development institutions once thought progressive.[80] James C. Scott's third book made 'seeing like a state' inefficient and implicitly oppressive.[81] A critique of the modern logic supporting state authority ran through intellectual streams of globalisation as national boundaries were collapsing under transnational flows; as Indian economists pushed for India's liberalisation from Yale and Columbia; as supporters for Khalistan, Eelam, and Hindutva raised funds in England, Canada, and the US; and as global media produced glossy images of the Indian middle class for Indian consumption. Moishe Postone summarised the changing historical context by saying that a new historical phase began, sometime after 1973, 'apparently characterised by the weakening and partial dissolution of the institutions and centres of power that had been at the heart of the state-interventionist mode [of capitalist development]: national state bureaucracies, industrial labour unions, and physically centralised, state dependent capitalist firms.'

> Those institutions have been undermined in two directions: by the emergence of a new plurality of social groupings, organisations, movements, parties, regions, and subcultures on the one hand and by a process of globalisation and concentration of capital on a new, very abstract level that is far removed from immediate experience and is apparently outside the effective control of the state machinery on the other.[82]

In this new context, the nation was being reconfigured, reimagined, re-theorised. Subaltern Studies became an original site for a new kind of history from below, a people's history free of national constraints, a post-nationalist reimagining of the Indian nation on the underside, at the margins, outside nationalism. Subaltern India emerged in fragments during the 1980s and 1990s,[83] and it changed form, as we will see; but from the outset, it rejected official nationalism and developed transnationally, as did its readership and its critical appreciation. It is the first international collaboration to make a sustained impact on South Asian studies, and its ideas are intricately tangled in recent world trends. In 1982, Ranajit Guha's assertion that the Indian nation had failed 'to come into its own' evoked failed revolution, but by 1990, it had new connotations. The fragmentation of the Soviet Union, Eastern Europe, and the Balkans was widely said to be the failure of Marxism, communism, and socialism. Nehru's regime was said to have failed the Indian nation. The failure of the modern state pervaded academic writing. New approaches to nationality came forward. In 1983, Benedict Anderson's *Imagined communities* sought to redress the failure of communists and Marxists to understand nationalism; and the rising prominence of his book in academic circles reflects a broad intellectual trend: political nationalism lost its grip on the historical imagination as nations were reinvented as 'imagined communities.'[84]

Subaltern Studies also became entangled with efforts to reimagine history itself, which became more compelling at the Cold War's end. Thomas Haskell repeated a popular, typically hyperbolic, American cliché about this turning point for history when he said, 'The bloody contest between capitalism and socialism unexpectedly came to an end in 1989 after a struggle that gripped the world for a century and a half.'[85] Eric Hobsbawm called 1989 the end of 'the age of extremes' and said about the 1990s that 'citizens of the *fin de siecle* tapped their way through the global fog that surrounded them, into the third millennium . . . certain . . . that an era of history had ended.' But, he said, 'They knew very little else.'[86] Epistemologies and ways of knowing history came under scrutiny as social theory took a linguistic, literary turn. Cultural studies became increasingly prominent. Cultural criticism became cultural politics.[87] Discursively deconstructing cultural power and recuperating everyday resistance became compelling projects for scholars who discovered the failures and betrayals of modernity, positivism, and the Enlightenment. Old empirical certainties of modernisation, capitalist development, and national progress were disassembled in the radical newness of post-modern and post-colonial writing.[88] The politics of language, media, and representations came of age in a world of globalisation.

Inventing Originality: Rejection, Crossroads, and New Departures

The original substance of *Subaltern Studies* emerged from work-in-progress in the late 1970s. Eleven authors in the first three volumes—Shahid Amin, David Arnold, Gautam Bhadra, Dipesh Chakrabarty, N.K. Chandra, Partha Chatterjee, Arvind N. Das, David Hardiman, Stephen Henningham, Gyanendra Pandey, and Sumit Sarkar—were doing close empirical work in social, economic, and political history. The leader of the project, Ranajit Guha, was different. A 'difference of generations,' he says, 'sets me apart . . . by at least twenty-five years,'[89] but four other collaborators had also published books before 1982.[90] His academic work sets him apart as sharply. His first book, *A rule of property for Bengal: An essay on the idea of permanent settlement*,[91] was an intellectual history of colonial land policy.[92] His published work in the 1970s concerned intellectual trends surrounding one nineteenth-century text,[93] and his second monograph, *Elementary aspects of peasant insurgency* distilled data from studies of peasant revolts in the colonial period to evoke a theory of subaltern resistance. Since 1982, his major publications have appeared first in *Subaltern Studies*, with which he is most personally identified. In his accumulated writings, colonialism appears to be a single, unified, discursive structure of power inside a vast ethnographic present; and state institutions, texts, personnel, and discourse, including those of the nationalist movement, stand in stark opposition to subaltern India and its indigenous culture from the first day of British rule down to the rupture of *Subaltern Studies*.[94] Ranajit Guha might be said to be the Louis Dumont of colonialism, which in his writing attains a comprehensive power like that of caste in *Homo hierarchicus*.

By contrast, seven scholars listed by Ranajit Guha as members of the project since 1982 (Shahid Amin, David Arnold, Gautam Bhadra, Dipesh Chakrabarty, Partha Chatterjee, David Hardiman, and Gyanendra Pandey) began their careers doing specialised research on Uttar Pradesh, Bengal, Gujarat, and Tamil Nadu. Their continued collaboration has stabilised the project but they have worked separately and also published widely outside *Subaltern Studies*. They have not engaged in joint research or writing. A good metaphor would be a flock flying in formation, each author with his own compass, but all in tune. It would seem that over the years, their compass bearings have been set collectively in tune with Ranajit Guha's. They have flown collectively into currents of theory and research that were more his home territory than theirs when the project began. In addition to this close-knit group, the project includes an unruly band of thirty-six (and counting) other authors who have contributed essays to

Subaltern Studies. They collaborate loosely. They include outsiders who became Collective members, insiders who left the project, and students who came up through the ranks. Each brings something specific. To cite a few exemplars, Sumit Sarkar stands for the project's early commitment to social history; Gayatri Chakravorty Spivak launched a literary turn in the mid-1980s (followed by Sudipta Kaviraj, Amitav Ghosh, Gyan Prakash, and others); and Julie Stephens, Susie Tharu, Kamala Visweswaran, Tejaswini Niranjana, among others, brought gender into view.[95]

Subaltern Studies reinvented subalternity. In 1982, the term 'subaltern' had little meaning in South Asian studies. Its conceptual emptiness at the time was underlined when Ranajit Guha quoted the *Concise Oxford dictionary* on the first page of *Subaltern Studies I* and then remained silent on Gramsci's use of the term. Readers who responded to early volumes focused particularly on problems of defining 'subaltern' in relation to Gramsci, which led to lively discussions outside *Subaltern Studies.*[96] But the project actually made itself original by divorcing itself from Gramsci to invent a distinctively *Indian* subalternity.[97] Guha also opened *Subaltern Studies* by declaring a clean break with most Indian historians, announcing the project's ambition 'to rectify the élitist bias' in a field 'dominated by élitism—colonialist élitism and bourgeois-nationalist élitism.' He did not elaborate, but his colonial élitists surely came from Oxford and Cambridge and his bourgeois-nationalist élites must include almost everyone else. Where the Marxists fit into his picture is unclear, but his brief discussion indicates that he believed colonialism spawned all historical writing about India before the rupture announced by *Subaltern Studies.* He suggests the same thing in *Elementary aspects of peasant insurgency*: it begins by asserting that, 'The historiography of peasant insurgency in colonial India is as old as colonialism itself' (p. 1); it then describes the 'discourse on peasant insurgency' as 'a discourse of power' under the Raj (p. 3); and it proceeds to cite interventions by Gramsci and Hobsbawm without mentioning Indian histories of peasant insurgency. Subaltern Studies launched itself with an act of rejection, denying South Asia's previous 'history from below.' The importance of this opening act is suggested by its republication in two anthologies of selected essays, in 1988 and 1997.[98] Subalternity thus became a novelty, invented *de novo* by Subaltern Studies, which gave old terms new meanings and marked a new beginning for historical studies. Domination, subordination, hegemony, resistance, revolt, and other old concepts could now be subalternised. By definition, subalternity had been ignored by all scholars in the past; thus, all the old research became élitist.[99]

Even readers who applauded Subaltern Studies found two features troubling. First and foremost, the new substance of subalternity emerged only on the underside of a rigid theoretical barrier between 'élite' and 'subaltern,' which resembles a concrete slab separating upper and lower space in a two-storey building.[100] This hard dichotomy alienated subalternity from *social histories* that include more than two storeys or which move among them; and not only histories rendered through the lens of class analysis, because subaltern social mobility disappeared along with class differentiation. Second, because subaltern politics was confined theoretically to the lower storey, it could not threaten a political structure. This alienated subalternity from *political histories* of popular movements and alienated subaltern groups from organised, transformative politics, in the past *and* in the present.[101] Not surprisingly, a rift soon opened between Subaltern Studies and Indian scholars committed to class analysis, political action, and popular histories of nationalism. Some critical responses appear in the first four reprints in this volume.

The project launched itself a second time, in 1985. David Hardiman (1986) called this critical juncture a 'crossroads.' Choices were made. In 1997, Brinda Bose alludes to it in her review of *Subaltern Studies IX.* Calling *Subaltern Studies* 'a touchstone for research in South Asian history, society and culture,' and reporting that 'each volume is ensured its loyal readership,' she says that readership 'has expanded beyond the horizons of students of (subaltern) history, which was where it all began many years back.'

> In recognition of this shift—or broadening—the more recent volumes have brought together essays that are no longer confined to the discipline of history, displaying, as the editors of this collection describe it, the Collective's 'engagements with more contemporary problems and theoretical

formations.' This expansion of critical and theoretical scope has benefited the fast growing body of South Asian sociocultural studies, providing it with the (predictable, but) dependable subalternist slant, routed, usefully, through history.[102]

Kate Currie called the move that Brinda Bose calls 'broadening' a shift *away* from studies of *subaltern politics* in the vein of E.P. Thompson and Antonio Gramsci, and *towards* cultural history, critical theory, and *representations of subaltern subjectivity* in the vein of Michel Foucault and Jacques Derrida.[103] Politics and representation are two aspects of subalternity, which historians study in records of action and discourse. Two sides of one coin, they both evoke anti-hegemonic possibilities.[104] In the 1980s, the gaze of the project shifted from one side of the coin to the other; and Hardiman's report from the 'crossroads' notwithstanding, project members today see no discontinuity in this shift. Ranajit Guha indirectly confirmed that a second point departure did occur by saying the project began 'roughly' in 1986 and by omitting from his account of the early years two authors whose approaches were most clearly at odds in the mid-1980s—bright signposts at the crossroads—Sumit Sarkar and Gayatri Chakravorty Spivak.[105]

We can suppose that before 1985 no consensus definition of subalternity had emerged in the project. Experiments were ongoing. Subalternity remained a fluid substance inside its two-storey structure. Then, in 1985, *Subaltern Studies IV* introduced the cultural perspectives of two prominent, US-based scholars, Bernard S. Cohn and Gayatri Chakravorty Spivak, who explored the language and textuality of discursive power, which Partha Chatterjee and Ranajit Guha, in particular, but also Dipesh Chakrabarty and some others had discussed in earlier volumes. *Subaltern Studies IV* also opened with a blunt statement of Ranajit Guha's annoyance with outside critics,[106] and ended with Dipesh Chakrabarty's 'Invitation to a dialogue,' the first extended response to critics in the pages of *Subaltern Studies* (specifically, to *Singh *et al.* 1984). Thus it appears, as Hardiman indicates, that the project was forming its intellectual identity as the first three volumes of *Subaltern Studies* were leading into a second three. What outsiders wrote, particularly in some essays reprinted here, seems to have added pressure and provided a focal point for oppositions that helped to resolve internal ambiguities. Dipesh Chakrabarty's closing essay in *Subaltern Studies IV* indicates the na-ture of this resolution by affirming their basic concern with 'the thorny question of "consciousness" ' and by defining subalternity as 'the composite culture of resistance to and acceptance of domination and hierarchy.' This approximates an official definition, but Chakra-barty also says that members of the Editorial Collective 'are perhaps far more united in their rejection of certain academic positions and tendencies than in their acceptance of alternatives.'[107]

Subaltern consciousness had always been a critical feature of subalternity; and in 1987, Ajit K. Chaudhury reiterated that, 'The focus of *Subaltern Studies* is on the consciousness of the subaltern classes, specifically peasants.'[108] But how is consciousness to be studied historically? What kinds of sources, methods, and reasoning should we use? Around these questions, a shift in orientation certainly occurred. In 1988, Edward Said's Foreword to *Selected Subaltern Studies* described an academic tendency outside India, in the world of global circulation, which was being embraced by the project, saying, 'this group of scholars is a self-conscious part of the vast post-colonial cultural and critical effort that would also include novelists like Salman Rushdie, Garcia Marquez,' and others, as well as 'poets like Faiz Ahmad Faiz, Mahmud Darwish, Aime Cesaire, theoreticians and political philosophers . . . and a whole host of other figures. . . .' (pp. ix–x). Gayatri Chakravorty Spivak's Introduction to *Selected Subaltern Studies* (from *Subaltern Studies IV*) cites 'the colonial subject' as the basic concern of theorisation and says, 'The Subaltern Studies Collective . . . generally perceive their task as making a theory of consciousness or culture rather than specifically a theory of change' (p. 4). Post-colonial cultural criticism and literary theory had embraced Subaltern Studies.

After 1986, the substance of subalternity remained fluid and mixed, but it contained much less material drawn from struggles waged by particular subaltern groups in colonial India and much more literary evidence concerning colonial constructions of culture and power. In the first four volumes of *Subaltern Studies*, twenty essays treat peasant, worker, and tribal struggles; in the next six volumes, only five.

The 'subaltern classes, specifically peasants' gave way in practice to the textuality of colonialism and resistance. This coincided with a shift in the work of Subaltern Studies' collaborators who had begun their academic careers doing research on specific groups. The project's underlying theory may have remained constant, but constancy—in its increasingly global context—expanded the field of subalternity into the transnational study of colonialism. This was Ranajit Guha's academic home ground, and on it the intellectual continuity of the project was constructed. A starting point for the shift-in-continuity can be found in Guha's seminal essay, 'The prose of counter-insurgency' (*SSII*) which demonstrated how élite repression lurked in official accounts of popular struggles. Colonial representations had begun to overwhelm subaltern activity in his insistence that a critique of colonial discourse is the starting point for Subaltern Studies. Guha consolidates the continuity shift in his final essay for the last volume that he edited (*SSVI*), 'Dominance without hegemony and its historiography,' which provides a comprehensive template for Subaltern Studies under the discursive power of colonialism. In the interim, he had indicated in his introduction to a collection of essays by Bernard S. Cohn how Subaltern Studies would be wedded to anthropological history by an insistence on the primacy of opposition between 'indigenous' and 'colonial' knowledge.[109]

The meaning of subalternity in Subaltern Studies shifted as the framework of study increasingly stressed the clash of unequal cultures under colonialism and the dominance of colonial modernity over India's resistant, indigenous culture. Subalterns in India became fragments of a nation; their identity and consciousness reflected India's colonial subjugation. This approach has organised an impressive collection of enduring scholarship on colonial texts, vernacular resistance, bureaucracy, police, factories, communalism, ethnography, prisons, medicine, ethnography, science, and related topics. It has also enabled Subaltern Studies to speak as India's subaltern voice. Methodologically, recuperating subaltern subjectivity entails the analytical and rhetorical liberation of Indian culture from its domination by the colonial archive and by modernity. Ingenious methods for uncovering fragments of subaltern nationality became the project's particular speciality. Critical readings of colonial texts, oral histories, and ethnographic techniques are employed to reveal India's cultural roots in subaltern subjectivity. Subaltern Studies thus becomes a post-colonial critique of modern, European, and Enlightenment episte-mologies. A new kind of cultural essence for India is found in iconic residues of hidden identities, expressions of difference, and misunder-stood mentalities.

The originality of Subaltern Studies came to be its striving to re-write the nation outside the state-centred national discourse that replicates colonial power/knowledge in a world of globalisation. This new kind of national history consists of dispersed moments and frag-ments, which subaltern historians seek in the ethnographic present of colonialism. Writing such history constitutes subversive cultural politics because it exposes forms of power/knowledge that oppress subaltern peoples and also because it provides liberating alternatives. In this project, historians and post-colonial critics stand together against colonial modernity to secure a better future for subaltern peo-ples, learning to hear them, allowing them to speak, talking back to powers that marginalise them, documenting their past. A liberated imagined community can only come into its own, in this view, in sub-altern language and memory, which historians can strive to recuper-ate, however partially and tentatively. For this project, historians need to shake themselves free of modernity's master narrative and from the shackles of chronological, linear time. Subaltern Studies' growing diversity of research now coheres like the new cultural history.[110] Its search for hidden pasts evokes textual criticism, fragmentary testimo-nies, and lost moments, to restore the integrity of indigenous histories that appear naturally in non-linear, oral, symbolic, vernacular, and dramatic forms.[111]

Reading Dialogically:
Context, Assimilation, and Critique

Essays about Subaltern Studies reprinted here represent a small but useful sample. This book is only a starting place for reading subalternity historically. The two appendices list the contents of ten *Subaltern Studies* volumes and provide additional bibliography (to supplement footnotes) drawn primarily from an excellent Subaltern Studies web-site.[112] With this material in hand, readers can explore Subaltern Studies and read it dialogically to find what is said and not said, visible and missing. I have organised readings into three groups to suggest one opening gambit for strategic reading.

The first group of essays—by Javeed Alam, Sangeeta Singh *et al.*, Ranajit Das Gupta, and Binay Bhushan Chaudhuri—indicates critical assimilation in India before 1986. Though reviews appeared outside India in the early years,[113] most readings occurred in India, where reviewers were most concerned with the contribution of individual *Subaltern Studies* essays to Indian historical writing at the time. Problematic relations with Marxism, on the one hand, and national history, on the other, stand out. The political autonomy of subalternity was hotly contested as a general claim and in specific circumstances, but reviewers indicate that there was plenty of room for *Subaltern Studies* in the Indian historical profession, where its authors already had a place. Their intervention was in tune with contemporary concerns and most critical comments were more requests for clarification than hostile attacks. But at the crossroads of the project in the mid-1980s, harsh critics preoccupied the project, most of all, critics in *Social Scientist*, an influential Marxist journal. Critics' arguments that subaltern *political activity* could not be detached empirically or theoretically from 'élites'—even when detached from nationalist institutions—seem to have hit home; as apparently did critical quotes from authoritative Marxists like Gramsci and Rodney Hilton. These may have combined to irk Ranajit Guha and to induce Dipesh Chakrabarty to clarify that the Subaltern Studies' approach to 'the thorny question of "consciousness" ' centred on 'the composite culture of resistance to and acceptance of domination and hierarchy.'[114] Since he made this clarification, Chakrabarty has remained the subalternist most concerned with Marxism. Binay Bhushan Chaudhuri, the dean of agrarian historians in India, called his 'Invitation to a dialogue' 'lucid' and 'convincing,' again indicating that major scholars concerned with subaltern themes made room for Subaltern Studies in India without accepting it whole cloth.

The second set of essays, all published outside India, represents a decade when readers incorporated Subaltern Studies into what I call, for lack of a better phrase, 'the global academy,' represented here by academic institutions in the English-reading world. Subaltern globalisation took off at the project's second point of departure. In 1986, Rosalind O'Hanlon discussed the project at a Cambridge workshop on popular culture, a field in which Subaltern Studies was rapidly embraced. Her reprinted essay first appeared in 1988, the same year that Edward Said introduced the project to 'the Western reader,'[115] calling it a collection of post-colonial histories,[116] to flag another new audience. Interestingly, O'Hanlon's essay, one of the first major review articles of Subaltern Studies outside India,[117] appeared in *Modern Asian Studies*, the venerable house journal of the Cambridge School. Having said that 'it is widely accepted that the project of *Subaltern Studies* has provided the most provocative and interesting intervention in recent years,' she goes on to consider both the project and its critics. Thus putting insiders and outsiders into one Indian intellectual space, she locates the origin of their 'confused' dialogue in a shared Marxist heritage, which she implies imparted to 'the dichotomy between domination and resistance . . . all the marks of dominant discourse, in its insistence that resistance itself should necessarily take the virile form of a deliberate and violent onslaught.' She prefers Foucault's approach to power and echoes Scott's *Weapons of the weak* by exhorting historians 'to look for resistances . . . dispersed in fields that we do not conventionally associate with the political.' She thus points in the very direction that Subaltern Studies was moving in at the time, in tune with a broad academic shift into studies of everyday struggles, where gender assumed special significance— though women were then missing in Subaltern Studies, as she noted. O'Hanlon introduced the project to readers as a step in the right direction towards post-Marxist studies of popular culture that take power and resistance seriously.

A few years later, Jim Masselos had all six volumes edited by Ranajit Guha in front of him when he set out to criticise subalternity as a condition of rebellion and resistant victimisation. The subaltern seemed to him a stereotype of real subaltern people, though he valued the Indian history in Subaltern Studies. Like O'Hanlon, he pitched his arguments to an audience of readers broader than Indian historians. Subaltern Studies called for such treatment, as other schools of Indian history had not. Masselos expressed discomfort with the idea that power and resistance inhabit every nook and cranny of social existence which had become familiar during Foucault's rising popularity. He calls 'the subaltern . . . a creation, a reification of historians,' which 'combines a polarised social category with the mentality of opposition,' and which he distinguishes from real subaltern people, in the real world, like those studied by French historians of mentalities, with whom he approvingly associates Sumit Sarkar. He rejects Subaltern Studies' theoretical identification of subordinate social status with mentalities of resistance and literary penchant for dramatising class opposition, both of which he traces to 'the activist world of the late 1960s and early 1970s.' What he dislikes in Subaltern Studies he also dislikes in Marx, Gramsci, and other Marxists. In reality, he says, subaltern 'acts of resistance link up with, interact with, intersect with what is happening around them.' In his view, any theory of subaltern autonomy would tend to erase real subalterns from history.

I would say that Subaltern Studies arrived in the global mainstream in 1993, after Ranajit Guha's alignment with Bernard S. Cohn had made the project's cultural critique of colonialism an elixir of new vitality for American-style cultural history. In 1992, heated exchanges followed a programmatic assertion by Gyan Prakash that Subaltern Studies had superseded older modes of history writing by pursuing post-colonial theory into the Indian past.[118] Then controversy subsided. The project came to mean different but relatively uncontroversial things to different kinds of people (especially on the Leftish end of the political spectrum) in various disciplines. A boom also occurred in the number of international publications by core collaborators, including many reprints from *Subaltern Studies*; and more new authors contributed to *Subaltern Studies*, expanding its disciplinary range (as noticed by Brinda Bose). K. Sivaramakrishnan notes the dimming of the past at the start of his essay. He then uses both the project and its critics to discuss the disciplinary intersection of history and anthropology, where Bernard S. Cohn had been a pioneer and Sivaramakrishnan represents a new generation of scholars who want to bring material concerns with the environment and political economy back into the picture.[119] Frederick Cooper wrote his essay for a forum in the *American Historical Review*, which called for him to read Subaltern Studies in the context of African history. That assignment itself indicates an arrival of sorts, but Cooper makes Subaltern Studies work for him as a vehicle for discussing distinctive features of Africa's historical scholarship. Florencia Mallon did the same for Latin America. Thus academic contexts for global reading were becoming more diverse; and readings, more detached from the history of the project. Subalternity was becoming multicultural.

Henry Schwarz leads back to India, where the project remained firmly grounded; and in India, he points to a specific, literary context: cultural history as composed by Calcutta intellectuals. In the book chapter reprinted here, he considers Ranajit Guha as an author in and of Indian cultural history; and in this double context, he gives subalternity yet another new meaning, as metaphor. In Guha's 'Dominance without hegemony and its historiography,' this metaphor evokes a cultural imperative to recover a truly indigenous history, a native paradigm, 'which has perpetually lain unrecognised beneath the veneer of historiographical appropriation, whether by outright colonists or by well-intentioned inheritors of colonialist thought.' We can thus read the two-storey structure of subalternity as being essentially that of colonialism, because colonialism sustained and separated two paradigms, two modes of being, one Indian and one foreign. Between these two, the double consciousness of India's middle class was formed; and between these two, politically engaged intellectuals were torn—a formulation that recalls Ashis Nandy's influential book, *The intimate enemy: Loss and recovery of self under colonialism*, published in 1983.[120] Guha's prose thus becomes a literary moment inside a cultural predicament, and at the crossroads of Subaltern Studies in the mid-1980s, choices were made: the otherness of subalternity became a place on a bifurcated metaphorical map, a home for identity and solidarity against the permanence of colonialism in the world of globalisation.

The last group of essays indicates that inside India other subalternities developed in other struggles. K. Balagopal is one of many scholar-activists who focus research on everyday subaltern politics. His essay considers events in the late 1980s in Adilabad district, in Andhra Pradesh, and in this context, he considers the work of David Hardiman, one subalternist who stayed close to the ground in his research on tribal groups and moneylenders in Gujarat.[121] Even so, Balagopal finds that Hardiman's subaltern autonomy is unrealistic because it ignores leadership and the need for intellectual tools that cross élite–subaltern divisions. Naxalite communists remain prominent in Andhra agrarian politics, where conflict at the intersection of tribal self-assertion and state coercion recalls the work of Kathleen Gough and her colleagues in the 1970s rather than supporting ideas about autonomous subaltern 'moral outrage.' Vinay Bahl extends and elaborates basic elements of this critique on a world stage. Again she questions the utility of Subaltern Studies for scholars concerned with social justice. Her central target is cultural definitions of 'difference.' Women and Dalits are not 'different' from élites as cultural groups and thus in the same boat as other subaltern subjects; rather, she says, they participate politically in differences produced by material inequalities and collective activities that also differentiate subaltern groups. In addition, she argues for the need to locate subalternity inside the history of global capitalism. From this perspective, it becomes possible to reread 'colonial constructions' and 'élite paradigms' as ideological elements that do not describe structures of power even under colonialism; and to see power structures changing after independence, in the Cold War, and during recent globalisation, along with changes in world capitalism. In this view, approaching subalternity merely through a cultural critique of colonialism stultifies Indian history as it stymies subaltern politics.

The last reprint is by Sumit Sarkar, a turncoat subaltern who, like Ramachandra Guha (though they have little else in common), left the project to become its critic. Here he recounts its history and clarifies reasons for his departure and dissent. I have tried to minimise redundancies in this introduction, so my account of the project ended where he puts his emphasis, at the time when Partha Chatterjee began to author its 'most lucid and comprehensive' statements of (what he calls) 'redirection.' He also pays special attention to contested meanings of Subaltern Studies in a time of rising Hindu majoritarianism (Hindutva), to which I allude briefly above. He describes immeasurably better than I or any other foreigner could ever do what it can feel like as an Indian scholar working in India to have India spoken for by Subaltern Studies so authoritatively in the wide world of globalisation.

To conclude, it is important to stress that the bulk of research on subaltern subjects has always escaped Subaltern Studies. Two recent books provide a good opportunity for controlled comparison of contemporary historical theory and method inside and outside the project as applied to the study of tribal peoples in Western India.[122] They diverge especially on questions of autonomy, consciousness, and colonialism. They indicate rightly that historians outside the project tend to locate subalterns more carefully in changing environments that include economic, political, ecological, technological, and social history;[123] and in this perspective, they tend to see colonialism as a diverse, changing bundle of historical forces rather than as a comprehensive structure.[124] The borders between Subaltern Studies and its Others are vague, shifting, and contested, however, and there is much smuggling and border crossing, authorised and otherwise. Anthologies abound with essays from both sides. The very existence of an inside and outside is today questionable as the project diversifies internally and merges externally with comparative colonialism,[125] cultural studies,[126] historical anthropology,[127] and post-colonial studies.[128] Many authors use Subaltern Studies but also draw on other sources, and hybrid research is now most prominent in *Subaltern Studies*. Internally, the project continues to be creative, adaptive, and malleable. Dispersion and convergence, migration and assimilation, have made subalternity a moveable feast with jumbled tracks leading in many directions.

There is no one intellectual history of subalternity and never could be, because it lives on local ground in disparate readings. Geographical patterns may exist, however, because, in the world of globalisation that makes Subaltern Studies what it is today, disparities have patterns. South Asian sites are extremely diverse and diverge along national lines. Readers in Bangladesh, Nepal, Pakistan, and Sri Lanka might tend to read Subaltern Studies as an Indian national project, not their own. South Asian readers far from big city universities and research centres might feel most distant from the global academy and might tend to value the project's global success inversely to its local credibility. But locality is shifting: Brinda Bose and K. Balagopal represent two equally real, totally different, and equally local South Asian sites, in cultural studies and human rights, respectively, which also have global dimensions. Readers outside South Asia would be more likely to encounter South Asia in media, abstractly. In the global academy, moreover, venerable ideas constitute India as a singular, unitary, South Asian space, so readers can imagine the national 'fragments' in Subaltern Studies quite literally, because debates in South Asia about multiple, shifting, contested nationalities do not interfere with this reading. Globally, India also has a theoretical location inside binary oppositions between West and East, First and Third World, Europe and Non-Europe, modernity and tradition, colonisers and colonised, rich and poor, developed and underdeveloped, privileged and downtrodden, and so on. Because India stands for South Asia in the second term in each binary pair, Subaltern Studies fit neatly into prevalent ideas about India's place in the world. Indian subalterns can thus represent India metonymically. Readers who identify strongly with the first term in each binary pair might tend to embrace the claim that someone from the other side can speak for it. Speaking for (Indian) subalternity as (Indian) subaltern could thus become a professional academic niche. We could expect Subaltern Studies to attain authority as an authentic voice of the post-colonial East in self-consciously Western academic localities which have been shaped intellectually by Orientalism, area studies, and Cold War anti-communism, where scholars mobilise to oppose colonial forms of knowledge with post-orientalist critical theory, global cultural studies, and post-Marxist, post-colonial literary criticism. Essays in this volume and citations in the bibliography indicate many more reading possibilities. In years to come, we can expect a continued profusion of reading disparities in diverging local circumstances.

Notes and References

1. In this essay, the italicised phrase *Subaltern Studies* refers to the series of edited volumes that appear under the full title, *Subaltern Studies: Writings on South Asian history and society* (vol. VIII is subtitled *Essays in honour of Ranajit Guha*), published by Oxford University Press, from 1982 until 1999. Without italics, Subaltern Studies refers to all the texts inside and outside *Subaltern Studies* by authors in *Subaltern Studies*. 'The project' refers to the organised activity of the core group in *Subaltern Studies*, primarily its Editorial Collective, to develop Subaltern Studies as a body of knowledge. In the footnotes, *Subaltern Studies* volumes are abbreviated as *SSI, SSII*, etc. Their contents are listed in Appendix 1. Abbreviated author–date references with asterisks—e.g. Cooper *1994—indicate reprints in this book; without asterisks, they refer to bibliographic citations in Appendix 2. Spellings have been standardised to Indian academic usage for the sake of uniformity.

2. For *SS* volumes 1–7, the editorial team included Shahid Amin (1–7), David Arnold (1–7), Gautam Bhadra (2–7), Dipesh Chakrabarty (2–7), Partha Chatterjee (1–7), Ranajit Guha (1–7), David Hardiman (1–7), Gyanendra Pandey (1–7), and Sumit Sarkar (3–7). Change in the Collective after 1989 is indicated in prefatory citations and also by the editorship of later *SS* volumes.

3. In the following list of books by editorial team members, the number of articles that they contributed to *SSIVI* appears in parentheses: Shahid Amin (3): *Sugarcane and sugar in Gorakhpur: An inquiry into peasant production for capitalist enterprise in colonial India* (Delhi and New York: Oxford University Press, 1984); David Arnold (4): *Police power and colonial rule, Madras, 1859–1947* (Delhi and New York: Oxford University Press, 1986); Gautam Bhadra (3); Dipesh Chakrabarty (3): *Rethinking working-class history: Bengal, 1890–1940* (Princeton, NJ: Princeton University Press, 1989); Partha Chatterjee (4): *Bengal, 1920–1947: The land question* (Calcutta: Published for Centre for Studies in Social Sciences by K.P. Bagchi, 1984), and *Nationalist thought and the colonial world: A derivative discourse?* (London: Zed Books, 1986); Ranajit Guha (4): *Elementary aspects of peasant insurgency in colonial India* (Delhi: Oxford University Press, 1983), and *An Indian historiography of India: A nineteenth-century*

agenda and its implications (Calcutta: K.P. Bagchi, 1988); David Hardiman (4): *Peasant nationalists of Gujarat: Kheda district, 1917–1934* (Delhi and New York: Oxford University Press, 1981), and *The coming of the Devi: Adivasi assertion in Western India* (Delhi and New York: Oxford University Press, 1987); Gyanendra Pandey (4): *The ascendancy of the Congress in Uttar Pradesh, 1926–1934: A study in imperfect mobilization* (Delhi and New York: Oxford University Press, 1978), *The construction of communalism in colonial North India* (Delhi: Oxford University Press, 1990), and (editor), *The Indian nation in 1942* (Calcutta: K.P. Bagchi, 1988); and Sumit Sarkar (2): *A critique of colonial India* (Calcutta: Papyrus, 1985), *Modern India, 1885–1947* (Delhi: Macmillan, 1983), second edition with foreword by D.A. Low, New York: St Martin's Press, 1989), and *Popular movements and middle-class leadership in late colonial India: Perspectives and problems of a history from below* (Calcutta: K.P. Bagchi, 1983). Only one other author contributed more than one article to *SSI-VI*: Gayatri Chakravorty Spivak (3): *In other worlds: Essays in cultural politics* (New York: Methuen, 1987). The following authors had one article each and many also published important books in the 1980s: N.K. Chandra, Ajit K. Chaudhury, Bernard S. Cohn, Arvind N. Das, Veena Das, Swapan Dasgupta, Ramachandra Guha, Stephen Henningham, Tanika Sarkar, Asok Sen, Julie Stephens, and Susie Tharu. Ranajit Guha provides a list of books by 'members of the Collective since 1982,' in *A Subaltern Studies Reader, 1986–1995*, edited by Ranajit Guha (Minneapolis: University of Minnesota Press, 1997), p. xxii, note 9.

4. *A Subaltern Studies Reader*, p. xiv.

5. Latin American Subaltern Studies Group 1993, 110.

6. *SSXI* has been published in 2000 by Permanent Black. The following alphabetical list of forty-four *Subaltern Studies* authors comes from the *Subaltern Studies* website (*http://www.lib.virginia.edu/area-studies/subaltern/ssallau.htm*). It shows the number of publications listed there on May 15, 1999. This tally is not exhaustive. In this list, the relevant *SS* volume number appears next to authors who have only one *SS* publication. Authors who have left the *SS* project to become critics are marked with one asterisk (*). Two asterisks (**) mark the ten core members for *SSIVI* (see note 2). Authors marked with a plus sign (+) appear in volume x and were not listed on the website as of May 15, 1999:

   **Shahid Amin, 8; **David Arnold, 12; Upendra Baxi, 1 VII; **Gautam Bhadra, 6; **Dipesh Chakrabarty, 14; N.K. Chandra, 1 II; + Indrani Chatterjee, 1 X; **Partha Chatterjee, 18; Ajit K. Chaudhury, 1v; Bernard S. Cohn, 3; Arvind N. Das, 1 II; Veena Das, 1 VI; Swapan Dasgupta,

1 IV; Vivek Dhareshwar and R. Srivatsan, 1 IX; + Ishita Banerjee Dube, 1 X; Saurabh Dube, 1 VII; Amitav Ghosh, 1 VII; + Kaushik Ghosh, IX; Ramachandra Guha,* 1 IV; **Ranajit Guha, 22; **David Hardiman, 9; Stephen Henningham, 1 II; Kancha Ilaiah, 1 IX; + Sundesh Kaali, 1 X; Sudipta Kaviraj, 6; David Lloyd, 1 IX; Shail Mayaram, 2 IX; + Sudesh Mishra, 1 X; **Gyandendra Pandey, 12; MSS Pandian, 1; + Chrisopher Pinney, 1 X; Gyan Prakash, 6; + Vijay Prashad 1 X; **Sumit Sarkar* 4; Tanika Sarkar, 1 IV; + Rosemary Sayigh 1 X; Asok Sen 1 V; Ajay Skaria 1 IX; **Gayatri Chakravorty Spivak, 4; Julie Stephens, 1 VI; Tejaswini Naranjana, 1 IX; Susie Tharu, 2; Karnal Visweswaran, 1 IX.

7. Ranajit Guha's list of 'members since 1982' is this: Shahid Amin, David Arnold, Gautam Bhadra, Dipesh Chakrabarty, Partha Chatterjee, Ranajit Guha, David Hardiman, and Gyanendra Pandey. *A Subaltern Studies Reader*, p. xxii, n. 9.

8. *SSVIII*, Preface.

9. Stein 1990.

10. Bela Malik was the chief driving force behind this project. In writing this introduction and compiling reprints, I received invaluable assistance from Lauren Nauta. Additional assistance from Jeremie Dufault, Linda Oh, Teresa Watts, and Sue Yi speeded the project along. Dina Siddiqi and Neeladri Bhattacharya read drafts and provided constructive criticism. Partha Chatterjee, Gyan Prakash, and Gyan Pandey were generous with their time, insights, and recollections. David Nelson gave bibliographic help. Rukun Advani shared archival data and did the final editing at Permanent Black. Many others read parts of the manuscript and gave me good ideas. Many thanks to one and all.

11. See Cooper *1994, Mallon 1994, and Prakash 1994.

12. On Hindutva, see *Contesting the nation: Religion, community, and the politics of democracy in India*, edited by David Ludden (Philadelphia: University of Pennsylvania Press); published in India as *Making India Hindu: Community, conflict, and the politics of democracy* (Delhi: Oxford University Press, 1996).

13. Peter Gran, 'Subaltern Studies, racism, and class struggle: Examples from India and the United States,' unpublished paper from Working Paper Series, Department of Comparative American Cultures, Washington State University, Pullman: Washington, 1999. His comparative approach to political cultures, within which he locates readings of Subaltern Studies, is elaborated in his *Beyond eurocentrism: A new view of modern world history* (Syracuse: Syracuse University Press, 1996).

14. Raymond Williams, *Marxism and literature* (London: Oxford University Press, 1977).

15. See Todd Gitlin, 'Prime time ideology: The hegemonic process in television entertainment,' *Television: The critical view*, Horace Newcomb, editor, fifth edition (New York: Oxford University Press, 1994). Dominic Strinati, *An introduction to theories of popular culture* (London: Routledge, 1995).

16. Arnold 1984, Chopra 1982.

17. New York: Pantheon Books, 1963.

18. In the US, two pioneering books are Eugene Genovese, *Roll, Jordan, roll: The world the slaves made* (New York: Pantheon Books, 1974); and Dee Brown, *Bury my heart at wounded knee: An Indian history of the American West* (New York: Bantam Books, 1972).

19. Andrea Hinding, *Women's history sources: A guide to archives and manuscript collections in the United States* (New York: Bowker, 1979).

20. *Europe and the people without history* (Berkeley and Los Angeles: University of California Press, 1982).

21. R. Das Gupta *1985, R.B. Chaudhury 1985, Yang 1985.

22. *The Journal of Peasant Studies*, London, Frank Cass, began in 1973; and *The Peasant Studies Newsletter*, which became *Peasant Studies* (University of Pittsburgh), began in 1972.

23. David Ludden, 'Productive power in agriculture: A survey of work on the local history of British India,' in *Agrarian power and agricultural productivity in South Asia*, edited by Meghnad Desai, Susanne H. Rudolph, and Ashok Rudra (Berkeley and Los Angeles: University of California Press, 1984), pp. 51–99.

24. Eric Stokes, *The peasant and the Raj: Studies in agrarian society and peasant rebellion in colonial India* (Cambridge: Cambridge University Press, 1978).

25. Sirajul Islam, *Rural history of Bangladesh: A source study* (Dhaka: Tito Islam, 1977).

26. See K. Rajayyan, *South Indian rebellion: The first war of Independence, 1800–1801* (Mysore: Rao and Raghavan, 1971); and *Rise and fall of the poligars of Tamilnadu* (Madras: University of Madras, 1974).

27. Sumathi Ramaswamy, 'The dialogics of history: Consensus and contention in the tellings of a past,' unpublished Master's Thesis, Department of Anthropology, University of Pennsylvania, 1986.

28. After a national study, the ministry concluded that persisting inequalities 'may lead to a situation where the discontented elements are compelled to organise themselves and the extreme tensions building up with the "complex molecule" that is the Indian village may end in an explosion.' Ministry of Home Affairs, 'The causes and nature of current agrarian tensions,' in A.R. Desai, editor, *Agrarian struggles in India after Independence* (Delhi: Oxford University Press, 1986), pp. 36–43.

29. N.G. Ranga had been writing since the 1930s, but his most relevant work is *Revolutionary peasants* (Delhi: 1949). See also L. Natarajan, *Peasant uprisings in India, 1850–1900* (Bombay: 1953).

30. Atis K. Dasgupta, *The Fakir and Sannyasi uprisings* (Calcutta: K.P. Bagchi, 1992), p. 1, citing Jamini Mohan Ghosh's *Sannyasis in Mymensingh.*

31. Walter Hauser has documented one intellectual who changed popular thinking in *Sahajanand on agricultural labour and the rural poor: An edited translation of khet mazdoor* (Delhi: Manohar, 1994) and *Swami Sahajanand and the peasants of Jharkhand: A view from 1941, an edited translation of Jharkhand ke kisan* (Delhi: Manohar, 1995).

32. Hamza Alavi, 'Peasant classes and primordial loyalties,' *Peasant Studies*, 1, 1, 1973, 23–62.

33. *Rebellious prophets: A study of messianic movements in Indian religions* (Bombay, New York: Asia Publishing House, 1965). The specificity of tribal rebellion was established early on: see V. Raghavaiah, *Tribal revolts* (Nellore: Andhra Rastra Adimajati Sevak Sangh, 1971); and 'Tribal revolts in chronological order: 1778 to 1991,' reprinted in A.R. Desai, editor, *Peasant struggles in India* (Bombay: Oxford University Press, 1979), pp. 23–7.

34. Jagdish Chandra Jha, *The Kol insurrection of Chota-Nagpur* (Calcutta: Thacker & Spink, 1964).

35. *History of the Fara'Idi Movement in Bengal (1818–1906)* (Karachi: Pakistan Historical Society, 1965).

36. Kalyan Kumar Sengupta, 'Agrarian disturbances in Eastern and Central Bengal in the late nineteenth century,' *Indian Economic and Social History Review*, 8, 2, 1971, 192–212; and *Pabna disturbances and the politics of rent, 1873–1885* (New Delhi: People's Publishing House, 1974). Binay Bhushan Chaudhuri, 'Agrarian movements in Bihar and Bengal, 1919–39,' in *Socialism in India*, edited by B.R. Nanda (Delhi: Vikas Publications, 1972), pp. 190–229; and 'The story of a peasant revolt in a Bengal District,' *Bengal Past and Present*, 92, 2, 1973, 220–78. Sunil Kumar Sen, *Agrarian struggle in Bengal, 1946–1947* (New Delhi: People's Publishing House, 1972).

37. *Tribal revolts* (Nellore: 1971).

38. 'Traditional society and political mobilisation: The experience of the Bardoli Satyagraha (1920–8),' *Contributions to Indian Sociology*, NS 8 (1974).

39. See Sukhbir Choudhary, *Moplah uprising, 1921–1923* (Delhi: Agam Prakashan, 1977); Stephen F. Dale, 'The Mappilla outbreaks: Ideology and social conflict in nineteenth-century Kerala,' *Journal of Asian Studies*, 35, 1, 1975, 85–98; Conrad Wood, 'Peasant revolt: An interpretation of

Moplah violence in the nineteenth and twentieth centuries,' in *The imperial impact: Studies in the economic history of Africa and India*, edited by Clive Dewey and A.G. Hopkins (London: Athlone Press, 1978), pp. 132–51.

40. New York: Monthly Review Press, 1973,

41. Delhi: Oxford University Press, 1979, reprinted 1981, 1985.

42. Delhi: Oxford University Press, 1983.

43. Cambridge: Cambridge University Press, 1968.

44. For an early collection of articles, reprinted from *Modern Asian Studies*, see *Locality, province and nation: Essays on Indian politics 1870–1940*, edited by John Gallagher, Gordon Johnson and Anil Seal (Cambridge: Cambridge University Press, 1973).

45. Tapan Raychaudhuri, 'Indian nationalism as animal politics,' *The Historical Journal*, 22, 1979, 747–63. See also Howard Spodek, 'Pluralist politics in British India: The Cambridge cluster of historians of Modern India,' *The American Historical Review*, 84, 3, 1979, 688–707.

46. A.R. Desai had opened up this line of inquiry in 1948. His *Social background of Indian nationalism* (Bombay: Popular Prakashan, 1948, reprinted 1954, 1959, and 1966) was the first 'attempt to give a composite picture of the complex and variegated process of the rise of Indian nationalism and its various manifestations.' In a long chapter on the 'Rise of new social classes in India,' he argued that, 'one striking characteristic of the new social classes was their national character. This was due to the fact that *they were integral parts of a single national economy* of India and *further, they lived under a single state regime*. This engendered a community of economic, political and other interests [among] the members of each of the new social classes on an all-India national basis. . . . [T]hey felt an urge to organise themselves on an all-India scale and [to] start [a] movement to advance their common interests on a national basis [pp. xii, 214. Italics original].'

47. See Stein 1990; and more generally, Peter Novick, *That noble dream: The 'objectivity question' and the American historical profession* (Cambridge: Cambridge University Press, 1988).

48. See Bernard S. Cohn, *An Anthropologist among the historians and other essays* (New York and Delhi: Oxford University Press, 1987), with an introduction by Ranajit Guha.

49. James C. Scott, *The moral economy of the peasant: Rebellion and subsistence in Southeast Asia* (New Haven: Yale University Press, 1976). Samuel Popkin, *The rational peasant: The political economy of rural society in Vietnam* (Berkeley: University of California Press, 1979).

50. E.P. Thompson, 'The moral economy of the English crowd in the eighteenth century,' *Past and Present*, 50, 1971, 76–136. George Rude, *The*

crowd in history: A study of popular disturbances in France and England, 1730–1848 (New York: Pantheon, 1968).

51. See Eric R. Wolf, *Peasant wars in the twentieth century* (New York: Harper, 1969).

52. *Stratagems and spoils: A social anthropology of politics* (New York: Schocken Books, 1969).

53. London: Verso.

54. His inaugural essay in *SSI* containing this formulation is also the first essay on 'methodology' in the 1988 collection of seminal essays, *Selected Subaltern Studies*, in which the quote is on p. 40.

55. See David Ludden, 'Orientalist empiricism and transformations of colonial knowledge,' in *Orientalism and the post-colonial predicament*, edited by C.A. Breckenridge and Peter Van der Veer (Philadelphia: University of Pennsylvania Press, 1993), pp. 250–78.

56. Barrington Moore, *The social origins of dictatorship and democracy: Lord and peasant in the making of the modern world* (Boston: Beacon Press, 1966).

57. First English edition (London: Weidenfeld and Nicholson, 1966).

58. Kathleen Gough, 'Agrarian relations in Southeast India, 1750–1976,' *Review*, 2, 1, 1978, 25–54, and *Rural society in Southeast India* (New York: Cambridge University Press, 1971). See also Andre Beteille, *Caste, class, and power: Changing patterns of social stratification in a Tanjore village* (Berkeley: University of California Press, 1965); and Gerald D. Berreman, *Hindus of the Himalayas: Ethnography and change* (Berkeley: University of California Press, 1972).

59. Alam 1983, Copland 1983, *R. Das Gupta 1985.

60. Tariq Ali, *Can Pakistan survive?* (London: Verso, 1983).

61. See Peter Hardy, *The Muslims of British India* (Cambridge: Cambridge University Press, 1972), and *Communal and pan-Islamic trends in colonial India*, edited by Mushirul Hasan (Delhi: Manohar, 1981).

62. Mushirul Hasan, *Legacy of a divided nation: India's Muslims since independence* (Boulder: Westview Press, 1997).

63. Christopher Baker and David Washbrook, *South India: Political institutions and political change* (Cambridge: Cambridge University Press, 1975). Sugata Bose, *Agrarian Bengal: Economy, social structure, and politics* (Cambridge: Cambridge University Press, 1986). Ayesha Jalal, *The sole spokesman: Jinnah, the Muslim League and the demand for Pakistan* (Cambridge: Cambridge University Press, 1985). David Washbrook, *The emergence of provincial politics: The Madras Presidency, 1870–1920* (Cambridge: Cambridge University Press, 1976).

64. See John Broomfield, 'The regional élites: A theory of modern Indian history,' *Indian Economic and Social History Review*, 3, 3, 1966, 279–90.

65. See, however, Sumit Sarkar, 'Hindu–Moslem relations in Swadeshi Bengal,' *Indian Economic and Social History Review*, 9, 1972, 163–216.

66. D.N. Dhanagare, *Agrarian movements and Gandhian politics* (Agra: Institute of Social Sciences, Agra University, 1975), 'Peasant protest and politics: The Tebhaga movement in Bengal, 1946–7,' *Journal of Peasant Studies*, 3, 3, 1976, 360–78, and 'Agrarian conflict, religion and politics: The Moplah rebellions in Malabar in the nineteenth and early-twentieth centuries,' *Past and Present*, 74, 1977, 112–41. Majid Hayat Siddiqi, *Agrarian unrest in North India: The United Provinces, 1918–1922* (New Delhi: Vikas, 1978). Gyanendra Pandey, *The ascendancy of the Congress in Uttar Pradesh.*

67. On traditionalism and developmentalism in agrarian power relations, see David Ludden, *An agrarian history of South Asia* (Cambridge: Cambridge University Press, 1999).

68. Bipan Chandra, *The rise and growth of economic nationalism in India: Economic policies of the Indian national leadership, 1880–1905* (Delhi: People's Publishing House, 1966).

69. *A tryst with destiny: A study of economic policy resolutions of the Indian National Congress passed during the last 100 years*, edited by A. Moin Zaidi (New Delhi: Indian Institute of Applied Political Research, 1985), p. 54.

70. A good account of this environment is Francine Frankel, *India's political economy, 1947–1977: The gradual revolution* (Princeton: Princeton University Press, 1978). I have argued for the enduring connection between research in agrarian history and debates about development policy in 'Agricultural production and Indian history,' in *Agricultural production and Indian history*, edited by David Ludden, pp. 1–35

71. *Subaltern Studies Reader*, p. xii.

72. 1975–6 is taken to be the turning point in many discussions of recent trends in Indian political culture: see Uma Chakravarti, 'Saffroning the past: Of myths, histories, and right-wing agendas,' *Economic and Political Weekly*, January 31, 1998, 225–32.

73. Amrita Basu, 'Mass movement or élite conspiracy? The puzzle of Hindu nationalism,' in *Contesting the Nation*, pp. 55–80.

74. An excellent case study is Sanjib Baruah, *India against itself: Assam and the politics of nationality* (Philadelphia: University of Pennsylvania Press, 1999).

75. Gail Omvedt, *Reinventing revolution: New social movements and the socialist tradition in India* (Armonk: ME Sharpe, 1993). For comparable cases, see

Between resistance and revolution: Cultural politics and social protest, edited by Richard Fox and Orin Starn (New Brunswick: Rutgers University Press, 1997).

76. New Haven: Yale University Press, 1986.

77. *Contesting power: Resistance and everyday social relations in South Asia*, edited by Gyan Prakash and Douglas Haynes (Berkeley: University of California Press, 1991).

78. Frederic Jameson, *Post-modernism, or, the cultural logic of late capitalism* (Durham: Duke University Press, 1991).

79. Arturo Escobar, 'Imagining a post-development era? Critical thought, development and social movements,' *Social Text*, 31–3, 1992, 20–56, and *Encountering development: The making and unmaking of the third world* (Princeton: Princeton University Press, 1995).

80. See *The development dictionary: A guide to knowledge as power*, edited by Wolfgang Sachs (London: Zed Books, 1992).

81. James Scott, *Seeing like a state: How certain schemes to improve the human condition have failed* (New Haven: Yale University Press, 1998).

82. Moishe Postone, 'Political theory and historical analysis,' in *Habermas and the public sphere*, edited by Craig Calhoun (Cambridge and London: MIT Press, 1992), pp. 175–6.

83. Gyanendra Pandey 1992, Partha Chatterjee 1995.

84. Benedict Anderson, *Imagined communities: Reflections on the origin and spread of nationalism*, revised and extended edition (London and New York: Verso, 1991). The emergence of a new discourse of nationality is much discussed. A useful point of entry is David Lloyd, 'Nationalisms against the state,' in *The politics of culture in the shadow of capital*, edited by Lisa Lowe and David Lloyd (Durham: Duke University Press, 1997), pp. 173–98.

85. Thomas L. Haskell, 'The new aristocracy,' *New York Review of Books*, 4 December 4, 1997, p. 47.

86. Eric Hobsbawm, *The age of extremes: A history of the world, 1914–1991* (New York: Vintage, 1996, first edition 1994), pp. 558–9.

87. A good discussion in the South Asian context is 'Culture, nationalism, and the role of intellectuals: An interview,' in Aijaz Ahmad, *Lineages of the present: Political essays* (Delhi: Tulika, 1998), pp. 396–428.

88. A critical review of the general trend is in Bryan Palmer, *Descent into discourse: The reification of language and the writing of social history* (Philadelphia: Temple University Press, 1993).

89. *Subaltern Studies Reader*, p. ix.

90. David Arnold, *The Congress in Tamilnad: Nationalist politics in South*

India, 1919–1937 (London: Curzon Press, 1977). David Hardiman, *Peasant nationalists of Gujarat: Kheda district, 1917–1934* (Delhi and New York: Oxford University Press, 1981). Gyanendra Pandey, *The ascendancy of the Congress in Uttar Pradesh, 1926–1934: A study in imperfect mobilization* (Delhi and New York: Oxford University Press, 1978). Sumit Sarkar, *Swadeshi movement in Bengal 1903–1908* (New Delhi: People's Publishing House, 1973). Sumit Sarkar had also published a *Bibliographical survey of social reform movements in the eighteenth and nineteenth centuries* (New Delhi: Motilal Banarsidass, 1975).

91. Paris: 1963; second edition, Delhi: Orient Longman, 1982; reprinted with a foreword by Amartya Sen by Duke University Press, Durham NC, 1996.

92. Its counterpoint is Eric Stokes, *English utilitarians and India* (Oxford: Oxford University Press, 1959).

93. '*Neel-Darpan*: The image of a peasant revolt in a liberal mirror,' *Journal of Peasant Studies*, 2, 1, 1974, 1–46. He also wrote some other short pieces. For biography and publications, see *SSVIII*, pp. 222–8.

94. Sathyamurthy (1990) has the most extensive account of his work.

95. *Subaltern Studies XI* introduces a new editor, Pradeep Jeganathan, and is subtitled *Community, gender, and violence.*

96. *Alam 1983, Arnold 1984, Chatterjee 1983, Chopra 1982, Gupta 1985, *Das Gupta, *Singh *et al.* 1984.

97. See *Sivaramakrishnan 1995.

98. Concerning his act of rejection, Ranajit Guha says, 'a statement of this kind was irreverence approaching sheer impudence for many in authority,' *A Subaltern Studies Reader*, p. xiv.

s 99. *J. Alam 1983, *Bahl 1997, Bayly 1988, *Das Gupta 1986, Freitag 1984, Lochan 1987, *Masselos 1992, Mukherjee 1988, O'Hanlon and Washbrook 1992, Stein 1990.

100. *J. Alam 1983, S. Alam 1993, *Bahl 1997, *Balagopal 1989, Mishra 1983, *Singh *et al.* 1984, *Masselos 1992, Yadav 1989, *Cooper 1994, Mukherjee 1988, *Chaudhury 1986, Chaudhuri 1986, *Das Gupta 1986, Hauser 1991, Perusek 1992, and Siddiqi 1985.

101. *Das Gupta 1986, *Bahl 1997, Bayly 1988, *Sarkar 1997, *Balagopal 1989, Brass 1991, Mukherjee 1988, *O'Hanlon 1988, and O'Hanlon and Washbrook 1992.

102. *The Book Review*, 21, no. 6, June 1997, pp. 5–7.

103. Currie 1995.

104. See Craig Brandist, 'The official and the popular in Gramsci and Bakhtin,' *Theory, culture and society*, XIII, 2, May 1996, 59–74.

105. *Subaltern Studies Reader*, pp. ix, xxii, n. 9.

106. Ranajit Guha often gives the impression of a battle raging. The *SSIII* preface includes this: 'These publications, we are delighted to acknowledge, have not gone unnoticed. Although the big guns of the academic press are yet to open up—that old-fashioned artillery operates with the tardiness of a medieval siege and takes its time to be moved into position—a sufficient number of reviews have already appeared and raised a host of questions. . . . Negativity is therefore the *very raison d'etre* as well as the constitutive principle of our project. . . . It is this negativity, this critical drive, which enables Subaltern Studies to disturb the charmed and almost soporific smugness of established scholarship.'

107. Dipesh Chakrabarty, 'Invitation to a dialogue,' *SSIV*, pp. 364, 376. In his Introduction to *A Subaltern Studies Reader*, Ranajit Guha characterises the ethos of the Collective as an 'insistence on a solidarity that would not reduce individual voices, styles, and approaches to a flat and undifferentiated uniformity' (p. ix).

108. 'In search of a Subaltern Lenin,' *SSV*, p. 237

109. Introduction to Cohn, *An anthropologist among the historians*, especially pp. xx–xxiv.

110. . See *The new cultural history*, edited and with an introduction by Lynn Hunt (Berkeley: University of California Press, 1989), and *Telling the truth about history*, edited by Joyce Appleby, Lynn Hunt, and Margaret Jacob (New York: Norton, 1994).

111. Methodological statements are in Amin 1995, Chakrabarty 1992b, 1997, 1998, Chatterjee 1995, Pandey 1995, Prakash 1990b.

112. This site (*http://www.lib.virginia.edu/area-studies/subaltern/ssallau.htm*) was developed by Frank Conlon, Henry Schwarz, Philip McEldowney, and others. Relevant material is also available through my homepage, http://www.sas.upenn.edu/~dludden.

113. Freitag 1984, Brennan 1984, Yang 1985.

114. See note 107.

115. *Selected Subaltern Studies*, p. v. Gayatri Chakravorty Spivak's widely cited article, 'Can the Subaltern speak?' also appeared in 1988, in *Marxism and the interpretation of culture*, edited by Cary Nelson and Lawrence Grossberg (London: Macmillan), pp. 271–313.

116. This reframing of Indian history was later elaborated by new Collective member, Gyan Prakash 1990b, 1992a, 1994. For a critical discussion of post-colonial formulations, see Arif Dirlik, 'The post-colonial aura: Third world criticism in the age of global capitalism,' *Critical Inquiry*, 20, Winter 1994, 328–56.

117. Also McGuire 1986.

118. Brass 1991, O'Hanlon and Washbrook 1992, and Prakash 1990, 1992a, 1992b, 1994.

119. K. Sivaramakrishnan, *Modern forests: Statemaking and environmental change in colonial eastern India* (Stanford: Stanford University Press, 1999), and *Agrarian environments: Resources, representations, and rule in India,* edited by Arun Agarwal and K. Sivaramakrishnan (Durham: Duke University Press, 2000).

120. Delhi and New York: Oxford University Press.

121. Hardiman 1996.

122. Ajay Skaria, *Hybrid histories: Forests, frontiers, and wildness in Western India* (Delhi: Oxford University Press, 1999); and Sumit Guha, *Environment and ethnicity in India, 1200–1991* (Cambridge: Cambridge University Press, 1999).

123. Some recent illustrative examples (with relevant bibliographies) include Sumit Guha, *Environment and ethnicity*; K. Sivaramakrishnan, *Modern forests*; Chetan Singh, *Natural premises: Ecology and peasant life in the Western Himalaya, 1800–1950* (Delhi: Oxford University Press, 1998); and Nandini Sundar, *Subalterns and sovereigns: An anthropological history of Bastar, 1854–1996* (Delhi: Oxford University Press, 1997).

124. See Ludden, *An agrarian history of South Asia.*

125. *Colonialism and culture,* edited by Nicholas B. Dirks (Ann Arbor: University of Michigan Press, 1992).

126. Scott 1995, *Culture/Power/History: A reader in contemporary social theory,* edited by Nicholas B. Dirks, Geoff Eley, and Sherry B. Ortner (Princeton: Princeton University Press, 1994). *In near ruins: Cultural theory at the end of the century,* edited by Nicholas B. Dirks (Minneapolis: University of Minnesota Press, 1998). *The politics of culture in the shadow of capital,* edited by Lisa Lowe and David Lloyd, Durham: Duke University Press, 1997).

127. See Bernard S. Cohn, *Colonialism and its forms of knowledge: The British in India* (Princeton: Princeton University Press, 1996).

128. *Dangerous liaisons: Gender, nation, and post-colonial perspectives,* edited by Anne McClintock, Aamir Mufti, and Ella Shohat (Minneapolis: University of Minnesota Press, 1997).

PART I

Early Critiques in India

JAVEED ALAM

'Peasantry, Politics and Historiography: Critique of
New Trend in Relation to Marxism.'
Social Scientist, 11, 2 (February 1983), 43–54.

SANGEETA SINGH, MINAKSHI MENON,
PRADEEP KUMAR DATTA, BISWAMOY PATI,
RADHAKANTA BARIK, RADHIKA CHOPRA,
PARTHA DUTTA, AND SANJAY PRASAD

'*Subaltern Studies II*: A Review Article.'
Social Scientist, 12, 10 (October 1984), 2–41.

RANAJIT DAS GUPTA

'Significance of Non-subaltern Mediation,'
Indian Historical Review, 12, 1–2
(July 1985–January 1986), 383–90

BINAY BHUSHAN CHAUDHURI

'Subaltern Autonomy and the National Movement,'
Indian Historical Review, 12, 1-2
(July 1985–January 1986), 391–9.

CHAPTER I.1

Peasantry, Politics, and Historiography: Critique of New Trend in Relation to Marxism*

JAVEED ALAM

T HE PUBLICATION of *Subaltern Studies*[1] is an important event in the writing of the history of colonial India. This is so not just because of the thorough research into the wide range of problems that make up the volume. Nor is it only because the research wants to make us listen to the voice of the exploited and oppressed people. The focus of all the contributors is on the activities of the 'people,' in the present volume, the peasants. However, what makes for the difference of approach is that the contributors share a significant presupposition concerning the activities people engage in, which becomes the point of departure of this volume.

The presupposition is as follows: Between the world of politics on the one hand and the economic processes of capitalist transformation on the other, there is a kind of mental space within which the social

*A longer version of this critical note was read at the Peasant Seminar at the Centre for Studies in Social Sciences, Calcutta. The long and involved discussions with the participants helped the writer in reformulating his ideas and correcting the emphases. The author is indebted to all of them. Special thanks are due to Gyan Pandey for persuading the author to write out his views.

forms of existence and consciousness of the people are all their own—strong and enduring in their own right and therefore free of manipulations by the dominant groups. However much the ruling classes may control the themes and content of politics or the sources of history, the subalterns, that is, the people, will always manage to make themselves heard. In other words, this intermediate space represents the subjectivity; the active source of the political activity of the people and therefore the basis on which they act as subjects of history and not just its objects, being merely acted upon. It is the task of people's historians, if I have grasped the argument correctly, always to keep their antennae directed towards the intermediate space from where comes the voice of the people.

All the contributors are therefore convinced of the autonomy of the peasantry and concerned with demonstrating how in their struggles, whether in the sphere of productive activity or in the more directly political sphere of mass upsurges or revolts, the politics of the subalterns[2] constitutes an 'autonomous domain.' This theme is central to the arguments advanced in various contributions in this book. Variously expressed, it is almost axiomatic, a kind of meta-theoretical position. Its importance for the evaluation of popular movements even outside the temporal frame of this book needs no emphasis.

My discussion will be mainly concerned with building a critique around this theme, and certain other theoretically significant propositions related to this in the volume, especially in Partha Chatterjee's contribution.

A review of this volume by Suneet Chopra was published in *Social Scientist* (no. 111, August 1982, pp. 55–63). Suneet Chopra makes a number of very useful points and gives us a revealing insight into the way in which terms and categories employed in this book deviate from Gramsci's usage and methodological precision. However, I feel that he passes by some of the more significant themes and propositions in this book such as the one pointed out above. Or, let us take another instance. While it is important to know that 'élite' is not a pejorative term with Gramsci, it is not clear whether the attack on the dominant framework of 'élitism' in the writing of the history of modern India does in any significant way get affected by the deviation in the use of the term 'élite' that Suneet Chopra highlights. After all, Gramsci's use of the term is highly unusual and therefore should not detract from the general use one makes of common language terms.

Looked at in this way, Ranajit Guha's critique of the myopic vision of élitist historiography, which views the 'Indian nation,' its consciousness and nationalism as a product of the élite initiatives, emanating from British or Indian sources, does not get weakened by, let us say, his inadequate understanding of the Gramscian use of the term élite. His main point remains valid, namely, that élitism does not recognise, or minimise, the role of and the initiatives by the common people in the making of modern Indian history.

In so far as he points out this lacuna in bourgeois historiography there need be no disagreement with him; in fact such a critique is called for. But what is singularly striking in this writing by Guha is the complete absence of recognition of *any* historical understanding outside the 'élitist' tradition in its various incarnations. It seems obvious to me that in his categorisation of historiography the entire tradition of Marxist historical understanding in India is being clubbed together with élitism, probably in its nationalist and neo-nationalist variants; or else, it should have been treated, or, at least, mentioned as a distinctive viewpoint, however inadequate its reflection in academic circles. Such a dismissive attitude is deplorable.

'Autonomous Domain'

How and where is autonomy located, or, in other words, what are taken to be the empirical roots of autonomy? Definitionally, it is a domain which, first, 'neither originated from élite politics nor did its existence depend on the latter' (p. 3) and where, second, the politics was 'as modern as indigenous élite politics, it was distinguished by its relatively greater depth in time as well as structure' (p. 4).

Empirically the 'autonomous domain' of peasant politics is sought to be established on the basis of evidence which displays a consistent tendency towards resistance and a propensity to rebellion on the part of peasant masses, thereby outstripping the limits set by the ruling classes—'élites.' It is true as Ranajit Guha says that there is an 'invariant notion of resistance to élite domination' (p. 4) and this is due to, as he rightly remarks, the common condition of exploitation.

It however seems clear from the history of popular revolts that the notion or actual fact of resistance is not necessarily dependent upon overcoming a certain type of outlook. Resistance is possible given any kind of outlook—modern or archaic. Exploitation and oppression have been a perennial source of revolts. Much before becoming aware of historical research, even as children, we had heard of slave revolts of exceptional daring and ferocious violence. The feudal age in India too, as elsewhere, is full of accounts of revolts. Most class societies have some history of revolts even if the people involved had not outgrown the limitations of their archaic consciousness. But to infer from the fact of such sporadic upsurges that the domain of politics underlying such revolts is autonomous is a highly questionable proposition. In the context of nationalist politics, apart from everything else, such a simplistic equation begs the question instead of providing a lead towards the historical evaluation of peasant insurgency and developing a correct revolutionary stand in the struggle for emancipation.

There is a constant tension and discrepancy between the definition of the autonomous domain of politics and the location of its empirical basis. Because hundreds of thousands of peasant masses broke through the limits imposed by the 'élites' and took to militant action, as during the Rowlatt Satyagraha or Civil Disobedience Movement, what are we to assume from this? It is one thing to say, as Ranajit Guha does, and quite rightly, that one cannot look at such militant activity as a consequence of the influence or initiatives of the élites themselves and quite another to jump to far-reaching generalisations about the autonomy of peasant politics. Popular spontaneity can have contradictory historical consequences as can be clearly seen from the researches of Gyan Pandey and Partha Chatterjee. Partha Chatterjee shows that the mainspring of political action located within the consciousness of the 'peasant community' set the Hindus and Muslims apart from each other and at each other's throats and therefore can be looked upon as a divisive force. In the case Gyan Pandey reports, the same became the basis for growing militant unity in the course of the struggle as it brought different castes and communities together.

Yet both are used by the respective authors as instances of autonomous action and domain. Both could make the same theoretical claim, as does the editor, from such contradictory evidence because of their one-sided emphasis on the subjectivity of the peasantry. But then subjectivity itself is not a closed mental space. There are propensities, dispositions, fears and apprehensions, hopes and aspirations, and more or less clear awareness of the limits and possibilities about the future which are integral parts of the subjectivity of the people. These provide the grounds for progressive historical tendencies or backward reactionary pulls to work upon. It is true that in many an analysis the manipulation theme has been overemphasised but *Subaltern Studies*, in trying to correct it, more or less negate the possibility of manipulation, incitement and confusion. By doing so one logically also forecloses the possibilities of education, propaganda and agitation and thus make the unity of theory and practice an impossibility. Obviously, education and agitation—vanguard functions—succeed as much by situating themselves within the existing subjectivity as does manipulation and confusing people—the reactionary functions.

Whether spontaneous activity and militancy weaken or strengthen the existing basis of people's unity and the future prospects of the growth of mass and class organisations—the basis on which the people can become autonomous—seems to be immaterial to the nature of the arguments advanced in these pages. Logically speaking, such activity is autonomous so long as it emanates from the existing subjectivity of the people. The historical direction of the militancy is, at best, of secondary consideration. What is primary is the spontaneity and an internally located self-generating momentum. Extending the implications of the inherent logic of such a theoretical construction, it is a matter of indifference if it leads to communal rioting or united anti-feudal actions that overcome the initial limitations. Both happily indicate the autonomy of the peasantry.

In between these two instances lies the case of Gudem-Rampa tribals dealt with by David Arnold where rebellions are so completely bound down by the constraints of 'territoriality' that one cannot, going by the logic of description, even hope to see these developing common grounds with the struggles conducted in the wider structure of exploitation in Indian society.

What then are we to make of the meaning of autonomy? It is important for any serious historiography or a critique of existing historical understanding to overcome the imprecision of ambiguous terms, particularly when these provide the main terms of discourse. It is therefore legitimate to ask: Can autonomy be equated with episodic actions, whatever be the sources or motivational mainspring of action? Is it simply synonymous with a situation of asymmetry between the limited calculations of the 'élites' or bourgeois reformist nationalist leadership and the radical stirrings of the exploited and oppressed classes which outstrip the limits set by such a leadership?

In none of the studies do we find any evidence from which it could be inferred that the domain of peasant politics had come to acquire the character of a stable condition that defines the availability of concrete options and choices for these classes or strata in a long-term sense. It still needs to be demonstrated that any section of the exploited and toiling people had developed, at that time, the ability to consistently take the initiative to further their material and other interests, temporary defeats notwithstanding. Perhaps it was the absence of this ability that made it possible for the bourgeois reformist nationalist leadership to demobilise and disrupt many a peasant movement even while being able to draw the peasantry to itself.

As a consequence we find 'that the numerous peasant uprisings of the period, some of them massive in scope . . . waited in vain for a leadership to lift them up above localism and generalise them into a nation-wide anti-imperialist campaign' (pp. 6–7). This historical limitation of the peasantry, coupled with the absence of leadership— shall we say independent class and mass organisations and a centralised revolutionary party?—was the cause of 'spectacular retreat and nasty reversions in the form of sectarian or sectional strife' (p. 6).

If this represents an autonomous domain it can only be in the sense that it is located in the intermediate space which is the peasant world as yet unconquered by the bourgeois world outlook. It is here that one encounters the inherent conservatism of the presuppositions that underlie the outlook of the *Subaltern* scholarship. The specificity of peasant spontaneity, the mainspring of their political action, and the persistence of their identity are all located in the pre-capitalist consciousness and ideology. In that sense it is a historiography closely related to classical anthropology which also always looked to the unconquered, the 'exotic,' to find the autonomy and specificity of people's subjectivity.

My reading of the argument is fully sustained by the observation of the editor that the existence, or more appropriately the persistence, of the 'structural dichotomy' was due to 'the failure of the Indian bourgeoisie to speak for the nation' (p. 5), which, I presume, the bourgeoisie of advanced capitalist nations could. 'There were,' therefore, as he says, 'vast areas in the life and consciousness of the people which were never integrated into their hegemony' (p. 5).

Leaving aside questions of theory and terminology, let us look at the issue concretely in historical perspective. Is it necessary for the bourgeoisie to take the post-independence phase for the sake of clarification, to establish its 'hegemony' over the peasantry or over most areas of society to extract compliance or sustain a relatively stable domination? How does the bourgeoisie do so now?

It is possible to suggest that through different mechanisms and modalities but through the same class allies, it could do so at that time as it does now. Historians will agree that by the 1920s or so, after the Gandhian mobilisation techniques were accepted by the Congress, a class alliance between the rapidly expanding bourgeoisie and the upper strata of the landed interests was getting cemented. Gandhi was the only one among the nationalist leaders who could sense that if the simmering discontent among the peasant masses was not channellised under the Congress leadership it could become mobilised under radical leadership for anti-feudal struggles within an alternative nationalist programme. In fact this was happening in an incipient, halting manner as it became clear in the 1930s and the following period.

If so, then one cannot talk of bourgeois 'hegemony' without also raising the question of the concrete possibilities of the bourgeois–landlord alliance as a necessary tool of domination over the people. And, if the fact of the bourgeois–landlord alliance is tenable then the bourgeoisie or the colonial state at that time could use the landed vested interests, depending upon the complexion of issues in the struggles, as forces to disorganise or disrupt and thus contain peasant movements whenever they crossed the limits set by the leadership of the emerging ruling classes, even if these ruling classes were themselves subordinate to colonial authority at that time and therefore needed to struggle. Such movements created partial complementarities between them and the colonial authorities. In fact, the rich and insightful evidence contained in Gyan Pandey's differentiated presentation of respective perceptions of contending parties goes to show precisely this.

It is therefore important to note that the pre-capitalist structures, whatever their depth in time, and the ideologies that thrive on them do not give autonomy to the people but compel the leading class force—the aspiring bourgeoisie—to compromise and adjust with landlordism for joint domination. We will therefore always have spheres of social life, especially those within the agrarian economy or closely linked to it, not fully integrated into the bourgeois world outlook or outside of bourgeois 'social hegemony.'

Nevertheless, the point of importance here is that in such a situation, by the logic of compromise with landlordism operating within feudal structures, *if it gives autonomy to any group, it gives to the landlords*, at least as an initial condition. In the absence of independent class and mass organisation natural to its modes of struggle the peasantry remains deeply subjugated.

Moreover, speaking theoretically, it is important to be aware of the limits to a retarded and dependent capitalism, as in most Third World countries, establishing its sway over society. 'Hegemony,' in a precise Gramscian sense, is an outcome of the successful historical mission of the bourgeoisie. In cases of unsuccessful transition, bourgeois rule is always a case of infirm capitalism riding on the back of what is feudal; being the rider, to stretch the analogy, it channels the energies of pre-capitalist forces, however active they may be. To talk of bourgeois hegemony without at all relating it to the nature and content of capitalist transformation is to deal with an empty abstraction.

Gramsci, theorising out of his experience of work among the people, remarks: 'The history of subaltern groups is necessarily fragmented and *episodic*. There undoubtedly does exist a tendency to . . . unification in the historical activity of these groups, but this tendency is continually *interrupted* by the activity of ruling groups; . . . Subaltern groups are always subject to the activity of ruling groups, even when they rebel and rise up; only 'permanent' victory breaks their subordination. . . .'[3] Thus where Gramsci points to the great difficulties in the way of people becoming an independent force, Ranajit Guha, by a theoretical leap, transforms peasant politics into an 'autonomous domain.'

Autonomy can never be an inherited condition of the exploited and oppressed masses but a dialectical possibility born of struggle and revolutionary advance. In this epoch of socialist revolutions, autonomy of the exploited and the oppressed cannot be anything other than the advance made by revolutionary politics.

It therefore happens that by locating the source of autonomous political activity in what I have, for the sake of convenience, called a mental space, the studies in this volume do not sufficiently account for the extreme complexity of the content of the emerging consciousness of large formations of people. In these studies, it tends to get reduced to its simplest pre-reflective forms. What we look for but fail to encounter in any of these studies are the complex ways in which a variety of ideologies and their variants intermingle with pre-existing forms of consciousness to give rise to ever newer forms of self-awareness ranging from new perceptions of immediate surroundings to the widening horizons of what constitutes the surroundings. To be fair, there are important leads in the writings of Gyan Pandey and David Arnold but they seem hesitant to follow them up. This process of braiding of forms and content makes peasant conciousness potentially reflective and self-critical and thus makes them capable of alternative forms of thought, struggle and mobilisation.

Politically, these and other such questions are not inconsequential. Efforts to rework peasant history as a significant independent component of the anti-colonial struggle in India have to show how and where the nationalist ideology took shape and its slow refraction among the peasant masses. This obviously cannot be done by emphasising only the distinct consciousness of the peasant community or communities. Let us face the fact that the pre-reflective, *a critical* consciousness of the peasantry however much it could help resistance and rebellion against depredations, could not be the basis of new nationalist stirrings nor of anti-feudal sentiments unless newer ideologies—bourgeois or proletarian—got braided with the pre-capitalist peasant consciousness.

This failure to deal in a discriminating way with the problems of consciousness and to identify the long-term secularisation process associated with it is also reflected in the cursory and one-sided view of religion. One gets to know how religion constitutes a significant component of the peasant consciousness. But in the face of the disintegration of the peasantry as a result of capitalist penetration, it played varied roles. Ruling classes—both old and new—were trying to unify the different communities under their leadership. Given the disintegration of the peasantry due to the same processes of change, communalism, revivalism, etc., were *also* facets of this phenomenon. Religion as a factor was something different in popular upsurges, when spontaneously used by the people themselves, from what it was when whipped up into a frenzy by the intervention of the ruling classes. Both processes also intermingled in complex ways.

Conceptual Eclecticism

The asserted disjunction between the production process and the system of exploitation on the one hand and the structure of consciousness and ideological phenomena on the other is largely due to the implicit rejection of class categories. The studies cited here take recourse to all sorts of imprecise terms like 'élites,' 'dominant groups,' 'upper classes' but never to the term 'the ruling classes.' Why this eclecticism and the use of terms out of the bourgeois social science discourse?

This dissatisfaction with Marxist categories comes out in a pronounced manner in Partha Chatterjee's contribution. It is therefore worthwhile to dwell a little more on what he has to say. Let us take for instance his use of the concept of distinct 'Modes of Power' for the study of 'politics in the period of break-up of feudalism, or more generally of pre-capitalist societies in transition' (p. 15). This is aimed at overcoming the inadequacies of the conventionally used base–superstructure schema for the study of politics and related aspects like ideology, culture, etc. In a limited way he uses this in his contribution for explaining one facet of Bengal politics during 1926–35: the persistence of communal identity and its reflection in the widespread riots that swept through Bengal in the mid-1920s.

The key notion used by Partha Chatterjee is the 'peasant community' with the associated notion of a religion-based, community-oriented 'political authority' which is quite 'autonomous.' Its importance can be understood from its repeated use (pp. 11, 13, 14, 16, 17, 18, 19, 27, 32, 34, 36, 37). What is striking here is the absence of any notion of a differentiated class-based peasantry in the Lenin–Mao tradition. Given the primacy of the concept of the 'peasant community' over the 'conventionally used' class-differentiated notion of peasantry in Marxist writings, one of the main problematics in this essay is to locate the historical foundations of the peasant community. 'Modes of Power' as a conceptual schema is used precisely for this purpose.

Partha Chatterjee's complex argument goes something like this: Capitalism, unlike feudalism which can coexist with a communal mode of existence, destroys the peasant community and the basis of peasant communal identity. This fact is noted by Marxists when they talk of pre-capitalist ideologies giving way to the bourgeois world outlook. It is also implied in the notion, in use since the time of Lenin, of the bourgeois-democratic revolution.

But in the case of incomplete transition to capitalism the peasant community and its ideologies and culture survive. Furthermore, the strength or resilience of the peasant communities depends upon the extent of 'differentiation' within the peasantry. The survival of elements from the previous epochs gives an active force to the culture and ideology of the peasants and therefore to the assertion of communal identity in politics and hence to communalism.

We thus have political power in societies in transition to capitalism which is a coexistence of distinct modes of power—communal, feudal and bourgeois.

The problem here is: can one at all talk of 'modes of power' as a conceptual schema? It is one thing to employ 'modes of power' as a descriptive term in the same way as 'modes of dress' or 'mode of articulation' but it is quite another to use it in the sense of mode of production or mode of exploitation, that is, a conceptual schema to organise and unify a large number of relational activities in society.

The basic error in this conceptualisation flows from the notion that the survival of elements from the historical order of development can have the same significance in the making of political power in periods of capitalist transformation as they would before the beginning of capitalism. On the contrary, what is determinative in an age are the characteristically dominant relations and their contradictions.[4]

Partha Chatterjee's argument is flawed also because it looks at the coexistence of elements from different modes of production in a static, spatial sense and not in their changing rational salience. The fragments of the 'original peasant community' (p. 19) survived in the later colonial society only because the retarded process of capitalism was in no position to destroy pre-capitalist forces and modes of exploitation. The conditions of survival were not attributable to the resilience of the peasant community. The continued expansion of capitalism, however handicapped, caused increasing depredation in society. As it grew it created a whole range of new interests.

Such a situation gives rise to increasing incompatibilities between the pre-existing, pre-capitalist ideologies, communal in the case under consideration, and the emerging material interests. The 'original peasant community' is riven by contradictory material interests but can be potentially unified by appeals to these ideologies.

That the analytical framework itself is based on a notion of a static relationship between the various elements comes out clearly, for example, in Partha Chatterjee's conception of the bourgeois mode of power. It is based on abstractions which are essentially idealist in nature. The notion advanced is that the 'political domination of the bourgeoisie in the political process is sustained by the institutions of representative government' and 'the separation of the state from civil society, the elevation of the state into a neutral institution . . .' (p. 15). It is true that this was stated by Marx in his Critique of Hegel's Philosophy of Rights ('Introduction'), as the author notes. But it had a temporal–epochal reference. It was relevant to the phase of rising capitalism, and that too as a tendency rather than as an established fact, and, moreover, to a phase when the bourgeoisie had yet to face the organic challenge of the working class.

In the epoch of imperialism it is no longer valid. Once the rising challenge of the proletariat becomes a stable condition, the openly partisan character of the state becomes evident. More important, in the epoch of socialist revolution, fascism represents not a mere aberration but an organic response of capitalism to the threat of collapse at the hands of working class power. Abstracting the observations of Marx out of their historical context is to violate the dialectical unity which is the hallmark of the Marxist method. It is therefore easy to see how such an abstraction *conflates* the temporarily specific to a universal condition and *ignores* the great variations in the concrete social forms.

Thus the theoretical basis of Partha Chatterjee's exercise is very sketchy and it still needs to be demonstrated how it can satisfactorily replace the categories of base–superstructure or being-consciousness as developed by Marx. The application of his analytical framework for interpreting communalism and the riots in Bengal is full of problems but these cannot be gone into here.[5]

In looking for missing links—ideological currents, role of consciousness, the historical basis of subjectivity of the people, etc.—in the more mechanical application of Marxism, some of the studies cited above tend to rely too heavily on the superstructural elements as explanatory factors or the prime movers of popular movements. In this sense, the outlook of the authors cited above seems to be nearer to the Frankfurt School than to the Marxist revolutionary theory developed by Lenin and furthered by the experience of the world communist movement.

This criticism is not intended to detract from the insights and the provocative research contained in the volume. The volume stands on its own merit as an important contribution to historiography on colonial India.

Notes and References

1. Ranajit Guha (ed.), *Subaltern Studies I: Writings on South Asian history and society* (Oxford: Delhi, 1982). In the discussions that follow, I will be making references to the following contributions: Ranajit Guha, 'On some aspects of the historiography of colonial India'; Partha Chatterjee, 'Agrarian relations and communalism in Bengal, 1926–35'; Gyan Pandey, 'Peasant revolt and Indian nationalism: The peasant movement in Awadh, 1919–22,' and David Arnold, 'Rebellious hillmen: The Gudem-Rampa risings.'

I have not taken up Shahid Amin's 'Small peasant commodity production and rural indebtedness: The culture of sugarcane in eastern UP, *c.* 1880–1920' because the detailed and perceptive research on the process of small commodity production in semi-feudal setting, although it shares the basic outlook in the volume, is not central to my argument. David Hardiman's contribution on 'The Indian faction: A political theory examined' is itself a critique of some writings on the subject. Although I strongly disagree with his approach, I did not consider it necessary to do a critique of a critique. All page references to the contributions in this book are in parenthesis in the text.

2.   See note, p. 9, for the meaning and changing connotations of the term 'Subaltern' and other related terms.

3.   Antonio Gramsci, 'Notes on Italian history,' *Selections from the prison notebooks* (New York: International Publishers, 1971), pp. 54–5. Emphasis added.

4.   It is surprising that Partha Chatterjee who quotes so extensively from the *Grundrisse* to justify his proposed schema fails to note an important methodological injunction of Marx in the 'Introduction' of the same text. Marx writes:

> . . . nothing seems more natural than to begin with ground rent, with landed property, since this is bound up with the earth, the source of all production and of all being, and with the first form of production of all more or less settled societies . . . agriculture. But nothing would be more erroneous. In all forms of society there is one specific kind of production which predominates over the rest, whose relations thus assign rank and influence to the others . . .'
>
> Ground rent cannot be understood without capital. But capital can certainly be understood without ground rent. Capital is the all-dominating economic power of bourgeois society. It must form the starting-point as well as the finishing-point, and must be dealt with before landed property . . .
>
> It would therefore be unfeasible and wrong to let the economic categories follow one another in the same sequence as that in which they were historically decisive. Their sequence is determined, rather, by their relation to one another in modern bourgeois society, which is precisely the opposite of that which seems to be their natural order or which corresponds to historical development. The point is not the historic position of the economic relations in the succession of different forms of society . . . Karl Marx, *Grundrisse: Introduction to the critique of political economy* (Penguin Books, tr. Martin Nicolaus, 1973), pp. 106–7.

5.   I have done a detailed and substantive critique of Partha Chatterjee's contribution in this volume along with a few other of his writings pertaining to

this problem. I have tried to show there how his understanding of the 'agrarian situation' and 'differentiation', etc. is restrictive and how it deviates from that of Lenin with serious consequences for the understanding of communalism in pre-partition Bengal. See my 'Communalism in pre-partition Bengal: A critique on questions of approach,' *Journal of Social Studies* (Bangladesh), forthcoming.

Subaltern Studies II:
A Review Article

SANGEETA SINGH, MINAKSHI MENON,
PRADEEP KUMAR DUTTA,
BISWAMOY PATI, RADHAKANTA BARIK,
RADHIKA CHOPRA, PARTHA DUTTA
AND SANJAY PRASAD

RANAJIT GUHA, in 'The prose of counter-insurgency,'[1] has tried to analyse the historiography of peasant movements in colonial India. His basic argument is that historians who have studied these movements have not considered the specific consciousness of the peasantry. They have either characterised the revolts as spontaneous uprisings or have studied only their social and economic background. Guha's complaint is that these historians regard rebellion as 'external to the peasant's consciousness' (p. 3). According to him, this problem arises not only because of the uncritical use of official sources by the historians, but also because of the historians' projection of their own consciousness into the subject they are examining. However, despite these criticisms, Guha does not provide us with an alternative framework, and the very problems he poses can in fact be questioned.

To establish the peasants' own subjectivity as the valid object of historical enquiry, Guha attempts a critique of the view that ascribes spontaneity to peasant rebellions. He can do so only by caricaturing it. Spontaneity is equated with hysterical, irrational, apocalyptic outbursts. This however is not the commonly accepted meaning of spontaneity. Spontaneity is not unpremeditated action but political action based on the actually existing consciousness of the people. Gramsci, who participated actively in the processes of political mobilisation, is a better guide to the characterisation of spontaneity. According to him,

> It must be stressed that pure spontaneity does not exist in history: it would be the same thing as 'pure' mechanicity. In the most spontaneous movement it is simply the case that the elements of conscious leadership cannot be checked, these have not achieved any consciousness of the class for itself. . . . The fact that every spontaneous movement contains rudimentary elements of conscious leadership, of discipline, is indirectly demonstrated by the fact that there exist tendencies and groups who extol spontaneity as a method. . . . They are not the result of any systematic educational activity on the part of an already conscious leading group, but have been formed through everyday experience illuminated by commonsense, i.e. by the traditional popular conception of the world.[2]

According to Guha, spontaneity is synonymous with reflexive action, so that in order to rescue the peasants from 'spontaneity,' rebellion is posited as 'a motivated and conscious undertaking on the part of the rural masses' (p. 2). At the empirical level the assertion is true—all praxis is motivated and conscious goal-oriented activity. But at the level of historical analysis this truism is meaningless simply because it is universal and cannot be used to analyse specific situations. Spontaneity is action on the basis of traditional consciousness. Guha is very clear that rebellions occurred on the basis of traditional consciousness. Thus although he apparently rejects characterisation of peasant rebellions as spontaneous, the whole piece is an attempt to rehabilitate spontaneity as a political method. This emphasis on the spontaneous context of peasant movements is inherent in the linguistic methodology employed by Guha. This linguistic analysis moves in the grooves of phenomenological methodology which recognises just experience and existence as legitimate categories. This will be taken up in detail later on.

Guha's idealism can be seen most clearly in his attempt to criticise the analysis of the social and economic conditions which generate rebellion. According to him, 'factors of economic and political deprivation do not relate at all to the peasants' consciousness or do so negatively' (p. 3). The acceptance of the primacy of social existence over consciousness does not mean economic determinism in the least. Even Lévi-Strauss, who has devoted himself to the study of modes of thought and consciousness of cultures the world over, concedes the primacy of the economic infrastructure.[3] According to him, consciousness is not just the reflection of the economic base of a society but is constituted as a result of the interaction of several institutions and structures. Guha however does not even recognise these mediations. He thus accepts the basic premises of idealism; peasant consciousness is rendered supra-historical as it is not determined by any objective historical forces. It is at a par with the Hegelian 'geist' which is not determined by history, while the development of history is the march towards the self-realisation of this spirit. Guha's idealism consists not in emphasising the importance of consciousness, but in placing consciousness beyond the pale of historical determination or mediation. This leads to his assertion that the fundamental problem with the existing historiography of peasant rebellion is that 'Cause is made to stand in as a phantom surrogate for Reason, the logic of that consciousness' (p. 3).

The motivation for the study of causes, according to Guha, was to control rebellions. While this may be true of official historiography, it is doubtful whether it can be applied equally to present-day historiography. Here again Guha's understanding betrays the basic problematic of linguistic analysis in that it is incapable of proceeding beyond the discourse of the participants themselves. It is the basic premise of neo-positivism that all knowledge is to be derived from the experience of the subject. Further, the method of analysis restricts itself to the logical analysis of language. The discourse of the participants on analysis reveals the 'reason' for rebellion embedded in it. Following Wittgenstein, independent analysis of non-linguistic categories was forsaken.[4] Guha follows this methodology in wanting analysis to concentrate on Reason and not Cause, since reason is the participants' perception of the rebellion. This 'immediacy' of analysis links up with the advocation of spontaneity as a method.

The importation of the premises of linguistic analysis into history is crippling. For example, a similar analysis of the English Revolution of 1640–60, would mean no analysis of causes except in terms of the logic of the consciousness of the participants. In this myopic vision, the English Revolution disappears and it is replaced by the Civil War, and in many places the Civil War itself has been made to disappear. It is this revisionist tendency which has been recently criticised by Christopher Hill.[5] This tendency can also be seen in recent studies on the French Revolution which announce the demise of the revolution.[6]

The full effect of this methodology becomes apparent when we consider the national movement in India. If Guha's dictum is followed, the national movement vanishes and is replaced by so many struggles for local grievances. Methodologically there is little to distinguish this from the so-called 'Cambridge School' with its search for caste, religion and factional identities which constitute the logic of peasant consciousness.

Guha masks his idealism by formulating a critique of official, liberal and left historiography. The basic problem of existing historiography is that it does not consider the peasant rebel as 'an entity whose will and reason constituted the praxis called rebellion' (p. 2). The historiography of peasant rebellions is divided into three types of discourse—'primary, secondary and tertiary according to their order of appearance in time and filiation . . . differentiated from the other two by the degree of its formal and/or acknowledged (as opposed to real and/or tacit) identification with an official point of view, by the measure of its distance from the event to which it refers, and by the ratio of the distributive and integrative components in its narrative' (p. 3). The basic elements in this division of discourse are, first, the 'identification with an official point of view,' second, its distance from the event referred to, and third, an examination of the components of the discourse. It is our contention that these categories serve primarily to break up the existing historiography into redundant categories and thus mask Guha's own idealism which has much in common with official historiography.

According to Guha, the primary discourse is 'necessarily contingent on reasons of state' (p. 4) and is characterised by 'its immediacy.' A further characteristic of this discourse is the fact of its being written by 'participants' who include not only people involved in counter-insurgency but also those involved 'indirectly as onlookers' (p. 4). It is clear from this that there can be no primary discourse that is non-official in character. This is certainly a strong proposition to make. For the nineteenth century one can still talk of a paucity of insurgent discourse, but for the twentieth century this proposition is certainly invalid.

The 'massive documentation—"primary sources" as it is known in the trade' (p. 4) consists not merely of official documents, but includes, as every student of history knows, popular songs, ballads and stories, as also letters, diaries, and reminiscences of the insurgents themselves. For the twentieth century one can refer to the private papers of rebel leaders like Baba Ramchandra or the voluminous published works of the Kisan Sabha leaders like Awdheshwar Prasad Sinha, Sahajanand Saraswati, N.G. Ranga, Sunil Sen, etc., which deserve to be treated as primary sources.[7] From Guha's account it would seem that the historians of peasant movements make no use of such primary material. Guha's critique of the existing historiography of peasant movements is flawed from the start, as the use of the 'primary discourse' in historiography is criticised heavily as uncritical acceptance of the official prose of counter-insurgency. The way out, according to Guha, is to subject this official discourse to linguistic analysis (pp. 9, 10). However, in the same article when he criticises historians for ignoring the religious consciousness of the peasantry, he quotes uncritically from official reports (pp. 34, 35) without subjecting them to the same rigorous analysis of 'functions/indices,' linear sequences, metaphoric and metonymic relations, etc. for the absence of which he berates existing historiography.

The secondary discourse of peasant historiography consists, according to Guha, of memoirs and monographs written for public consumption. The main distinction between the primary and secondary discourse is that the latter is chronologically separate from the event described. However, both are 'linked with the system of power' (p. 7). Thus there can be no secondary discourse which is monographical in nature and not part of official historiography. Again, he includes both official and non-official writers as part of the tertiary discourse. The only criterion for the inclusion of the former is their being the 'farthest removed in time from the events' (p. 27). In this case, when does the secondary discourse end and the tertiary discourse begin?

The salutary feature of Guha's discussion of the official discourse is the stress on a critical examination of the sources and their functional insertion in an administrative and ideological structure. This point is a widely accepted dictum in historical writing. However, the method of critical scrutiny which Guha advocates should also be taken critically. The argument advanced is that the components of the discourse should be broken down into segments and the indicative and interpretative segments separated and analysed. The indicative statements provide an empirical picture while the interpretative statements provide a commentary on them. Not all discourse can however be separated on this basis. The indicative statements themselves are also interpretative and ideological. Syntagmatic or paradigmatic relationships, corresponding to functional and indicative codes, do not really help us in analysing the nature of the discourse. As Chomsky has emphasised, analysis of discourses cannot be carried out at the level of their empirical components alone. What has to be analysed are the larger signifying unities within which the symbols and signs create structures of sense.[8]

Further, the use of the syntagmatic and paradigmatic relationships is based on the work of Roland Barthes. This methodology of bidimensional analysis was developed in Ferdinand de Saussure and elaborated by Roman Jakobson. The problem with bidimensional analysis is that it is confined, as indicated above, to an empirical reading of the discourse. Barthes recognises this when he states that his analysis of *mythologies* depends on the analysis of images and texts not only at the empirical level but also at the second deeper level of signification.[9] He implicitly concedes that the first level of signification, including especially functional relations, is also ideological. The thrust of Barthes's work is towards the elaboration of the methods by which mythologies are created and sustained in society. It is only at the second level of signification that the ideological role of any text or image can be grasped. This is not attained by breaking up and analysing components of the discourse at the superficial level, where they can be both functional and indicative.[10] In later works, however, Barthes increasingly shifts from structural to sequential analysis, and assigns primacy to linguistics under which the science of semiology should be incorporated. As stressed earlier, this reflects the influence of the neo-positivists and Wittgenstein, with their focus on language as the source of all knowledge. Certain contradictory features emerge in his work and categories like 'functions' and 'indices' are developed and used for the analysis of narrative, as for instance, of Ian Fleming's *Goldfinger*. Sequential analysis, the mixing of systems personal and apersonal, remains confined to the level of the text, and is unacceptable as far as historical analysis is concerned because the discourse of the historian is the only object of analysis. The method of sequential analysis has been found inadequate also in standard literary criticism which increasingly stresses the need to study the conditions of literary creation, the reception of the text in its time and also the context of the text, its reader and its concretisation.[11] Barthes's analysis of James Bond does not tell us anything about the conditions of its creation, the social conditions it embodies like the Cold War, or even what it signifies to the reader.[12] These are precisely the pitfalls of getting caught up in the analyses of 'micro-sequence' (pp. 10–11). The pointlessness of this reductive tendency has been subjected to severe criticism by Pierre Macherey, according to whom all texts are 'decentered' texts. Their analysis has to consider not only what they state, but also the 'invisible presence' of what they do not state. However, sequential analysis results in accepting the text on its own terms.[13]

Thus, Mao's dichotomy of 'it's terrible' and 'it's fine' is developed by Guha totally within the paradigmatic/interpretative framework. Guha accepts the functional/metonymic/syntagmatic relationship as a true picture of the concrete reality. The official texts minus their interpretative context (terrible/fine) are taken at their face value. Guha makes the mistake of which he is accusing official historiography. This point is fundamental. Instances can be multiplied *ad nauseum* of primary and secondary discourses (in Guha's sense of the terms) which are ideologically biased not only in their interpretative/metaphoric relationships but also in terms of the functional/metonymic relationships. Official sources not only suppress information but also indulge in distortion and falsehood and this is specially true of the secondary discourse meant for public consumption. For instance, W.W. Hunter's *Annals of rural Bengal,* used heavily by Guha, says that as a result of British intervention the Santals stopped their insurgent activities in the early nineteenth century and took to plough agriculture. The reference, obvious to anyone familiar with Santal history, is not the Santals (plough agriculturists who migrated to the Santal Parganas from neighbouring districts under British aegis) but to the tribe of the Paharias whose insurrection was suppressed by the East India Company in the late eighteenth century. After this, their ecological habitat, which sustained shifting cultivation, hunting and gathering, was invaded by the Santals and they were pushed on to the inner forests and hilltops. The history of this tribe reveals a tragic story of deculturation, destruction and depopulation. The repression of the Paharias and the migration of the Santals into the area is fused by Hunter into a single event in the history of the Santals. The main aim of this fusion was to demonstrate the pacificatory benevolence of the British who transformed a 'criminal' tribe into peaceful peasants. The resulting concoction is not just ideological but is totally false.[14] Guha has in fact approvingly summarised Hunter's references to the Santals (pp. 21–6), but fails to note this contradiction. Guha's methodology of sequential analysis can identify only one thing wrong with the text, that 'the syntagma is broken up again by dystaxia and interpretation filters through to assemble the segments into a meaningful whole of a primarily metaphorical character' (pp. 21–2). The inference is that the functional/syntagmatic/metonymic relationships are valid. The text therefore can be accepted at its face value after the prejudices of the author have been discounted, that is, the adjectives expunged and the verbs retained. This leads to a certain carelessness in the handling of sources which are not cross-checked and verified. Guha criticises existing historiography for not being critical of sources, but the methodology he adopts is itself uncritical, and places him closer to the official discourse of power.

Coming finally to the tertiary discourse, this is clearly the most nebulous of the three categorisations, being based solely on the criterion of time, and, as we have already seen above, includes official, non-official, liberal and left writings. The basic proposition advanced by Guha is that historians have not considered the specific nature of peasant consciousness as exemplified in rebellion in particular. The discussion on the primary and secondary discourses is not an end in itself in the article, but is only important as an examination of 'those cuts, seams and stitches—those cobbling marks—which tell us about the material it (tertiary discourse) is made of and the manner of its absorption in the fabric of writing' (p. 3). One would therefore expect that detailed consideration of existing historiography would be taken up. However, Guha gives no examples from liberal nationalist historiography though he makes several sweeping generalisations. For instance, he says that the Indian bourgeoisie is the subject of 'tertiary discourse of the History-of-the-Freedom-Struggle genre' (p. 33). The lacuna is certainly not due to oversight. The absence of examples has to be taken into account if we read Guha's text not casually but symptomatically to search for the invisible presence. Probably texts that correspond to Guha's criteria do not exist.

Again, as far as radical historiography is concerned, Guha claims that the peasant does not exist as a subject in its discourse, having been replaced by 'an *abstraction* called the worker and peasant, *an ideal rather than the real* historical personality of the insurgent' (p. 33). Immediately obvious is the lack of any correspondence between the generalisations and the supporting evidence. The only example taken up for discussion is that of the Santal rebellion of 1855 and its discussion in S. Ray's *Bharater krishak bidroha o ganatantrik sangram* (1966). The choice could not have been worse because the only monographical work on the Santal rebellion is that of K.K. Datta.[15] The other works fall into two categories—either general studies of the Santal tribe with chapters on Santal history, or general works on peasant movement in India again with a chapter or less on the Santal *hool.* These non-specialised studies on the *hool* are dependent either on secondary sources or on the most easily accessible primary sources, like Hunter or the *Calcutta Review* article. No general conclusions on radical historiography could be justified on the basis of such works. Instances of radical historians studying the peasants' consciousness as it existed are not lacking. In fact, many insurgents, as indicated above, had written on peasant rebellions and movements, good examples being Sahajanand Saraswati's *Kisan sabha ke sansmaran, mera jivan sangharsh*, and numerous other articles, Awdheshwar Prasad Sinha's *Bihar prantiya kisan sabha ki report 1929–1935*, and Sunil Sen's *Agrarian struggle in Bengal 1946–1947*. These works are not only a part of radical historiography, but are also part of what are termed 'primary sources.' In addition, there are a number of historical studies both liberal and radical (the terms have been used heuristically) which are very critical of the primary and secondary discourses described by Guha and are separated from them by more than what Guha calls a 'declaration of sentiment' (p. 40).

A further problem with Guha's examples is that they are selectively drawn, predominantly from the nineteenth century. In this phase the attitude of the British colonialism to agrarian disturbances was one of paternalism whose ideological function Guha recognises (pp. 23–7). Therefore, primary and secondary discourses are full of protective references to the peasantry. In the case of the Santal *hool* taken up by Guha, this paternalism can masquerade as one of looking after the interests of the noble savage against the Bengali moneylender and *zamindar*. This is reflected at another level by the official caricature of the job-hungry Bengali *baboos*. The same historical representations thus serve the ends of ideological domination. This paternal ideology can be seen at work in most of the major peasant movements of the nineteenth century, the Deccan riots of 1875, the Pabna rebellion, etc., where, after suppressing the movements, the state held inquiries into the agrarian causes of the same, and even carried out legislation in the interests of the peasantry. By the twentieth century, however, with the coalescence of the nationalist, worker and peasant protest the state reaction was very different. Ideological domination was increasingly replaced by physical domination; landlord associations were organised to counter the now well-knit Kisan Sabha and other peasant bodies. The contradiction between primary and secondary discourses on the one hand and the tertiary discourse on the other is much more glaring in the twentieth century. The simplistic homologies developed by Guha with the *hool* as a backdrop are thus hardly representative.

The problem of 'immediacy' and the linguistic method in Guha's own study of peasant consciousness is symptomatic of his problematic. When analysing the Santal *hool*, Guha comes to the conclusion that 'religiosity was by all accounts central to the hool' and further that the rebellion was not related to any particular grievance. From this he infers that 'it is not possible to speak of insurgency except as religious consciousness' (p. 34). Rebellion is thus analysed purely in terms of the meaning the participants attach to it. He quotes from official documents to prove his point. But these statements on the religiosity of the peasantry, surely interpretative/metaphorical statements which should, by his own standards, be submitted to scrutiny, are taken at their face value. In fact, liberal and radical historiography is criticised for not having noticed the fact that the consciousness of the peasantry is profoundly religious. The religious consciousness of the peasantry is not subjected to any determinations and is made supra-historical. It is assumed that the peasantry has an ideal form of paradigmatically pure peasant consciousness. The implication is that peasant consciousness marked by religiosity existed in a pure state especially in the nineteenth century.[16] Could anything be more idealistic than this?

Religion also, following the critical structural method, is not merely religiosity but is tied up with the forces and relations of production. Religion is important for peasant consciousness not because peasant consciousness is inherently religious, but because religion is part of the ideological superstructure.

Rodney Hilton, in his analysis of peasant rebellions in Europe, notes that religion was not one of the important constituents of rebel consciousness.[17] The religious aspect of rebel consciousness was emphasised by British officials to the exclusion of the social, economic or political content of that consciousness. Colonialism was thus absolved of its oppressive role, and rebellions were attributed to the inherent irrationality of the peasantry. As we have indicated above, by accepting this characterisation, Guha places himself closer to the official historiography which he appears to be criticising.

Guha criticises historians for being 'blinded by the glare of a perfect and immaculate consciousness' (p. 39), even though his own characterisation is an abstraction. In a peasantry existing in a class-divided society, it is difficult to believe that religious consciousness could be something internal to its own subjectivity and not hegemonic in nature. Any exclusive analysis limited to consciousness at a given moment conveys very little. As L. Goldman, who stresses the importance of studying consciousness as part of social totality, emphasises that no analysis of the real consciousness of the Russian peasants in 1912, for instance, would help in predicting their consciousness and actions between 1917 and 1921, and if our analysis was restricted merely to linguistic categories we would never be able to move from the study of actual to possible elements of consciousness based on the historical moment, which would severely limit our understanding.[18]

Further, looking at analytical categories only in terms of meaning attached to them by the participants is, as has been stressed, a form of positivism. Such an experiential epistemology has a long history that can be traced back to Berkeley in the early eighteenth century. It has already been subjected to a withering attack by Lenin in his *Materialism and emperio-criticism.*[19] The restrictive effect of a historiography based on such an epistemology is immediately apparent in a consideration of its imposition in other disciplines studying society. The works of Marcel Mauss and Lévi-Strauss which emphasise the integrative aspect of exchange of gifts and women, and of Lévi-Strauss and Maurice Godelier on myths, would be illegitimate inferences as the participants themselves are not conscious of these integrative and reifying aspects.[20] In economics the whole discussion of fetishisation of commodities and the generation of surplus value in Marx's *Capital* and *Theories of surplus value* is based on the critique of the phenomenological method. Meaningful analysis cannot be carried out unless the apparent empirical level is transcended and hidden relationships revealed. Marx states, '. . . vulgar economy feels particularly at home in the estranged outward appearances of economic relations . . . all science would be superfluous if the outward appearance and the essence of things directly coincided.'[21]

One of the major issues of concern for Guha is that official historiography does not have a place for the rebel 'as the subject of rebellion' (p. 27). Liberal and radical historians also do not consider the rebel as a subject and the representation of the rebel in their discourse is, according to Guha, an inverted form of official discourse in which the peasantry is arranged 'along the alternative axis of a protracted campaign for freedom and socialism . . . this too amounts to an act of appropriation which excludes the rebel as the conscious subject of his own history and incorporates the latter as only a contingent element in another history with another subject' (p. 33). Posing the problem in terms of the subject–object dichotomy is however a pointless exercise. As far as scientific analysis is concerned, the subject form is valid for every individual in history since his acts constitute social practice. No historian can obviously deny subjectivity to the people he is studying. At the philosophical level, however, the whole problematic centred around the subject is part of what Althusser, in his debate with John Lewis, calls the discourse of idealist philosophy.[22] This is because the subject of phenomenological and existential discourse is a person who has internalised the movement of history and, by the ascription of subjectivity, is made responsible for this movement. But man is only a subject transforming history; the mode of his intervention is determined by the objective conditions in which he is placed. There is no supra-historical transcendental subject. It is not by a phenomenological analysis of the human essence that an understanding of social relations is gained; on the contrary, it is scientific investigation of social relations which makes for an understanding of the human essence for, after all, human essence is the ensemble of social relations, a product of history. To understand man's capacity to change these social relations, and evaluate the efficacy of continuing attempts to bring about such changes, one has to go beyond subjectivity and such false dichotomies as determinism and liberty, and concentrate instead on the study of the concrete.

Guha's phenomenological bias is clearly visible when we consider existing historiography which, according to Guha, has appropriated the rebel to its own discourse. Guha wants analysis to be restricted to the categories of experience within which participants are viewing them. However, in the materialist method, all knowledge is appropriation. According to Marx, '. . . thought appropriates the concrete reproducing it as the concrete in the mind . . . the concrete totality is a totality of thoughts, concrete is thought, in fact a product of thinking and comprehending.'[23] Since all knowledge is appropriation, there is nothing very special about the liberal or radical historiography appropriating the peasantry (technically what is appropriated to their discourse in the knowledge of the peasantry).

It follows that Guha's reconstruction of the consciousness of the peasantry is also an act of appropriation, In fact, it cannot but be otherwise. Guha realises that the problem is insurmountable because of the chronological distance between the event and the historian, and suggests that a realisation of this subjectivity would help. But this awareness of the historian's own historicity is something that has become conventional knowledge since at least E.H. Carr's *What is history?* The failure to evolve any alternative paradigm mars Guha's whole historiographical critique. From a consideration of sequential analysis of sources down to the plea that the peasant be treated as a subject of his own history, whose consciousness must be analysed in terms of categories valid to it, the critique finally concludes as a historian's self-awareness of the unrealisability of the project. The problems posed by Guha may have some validity but they certainly have not been satisfactorily formulated or resolved.

II

Gautam Bhadra's 'Two frontier unprisings in Mughal India' is the shortest and perhaps the most unpretentious contribution to this volume.

Studies on the agrarian structure and peasant protest in medieval India have come into their own in a big way recently, and Bhadra's essay is of interest chiefly because it focuses on a region regarding which comparatively little is known—medieval north-eastern India, specifically the area of Kamrup–Goalpara in present-day Assam.

While conceding the paucity of indigenous source material on seventeenth-century Assam (most Buranjis and other literature deal with a later period), Bhadra, it would seem, has consciously confined himself to a Persian chronicle, Mirza Nathan's *Baharistan-i-ghaybi*, a standard seventeenth-century account of the region, for his discussion of the two rebellions.[24]

Bhadra's aim is two-fold: to project Mughal–Koch relations as two opposing totalities, that is, the 'élite' Mughals *vs.* the 'subaltern' group of the ruling chieftains and the people of Kamrup, and in conjunction with this, to attempt to delineate 'a tradition of peasant resistance that was invoked again and again in various forms against Mir Jumla, against the Ahoms during the Moamaria revolt and against British rule in the late nineteenth century' (p. 59).

In order to achieve his object, Bhadra has attempted to depict the pre-Ahom Koch polity as an undifferentiated unity in its response to the Mughal challenge, as well as deliberately playing down the tumultuous political history of the region, in this period. And finally, having done so in his analysis of the character of these two rebellions, he projects them as pre-eminently peasant in their orientation, although as regards participation and mobilisation, 'some of the rebellions had an obviously aristocratic linkage' (p. 55), due to the operation of vertical linkages such as kinship and caste ties.

As regards the agrarian economy and social organisation of Kuch-Bihar, what Bhadra wishes to convey is that while the *paikan* system was as important for agrarian organisation in Kuch-Bihar as for the Ahom kingdom, the level of social differentiation which existed in the latter was the product of Ahom and Mughal impact in Kuch-Bihar, and as such developed in a later period, namely, the seventeenth and eighteenth centuries. He offers no evidence at all for this assertion, except to state the non-availability of any indigenous sources on Kamrup for this period. This is turn allows him to assume that 'the community bondage among the *paiks*, soldiers as well as cultivators, was perhaps stronger within a less differentiated agrarian society, especially where the bulk of the cultivators belonged to the same caste group' (pp. 53–4). Thus the Mughal–Koch conflicts were, for Bhadra, a confrontation between a socially and economically liberal society and a stratified economically oppressive one. Koch reaction to the Mughal displayed a unity of action of the Koch people, due mainly to this lack of social differentiation. Apart from the fact that such an argument is theoretically untenable, there are no real grounds for supposing that the Koch social system was in any sense different from that which prevailed in the neighbouring Ahom territory. Indeed, a stronger case can be made on the basis of available evidence for mutual socio-economic and cultural interaction and influence. We know of the existence of a well-established trade between the Koch and Ahom kingdoms. While referring to a later period, Amalendu Guha has discussed how the impact of the imposition of the Mughal revenue system in Kuch-Bihar, and in the occupied areas of Assam, was transmitted to the region as a whole,[25] especially the Ahom territory.

With reference to Bhadra's period, the existence of well-developed social differentiation in the Koch territory is hinted at by the marriage of the daughter of Raja Parikshit in 1608 to the Ahom ruler Pratap Singha (Hso-Hseng-Hpa). It is mentioned that the Koch king sent with his daughter twenty families of slaves and twenty families of domestics as dowry.[26] What appears very likely is that the existence of a well-developed social stratification in the Ahom territory was paralleled by similar differentiation in the Koch kingdom.

Amalendu Guha has mentioned the nature of the exploitation within the Ahom polity: the existence of slavery, both domestic and agrestic, as well as serfdom. He estimates that slaves, serfs and bondsmen constituted between five and nine per cent of the population.[27] Apart from this, he discusses the state of the peasants, who, in their capacity as *paiks*, were allotted to the estates and homes of office holders, 'with full exposure to their cruelties and extortions. (Nearly) . . . one-fourth to one-third of the mobilised *paiks* were allotted as *likechaus*. Available as they were for a limited period, exploitation was more ruthless in their case than in the case of slaves.'[28]

Such being the case, it is not surprising that the adoption of the Mughal land revenue administration in the Ahom territory, later in the seventeenth century, provoked no opposition. Indeed, this came about because a relatively affluent section of Assamese *paiks* looked forward to the commutation of the service obligation to the state into kind or cash payment, and the government was forced to concede such demands.[29] Indeed, the Ahoms even retained the Mughal revenue system in areas such as Kuch-Hajo, from where they succeeded in dislodging the Mughals in a subsequent period.

If, as we have reasoned, the Kochs had a socio-economic system similar to that of the Ahoms, it would be difficult to accept Bhadra's depiction of the nature of the confrontation between the Mughals and the Kochs: 'Hence in this type of agrarian society, where most of the cultivators as well as their chiefs belonged to the same caste group, mobilisation often followed the lines of social linkages binding rajas, *sardars* and cultivators in a common struggle. Dishonourable treatment meted to a royal house or a breach of trust with respect to the latter, could easily have been construed as an affront to the prestige of the community, particularly to that of the chiefs' (p. 57). Bhadra's inference is clear: even if the rebellion under Sanatan, for instance, had a *zamindar* leadership, its impetus and thrust was peasant in character, since they were equally threatened by Mughal paramountcy.

According to this argument, the peasantry was faced with the economic oppression of Mughal revenue practices, the local *sardars* by their attempted political domination. Both of these oppressed 'subaltern' groups were bound together by kinship and caste ties. Once we consider the existence of differentiation and economic exploitation internal to the Koch polity itself, however, this manner of reasoning appears difficult to accept.

Allied to this is Bhadra's neglect of the political scenario of the region in the period. The paradigm of 'subalternism' cannot comfortably accommodate the fact that the politics of the region—the rivalry between the rulers of Kuch-Bihar and Kamrup, as well as the drive for suzerainty over this area by the Ahoms, and the attempts of the Mughals to expand the boundaries of *suba* Bengal eastwards—resulted in sudden changes of political alliances. It is against this shifting background of alliances, defined by the Mughal–Ahom confrontations for hegemony in the region, that the series of border rebellions in the early seventeenth century must be analysed. The endemic agrarian unrest and the 'peasant' uprisings which occurred, cannot be viewed in isolation from the clashes for political supremacy among the ruling groups of the region.

The nature of these political alignments is ignored perhaps because this would deflect the main line of Bhadra's reasoning—that of a tradition of 'subaltern' resistance to 'élite' Mughal authority, in conjunction with the essentially 'peasant' character of this protest. In this connection, he makes two interesting statements. With reference to the rebellions in Kamrup in 1616–17, he says: '. . . the peasants killed the *karoris* and *mustajars*. The Kuch nobles joined their rebellion and proclaimed one of themselves as the raja' (p. 47). And again, with reference to the Hathikheda uprising, after referring to the special categories of *paiks* (i.e., *palis* and *gharduwaris*) who were involved in it, he remarks: 'The rebellion spread to other classes. Bhaba Singh, the Kuch noble and brother of Raja Parikshit, became involved in it' (p. 50). If this were so, we would have two quite unique instances in the history of protest and dissent in Mughal India—of peasant upsurges joined in the later stages by the local chieftains. The usual pattern appears to be one where peasant unrest was subsumed, after a stage, by the aggressive activities of recalcitrant *zamindars*.

Bhadra's approach thus necessitates two divergent lines of reasoning: on the one hand he posits a less differentiated society in the Kuch kingdom, to account for a unity of action by different social groups *vis-à-vis* the Mughals. On the other hand, he attempts to establish these rebellions as primarily peasant in origin, joined at later stages by other superior classes. This latter delinking is of course necessary to establish the autonomy of peasant action even if it later coalesced with the protests of other affected groups. This is reinforced by a lack of detail regarding political affairs of the period.

In actual fact, the rivalry between the two houses of Kuch-Bihar and Kuch-Hajo, allowed the Mughals to obtain a foothold in the region, since Laksminarayan of Kuch-Bihar was forced to accept Mughal suzerainty in order to arm himself against Kamrup, which, under Raghudev and Parikshitnarayan, was successively allied with the Pathan, Isa Khan, and then with the Ahoms. The Ahoms, alarmed by Mughal expansionism in the region, were conscious of the necessity of maintaining Kamrup as a buffer state. Pratap Singha, it should be noted, installed Balinarayan (1615–37), brother of Parikshitnarayan, as the vassal ruler of Darrang, and then set about drawing all the neighbouring rulers to his side by war, marriage, friendly alliance and extension of protective vassalage.[30] His growing power induced most petty chiefs to accept his overlordship. The internal problems of subaltern methodology are thus made very clear. Did the aggressive designs of the ruler of Gargaon, and his attempts to consolidate Ahom power over the other petty states of the north-east qualify the Ahoms to be described, in turn, as an élite power group?

Sanatan, a headman of the *paiks*, is described by Bhadra as the leader of a spontaneous peasant rebellion against the oppressive practices of the Mughals. This Koch chief made Sheikh Ibrahim, the *karori*, his principal target, and protested vehemently against his revenue abuses and general harassment of the peasantry (pp. 48–9). But when Sheikh Ibrahim, in order to avoid the consequences of his misappropriation of imperial revenues, appealed to Pratap Singha, the Ahom ruler, for help,[31] his chief aid came in the form of a Koch force under Sanatan.[32] Sanatan's involvement in the power politics of the region is thus indicated. It is further recorded that when Sanatan attacked the Mughal *thana* of Dhamdhama, Mirza Salih Arghun, who was in charge of the garrison there, 'received the help and cooperation of the local zamindars with whom he was on very friendly terms.'[33]

As regards the agrarian unrest against the Mughals in Khuntaghat in this period, S.C. Dutta notes the instigation of a series of rebellions in Khuntaghat by the Ahoms and their vassals, especially Balinarayan of Darrang.[34]

The entire period commencing with the campaigns of Mirza Nathan in the reign of Jehangir to the end of Mir Jumla's expeditions against the Ahoms, was characterised by a situation of extreme political dislocation in the region. Political instability, border raids and constant plundering expeditions by both sides resulted in agrarian upheaval. It would, therefore, be a mistake to view this solely as peasant protest against Mughal oppression.

Who, after all, were the real losers as a result of the establishment of Mughal suzerainty and the co-option of hitherto independent regions of the subcontinent into the centralised Mughal administrative framework? In every case it has been shown to be the local ruling groups, who were reduced to the position of revenue collecting intermediaries, or at best to vassal chieftains, owing a material and moral allegiance to the paramount power. The political power of these independent rulers was firmly quelled by the Mughal sovereign and an elaborate central administrative machinery was established to keep them well under control.[35] There was a resurgence of these local ruling groups in most parts of the empire with the decline of Mughal authority.[36]

What appears likely, given the factual evidence, is that in the confrontation between the Mughals and the Ahoms for control over the Koch territory, the local chieftains were able to mobilise the peasantry against their rivals. This is logical, given the operation of the *paik* system, and the fact that a section of the peasantry (amounting to 50 per cent of the cultivators in situations of emergency) was always in the military service of the chief.

Kinship and lineage were doubtless factors in promoting a degree of cohesion against external threat. But what probably happened was that agrarian unrest, such as it was, was subsumed in the political ambition of the local rulers in their struggle against the Mughals, and with each other. This would be in consonance with our information regarding agrarian revolts in the seventeenth century in other parts of the Mughal empire.[37]

The character of peasant unrest in medieval India was thus diluted by the intervention of *zamindars* and other superior right holders, who channelled peasant unrest in the direction of their partisan political ambitions. Moreover, as Irfan Habib has remarked, the peasantry was so intensely divided on lines of caste and so heavily differentiated that the idea of equality at any plane, essential for any recognisable level of class consciousness, could not flourish.[38]

Nothing could be more positivist than an attempt to project the history of the region of Kamrup in the seventeenth century as a united popular protest of the 'people' against the encroaching Mughal power. For this does not take into account the contradictions within the structure of the Koch polity, or the complex political relations between the Ahoms, the Mughals and the Kochs.

Bhadra's piece is a good illustration of the potential for myth-making inherent in the concept of the 'subaltern.' By positing a unity of action by the people of the region against 'élite' Mughal authority, it sidesteps the necessity for an analysis of the agrarian structure of the region and the social relationships generated by it. When studies of medieval agrarian history and agrarian protest are moving towards further complexity of analysis and characterisation, 'subalternism' constitutes a methodological regression to the days of W.C. Smith, when all uprisings against Mughal authority were characterised as 'lower class uprisings.'

III

Gyan Pandey's 'Rallying round the cow: Sectarian strife in the Bhojpuri region, *c.* 1888–1917' deals with the much-discussed question of communalism from a new angle. Its contribution lies both in exploring an originality of research (for this subject) as well as in the questions it raises.

The originality of this essay stems from its recognition that communalism is not a socially autonomous process; that, besides material factors, it is linked to other problems like caste, which have been accentuated by colonial economic development. This gives to the essay a certain comprehensiveness of analysis, which, if extended, can throw even more light on the specific ways in which a semi-feudal society interacts with capitalist penetration.

Equally important, in contrast to the standard historiographical approach to communalism, Pandey is able to establish the possibilist nature of the situation: the fact that the communal contradiction was simply one of the many contradictions latent in Indian society. The problem with the usual historiography of communalism is that it deals only with the national level of communal politics. As a result, the understanding often becomes necessitarian. After all, as is well known, the basic parameters of nationalist ideology could not transcend religion. In fact, it largely contributed to the virulent growth of communalism and the clarity of its articulation. The problem is actually in-built in the whole historical circumstances of a national movement led by the bourgeoisie linked to the feudal order, as in our country. However, by revealing a disjunction between the 'national' and 'popular' levels, Pandey does break new ground to show that the situation at the grassroots was not inevitably progressing towards a clear communal divide.

Amongst the new perceptions that this essay offers is the fact that rural areas are not immune to communal contagion. This point is very important, especially in the context of our own times, when communalism is showing no signs of abatement. The other original assertion in this essay is that it decisively debunks the idea of the 'religious fanaticism' of the masses, and clearly establishes that there were different motivations behind the flare-ups.

Despite these important contributions, Pandey does not offer a complete explanation for the central problem of this essay: why the communal contradiction got accentuated despite the existence of other equally severe contradictions. As Abdul Majid's diary (cited by Pandey, pp. 77–8) indicates, the division between *bade* and *chote log* dominated over the religious divide. In that case why did the communal riots slide back?

A large part of the answer to this question can be found in the quote from Majid itself. Majid recognises the fact that they were manipulated by the *zamindars*. Pandey himself notes that communal demands were 'injected' into the Bhojpuri region. If this was the case, then Pandey should have dealt with the Gaurakshini Sabha and its activities in greater detail. This would have led to a better understanding of the whole process of communal transmission, from the national level downwards.

This lacuna in Pandey's argument is related to a fundamental problem of 'subaltern' scholarship. By trying to abstract the 'subaltern' from the 'élite,' one cannot really explore the ways in which these two levels interact. Moreover, this approach also begs the question of leadership and its different levels, ranging from the local to the decisive level of national politics. Ultimately, both issues are related to the problem of why subalterns remain in their subject position.

Part of the 'subaltern' prejudice militates against the urban petit bourgeoisie. This is clearly evident in the essay. While establishing the intimate connections and continuities between town and country in the Bhojpuri region, Pandey also observes another fact. By the late nineteenth century there was a growing class of urban petit bourgeoisie. Later he notes that they played an initiating role in transmitting Gaurakshini propaganda. These facts certainly make them more important than the limited space given to them might indicate. As a result, certain important questions regarding how this urban culture was changing and becoming the centre of Gaurakshini activity, the question of the relationship between different sections of the petit bourgeoisie, and finally the relationship between this urban class and the *zamindars* are ignored.

On the other hand lies the problem of autonomy. Besides the fundamental problem as to whether any single historical process can be truly autonomous, at the level of the essay itself Pandey does not seem very confident about this term. In the space of a single paragraph Pandey characterises the Ahir action as being both 'relatively independent' and 'autonomous' (p. 104). Surely the two terms do not mean the same thing.

In fact, there seems to be a conscious desire to abstract the Ahirs from the other processes of encouraging the growth of communalism in this region. Even if it is granted that they were reaching out for a higher social status, this does not explain why they should have had to indulge in communal riots. After all they could have simply built temples or *gaushalas*.

A good deal of light could have been thrown on this problem if Pandey had dealt more extensively with the specific ways in which Gaurakshini propaganda interacted with Ahir discontent. This would also have provided a means of explicating their relationship with the *zamindars* and more specifically of showing why, with the exception of some situations, they seem to have accepted the overall leadership of the *zamindars*. Surely their united front with the *zamindars* on this question cannot simply be attributed to a historical coincidence of interests.

This brings us to the question of ideology and mentalities. Strangely, for a topic such as communalism, for which it is so important to understand the culture and mentality as the material factors, Pandey pays scant attention to the use of symbols and slogans. His account confines itself to methods of transmission and descriptions of riots caused by violations of communal symbols. Both aspects are in a sense redundant, because the issues they raise have already been covered. Regarding the symbol of the cow itself, Pandey reiterates the obvious: that its sanctity was emphasised.

We would have acquired a better understanding of the peasant mentality, of a fundamental condition of communal unity, had Pandey delved deeper into the symbol of the cow. After all the cow was not simply a symbol; it was a world-view condensed into a symbol. This can be deduced from Pandey's observations that all the gods were telescoped into the cow. Moreover, being a material creature, the cow could provide supernatural ratification for the material actions which violated other codes of the Hindu religion which advocated acceptance and non-violence.

At the same time it is interesting to note the basic issues raised to prominence through the symbol of the cow. Significantly, the Hindus—as emerges from the *patias* quoted by Pandey—did not regard their objective as one of expanding hegemony, of forcibly converting the Muslims to the cause of the cow. They viewed it as a defensive battle against oppression and injustice as palpably expressed in cow-slaughter. As such their religious motivation corresponded to their basic sense of insecurity, which, as Pandey himself shows, was the outgrowth of the whole impact of colonialism.

This leads us to two related problems which have received inadequate treatment: the ferocity of the attacks and the latent anti-imperialism within the communal consciousness.

What was responsible for the intensity of the attacks? Can it be explained, as Pandey offers to do, merely by the fact of issues becoming entangled with personal quarrels? True, these quarrels have more resonance in a rural society, especially in the specific circumstances delineated. But why should it take on the character of a civil war? Nor can this be attributed simply to the momentum of action. The wedding incident in 1893 (p. 85) clearly suggests a high degree of premeditation in the savagery.

This intensity can possibly be better understood if the latent, subverted anti-imperialist thrust of their actions is taken into account. After all, if the cow becomes a bulwark against a vulnerable existence, then it was also a symbol representative of resistance to colonialism which had created these conditions. This would raise the more specific problem of Gaurakshini propaganda: Was it simply a defence of religion or did it also link this with the whole colonial context of flux and insecurity?

It is in fact remarkably short-sighted of Pandey not to have dealt with this aspect. This is worth remarking precisely because Pandey does make stray observations regarding the conjunction of cow protection propaganda with Home Rule activity and rumours of the imminent collapse of the Raj (p. 90). Even more significantly, in the second *patia* quoted by Pandey (p. 91), there is a direct reference to the alleged help forthcoming from the German king, the Chhattris and the Bengalis (p. 110). Given the context of the First World War and popular memories of the Swadeshi movement, amongst other things, this obviously points to the somewhat ambiguous political significance of the cow.

At the same time, Pandey's delineation of the impact of colonial rule seems insufficient. The structural changes in the society and economy of the Bhojpuri region as a consequence of colonial rule are competently sketched. Where Pandey falters is in trying to analyse the politics of colonialism in furthering the communal divide. There are some observations on how officials provoked riots in Shahabad and some generalisations about British policy (p. 122), but the stress seems to be on the idiosyncrasies of official action. Part of the problem may be due to the fact of undertaking a micro study which would tend to enlarge the importance of individual actions. However, in the ultimate analysis, this cannot be a justification for the absence of a clearer assertion of the relationship between colonial policies and the actions of individual officials.

In conclusion, it may be remarked that these problems and lacunae in the essay are finally a product of the limitations of the 'subaltern' approach. For, this approach ultimately inverts the world of historiography, as against the importance given to the 'élites,' the 'subalterns' are given pride of place. The result of this inversion is that the international and national levels of history are at best treated as a passive backdrop. Precisely because of this approach, subaltern history itself starts showing many gaps.

This finally relates to the question of political responsibility. If one is simply investigating communalism as an academic exercise, the avoidance of interlinked issues may be understood. But for historians like Pandey, whose anti-communal bias is evident, it is crucial to understand the phenomenon of communalism in its totality. The process of understanding itself has to be an instrument in the battle against communalism. And, as is clear from our contemporary situation, we can no longer afford the indulgence of partial enlightenment.

IV

Stephen Henningham's 'Quit India in Bihar and the Eastern United Provinces: The dual revolt' shows clearly the dangers involved in relying solely on the 'prose of counter-insurgency' to reconstruct a movement as complex and fascinating as the Quit India revolt in eastern Uttar Pradesh and Bihar. It is indeed an irony that historians professing to rescue the 'people' from the clutches of bourgeois-nationalist historiography fall back primarily on imperialist sources to accomplish their task. Can one talk of serious problems related to the not-so-remote past without using oral evidence? Henningham overlooks the land question and vital issues such as peasant stratification, except for stray references to prove a point or refute another. Can one really look upon the 'subalterns' as a historical category or a class in colonial India?

Henningham's mistakes, then, originate in certain methodological problems which get reflected in the essay.

Can one overlook the Congress and its call for the 1942 movement? Henningham himself notes at the outset that the movement, in fact, was sparked when the colonial government reacted sharply to the AICC's 'Quit India' resolution of August 8, 1942 (p. 131). The dialectical linkages between the call for the struggle and the slogans unleashed by the 'messiah from above' (i.e., Gandhi) and the stratified peasantry in the middle Gangetic plain with its problems and perceptions of the 'saviour' and *swaraj* are overlooked. 'Do or Die,' 'Let every Indian consider himself to be a free man,' etc., were slogans that did provide a signal for the launching of the 1942 movement. Unless one grasps these basic features it is not possible to explain things without confusion. 'People' did not see a 'breakdown' through rumours alone (p. 141), but through the dialectical interaction between, on the one hand, the problems affecting them, which the author mentions (pp. 137–42), and, on the other, perceptions of *swaraj* as a distinct possibility of a way out.

In his eagerness to create a 'historic bloc' of the subalterns, the author makes the mistake of not seriously taking into account what his own work shows: (a) the increasing influence of the Congress in the pre-1942 context and (b) the importance of 'less important' Congress leaders at the local level who survived the arrests. As regards the latter, it should be pointed out that in Bihar, for example, these leaders included a fisherman, students and teachers and an ex-minister of the 1937–9 ministry—all of them associated with the Congress (pp. 149–50). The author also mentions the passive support of landed elements like the Maharaja of Darbhanga (p. 160). As can be seen, (a) and (b) provided the links between the bourgeois-led Congress and the revolt. Besides, the author's evidence clearly shows that different sections in the countryside, including the agricultural labourers (p. 151), joined the movement. The Congress became a symbol of struggle for them, although the latter's responses to *swaraj* and the Mahatma had *their own specificities.*

Henningham's attempts to split the 1942 movement into two nationalisms (?) follows from the mistakes already outlined. As he himself puts it, there were . . . 'very few attacks on property other than that belonging to the government' (p. 159). But he does not cite a single instance of an attack on the property of the landlords. Moreover, he looks upon the revolt as expressing (a) '. . . moral protest against the "Sarkar" (which was) . . . regarded . . . as *ultimately responsible* for the conditions of economic deprivation within which they (i.e., the 'subaltern' groups) found themselves' (p. 159; emphasis added); (b) the lack of any agrarian movement before or immediately after the 1942 movement (p. 159); and (c) forms of protest like sabotage which were Congress-inspired, coexisting with popular forms such as *hat* lootings, and belief in invulnerability since Gandhi had rendered the rebels bulletproof (p. 153).

While acknowledging the specificities of different class interests, it is, however, difficult to accept the '. . . duality of the insurrection . . .' which, according to the author, '. . . consisted of an élite nationalist uprising combined with a subaltern revolt' (p. 164). Henningham's facts refute his own conclusions. Worse still, his position echoes the basic position of the 'old' and 'new' imperialist historians.

Failing to grasp these fundamental problems the author does not recognise the political significance of the 'subalterns' in revolt. Why did his 'subaltern' rise in the 1942 movement? Acts of sabotage and looting seem to be Henningham's answer. Behind this lurks the presupposition that peasants and agricultural labourers could not relate their issues and concepts to the anti-imperialist struggle.

V

Arvind N. Das, in his essay 'Agrarian change from above and below: Bihar 1947–78,' has attempted a study of agrarian changes in Bihar in the post-independence period. Bihar is a region which has a history of militant peasant struggles during the pre-independence period. The author examines two major attempts 'from above': (i) the *zamindari* abolition, and (ii) the Bhoodan movement. He also attempts to link these with the 'green revolution.' In the efforts 'from below' he takes up the contemporary struggles waged by the Bihar peasantry under the CPI, the CPI (M) and the CPI (M-L).

The changes from above, Das rightly argues, were 'not a process unilaterally initiated and sponsored by the élite' but a 'response to long-drawn-out and militant peasant struggles' (p. 180). These attempts were efforts which provided the ruling party with a face-saving device, in relation to its pre-independence promises to the masses—now the electorate—and, at the same time, to check the advance of the militant forces in the countryside. The reforms from above were 'implemented' haltingly and in a manner which left ample scope for the ruling party leaders and their mentors and allies to safeguard their own class interests.

If Bihar was the first state legally to abolish *zamindari* (Das overplays the role of K.B. Sahay in this context), it nonetheless remains the foremost state in independent India where *zamindars* have successfully established their hegemony over the Congress organisation, and their interests are served excellently.

The author has successfully shown the manoeuvres of the state and the landlords to stall the process of reform but he should have further elaborated the links between the ruling party and the landed interests, particularly since 1937, when, for the first time, the Congress signed an agreement with the *zamindars*. Occasional references notwithstanding, an in-depth study of this relationship is missing. This would have clearly explained why the state has repeatedly attacked the poor on behalf of the landlords.

The author mentions the pressure of the nascent bourgeoisie as a factor leading to agrarian reforms, but neglects the important question of the stagnation of the regional bourgeoisie in Bihar.

Given the emphasis on the 'subaltern,' one expected Das to say much more about the response the Bhoodan movement elicited from the peasantry. Moreover, he could have examined the extent to which the Sarvodayites indirectly helped the landlords, since their movement was, to a certain extent, aimed at arresting and diverting the growth of an organised peasant movement. The caste–class relationship in a caste-ridden society like Bihar should have been examined in greater detail.

The author states that any attempt on the part of the poor to resist the landowners is seen as a Naxal-inspired movement which is ruthlessly crushed (pp. 218, 224–5). However, Das does not mention the fact that this is not because the activities of the Naxalites (in Bhojpur) had induced any stable changes 'from below' but because the state has found a convenient excuse to act against the struggling poor on the pretext of curbing Naxalism.

The essay suffers from a factual error. The author suggests in the conclusion: 'In fact, only towards the end of his (Swami Sahajanand Saraswati's) life did he come to acknowledge the need for the peasantry to acquire class allies in its struggle' (p. 226). However, Sahajanand had vigorously advocated a worker–peasant alliance from 1936 onwards. The *Bulletin of the All India Kisan Sabha* from 1936 to 1939 bear, this out. The worker-peasant alliance in the strikes in the Bihta Sugar Mills (Bihar) under his guidance in the late 1930s and early 1940s are a well-known historical fact. Besides advocating worker–peasant unity, Sahajanand also maintained that the 'industrial labourers are kisans par excellence' as a 'very significant proportion' of the city proletariat consists of *kisans* who go to mills and factories 'in search of some relief from the sufferings that confront them in their village homes.'[39]

VI

N.K. Chandra's 'Agricultural workers in Burdwan' focuses attention on three villages—Karulia, Nalhati and Mirzapur (the last is a division of the large *mouza* or revenue village of Nalhati)—of the agriculturally progressive block, Abanti, in Burdwan district. Abanti was an area chosen for the Intensive Area Development Programme (IADP) in 1962, and a great deal of attention was paid to providing technology to boost agricultural production.

The three villages are agriculturally fairly distinct, with Karulia classified as 'quite advanced,' Nalhati as 'fairly backward' and Mirzapur as 'more progressive' (p. 231). Most of the land is owner cultivated, although in Nalhati 40 per cent of the land is owned by two families. In the other two villages, the concentration is less skewed.

Chandra makes a broad division between the 'upper-classes' and the 'lower classes'; in the latter he includes landless agricultural labourers and small and marginal peasants. He concentrates upon describing the economic condition of this 'lower class' under various sections (types of labour contracts, working conditions, standard and actual wages, credit relations) and finally makes an 'analysis of poverty' (pp. 251–5) based on nutritional standards, education and literacy.

The agricultural labourers are categorised according to their degree of attachment to their employers. On the one hand there is the yearly contract for *mahindars*, which is often renewed because the employer finds it 'tedious and vexatious' (p. 248) to continually switch between individual labourers, while, for the labourers 'because of the security it offers, the *mahindars* job is much sought after' (p. 234). At the other end of the scale are the casual or daily labourers who can, theoretically, work for different employers every day. In between the two are a variety of semi-permanent or semi-attached labourers, the *nagare*, the *botare* (specialist ploughmen), 'cowboys' who tend the landlord's cattle, and the migrant Santal tribals.

The payments vary widely, not only in the manner in which they are paid (i.e., the cash–kind ratio), but also in the time at which they may be made, from seasonal, half-yearly payments to daily rations and wages. The cash component is a very small part of the total wages, and only in Mirzapur do casual agricultural labourers earn more cash than kind as part of their average daily wage. In the other two villages cash payments are less than half of the payments in kind (pp. 244–5). The cash earnings of *mahindars, nagares,* 'cowboys' and domestic servants (who are largely women) are extremely low.

This is the most systematic part of Chandra's essay. The rest of the essay is a confused amalgam of sometimes contradictory statements which seek to elucidate the response of agricultural labourers and poor peasants to their condition.

We are told that the employers 'were not generally satisfied with the quality and quantity of work put in by the workers' and thought that the labourers were 'prone to idle away their time' (p. 238). Which employer has ever praised his workers, especially to outsiders who come to their village for such a brief period? Only three months (p. 228) were spent in the three villages, and therefore the time spent in each village would be even less than one month. The labourers' morale, on the other hand, was so low that 'they do not feel too humiliated' (p. 239) when thrashed by their employers.

Yet in Karulia the lower classes who 'seemed to be quite subdued, if not firmly under the control of their masters' (p. 233), went on a strike to improve their wages and working conditions, and refused to follow the advice of the local *kisan* leader, Haridhan Banerji, who upheld the employers' point of view. Why labourers should follow a *kisan* leader at all is left unexplained by Chandra; neither are we told of Banerji's class, caste or general social position in the rural structure. Instead, one is left wondering as to who were the people who initiated the strike since the lower classes could 'hardly afford to engage in such a project in a state of absent-mindedness' (as R. Guha puts it in his piece, p. 1).

Chandra's data probably contain many more examples of conscious resistance than he has cared to mention here. The rejection of Haridhan Banerji is only one instance. The labourers' insistence on eating their midday meal in their own homes (p. 237), the casual labourers' wives demanding payment of the wage at the start, rather than at the end of the day (p. 250), and the labourers' rejection of the authority of their *malik's* relative (p. 238), are a few other examples which indicate a non-militant but clearly conscious attempt at making a stand.

But the incidents themselves are poorly elaborated in the essay, and they are not helped by Chandra's commentary. 'Their poverty and a desire to assert their independence are the main reasons why food is being consumed today at the workers' own homes' (p. 237). One can understand the will to assert independence, but what has the labourers' poverty to do with their eating food at home?

Chandra quotes Haridhan Banerji's condemnation of the labourers' wives nagging their employers for their husbands' wages. He does not, however, give any explanation why the labourers do this, or their point of view.

Instead, the labourers are asked 'why there was no organised protest or strike' (p. 520), and they listed their reasons. Listing reasons itself is a conscious realisation of one's vulnerability and one's position; it is also a step towards acting for oneself. More important, the question asked is insensitive and by no means neutral. Besides, Chandra has noted militant action by the lower classes in the villages surveyed (pp. 233, 251). The memory of these actions is not explored, though it can be a most potent element in shaping perceptions.

There are some particular facts which are noted but are left unaccounted for, and one can only list them here.

(i) Karulia has 22 domestic servants from its agricultural labourer population, and the other villages have none. No explanation is provided.

(ii) While Nalhati and Karulia have an equal number of male and female casual labourers (18 and 28 respectively), Mirzapur has 10 men and only one woman casual labourer. No explanation is given.

(iii) There is no account of how the average number of days per worker per year is calculated. Since the number of days is one of the major bases for payments and earnings, one would like to know how Chandra has attempted this exercise.

(iv) An incident where labourers were severely beaten by their employer is mentioned (p. 238), but one is not told in which village it occurred.

One cannot argue with an anthropologist's description of his field material, but one can argue against a slipshod and impressionistic presentation of the field material. What should have been the core of the discussion, that is, the perceptions and the responses of the 'lower classes,' is the weakest part of the essay.

VII

The fact that *Subaltern Studies I* did not have a single essay on labour has already been lamented by Sabyasachi Bhattacharya in his 'History from below' (*Social Scientist*, no. 119, fn 23). *Subaltern Studies II* seems to have made up for this absence by including Dipesh Chakrabarty's 'Conditions for knowledge of working-class conditions: Employers, government and the jute workers of Calcutta, 1890–1940.' Chakrabarty, whose previous essay, 'Communal riots and labour: Bengal's jute mill-hands in the 1890s' (*Past and Present*, May 1981) we are familiar with (including the less-known debate with Ranajit Das Gupta—CSSS Occasional Papers), has ambitiously called his essay 'Conditions for the knowledge of working-class conditions.' The sophisticated tools of French Structuralism (Michel Foucault's *Discipline and punish: The birth of the prison* is quoted approvingly) are grafted to a broad Marxian framework and meaningful insights are gained on the working class for the period 1890 to 1940.

Chakrabarty sees the relation of labour and capital as one of domination/subordination within a system of power. An 'autonomous' culture of the oppressed is postulated and it is argued that it is important to understand this culture if we are to seek the conditions for knowledge of working class conditions. It is here that Chakrabarty stresses the existence of a pre-industrial culture among the working class in the jute mills (what he calls 'community consciousness') and contrasts it with the English working class which entered the experience of Industrial Revolution with a rich tradition of artisan radicalism and the 'notion of equality before law.'

Chakrabarty's argument (borrowed from Marx) is that the centralising nature of capitalist industry made it necessary that it produced a body of knowledge to regulate labour. This 'knowledge' found in the documents of the English State (Factory Acts, etc.) served the capitalists in two important ways. First, they sought to make 'conditions of competition' between different factories uniform, that is, equal restraint on all exploitation of labour. Second, by regulating the working day as regards its length, pauses, beginning and end, they forced into existence a more developed and complex machinery and hence by implication, a more efficient working class. For Marx, the 'cruelties' of early capitalism, the humanistic impulses arising therefrom resulted in factory inspection reports which spoke for the 'political will' that the English State was capable of mustering, the will that allowed it to distance itself from particular capitalists and yet serve English capitalism in general. In the process of regulating the labour force, the interests of the individual capitalists and those of the State were meshed, since in England, the pressure towards discipline arose both from within and without the factory. Discipline has two components. It entailed a technical subordination of the workman to the uniform motion of the instruments of labour, hence the need for training, education, etc. Third, it made supervision—the labour of overseeing— an integral part of capitalist relations of production. Supervision, so crucial to the working of capitalist authority, was based on legislation and produced documents in turn. The everyday functioning of the capitalist factory, therefore, produced documents, hence knowledge, about working class conditions.

Chakrabarty rightly stresses the relevance of Marx's arguments for historians studying the working class in India. Here Chakrabarty raises the important questions of the general paucity of sources for working class in India and argues that ruling class documents are important for what they say and for their 'silences.' An attempt to understand their silences cannot stop at the purely economic explanation—but has to push itself into the realm of working class culture.

For the period Chakrabarty is studying, evidence becomes less scarce from the period of the First World War. The Russian Revolution was still fresh in memory. India was showing rapid industrial growth. With these considerations in mind an effort was made for the 'steady betterment of the conditions of labour' (p. 266). Factory Acts were awarded. The Bengal government established in July 1920 a post of

Labour Intelligence Officer. Factory managers were asked to maintain regular attendance registers. As Chakrabarty has shown by carefully sifting the evidence, the conditions of the jute mill labour in Bengal never fully received the documentation that the Government of India had arranged to give them. Investigation into labour conditions was seen as sympathy for labour. The Intelligence Office was saddled with other important duties. Investigation was heavily biased. For example, none of the mentioned diseases to be treated free by doctors was of nutritional origin; only epidemics disrupting work were recorded. Besides, the government of Bengal was unashamedly 'pro-capitalist,' refusing to distance itself from the particular interests of the industrialists. Thus, even the attendance register that the 1922 Factories Act required the factories to maintain was modified in Bengal to suit the convenience of the jute mill managers. Thus, the industry never produced the necessary documents; and the government lacked the 'political will' to carry out its own investigations. Why was this so?

One reason could be the tight racial bonds between the government and the capitalists. Yet there was no attempt at standardising the 'conditions of competition.' Another reason was that the jute industries found no international competition, and they accepted 'individualism' as a price for organisational unity and monopoly control. In an interesting argument, Chakrabarty shows that 'conditions of competition' were more or less at a par with each other (in spite of difference in wage rates). Thus, the mills which payed lower wages spent more on housing, etc., and vice versa. A lack of standardisation in wage rates therefore did not necessarily reflect an absence of competitive situation among the mills regarding their labour conditions. The state therefore reproduced in its documents the blinkered vision of capital (p. 281). Why was this vision of capital 'blinkered'?

Chakrabarty now moves a step further and brings in the useful concept of discipline, considering the nature of work, and technology and the role of supervision. The technology used is found to be extremely primitive, and given the fact that there is always a cheap supply of labour, there was no need to educate the labourer. The worker's relationship with the machine, instead of being mediated through technical knowledge, was mediated through the north Indian peasant's conception of his tools, where the tools often took on magical and godly qualities. The importance of the *sardari* system is now brought to focus. Here the importance of the strong primordial loyalties of community, language, religion, caste and kinship is shown and light is thrown on the corrupt practices of the *sardars* in keeping the workers in order. One reason why this was tolerated was that *sardari* control was cheaper than housing, health care or an articulated body of rules guiding the conditions of work. The legally required factory documents on working class conditions were thus largely irrelevant to the exercise of the *sardar's* authority, which was in the nature of pre-capitalist domination. The *sardar* proved his power by bending rules and falsifying documents. Hence the existence of 'silences' and unreliable documents.

Chakrabarty's arguments have been set out in detail for they throw important light on a particular industry during the colonial period of our history. The distortions in this industrialising process are not merely a result of the deliberate policy of colonialists but also due to the existence of a pre-industrial culture among the working class, strengthened by the peculiar conditions under colonialism.

Given the long period that Chakrabarty covers in his essay, 1890–1940 (practically the entire period of Indian national movement), it is a little difficult to swallow the fact that the jute mill worker remained mainly 'community conscious' (we borrow this term from Chakrabarty's earlier essay, op. cit., *Past and Present*) and under the control of the *sardar*. True, the existing legislation did not show any significant change in trying to accommodate a more 'class conscious' worker. But surely ruling class documents are hardly always an adequate guide for 'conditions for knowledge of working class conditions.' For instance, there is little attempt to show the changing nature of working class demands. Ranajit Das Gupta (CSSS Occasional Papers, op. cit) has shown how the articulation of demands by workers shows a gradual shift from merely community to incipient class consciousness. For example, there was a gradual shift from demands for religious holidays to demands for increase in wages. In a complex situation like this, notions of class and community tend to get fuzzed up, but over a long period one can discern the growth of a more articulate working class. Do the ruling class documents show any of this change? Chakrabarty does not tell us anything about this. One is left with the impression that their consciousness did not show much change and this too in a period characterised by strikes and in a region which saw the first organised left movement in the country. How will Chakrabarty explain the massive strikes which erupted in the 1946–7 phase?

Then there is the question of the control that the *sardar* exercised over his workers. R. Newman, in his valuable study, *Workers and unions in Bombay, 1918–1929*, has shown how, with the passage of years and changing economic condition, the hold of the *sardar* gradually weakened. This was in part due to the *badli* system and in part due to the rising political consciousness of the working class. Was the role of the *sardar* changing in Calcutta? Is there any record of this in the ruling class documents? Could not the 'gaps' in the ruling class records be narrowed if the worker is not just seen as possessing a consciousness that was pre-industrial in nature but a consciousness that was gradually changing with time? Similarly, one gets the impression that the colonial state and foreign capitalists had only one view of the worker. Surely there must be ruling class documents showing the offensives and retreats that they made, accommodating their interests to a developing national movement and its impact on the working class. One comes away from Chakrabarty's argument with the feeling that there was little change in the attitudes of both the workers and the industrialists during the entire period. One hopes that in future he will fill in more of the 'gaps' that are the 'conditions for knowledge of working class conditions.'

VIII

Partha Chatterjee's 'More on modes of power and the peasantry' is an elaboration of the theoretical portions of his previous piece on 'Agrarian Relations and Communalism in Bengal, 1926-1935' in *Subaltern Studies I*. The substance of the argument is not different; it has only been taken up again by the author as the conceptualisations in the earlier essay were too cryptic. As a corollary, the critique advanced in this review is also equally applicable to the earlier essay.

First, what is meant by a mode of power? According to Chatterjee they are 'distinguished in terms of the *basis* of the specification of the "property" connection (the relations of production) in the ordered and repeated performance of social activities, i.e., the particular pattern of allocations of rights or entitlements over material objects (sometimes extended to non-material objects such as knowledge) within a definite system of social production. The three modes of power I called the *communal,* the *feudal* and the *bourgeois* modes' (p. 317). Chatterjee relates this concept of mode of power to the concept of mode of production. Chatterjee says that 'the "real appropriation" connection is the specific field of social production in its techno-economic aspects for the study of which there are appropriate categories and analytical relations,' What he is concerned with are the categories and relations relevant to the analysis of the 'property' connection (p. 316). The whole argument thereafter is the elaboration of this concept of modes of power which corresponds, according to Chatterjee, to the property connection.

The analysis of any mode of production can only be carried out by taking both these factors, the forces and relations of production, into account. In fact, the division of labour takes place at two levels analytically—technical and social. Both these levels are indivisible and no one-dimensional study is possible. In *Capital,* volume I, for instance, Marx has taken pains to go into details of the technical division of labour. in the immediate process of production and the generation of surplus value through this process.[40] But for Chatterjee all this is 'the bog of techno-economic determinism' (p. 314). As we will see later on, because the conceptual tools developed by Chatterjee are delinked from the process of production, they are also delinked from determination by the modes of production.

The reason for this separation of process of production and relations of production in Chatterjee's argument is not difficult to understand. From the property connection being used as shorthand for the relations of production what he does is to use the concept of property in its legal-juridical sense. He declares that the analysis of the property connection is 'the question of rights or entitlements in society, of the resultant power relationship, of law and politics, of the process of legitimation of power relation, etc.' (p. 316). It is therefore very clear that what is being analysed is not the structure of production relations which is internal to the economic infrastructure of society, but the political-juridical structures which are part of the superstructure. Playing on the apparently common words signifying two different relationships he tries to legitimise his concept of modes of power. He righteously declares that it is related to the property connection which are the relations of production, but what he actually means is the study of merely the political forms existing in society. He declares that the study of the process of production is 'techno-economic determinism.' But what in effect he is criticising is not just the study of forces of production, but also the relations of production to which his property connection in no way corresponds despite his assertions. It is because of this that he starts his essay with an appreciative summary of Robert Brenner's recent contributions to the debates on the transition from feudalism to capitalism. For Chatterjee, Brenner's contribution is important because it locates 'the element of "indeterminacy" in the transition problem in the specific *political* form of the class struggle' (p. 315). The question which emerges for Chatterjee is: 'What are the distinctive categories with the help of which specific political problems . . . can be posed within a general framework of theory?' (p. 316). The modes of power is the specific category developed in reply to this question. The concept of modes of power does not therefore relate to the study of relations of production, but to that of the political superstructure. Because of this Chatterjee can develop his analysis without recourse to the concept of modes of production and the concept of the determination of the political and ideological levels in the last instance by the economic level. This is not the occasion to go into the complexities of the debate on the transition from feudalism to capitalism in Europe, but it should be noted in passing that Brenner has been criticised by Guy Bois for precisely this lack of any conception of what constitutes a mode of production.[41]

Coming now to the specificities of the categories developed by Chatterjee: '*Communal* mode of power exists where individual or sectoral rights, entitlements and obligations are allocated on the authority of the entire social collectivity, i.e., the community' (p. 317). The theoretical foundation on which this category is developed is the section on 'forms which precede capitalist production' in the texts which Marx wrote in preparation for *Capital,* now published as the *Grundrisse.*[42] The sections on pre-capitalist formations in the *Grundrisse* are some of the most stimulating texts written by Marx, but they are also the most controversial. As far as the status of these texts is concerned, they were written not in order to elaborate a theory of pre-capitalist modes of production but in order to explain the genesis of capitalism. According to Hobsbawm and Texier, pre-capitalist formations were important in a negative way only in so far as they contained the preconditions of capitalism.[43]

According to Marx, the fundamental difference between pre-capitalist and capitalist modes of production was that in the pre-capitalist formations there was no separation of the producer and the means of production. Because of this Marx has lumped together all the pre-capitalist formations though it is obvious that he did not believe that they had the same socio-economic structures. According to Marx, the first form of property was tribal property and other forms of property were developments from this. The four main forms of development from tribal property were the Asiatic, the Slavonic, the Germanic and the Classical Ancient forms. Chatterjee theorises that these four forms were based on communal property and therefore stood in opposition to the feudal mode of power which was 'characterised fundamentally by sheer superiority of physical force, i.e., a relation of domination' (p. 317). Feudal power which includes slavery as well as serfdom as relations of production realised within it was marked 'in terms of the categorical opposites *community/external domination*' (pp. 333–4). However, as indicated above, what Marx was concerned about in these manuscripts was not the characterisation of pre-capitalist modes of production, but of only their opposition to the capitalist mode of production. It is very strange that the Ancient mode of production based on slavery is grouped by Chatterjee in the communal mode of power, while at the same time slavery and serfdom are taken to be constitutive of the feudal mode of power, with its opposition between community and feudal power. As is obvious, these two positions are internally inconsistent. According to Marx, all pre-capitalist modes of production were based on the community. Slavery and feudalism were also part of this 'communal organisation' which included 'all these forms where landed property and agriculture form the basis of the economic order and consequently the economic effect is the production of use values. . . .'[44] We have seen that Marx had relegated the slave-based Ancient mode of production to communal power. This was because in ancient Greece and Rome it was the political level of citizenship which determined ownership of land. It did not mean that the society was not a class society. Recently, de Ste Croix, in his *The class struggle in the ancient Greek world*, has demonstrated conclusively that classes and class struggle existed in ancient society.[45] As far as feudalism is concerned, Marx again envisaged it as part of the original categorisation of the four basic variants of the original form of property. This can be seen from his assertion that 'the middle ages (Germanic period) starts with the countryside as the location of history. . . .'[46] In a long passage, Marx stated clearly that slavery and serfdom were also forms of pre-capitalist property which were communal in nature.

'*The extra-economic* origin of property is the *pre-bourgeois* relationship of the individual to the objective conditions of labour, and in the first instance to the *nature* of objective condition of labour the *original conditions of production cannot initially be themselves* produced . . . what we must explain is the *separation* of these inorganic conditions of human existence from this active existence, a separation which is only fully completed in the relationship between wage labour and capital. In the relationship of slavery and serfdom there is no such separation . . . the original conditions of production appear as natural prerequisites, *natural conditions of existence of* the producer . . . his *property*, i.e., his relations to the natural prerequisites of his production as *his own* is mediated by his natural membership of a community.'[47]

That this is not an isolated reference but was central to Marx's conceptualisation of pre-capitalist society in general can be seen from the following passage from the *German ideology*: 'The first form of ownership is tribal ownership . . . the second form is the ancient communal and state ownership. It is the communal private property which compels active citizens to remain in this natural form of *association over against* their slaves. The third form of ownership is feudal or estate property . . . like Tribal and communal ownership, it is based again on a community but the directly producing class standing over against it is not, as is the case of ancient community, the slaves, but the enserfed small peasantry. . . .'[48] What Marx is trying to work out in the manuscripts is that it is only under capitalism that the labourer and the means of production are separated. In the pre-capitalist modes of production there is a natural unity between the labourer and his means of production which is structured and mediated by the community. Obviously everything here rests on the characterisation of this community. From the community we cannot jump to the 'communal mode of power.' What Marx is emphasising is that property is not an individual but a social relationship which depends on the social relations of production. He compares property with language which also is a profoundly social act.

'The individual is related to his language as *his own* only as the natural member of a human community. Language as the product of an individual is an absurdity. But so also is property . . . *property* therefore means belonging to a tribe.'[49] If the same relationship posited by Chatterjee for property is applied to language it would mean that all societies where language is spoken would fall under the communal mode of power, since language is a communal activity.

Chatterjee gives a number of concrete examples of stateless communal societies with special reference to Africa. Here again the basic problematic of Chatterjee becomes apparent and that is a consideration of the property connection at the politico-juridical level without any consideration of the economic basis of these communal forms. Evans-Pritchard, whose texts are appreciatively quoted by Chatterjee, clearly states in his study of segmentary lineage system of *The Nuer* that 'we have tried to show how the lines of political cleavage tend to follow distribution in relation to modes of livelihood.'[50] It is significant that though Chatterjee traces his own methodology to the concept of modes of production, recent studies on classless societies which have utilised this concept have been largely ignored by him. The methodology of the functionalist scholars who are generally cited, has an in-built bias towards portrayal of stateless societies as idyllic structures in which there is a perfect situational symmetry of forces. The gross inequality and exploitation which exists in stateless societies is glossed over. The lineage society studied in the twentieth century was already in a process of change and cannot be regarded as merely primitive communism or primeval society. As Georges Dupre and Pierre Philippe Rey have emphasised, lineage society maintained itself through participation in the slave trade for over four centuries. Europeans obtained their supply of slaves largely by manipulating lineage societies in which this trade strengthened the hold of the lineage elders. Other studies have shown that certain segmentary societies subsisted only on the basis of slave trade. In certain lineage-based societies, slaves accounted for 20–60 per cent of the population, but the formal organisation was still segmentary.[51] Chatterjee notes the existence of inequality in lineage society, but for him this was the result of domination imposed by conquering groups. Where lineage society contained external exploitation it was already on the way to becoming a society with institutionalised coercive apparatus (pp. 324–5). With agricultural production the hunting–gathering bonds are transformed to tribal society which becomes more and more hierarchical in nature. The tribe itself is a residuary category between hunting–gathering bands and state societies. Too much cannot be read into the existence of apparently egalitarian tribal communities.[52]

Anyway, the concept of tribe and the importance of kinship in these societies is not something which can be located in the evolution of the political process alone, but has to be situated in the context of determinate mode of production. According to Emmanuel Terray, 'lineage is the realisation, of the *production community*,' and that kinship relations are the product of the structural causality of the economic politico-juridical and ideological determinates of a mode of production.[53] According to Maurice Godelier, also, even if kinship or politics is the dominant structure, the determining structure continues to be that of the production relations.[54]

Let us turn now to the feudal mode of power which, according to Chatterjee, was 'characterised fundamentally by sheer superiority of physical force, i.e., a relationship of domination' (p. 317). The feudal mode includes within itself not only serfdom but also slavery. In this he has based himself on the lumping together by Marx of slavery and feudalism as two paths to development of tribal property. From this Chatterjee wrongly concludes that slavery and serfdom were characterised by a similar mode of power and that therefore they correspond to the same mode of production. But this cannot be, for, after all, mode of power, according to Chatterjee, is linked to the property connection corresponding to the relations of production. It would mean that slavery and petty peasant production are the same. Even if the alternative usage of mode of power as corresponding to the political superstructure of a mode of production is used, it means that slavery and feudalism are the same mode of production since, if the determined political form is exactly the same, the determining levels also are the same. It is improbable that any historian today holds the view that slavery and serfdom are the same relations, and the political structures corresponding to these relations are the same. According to Chatterjee, the lord's right to rent is a function of the lord's control of the person of the labourer. 'The labourer is a part of the landlord's property' (p. 335). However, such rights were only a part of the landlord's total privileges. Other forms of domination included monopoly over land and jurisdictional rights. Feudalism has been defined by Guy Bois as the 'hegemony of small scale production plus the seigneurial levy which is secured by a constraint of extra economic or political nature.'[55]

The basic point is that feudalism is decisively different from slavery in that under slavery the reproduction of labour power is dependent on the slave owner's control of the production process. On the other hand, under feudalism, the reproduction of labour power is carried on independently of seigneurial control. This is true whether the peasant is free or dependent or whether rents are paid through labour or in cash.

Chatterjee seems to believe that the opposition between small peasants and lords under feudalism was something which was characteristic of feudalism being imposed on the small peasantry. According to him, this can be expressed in the opposition between community and feudal power. However, as Marc Bloch and Georges Duby have pointed out, the peasantry characteristic of feudalism was not a legacy of a mythical communal past, but was a result of the fusion of the slaves and free peasants into a uniform class of dependent peasantry.[56]

But for these problems which are inherent in the very category of modes of power, the sections on feudalism are the best parts of the essay. The opposition between the institutionalised power of the nobility crystallised in certain formations in the state and the peasants organised in terms of village communities is incisively analysed. The formation of peasant consciousness and its functions in different situations, especially rebellions, has been well brought out. Perhaps the reason why the contradictions of feudalism are well brought out is because the level of rent being determined by the objective balance of class force between the peasants and the lords has been emphasised.

In the consideration of the transition from feudalism to capitalism, he proceeds to enumerate the 'main elements which describe the class struggles in this period, a feudalism in crisis, a rising bourgeoisie, the absolutist state, varying levels of solidarity among the peasantry' (p. 346). Here the methodological weakness of Chatterjee's approach which focuses on the opposition between the peasantry and lords is very clear. According to him the crisis of feudalism and the emergence of the bourgeoisie are 'new elements' which 'together create the conditions of a possibility for a transition' (p. 346). But as feudalism has been characterised as only the opposition of the peasants and the lords, the reason for the sudden emergence of these new elements is left unclear. It cannot be reconciled with the concept of power, especially as earlier he has praised Brenner for having transformed the terms of the transition debate by extricating it from 'the bog of techno-economic determinism of depopulation, declines of productivity . . .' etc. (p. 314). In fact classes constitute themselves as such only on the basis of social relations of production which again are linked to the production process. Seeing the transition only in terms of the opposition between the feudal mode of power and the peasant communal mode of power is a profoundly Hegelian view of the totality which includes two paradigmatically opposed forces. It cannot account for the development of a new mode of production, that is, capitalism, since it cannot explain why capitalist relations of production, in which peasants lost control of the means of production, should develop out of a situation of supposedly successful class struggle of the peasantry. In fact, as Rodney Hilton has emphasised, peasant movements were invariably led by rich peasants who themselves later formed part of the capitalist class.[57]

This brings us to the second point concerned with the existence of the peasantry in the capitalist mode of production. According to Chatterjee, 'To the extent that a peasantry continues to exist as peasantry in a society dominated by capitalism, it represents a limit to bourgeois hegemony' (p. 347). This again is difficult to accept. The peasantry which is self-employed on the family farm can coexist with advanced capitalism. The family farms take on the economic rationality of small enterprise dominated by large industrial units. The peasantry continues to exist as a distinct category for instance, in France, Greece, Japan, the US, etc. In no case is it in antagonistic contradiction with capitalism. In fact, as indicated above, the peasantry's contradiction with feudalism becomes acute and historically important only when the peasantry is closely articulated to the capitalist economy. It is because of this articulation that the peasantry of late medieval West Europe struggled against feudal constraints and thus was instrumental in the transition from feudalism to capitalism.

This brings us to the final weakness of the whole concept of modes of power. The development of history seems to be a dialectical relationship of two modes of power contending with each other. This is a very partial view of history, if only because it cannot really account for progressive development since everything is contained in the evolution of the communal mode of power which, like the Hegelian giest, is throughout history striving for its self-realisation. Finally, it should be reiterated that despite Chatterjee's attempt to situate the concept of modes of power in the context of modes of production, the two concepts are fundamentally incompatible. This is because modes of power do not allow for the combined effect on any level of the various structures contained within a mode of production. The concept of political power isolated from the economic domain is a Nietzschean concept which has recently found favour with the neo-rationalists and neo-positivists and an attempt to combine this with the concept of modes of production is bound to flounder.

Notes and References

1. Ranajit Guha (ed.), *Subaltern Studies II: Writings on South Asian history and society* (Delhi, Oxford University Press, 1983).

2. Antonio Gramsci, *Selections from the prison notebooks* (New York, 1971), pp. 196–9.

3. Raymond Williams, *Marxism and literature* (Oxford, 1977), and 'Base and superstructure in Marxist theory,' in *Problems in materialism and culture* (London, 1980), Lucien Goldman, *Le Dieu Cache* (Gallimard, 1959); Lévi-Strauss, *La Pensee Sauvee* (Paris, 1962), especially, p. 155; Althusser, *Essays in self-criticism* (London, 1976).

4. Michel Vadee, 'L'epistemologie dans la philosophie Occidentale contemporaine,' *La Pensee*, no. 220, 1981, 85–97; Bernard Michaux, 'Neo Positivism: Heritage et critique,' *La Pensee*, no. 230, 1982, 69–76; Ludevico Geymonat, 'Du Neopositivisme au materialisme dialectique,' ibid., pp. 77–84; Wittgenstein, *Tractacus Logico-Philosophicus* (New York, 1961).

5. Christopher Hill, 'People and parliament in seventeenth-century England,' *Past and Present*, no. 62, 1981.

6. For example, T.J.A. Le Goff and D.M.G. Sutherland, 'The social origins of counter-revolution in Western France,' *Past and Present*, no. 99, 1983, 65–87.

7. For example, Baba Ramchandra's private papers in the Private Papers Section of Nehru Memorial Museum and Library (New Delhi); Awdheshwar Prasad Sinha, *Bihar prantiya kisan sabhaki report (1929–1935)* (Patna, 1935); Swami Sahajanand Saraswati, *Mera jeevan sangharsh* (Bihta, 1974); N.G. Ranga, *The modern Indian peasant* (Madras, 1936); and Sunil Sen, *Agrarian struggle in Bengal (1946–1947)* (New Delhi, 1972).

8. Henri Lefebvre, *Le Langage et la societe* (Paris, 1966), especially pp. 137–44.

9. Roland Barthes, 'Myth today,' in *Mythologies* (London, 1974), especially pp. 116, 122, 125–6.

10. Roland Barthes, 'Change the object itself—mythology today,' in *Image music text* (Glasgow, 1977), pp. 164–9; Edwin Ardener, 'Introductory essay: Social anthropology and language,' in Ardener (ed.), *Social anthropology and language* (London, 1971).

11. Yves Gilli, 'Les rapports textes—historie et l'esthetique de la reception en RFA,' *La Pensee*, no. 223, 1983, 117–25; G. Pagbiano Ungari, 'Le dialogue oeuvre—Lecture,' in *Le structuralisme genetique l'oeuvre et influence de L. Goldman* (Paris, 1977), pp. 137–42.

12. Roland Barthes, 'Structural analysis of narratives' in *Image/music/text*, pp. 79–124.

13. Pierre Macherey, 'L'analyse litteraire, tombeau des structures,' in *Pour une Theorie de la Production, Litteraire* (Paris, 1968), pp. 159–80.

14. W.W. Hunter, *Annals of rural Bengal* (London, 1868), pp. 219–21. For an account of the suppression of this rebellion, see Major J. Browne, *India tracts: Containing a description of the jungle terry districts, their revenues, trade and government with a plan for the improvement of them all* (Black Friars). For an analysis, see K.K. Dutta, 'The Santhal insurrection of 1855–7,' in *Anti-British riots and movement before 1857* (Meerut, 1970), pp. 43–152.

15. Ibid.

16. Ranajit Guha, *Elementary aspects of peasant insurgency in colonial India* (Oxford, 1983), p. 13.

17. Rodney Hilton, *Bond men made free* (London, 1977), pp. 124–5, 207.

18. Lucien Goldman, 'Conscience realle et conscience possible, conscience adequate et fausse conscience,' in *Marxism et sciences Humaines* (Gallimard, 1970), pp. 121–9.

19. Lenin, *Materialism and empirio-criticism: Critical comments on a reactionary philosophy* (Moscow, 1970). Also Pierre Macherey, 'L'histoire de la philosophie consideree comme une lutce de tendences,' *La Pensee*, no. 185, 1976, 3–25.

20. Marcel Mauss, *The gift* (London, 1954); Claude Lévi-Strauss, *Structural anthropology* (New York, 1963); Maurice Godelier, 'The phantasmatic nature of social relations,' in *Perspectives in Marxist anthropology* (Cambridge, 1978), pp. 169–220.

21. Marx, *Capital*, vol. 3 (Moscow, 1974), p. 817; the same point is developed by Lukacs, *History and class consciousness* (London, 1971).

22. Althusser, *Essays in . . .*, op cit., pp. 44–9.

23. Marx, *Grundrisse* (Harmondsworth, 1973)—the introduction; Althusser, 'Contradiction and overestimation,' in *For Marx* (London, 1969), pp. 87–128; and Althusser and Balibar, *Reading capital* (London, 1975), pp. 11–70.

24. That the scarcity of source material on the seventeenth century specifically need not be a drawback is evident from the work of Amalendu Guha, who has competently discussed different aspects of the society and economy of this region; see, for example, Amalendu Guha, 'Appendix: The medieval economy of Assam,' in Tapan Raychaudhuri and Irfan Habib (eds), *The Cambridge economic history of India*, 1982, vol. 2, pp. 418–505; also his 'Land rights and social classes in medieval Assam,' *Indian Economic and Social History Review*, vol. III, 1966.

25. Amalendu Guha, 'Medieval north-east India (1200–1750),' Occasional Paper no. 19, Centre for Studies in Social Science, Calcutta, 11.

26. E.A. Gait, *A history of Assam* (1926), p. 64.

27. Guha, *Cambridge economic history*, p. 503.
28. Ibid., pp. 502–3; also his 'Tribalism to feudalism in Assam, 1600–1750,' *Indian Historical Review*, vol. I, 1974.
29. Amalendu Guha, Occasional Paper, no. 19, op. cit., p. 11.
30. S.C. Dutta, *The north-east and the Mughals, 1661–1784*, 1984, intro, p. 24.
31. Padmeshwar Gogoi, *The Tai and the Tai kingdoms* (1968), p. 356.
32. Ibid., p. 357.
33. Ibid.
34. Dutta, op cit., p. 24.
35. A.R. Khan, *Chieftains in the Mughal empire during the reign of Akbar* (1977), especially the introduction and the conclusion. It is worth noting here that while centralising and uniformly regulating the revenue assessment and collection framework, in all the newly conquered *subas*, and revamping the judicial administration concomitant with it, the Mughal emperors, by and large, left local customs and social relations undisturbed.
36. See Tapan Raychaudhuri, 'The state and the economy,' in Raychaudhuri and Habib (eds), *The Cambridge economic history*, p. 178; also R.P. Rana, 'Agrarian revolts in northern India during the late seventeenth and early eighteenth centuries,' *Indian Economic and Social History Review*, XVIII, 3 and 4.
37. See, for example, Irfan Habib, *Agrarian system of Mughal India* (1963) and his 'Forms of class struggle in Mughal India,' Aligarh Muslim University, Dept. of History, mimeo, p. 47. R.P. Rana, op cit., reinforces this position in his study of agrarian unrest in *subas* of Agra and Ajmer.
38. Habib, 'Forms of class . . .,' pp. 54–5.
39. *Congress Socialist*, December 26, 1936.
40. Karl Marx, 'Appendix: The results of the immediate process of production,' in *Capital*, vol. I (Harmondsworth). Also see part III, 'The production of absolute surplus value,' part IV, 'The production of relative surplus value,' in ibid.
41. Guy Bois, 'Against the neo-Malthusian orthodoxy: Symposium on agrarian class structure and economic development in pre-industrial Europe,' *Past and Present*, no. 79, 1978, pp. 67–9.
42. 'Forms which precede capitalist production,' in Marx, *Grundrisse* (Harmondsworth, 1973), pp. 471–5, translated by Martin Nicolaus.
43. 'Introduction,' in Hobsbawm (ed.). *Karl Marx: Precapitalist economic formations* (New York, 1972), p. 43; Jacques Texier, 'Le privilege epistemo-logique du present et la necessite du moment genetique dans les Grundrisses de Karl Marx,' *La Pensee*, no. 225, 1982, 40–52. I am grateful to Sangeeta Singh for researching and discussing the French texts with me. Also see

Sudipta Kaviraj, 'On the status of Marx's writings on India,' *Social Scientist*, vol. 11, no. 9, September 1983, pp. 36–41.

44. Marx in Hobsbawm (ed.), pp. 80–1.
45. G.E.M. de Ste Croix, *The class struggle in the ancient Greek world* (London, 1981).
46. Marx in Hobsbawm (ed.), pp. 77–8.
47. Ibid., pp. 85–8. Emphasis added.
48. Marx and Engels, 'The German ideology,' in Hobsbawm (ed.), pp. 122–5. Emphasis added.
49. Ibid., pp. 88, 90.
50. E. Evans-Pritchard, *The Nuer* (New York, 1978), p. 190.
51. Georges Dupre and Pierre Philippe Rey, 'Reflection on the relevance of a theory of the history of exchange,' in Seldon (ed.), *Relations of production: Marxist approaches to economic anthropology* (London, 1978), pp. 171–208.
52. For a study of exploitation based on sexual domination, see Maurice Godelier, *La production des Grands Hommes: Pouvoir et domination masculine Cheziles Baruya de-Nouvelle Guinee* (Fayard, 1981).
53. Terray, pp. 126, 143–5.
54. M. Godelier, *Rationality and irrationality in economics* (New York, 1972), pp. ix, 92–5.
55. Guy Bois, conclusion of 'Crisis in feudalism' (manuscript of the English translation in the JNU Library, New Delhi).
56. Marc Bloch, 'The rise of dependent cultivation and seignorial institutions' in *Cambridge economic history of Europe*, vol. I, and Georges Duby, *The early growth of the European economy: Warriors and peasants from seventh to twelfth centuries.*
57. Rodney Hilton, 'Medieval peasants: Any lessons,' *Journal of Peasant Studies*, vol. I, 1973–74.

Significance of Non-subaltern Mediation*

RANAJIT DAS GUPTA

S UBALTERN HISTORIOGRAPHY has emerged as a significant, though sharply controversial, trend since 1982 and has provided a new analytical thrust to many recent writings on modern Indian history and society. In contrast to dominant tendencies which have obscured and even ignored the place and role of the consciousness and politics of the lower orders or subaltern groups, the central focus of the *Subaltern Studies* is on these groups and their activities. A fundamental theme running through all the published volumes including the present one is to view the subaltern as the subject of history, 'the maker of his own destiny' (p. vii).

Some historians not belonging to the subaltern history group have undoubtedly made important contributions to the writing of history from below and many of these have pre-dated the subaltern enterprise. But a major difference between the two lies in the crucial importance accorded by the latter to politics of the subalterns and relationship of power. Further, Ranajit Guha and the group associated with him have been less concerned than others with multi-class braiding of different streams and broad front political strategy. Another important difference arises from the claims made by the subaltern historians regarding the existence of an autonomous domain of the subalterns

*Based on Ranajit Guha, ed., *Subaltern Studies III: Writings on South Asian history and society* (Delhi: Oxford University Press, 1984), pp. xii + 327.

with its own coherent manifestations of consciousness, protest and organisation.

To what extent the existence of an autonomous domain has been established or proved by the subaltern historians is an open question. Moreover, the meaning of such a domain has not been made adequately clear. However, the idea of 'subalternity' is particularly relevant for historical circumstances in colonial India where the processes of class formation and class categories have never been adequately clarified and free from ambiguities. The term 'subaltern' is not just a substitute for peasantry or labouring poor or common people but a concept implying a dialectical relationship of superordination and subordination, a concept which is of importance in analysing the interplay of this relationship. In their enterprise the subaltern historians have validly stressed the significance of, to borrow from Antonio Gramsci, 'every trace of independent initiative on the part of subaltern groups,'[1] even though it was marked by fragmentation and remained remote from clarity of confrontation. In their writings they have drawn attention to the distinctive quality of the subaltern consciousness, perception and action and analysed these in their multiple ramifications and also in their various phases and levels of change.

Another major theme with which they have been concerned is the existence of two domains of politics—the domain of the subalterns and that of the dominant classes and groups or élites. And a challenging task undertaken by the subaltern historians is the analysis of the interaction between the two domains. Yet one more significant focus is on the wide range of social collectivities or bonds other than class, such as ties of kinship, religion, caste, community, tribe or language and the extent and nature of changes in relation to these ties. The importance of this arises from the reality that despite many far-reaching changes in both rural and urban social life and formation of new social groups and institutions under the aegis of British rule, such social collectivities have continued to exist vigorously and even developed new forms and content.

The volumes so far brought out under the series have greatly enlarged and deepened our understanding of the actual working of the political processes in colonial India and particularly of experiences, consciousness and activities of the subaltern groups. They throw new light not only on an unknown past, but partly also on a transformative potential that has remained unrealised. And a few of the subaltern historians have sought to explain why such potential has not been realised.

While noting the significance and distinctiveness of the rich contributions made by the subaltern historians, the present reviewer has the feeling that they have been less than fair to historians of the politics of lower classes of earlier years (for example, R.P. Dutt or L. Natarajan or Suprakash Roy and several historians of the 1960s and 1970s). A more fundamental point is that some of the subaltern historians have tended to concentrate on moments of conflict and protest, and in their writings the dialectics of collaboration and acquiescence on the part of the subalterns and the wide range of relationships and attitudes between resignation and revolt have by and large been underplayed.

In the legitimate concern with the subaltern concept and social collectivities other than class it is possible to discern a danger of dis-placement of class categories and class struggle. But while élite–sub-altern relationship is of immense value in understanding some of the crucial aspects of historical processes in the circumstances of the colo-nial economy and society of India, this must not be viewed as a substi-tute for class relationships. However, several contributors to the volume under review, particularly David Arnold and Sumit Sarkar, have shown an awareness of this problem. There is also the danger of exaggerating the autonomy of the subalterns resulting, for example, in the total negation of the significance of non-subaltern mediation or of organic link between the unorganised domain and organised domain.

II

The seven essays included in the volume are as follows: Shahid Amin, 'Gandhi as mahatma: Gorakhpur District, Eastern UP, 1921–2'; David Arnold, 'Famine in peasant consciousness and peasant action: Madras, 1976–82'; Dipesh Chakrabarty, 'Trade unions in a hierarchi-cal culture: The jute workers of Calcutta, 1920–50'; Partha Chatterjee,

'Gandhi and the critique of civil society'; David Hardiman, 'Adivasi assertion in South Gujarat: The Devi movement of 1922–3'; Gyanendra Pandey, '"Encounters and calamities": The history of a North Indian *qasba* in the nineteenth century'; and Sumit Sarkar, 'The conditions and nature of subaltern militancy: Bengal from Swadeshi to Non-Cooperation, *c.* 1905–22.'

Within the broad theme of 'subalternism' these essays deal with diverse areas. Shahid Amin, David Arnold and David Hardiman consider the subject of peasant consciousness and action. Sumit Sarkar is concerned with various manifestations of subaltern militancy and interaction between the two political domains. Gyanendra Pandey concentrates on textual analysis. The area covered by Dipesh Chakrabarty is that of interface between factory workers and middle-class leadership. Partha Chatterjee examines the nature of nationalism in India and particularly Gandhi's ideology in relation to the peasantry.

In his essay Amin makes a careful analysis of the reception of Gandhi's message by the peasant masses of Gorakhpur during the years of the Non-Cooperation Movement and the transformation and assimilation of it in the light of their own beliefs, experiences and practices. He has shown by an examination of the rumours that were in circulation that what Gandhi actually said during his visit to Gorakhpur and what the peasants perceived as his sayings were not necessarily the same. Amin states that some of the rumours and re-interpretations, for example, popular notion of Gandhi's Swaraj (pp. 51–2, the *Swaraj ka danka* episode narrated by him (p. 52) and its association with the miracle of Gandhi's passage through fire, rumour of an impending clash between the peasants and the landlords (p. 52) or the substitution of the *jaikar Mahatma Gandhi ki jai* by the orthodox war cry of *Jai Mahavir* or *Bam Bam Mahadeo* had a distinct militant tone (p. 54), went directly against Gandhi's injunctions listed by Amin (pp. 22–3) and anticipated the violence at Chauri Chaura. Yet can it be said that the perceived injunctions went directly against Gandhi's message of nationalism?

David Arnold uses colonial records on the Madras famine of 1876–8 to examine the nature of the perception of the peasants of famine and their responses to it. He argues against the widely prevalent view that peasants in India 'are, as a rule, inert and passive.' He seeks to show that they were not mere 'passive, fatalistic and powerless victims' and stresses that they were actors with their own sense of justice and expectation of relief from the upper classes in times of crisis.

Arnold makes use of 'the crisis of the famine as a window onto subaltern consciousness and action' (p. 64). In many respects the peasant's response to subsistence crises and famine exhibited 'close parallels' with peasant insurgency. In both conditions of 'heightened social realities' peasant action 'reflected a single underlying consciousness, employed a single vocabulary of expression and drew upon a basic, limited store of beliefs and symbols' (pp. 112–13). Their actions came to be marked by self-mobilisation in various forms, such as rumour, looting of grain stores and bazars and attacks on moneylenders and grain hoarders, 'a peasant sense of territoriality' and peasant solidarity or collectivity. The peasants were also conscious of the 'relationship of power, of command and control' (p. 78) to which they were subjected.

This study of the famine also demonstrates that peasant consciousness and action were informed by a sense of collectivity at several levels. But they 'were far from being aspiring revolutionaries seeking to overturn the existing order. On the contrary they were in effect reaffirming that order . . .' (p. 114). He points out that while a famine, like an insurrectionary situation, brings out many facets of peasant consciousness and action, its net effect 'was to render even more emphatic the peasant's subordination' (p. 115). But this reveals a fundamental limitation of peasant consciousness and action. This also raises the issue of the potentiality of unmediated peasantry to transform society. Arnold, however, has not indicated the sources and basis for making certain observations, for instance, the ones that 'the belief was prevalent . . .' (p. 85) or that 'subalterns felt themselves entitled to appropriate what they needed for themselves' (p. 85).

David Hardiman makes an in-depth study of a tribal movement and uses oral evidence collected in interviews in tribal villages and also other historical materials. The Devi movement was distinguished by a solidarity among the Adivasi or tribal peasants in which the orders of a goddess or the Devi were spread through select men who were under her spell. It began as an autonomous movement and had many features in common with tribal movements in other parts of India during the late nineteenth and early twentieth centuries.

It is possible to analyse the Devi movement within the framework of the 'Sanskritisation' theory advanced by M.N. Srinivas. But Hardiman questions the validity of this theory, which, while recognising the existence of conflict in Indian society, takes the position that it is not fundamental and that it can be resolved or at least assimilated through the accommodating structure of Hinduism and the castes. He stresses its failure to take account of the powerful challenge to the existing social order which constitutes a necessary dimension of such movements and hence the fundamental inadequacy of this theory as a tool for understanding the nature of the Devi movement and advances an alternative approach in terms not of values, as in the case of the Sanskritisation model, but in terms of relationships of power.

Basing himself on such an approach Hardiman discusses in detail the Devi movement and demonstrates that the divine commands reflected 'a powerful programme for Adivasi assertion' (p. 219). It had an unsettling impact on all those who wanted to preserve the *status quo* in the Ranimahals, the specific locality of the movement, and in particular it sought to dislodge the domination of Parsi landlords, liquor dealers and moneylenders through the collective reform of their customary social life.

Though the movement began as an autonomous one, soon Congressmen became interested in the movement and a process began to unfold which 'looked like an emerging alliance' (p. 224) between the tribals and the Gandhian nationalists and it caused concern to the British. Gradually the Congress politicians including Vallabhbhai Patel and Kasturba Gandhi came to gain considerable influence over the movement and they encouraged the tribal peasants to adopt some elements of Gandhi's teachings while watering down that aspect of the movement which was considered by the former as socially divisive and militant. Although by 1924 the movement had petered out, it was able to achieve considerable success for the Adivasis against powerfully entrenched interests. Hardiman, however, shows that it was 'on the one hand a great liberation but on the other a movement which laid the foundations for new forms of exploitation' (p. 230).

In an essay rich in historical materials and analyses, Sumit Sarkar concentrates on involvement of the subalterns in the Swadeshi Movement of 1905–8 and the Non-Cooperation Movement led by Gandhi in 1920–2, makes a comparative study of the two movements and emphasises the complex interactions between the élite and subaltern domains of politics by referring to the 'relative autonomy' of the subalterns. As Sarkar shows, the outbreak of a subaltern movement, though not launched or guided by élite politicians, might still be prompted by an awareness of a crisis within the élite domain—a crisis in the form of conflict among the élites and in the form of rumour of collapse of all existing authority—rousing hopes of an end to oppression and misery and 'emergence of a new symbolic power-centre like the Gandhi raj of 1921–2' (p. 307). Popular militancy, in turn, though it might not be more than limited under direction of élite leadership, could nevertheless add to the assertiveness and effectiveness of the anti-imperialist struggle and contribute to the long-term weakening of the colonial authority and power. A major task before the subaltern historians is the exploration of the interrelations and interactions between the élites and subalterns bearing in mind historical specificities.

In view of the fact that usually moments of conflict have received much attention, Sarkar emphasises that for having an adequate understanding of the history of the subalterns it is necessary to accord greater attention to 'the vast and complex continuum of intermediate attitudes' (p. 274) between total subordination and open revolt. One of his major concerns is to depict and explain 'the coexistence and complex interpenetration of extremely varied types of consciousness and activity' (p. 274) and he does this by drawing upon historical evidence from the period under study. He analyses 'some of the dimensions of collective mentality underlying . . . very different forms of popular militancy' (p. 277) and some of the features of the mentality unravelled by him do have certain recurrent patterns.

Sumit Sarkar also emphasises the important role that religion not infrequently plays in the resistance of the subaltern classes against their economic and political subordination 'in a peasant society which has not undergone the process of "disenchantment of the world" partially brought about in the West in the post-Reformation era' (p. 308). He points out the relevance of the religious dimension

including its 'magico-religious' character for having a proper understanding of four crucial features of subaltern movements in the early
Gandhian era: the significance of rumour, the ethical norms and obligations associated with the cult of Gandhi, the mood of renunciation
and sacrifice, and the persistence of faith in Gandhi. The role of
religion as an expression of the collectivity of the Indian peasantry is
also mentioned and discussed in the essays contributed by Arnold,
Hardiman and Amin with variations in focus and in varying degrees.

Gyanendra Pandey's essay involves critical examination of texts.
He analyses a local chronicle of events entitled *Waqeat-o-Hadesat*
written in Urdu by a Muslim zamindar of Mubarakpur in eastern
Uttar Pradesh and compares it with British colonial records. The
comparison points to important differences in perception and perspective between the élite Muslim groups in many parts of northern India
and the British official élites.

Pandey also examines two sketchy documents that come from the
Muslim weavers of Mubarakpur—one a petition drawn by the weavers
in 1813 and the other, the fragments of a Muslim weaver's diary
dating from the late nineteenth century. The diary provides glimpses
of what was going on in the minds of the ordinary labouring people
of the *qasba* and enables us to enlarge the comparison. It shows that
Islamic values had permeated to the bottom of the Muslim society
and that bonds of religion and community tied together the exploited
Muslim weavers and Muslim landed élite. It is, however, significant
that in spite of the religious bond and important areas of common
concern, in several respects there was an important difference between
the weavers and other lower classes on the one hand and élite Muslims
of the upper classes on the other. While both the élite Muslims and
poor Muslims 'speak of . . . a fight on several fronts for self-respect
and human dignity' (p. 269), the weaver's diary indicates 'the assertion
of the rights of the *chote log*' (p. 270).

Dipesh Chakrabarty seeks to explain why the often highly militant
jute workers of Calcutta failed to develop any durable, democratically
functioning trade union organisation or why their organisations
remained essentially an *ad hoc* affair during the period 1920–50. The
reason for this state of affairs, as Chakrabarty argues, was that the
union leaders came invariably from the *babu* or Bengali *bhadralok*

background and that the bond between the middle-class leaders and workers was that of *babu–coolie*. It was a relationship that remained profoundly 'hierarchical' and 'steeped in feudal morality' and values. The consequence of this was a sharp disjunction between a radical ideology and a traditional culture which accounted for the fundamental weakness of the trade union movement.

The distinctiveness of Chakrabarty's analysis lies in some of the issues of culture and consciousness raised by him. But in doing that the autonomy of workers is considerably underplayed and even denied and he tends to argue that the workers could have been rescued only through reforms of *babu* culture. One cannot but wonder whether this line of reasoning is in conformity with the subaltern theme. Further, he seems to impart a changeless quality to the culture of the workers coming from the rural areas and also to that of the trade union leaders coming from the ranks of the Bengali intelligentsia. But despite the persistence of many of the traditional social relationships and values, was there no noticeable change? Is there no evidence of formation of new social network and germination and development of new culture and consciousness, even if of an incipient form and discontinuous nature, in the Calcutta jute mill areas? Is it not possible to discern a process of transition from the social-welfarist position of Sasipada Banerjee through Aswini Kumar Banerjee or S.N. Haldar-type of legal adviser-cum-labour leader or Swarajist Santosh Kumari Gupta to the radical and Marxist position of Gopen Chakrabarty or Radharaman Mitra or Abdul Momen or Bankim Mukherjee? Indeed the relationship between the workers and the radical intelligentsia union leader was an essentially new one indicating a significant change. Within the labour force, too, new social relations and attitudes were being formed.

There were at least some instances of worker unions, the most striking one being that of the Calcutta Tramways Workers' Union, which had a long record of continued and vigorous existence based on active participation of the workers and also on new types of links between the tramway workers and middle-class 'outsider' leaders.[2] In view of such examples can the kind of generalisation made by Chakrabarty on the basis of a single case study and, further, of only a few aspects taken out of their context be done?

To explain the absence of vigorous union movement among the jute mill workers it is necessary to closely consider the specificities of the jute industry and certain aspects of its labour force. Among other things, it was an extrovert, externally oriented industry marked by sharp market instabilities and fluctuations in labour demand. This was most strikingly illustrated by the dismissal of about 60,000 workers out of a 3,00,000-strong labour force on just one single day in February 1931 under the impact of the Depression.[3] This may be viewed as too dramatic an example. But this points to the kind of formidable problems with which the jute mill workers and their middle class leaders were confronted. These are not referred to deny or even to underplay all the issues raised by Chakrabarty. It is, however, necessary to have better comprehension of the strength of traditional culture and its consequences and also of issues relating to the nature and forms of links between the working class and union organisers and leaders coming from the middle-class background.

Partha Chatterjee's essay 'Gandhi and the critique of civil society' is of a nature which is largely different from the other six essays. He has tried to lay down the theoretical conditions which provided the basis for Gandhi's popularity amongst the subaltern classes, particularly the peasantry. How did this actually operate in practice? How was Gandhi's system of thought related to the subaltern groups? Chatterjee has not addressed these questions in this essay. Here he is largely concerned with an examination of the political philosophy of Gandhi and also some of its implications.

Through a rigorous analysis of Gandhi's message Chatterjee shows how Gandhi's critique of all aspects of civil society and industry 'while subverting [the] structure of élite-nationalist thought, provided at the same time the historical opportunity for the political appropriation of the popular classes within the evolving forms of the new Indian state' (p. 156). Chatterjee argues that Gandhi's anti-capitalist, anarchist and communitarian ideas were divided from indigenous social context and not from any Western sources, not even from Edward Carpenter or John Ruskin or Tolstoy or Russian populists with all of whom he had important similarities in varying degrees, and thus his ideas were 'situated *outside* the thematic of post-enlightenment thought' (p. 176). According to Chatterjee, it would also be erroneous to consider Gandhian ideology as a direct manifestation of peasant ideology or regard him as another 'peasant intellectual.' He argues, 'Despite the inherently "peasant-communal" character of its critique of civil society, the correct framework for understanding the Gandhian ideology as a whole is still that of the historical development of the élite-nationalist thought in India. . . . It was an ideology conceived as an intervention in the élite-nationalist discourse of the time and was formed and shaped by the experience of a specifically national movement' (p. 176).

Gandhi's emphasis on communitarian, particularly 'peasant-communal' morality as against that of a society which views man as a limitless consumer signified an important break in the nationalist thought and there lay the source of his strength. He formulated an ideology and political programme that touched a responsive chord in popular mind and, further, made it possible to broaden the range and sweep of Indian nationalism, particularly its mass peasant following. At the same time, as Chatterjee's analysis shows, 'Gandhism succeeded in opening up the historical possibility by which the largest popular element of the nation, namely the peasantry, could be appropriated' (p. 193) by the Congress leadership. Further, 'the working out of the politics of non-violence . . . made it abundantly clear that the object of political mobilisation of the peasantry was not at all what Gandhi claimed on its behalf, to 'train the masses in self-consciousness and attainment of power.' Rather the peasantry was meant to become a willing participant in a struggle wholly conceived and directed by others' (p. 193). Chatterjee emphasises that within the Gandhian framework of national politics *kisans* and labour were to be mobilised but not activised as conscious participants. He firmly refused to involve himself in the mass struggles against exploitation and oppression and failed to go beyond the limits of the class interests of the bourgeoisie. Proceeding from this analysis, Chatterjee maintains that explanation of 'the specific historical process by which [the] political possibilities that were inherent in the Gandhian ideology became the ideological weapons in the hands of the [non-hegemonic] Indian bourgeoisie in its attempt to create a viable state structure' (p. 194) remains a major task of modern Indian historiography. And it is a challenging task.

III

In general the contributions in the volume under review have immensely enriched our knowledge and understanding about the history of subaltern consciousness and subaltern initiative and struggle and also the dialectical relationship between domination and subordination. In view of the fact that these dimensions have usually been neglected and even ignored in the prevalent historiography of India, particularly in the colonialist/Cambridge version, some of the nationalist versions and even in some variants of Marxian history writing, to start with, the subaltern historians have been primarily concerned with revolts and calamities. But that it is not enough is explicitly stated by Sumit Sarkar (pp. 273–4).

Most of the contributions reveal that without the help of effective leadership the subalterns, particularly the peasants, have shown their inability to transform the initiatives originating from the subaltern domain to transform these into nation-wide organic and total struggles against exploitation and oppression. This points to the need for exploration of the nature and forms of links between the two domains of politics and for forging organic links.

NOTES AND REFERENCES

1. Antonio Gramsci, *Selections from prison notebooks* (London, 1971), p. 55.
2. See Siddhartha Guha Roy, 'Tramwaymen of Calcutta: Their movement and organisation, 1920–47,' in Chittabrata Palit, ed., *Revolt Studies*, vol. I, no. 2, December 1985.
3. R.N. Gilchrist, *Indian labour and the land* (Calcutta: Government of Bengal, 1932), p. 23.

Subaltern Autonomy and the National Movement*

B.B. Chaudhuri

A LTOGETHER NINE essays have been included in this volume: David Arnold, 'Bureaucratic recruitment and subordination in colonial India: The Madras constabulary, 1859–1947'; Ramachandra Guha, 'Forestry and social protest in British Kumaun, 1893–1921'; Swapan Dasgupta, 'Adivasi politics in Midnapur, c. 1760–1924'; Tanika Sarkar, 'Jitu Santal's movement in Malda, 1924–32'; David Hardiman, 'From custom to crime: The politics of drinking in colonial South Gujarat'; Gautam Bhadra, 'Four rebels of eighteen-fifty-seven'; Bernard S. Cohn, 'The command of language and the language of command'; Gayatri Chakravorty Spivak, 'Subaltern Studies: Deconstructing historiography'; and Dipesh Chakrabarty, 'Invitation to a dialogue.' Considerations of space prevent me from critically reviewing all of them. I would prefer to concentrate on the essays dealing with a major theme of the 'subaltern' historiography: popular protest movements and their relationship with the wider political movements of the time.

Since the contributions of Arnold and Cohn do not belong to this genre, I would only briefly indicate their arguments. Arnold does deal with a subaltern group—the constabulary constituting the 'bottom

*Based on Ranajit Guha, ed., *Subaltern Studies IV: Writings on South Asian history and society* (Delhi: Oxford University Press, 1985), pp. x+383.

tier of the bureaucratic hierarchy' and performing 'the most menial policing duties in return for the lowest scales of pay.' In material terms they 'shared in the poverty and exploitation of the subaltern classes.' The colonial state sought to 'discipline' them, but failed to establish a complete institutional and ideological control over them. This made possible occasional protests against their lowly position. They even formed unions for the purpose. However, they seldom questioned the authority of the colonial state. Their collective action could not become 'a basis for wider solidarity with other subaltern groups,' for they used their limited powers derived from the state for their own selfish ends. Illegal exactions and bribe-taking alienated them from the rural and urban poor and 'aligned them more closely with the wealthier and more powerful classes who could purchase or command their services.' They were not 'collaborators' with the imperial government as they did not subscribe to its objectives. This, however, did not make them friends of the people, since, though an 'exploited' group, they were also 'exploiters'; 'the oppressed were also oppressors.'

The vastly erudite and well-argued essay by Cohn seeks to explain the reason why the British were keen on learning Indian languages after they had established their political domination in Bengal and other parts of India. Cohn also shows how the specificities of the learning process had wider cultural implications unconnected with the immediate aims of the learners. It was the command of languages, Cohn argues, which provided to the masters precise knowledge of the subject race—its material resources, manners, customs and laws. Knowledge was power. It 'was to be the instrumentality' through which the masters 'issued commands' and collected ever-increasing amounts of information. 'This information was needed to create or locate cheap and effective means to assess and collect taxes, maintain law and order, and it served as a way to identify and classify groups within Indian society. . . . The vast world that was India had to be classified, categorised and bounded before it could be hierarchised' (pp. 283–4). Knowledge was all the more vital initially since the Company's government decided to 'adapt our regulations to the manners and understanding of the people . . . adhering as closely as we are able to their ancient uses and institutions.'

The British conquest of India was thus also 'a conquest of knowledge.' However, the process of learning Indian languages had its own rules, its compulsions. The British tried to comprehend the strange world that was India using their own forms of knowing and thinking. Apart from anything else, the Europeans inevitably adopted the rules governing the structure of their own languages. Over the years developed comparative philology which 'in turn supplied the scientific model for the comparative study of law, religion and society.' The Europeans were now 'prepared to give to the Indians the greatest gift they could give anyone—the Indian would receive a *history.*'

Of the remaining essays the last two form a group apart—'discussions' rather than analysis of any specific historical theme. Dipesh Chakrabarty answers criticisms of some earlier 'subaltern studies.' His exposition is, as usual, remarkably lucid. It is all the more convincing since he seldom condescendingly responds to the critics. He mainly asserts the position of the 'subaltern' historians. However, from the point of view of the historiography of popular protest movements he contributes a new argument (which, at least, was not as explicitly made as he has done here). The persistence of the primacy given to economic factors he would associate with the 'popular revival' in the 1970s of the 'Nehruvian (Marxist-nationalist) critique of colonialism' (p. 370). Early nationalists sought to understand India's poverty, and not the poor, and blamed the poverty on colonialism. A considerable number of the writings in the 1970s and later on popular movements were essentially neo-nationalist. The movements were explained in terms of an 'inexorable economic rationality.' Even where popular protest was articulated in religious idioms, it was explained away merely as a matter of form which only obscured, it was argued, the essentially economic content of the protest.

The 'theoretical intervention' by Gayatri Chakravorty Spivak is as abstruse as Dipesh Chakrabarty's 'discussion' is lucid. She examines some postulates of the 'subaltern' historiography in the light of recent advances in linguistics. However, she addresses readers as a specialist would talk to a small coterie of specialists. Since the present reviewer does not belong to this charmed circle, he feels it would be foolhardy of him to try to glean any pearl from the depth of this bafflingly obscure piece of composition.

The five remaining essays deal with popular protests in different parts of colonial India. We first take up the contributions by Guha, Dasgupta, Sarkar and Hardiman, all of them examining, among others, a common theme: the nature of the autonomy of subaltern movements in relation to the nationalist movement of the time.

Guha's theme is the intensification of peasant protest (1893–1921) in Kumaun against the encroachment by the colonial state on the forest rights of the peasantry and against practices such as forced labour (*utar*) which the enforcement of the new forest laws necessitated. Guha's study of the encroachment is an excellent piece of research. We are, however, more concerned with the protest movement. Two aspects of it need to be re-examined: How did the gradual radicalisation of the movement occur? How do we explain the 'absence, comparatively speaking, of violence, certainly of physical violence' (p. 96)?

Guha identifies the major elements in the radicalisation process during the years 1920–2. Forced labour ceased to be the primary issue of the movement. Retrieving the lost forest rights now became the dominant aim. The rebels had, perhaps for the first time, the vision of a 'free India.' The organisation of the movement was suitably oriented to the radical aims. Guha thus comments on this organisation and on the nature of its relation with the contemporary nationalist movement: 'While this unity and sense of purpose necessarily made their actions political, the politics of the peasantry was clearly not derivative of the politics of urban nationalism. Apart from a hazy perception of Gandhi as a saint whose qualities of heroic sacrifice were invoked against the powers of government, the *utar* movements had little in the nature of an identification with the Congress as such' (p. 87).

Guha does not quite explain the radicalisation. 'Enhancement of the customary services' in the recent years scarcely explains why the radical tone in the movement became most pronounced in the year 1920–2. (We wish his note on the Kumaun Parishad, an 'association of local journalists, lawyers and intellectuals,' which had a leading role in the movement, were more elaborate. What was the nature of its links, particularly the key figure Badridutt Pande's relations, with the Congress organisation and movement of the time?) The evidence that Guha cites seems to be inconsistent with his conclusion. It is true that 'urban nationalism' did not have the initiative in organising the Kumaun movement. The question to decide is whether the widespread political ferment at the time affected the movement at all. The ferment is, of course, not the same thing as the role of a specific group of individuals. The Kumaun peasants might also have interpreted in their own way the political message that created the ferment. However, if its source lay outside the peasant society, it would be worthwhile to identify the way the ferment affected the peasant politics.

The idioms in which this politics was now articulated were strikingly new. For instance, at the crucial gathering of over ten thousand at a local fair Badridutt Pande passed on a message from Gandhi that he would come and save them from oppression as he did in Champaran. It was at the fair that peasants firmly resolved not to provide *begar* any longer and to combine for the restoration of their lost forest rights. 'Slogans in praise of Mahatma Gandhi and "Swatantra Bharat" and cries that the government was *anniyayi* (unjust) rent the air.' Incendiarism, that is, setting forests on fire, now became part of a 'systematic campaign.' Guha had not cared to explain such new forms of peasant protest. The bland formulation that peasant politics 'was clearly not derivative of the politics of urban nationalism' precludes consideration of their possible links with the nationalist movement of the time.

How to explain the near-absence of physical violence? Large-scale violence to property did occur. Guha does not tell us why the absence of only one form of violence needs to be explained. (We get an impression that he tends to assume the absence of violence of any kind as a form of protest.) His explanations of the phenomenon do not quite convince. He relates it partly to the absence in Kumaun of 'an intermediate class enjoying a vested interest in land,' 'a culturally distinct buffer class, as the Hindu zamindars were to the tribals, between the body of cultivating proprietors and the state,' and partly to the 'distinctive history of peasant protest' of the pre-British days which the practice known as *dhandak* exemplified.

Guha's assumption is that the extent of violence is correlated to 'different forms of domination.' One may argue that the absence of an intermediate landed class in Kumaun did not mean the absence of domination altogether. The new forest administration, 'the affirm-ation of state monopoly,' did represent a stable structure of domination. More significantly, violence could occur even in the absence of the domination of an intermediate landed class. (The Santal revolt of 1855 first broke out in the Damin-i-Koh, where such a class was non-existent.) Normally, tribal protest turned violent mainly when the tribals realised, under specific circumstances, that the colonial state (often its local representatives) had gone over to the side of their ad-versaries, so that they had nothing to expect from it towards redressing their grievances. Needless to say, this perception *alone* did not lead to an organised tribal movement.

Dhandak, the typical collective peasant protest in pre-colonial Kumaun, directed primarily against specific wrong-doers and rarely against the authority of the king, had two major forms: defiance of their authority and an appeal to the king to remove them where the peasant initiative was not enough to make them mend their ways. This form of protest did not perhaps persist. It was devised under specific historical conditions, particularly a firm belief of the people that the king would either tame their oppressors or altogether remove them. Guha does admit that 'its socio-cultural idiom was predicated firmly on the traditional relationship between the *raja* and *praja*' (p. 84). The new power structure was hardly compatible with such a belief.

Swapan Dasgupta's conclusion that the tribal politics in the Jungle Mahals of Midnapur was far from the 'exclusive handiwork of Cong-ress politics' is indisputable. However, he does not seem to have made up his mind as to how exactly the tribal politics was related to the Congress politics. The assertion such as the following is unequivocal: 'Élite politics in Midnapur has thus only a very tenuous connection with the autonomous mobilisation of this particular section of the subaltern. Adivasi insurgency belonged on the whole to another do-main of politics' (p. 135). (By 'élite politics' Dasgupta presumably means the Congress politics.) He also makes qualified assertions. To the question he asks (in connection with the resistance of the tribals to the Midnapur Zamindari Company): 'If Congress did not introduce "politics" to the Adivasis, did it merely appropriate their autonomous political initiatives?' his answer is as follows: 'The answers are not clear-cut' (p. 126).

In fact, his narrative of the 'first wave' of tribal resistance to the Midnapur Zamindari Company (MZC) proves beyond any doubt that the so-called élite politics was scarcely peripheral to the resistance. He finds a continuity between the *hat* (country market) looting of 1918 and this resistance (1921–2). He would even suggest: 'The events of 1918 are central to our understanding of subsequent events, especially the politics of nationalism . . . there is sufficient justification for believing that there was an already existing subaltern consciousness which was seized upon, appropriated, and of course in certain cases advanced by the élite' (p. 124). As a conscious activity of tribals, *hat* lootings, sporadic, isolated and often spontaneous, qualitatively differed from the organised resistance to the MZC, an infinitely more formidable enemy than the petty shopkeepers and traders in essential commodities whose demand of an abruptly increased price infuriated the tribals. Dasgupta did not come across any 'recorded instances of popular agitation against the MZC' prior to 1921–2. And he has the following explanation to offer: 'Overawed perhaps by the MZC's power, the Santals did not act in the same idiom upon which Birsa Munda, for example, had drawn. Their awareness of their own condition and the power relations responsible for it was not enough to activate them.' Dasgupta does admit the cruciality of the role of the Congressmen in the organisation of the opposition to the MZC: 'In this respect Congress propaganda, fuelled by thriving rumours of the impending collapse of the British Raj, provided the necessary stimulus' (p. 127).

Yet Dasgupta would accuse the Congressmen of not consistently upholding the tribal cause. Indeed he would even conclude: 'On other occasions the role of the Congress seems to suggest a *conscious subversion* of autonomous adivasi initiative' (p. 128) (emphasis mine). He cites just a single occasion. Even that does not establish his argument. The occasion was as follows. While the Santals 'were collectively reasserting lost traditional rights as a conscious political act of insurgency,' Roy, an active Congress worker there, 'was intent on negotiating with the District Magistrate and the MZC.' Roy's motive, according to Dasgupta, was 'to ensure Congress supervision over the labour process to make landlordism more humane.' He does not provide any evidence whatsoever in support of this crucial assertion. On the contrary he himself points out that the District Magistrate's 'attempt at a compromise failed due to the intransigence of Roy. Roy in fact pressurised the MZC to come to terms with the Congress on the latter's terms.' How did, then, Roy 'consciously' subvert the autonomous Adivasi initiative? What does 'Congress supervision over the labour process' actually mean? Dasgupta has only perfunctorily dealt with such questions. The manner in which Congressmen came to be involved in the specific tribal struggle implies that the Congress politics there had ceased to be 'élite politics,' in the sense in which he understands it.

It is true that the Congress role in the 'second wave' of the movement (beginning sometime in August 1922) was much less decisive. However, the Congress continued to be associated with it. The Congressmen, on Dasgupta's own admission, 'did not alienate themselves from the tribal people.' During a Congress worker's trial 'not a single Santal or anyone else came forward to serve as witness for the prosecution.' Following the arrest of a prominent Congress leader 'the Adivasis destroyed the MZC office.' Yet Dasgupta sees 'only a very tenuous connection' of the Congress politics with the tribal movement there. This seems to be an instance of a tension between the *idee fixe* of a historian and his compulsion not to ignore the historical data he handles.

Tanika Sarkar's is an illuminating study of ambiguities in the consciousness of a subaltern group—immigrant Santals in Malda, mostly sharecroppers. (The story of the Santal movement against landlords, which forms an important part of the study, is the context in which the ambiguities become intelligible.) Recurrence of religious revitalisation movements among tribals in different parts of British India is by now a well-known phenomenon. So is the decisiveness of the influence of Hindu ideas on some of them. The originality of Sarkar's study of the Santal revitalisation movement is that she points to striking ambiguities in its ideology.

The influence of Hindu ideas on the leader, Jitu, and his 'Sannyasi

Dol' was far from peripheral. The leader and his followers were actually Hinduised. The Santal movement of the time (1926–32) 'seemed, at least on the surface, to amount to a rejection of the Santal identity in an endeavour to raise their status through integration with the same Hindu society that had always oppressed them' (p. 149). One of Jitu's followers openly proclaimed: 'We shall not keep either Santals or Muhamadans any longer.' The Hinduisation process was occasionally understandably associated with use of force. Naturally certain aspects of the hierarchical Hindu caste system strongly influenced the ideology of Jitu and his followers. For instance, they aspired to the *jal-chal* status (so that high caste Hindus would accept offer of drink from them without fear of pollution). Hinduisation also probably largely accounted for Jitu's 'contemptuous references' to the lower castes and the untouchables. Jitu's strong antipathy towards the Muslims was also partly due to the communal preachings of the Hindu Mahasabha at the time.

However, the Hindu influence did not go far enough. Indeed, the distinctively Santal identity constantly reappeared in Jitu's perceptions and deeds. For instance, conversion to Hinduism did not necessitate abandonment of the traditional Santal worship of spirits (*bongas*). The usual Santal festivals and celebrations, based on the Santal notion of pleasure, were retained throughout. Jitu's message was addressed exclusively to the Santals. It was communicated too in the Santali language. More significantly, the message essentially derived from Jitu's perceptions of the roots of the Santal subordination. He would repeatedly tell the Santals that they would soon regain their *Desh* (homeland) where all 'intermediate layers of authority created by the colonial government' between the common Santal and the village head would disappear.

These apparent ambiguities in the consciousness of the Hinduised Santals are explicable. Conversion to Hinduism was not merely a matter of substituting one religious faith for another. It was largely motivated by a sincere conviction that it was an essential precondition for the coming of the millennium. The practice of keeping pigs and fowls was abandoned not just because the Hindus considered it unclean. Jitu believed that revitalisation of the Santal culture and religion through this abandonment would make the Santals a match for their adversaries. The new *jal-chal* status was a means of the appropriation of the symbols of status of the caste Hindus, and would thus make them feel equal to their enemies. The religious revitalisation movements of the Santals are inseparable from their continuing political struggle.

This phase of the religious movement of the Santals should not, however, be regarded as a continuation of such movements earlier. The Santals did come under Hindu influences before, but they were not formally Hinduised. Nor did they think it a matter of pride to call themselves Hindus, to the extent of rejecting their Santal identity. They were then hardly keen on finding a place for themselves in the Hindu caste system; Hindu influences only reinforced their search for an enduring Santal identity.

Hardiman's essay divides into two distinct parts. The longer one convincingly shows how the intervention by the colonial government in the production and distribution of 'drinks' tended to force the poor tribals of south Gujarat to abandon the increasingly expensive drinks and to shift to cheaper but impure stuff (made not of the traditional ingredients such as the juice of certain trees or of certain flowers). The tribals did not allow this to happen without a protest. Its usual form was not opposition to the strangers connected with the new apparatus of colonial control, but 'illicit' distillation and smuggling. An activity, which in the tribal consciousness had nothing whatsoever to do with the commission of a crime, appeared now as a crime. The second part analyses the changing attitudes of the tribals to drinking. This seems to be more significant from the point of view of the 'subaltern' historiography. Drinking for the tribals was not just a way of finding an escape from the stresses produced by a hard day's work. It 'occupied a central place in their culture' (p. 173). 'In all spheres of their life, drink had positive associations. It was a food of the gods which possessed an element of divine power; it set a seal on negotiations and legitimised family ceremonies; it enhanced the pleasures of social gatherings and public festivities; it provided succour during times of scarcity. Drink . . . lubricated the whole cycle of life of the peasants' (p. 177).

However, under the altered conditions created by the intervention of the colonial authority the tribals themselves tended to regard drinking as an evil, associating with it their ever-increasing indebtedness to the Parsis and the consequent immiserisation. Hence attempts were made within the tribal society itself to persuade the tribals to get rid of the evil. Even before British rule some well-to-do families gave up drinking 'in the belief that this would raise their status in the wider society.' It was presumably an effect of the influence of the Brahmanic culture in which 'abstention from spirituous drinks was considered a great virtue.'

The temperance movement in the tribal society from about the last quarter of the nineteenth century basically differed from such isolated individual acts of renunciation. Now entire communities undergoing a process of pauperisation became involved in it. Fairly widespread movements appeared in the years 1905–6. The most organised one (known as the Devi movement) occurred during the Non-Cooperation Movement, but did not survive its withdrawal by Gandhi. An 'influential class of upwardly-mobile Adivasis' sought to prevent the movement from flagging. But the old tribal mores largely reasserted themselves. Hardiman has not adequately explained this significant phenomenon. In an earlier essay on the Devi movement (included in volume III of *Subaltern Studies*) Hardiman identified as one of the primary impulses behind the movement a collective will to appropriate the symbols of ritual status of the dominant groups in order to undermine their cultural domination. Why did this will weaken and disappear before long?

Adivasis 'felt that drinking was a part of their culture, a custom hallowed by tradition, something indeed which was a part of their very identity' (p. 222). This explanation is only partly tenable. Other tribal societies did jettison customs 'hallowed by tradition,' once they were convinced that the renunciation would help them retrieve their lost independence. (Needless to say, the whole of a tribal community could not be persuaded to the new style of life. Hence the continuing conflict in the tribal society committed to a new culture and ethical code.) The sense of identity and communal solidarity need not necessarily have derived from one continuing tradition. It could have multiple roots, since the tradition by itself did not preclude exposure to new cultural influences, which might have created a more enduring sense of solidarity. It would be tautological to say that the tribals returned to their old practices, just because they were 'hallowed by tradition.'

Gautam Bhadra rehabilitates four little-known rebels of the 'Mutiny': Shah Mal (a small landlord), Devi Singh (a cultivator belonging to a substantial peasant community), Gonoo (an ordinary cultivator of Singhbhum) and Maulavi Ahmadullah Shah (an itinerant preacher). He rejects the usual élitist bias in the traditional historiography of the Mutiny and seeks to refute one of its central assumptions that 'the mass of the population appeared to have played little part or at most tamely followed the behests of the caste superiors' (p. 230). He concentrates on the people's perception of alien rule and of the wide-ranging implications of the Mutiny, and on the independent initiative of the people in organising local rebellions against the Raj.

The most remarkable part of the essay is his explanation of how relatively 'ordinary' rebels came to lead the popular rebellions. The crucial factor was the pervasive popular belief that the mighty British Raj, which represented in the people's consciousness a formidable instrument of repression, had irretrievably collapsed. It was now time for the people to take the initiative which had for long been denied to them. Creation of an alternative structure of authority and power embodied this initiative and also the people's aspirations. Anger against exploiters was formerly often expressed in the form of sporadic crimes. Violence, now collectively organised and sustained by the new authority structure, was designed to achieve collective aims. However, the rebels' vision ranged far beyond their immediate grievances. The remote past was now recalled. This revived communal memories, which had often little relevance to the contemporary reality. The leader here was carrying out the will of the people and not imposing his will on the people.

In at least one case, that of the maulavi, the people's choice of the leader had much to do with his extraordinariness. Bhadra infers the 'ordinariness' of the maulavi from his limited 'learning' and command over Arabic and Persian. This was hardly a measure of his stature as a leader. Bhadra's references to contemporary assessments of the Maulavi point unmistakably to the sources of his moral authority: 'his holy character' (p. 266); 'the Mahomedans had great faith in him as an inspired prophet' (p. 267); his troops 'believed in his invulnerability, even after a bullet . . . smashed his thumb' (ibid.), and they also believed that 'his Whip and Handkerchief possessed magical qualities' (ibid.). Other leaders were scarcely adored in this manner.

It is refreshing to find 'subaltern' historians handling strikingly original themes. The present reviewer has, however, some reservations about their treatment of the question of 'autonomy' of subaltern movements. Some studies included in the present volume show that the rigidity of the first formulation on the theme still persists. Subaltern movements did, understandably, have their distinctive elements. However, the distinctiveness might not necessarily have derived from their autonomy. On the other hand, persons formally associated with 'élite politics' could be involved in subaltern movements in such a manner that the élite politics ceased to be so. It would be worthwhile to investigate how the content of the so-called élite politics could be thus significantly altered.

PART II

Critical Incorporation in the Global Academy

ROSALIND O'HANLON
'Recovering the Subject: Subaltern Studies and Histories of
Resistance in Colonial South Asia.'
Modern Asian Studies, 22, 1, 1988, 189–22.

JIM MASSELOS
'The Dis/appearance of Subalterns: A Reading of a Decade
of Subaltern Studies.'
South Asia, 15, 1, 1992, 105–25.

K. SIVARAMAKRISHNAN
'Situating the Subaltern: History and Anthropology in the
Subaltern Studies Project.'
Journal of Historical Sociology, 8 (December 1995),
395-429.

FREDERICK COOPER
'Conflict and Connection: Rethinking African History,'
American Historical Review, 99,
December 1994, 1516–45.

HENRY SCHWARZ
'Subaltern Studies: Radical History in the
Metaphoric Mode,' in *Writing Cultural History in Colonial
and Post-colonial India.* Philadelphia: University of
Pennsylvania Press (1997), pp. 128-61.

Recovering the Subject:
Subaltern Studies and Histories of Resistance in Colonial South Asia

ROSALIND O'HANLON*

I N THE field of social and cultural anthropology, the issues raised by European representations of non-European 'others'—of the control of discourses, the production of professional canons for the representation of truth about the other, the epistemological and ethical ambiguities in the position of the ethnographic observer—have recently received an enormous amount of critical attention. This intensified critical awareness goes beyond the familiar ethnographic concern with the development of cultural empathy, to a much more fundamental exploration of the epistemological constitution of non-European and colonial societies as objects of knowledge within the

*I am indebted to David Arnold, Crispin Bates, Chris Bayly, Nick Dirks, David Hardiman, Gyan Prakash and David Washbrook for having taken the time to provide detailed commentaries on the arguments made here and also to the participants at seminars where parts of it were presented as papers: at the South Asian Studies seminar at St Antony's College, Oxford, at a workshop on popular culture in South Asia held at the Centre of South Asian Studies, Cambridge, in March 1986, and at a symposium on colonialism and the nation-state at the California Institute of Technology in May 1987.

disciplines of Western social science. The development of these concerns, and the acceptance and exploration in the last decade of the links between colonialism and the emergence of anthropology as a discipline are traceable in no small part to the attempted iconoclasms of structuralism and its post-structuralist and deconstructive turns, and to the latter's ferocious and many-sided attack upon the presumed sovereignty and universality of the Western intellectual tradition: in particular, upon the Enlightenment faith in a rational human subject and an effective human agency. These themes have been brought together with greatest political and theoretical effect, of course, in Edward Said's assault upon the production of histories in which 'the one human history uniting humanity either culminated in or was observed from the vantage point of Europe.'[1] These concerns have been rather less well explored for the writing of social history of non-European or colonial societies, except where these social histories are argued, as they are now with increasing frequency, to be most usefully subsumed under the new category of historical anthropology or ethnohistory.[2]

My purpose here is to explore these themes in the context of the social historiography of colonial South Asia, where I think it is now widely accepted that the project of *Subaltern Studies* has provided the most provocative and interesting intervention in recent years. I intend the present essay in part to be a general review, but my more central purpose is to rethink the issues raised and fruitfully restated by the series in the context of the themes sketched out above. I aim both to suggest how we may place the series, and what I believe to be its limitations, in a critical and intellectual context, and to indicate some of the further categories and conceptual schemes which must be developed as a part of the project of restoring 'suppressed' histories—of women, non-whites, non-Europeans—as well as the subordinate of colonial South Asia. It needs hardly to be said that a commentary of this kind is in many ways a parasitic exercise, made possible in large part by the insights and critical stance developed by the contributors themselves.

The central concern of the project has been the possibility of writing a history which is not only from Europe's 'periphery' in its rejection of the neocolonialist, neo-nationalist and economistic Marxist modes of historiography argued to dominate the contemporary field, but which also takes as its focus the dispossessed of that periphery. Their own particular forms of subjectivity, experience and agency, at present subjugated by these universalising modes, are to be reconstituted and thus restored to history. This project in turn engages the contributors with further issues: with the identification of forms of power in fields and relations far removed from the domain of the political as we familiarly understand it, such as colonialism's production of new forms of knowledge of South Asian societies; with ways of conceptualising the nature of resistance and its possibilities in a deeply coercive social context; and, in the overt commitments of the project and particularly of its editor with the political status of the historian or critic. The extraordinary interest of the project viewed in this way is thus that it illustrates both the present possibilities of, and the likely limitations in a challenge to the kind of rationalist and universalising historicism identified by Edward Said: a challenge which, although it incorporates many of their themes, is made neither from the ground of post-structuralism nor from that of classical Marxism, but from the point of view of the subordinate of colonial society.

Both the rejection of an ethnocentric historicism and, perhaps less uncontroversially, a decentring of our familiar notions of power and the political, seem to me wholly to be welcomed. This does not mean, however, that we enter a world free of determination or necessity, for the emphasis on difference is informed by a much sharper awareness of the various forms which power and domination may take, of the possibility of its appearance even in those social contexts associated in programmatic political radicalism with emancipation. In epistemological terms, moreover, the very focus on ways in which non-European objects of knowledge have been and are constituted in the social scientific disciplines of the West separates this perspective from empiricism. My main concern here, however, is with the nature of the reconstruction attempted in the Subaltern project. At the very moment of this assault upon Western historicism, the classic figure of Western humanism—the self-originating, self-determining individual, who is at once a subject in his possession of a sovereign consciousness whose defining quality is reason, and an agent in his power of freedom—is readmitted through the back door in the figure of the subaltern himself, as he is restored to history in the reconstructions of the Subaltern project. The consequence of this is to limit and distort the conceptualisation of the contributors' own chosen themes of domination and resistance. What they raise for us, however, is a critically important question. If we accept, as I assume we should, that no hegemony can be so penetrative and pervasive as to eliminate all ground for contestation or resistance, this leaves us with the question as to how we are to configure their presence, if it is not to be in terms of liberal humanist notions of subjectivity and agency. Much of the material with which the contributors work, particularly that concerning the construction of subjectivity through negation, does help to provide us with some basis for the construction of subjectivities of a kind very different from the universal constitutive subject of the Western tradition. A similar tension appears in the conceptual status accorded to the category of experience. While a Marxist teleology which emp-ties subaltern movements of their specific types of consciousness and experience forms a principal target of the project, the notion of a cumulative subjective change through struggle towards a recognisable class consciousness forms a principal theme in some of the studies. I situate this tension within similar debates amongst Marxists in the European context and suggest that the problem of experience, separated from that of agency, might be more fruitfully thought without the notion of universal human subjectivities. Finally, I examine the notion of political commitment in the project, and what I see as the tension between the desire to find a resistant presence, and the neces-sity of preserving difference and otherness in the figure of the subaltern.

In addition to the first four volumes of *Subaltern Studies*, I should also like to make reference to Ranajit Guha's *Elementary aspects of peasant insurgency in colonial India*, both because Guha is editor of the series, and because the two seem to me to illuminate each other in important ways. At the time of writing, some eighteen scholars have contributed to the series, in essays ranging over a period from the early seventeenth century to the 1970s, and including in the subordinate groups surveyed peasants, agricultural labourers, factory workers and tribals. The contributions also range in theoretical sophistication from empirical accumulations of detail concerning these groups and their resistances, to the most ambitious attempts to redraw the basic explanatory procedures of Marxist historical theory. What they all share in common, however, is their critical intent, and indeed it is the critique of the conventional genres of nationalist, colonialist and Marxist historiography which is now the most familiar and impressive feature of the series. The attack upon élite historiography in its three forms is, of course, that these have treated the subordinate peoples of South Asian society as if they had no consciousness of their own, and hence no ability to make their own history. In the case of neocolonial historiography, as Guha has put it, Indian nationalism is represented 'as the sum of the activities and ideas by which the Indian élite responded to the institutions, opportunities, resources, etc., generated by colonialism.'[3] Of course, this criticism of the Namierite character of much of the history of South Asia written from outside the region is not new, and the 'Cambridge school' is now a familiar figure in a variety of radical demonologies. Yet such criticism has rarely been supported by the systematic and substantive investigation into what went on beyond the narrow circles of élite politics, with which some of the contributors have furnished us.

The attack on neo-nationalist historiography is now also familiar. This genre has read every moment and variety of popular resistance in terms of its own anti-colonial struggle, appropriating all of them to a new 'great tradition' of the Indian freedom movement, in which the Indian National Congress not only spoke for all of the people, but generated and led all of the 'genuinely' political movements in which they were engaged. In response, the contributors have attempted to establish, in a variety of contexts, the specific rootedness in bourgeois political ambition and ideology of many Congress and Gandhian campaigns, and to show that far from leading movements of subordinate resistance, Congress activists frequently moved in and attempted to appropriate and divert movements which were generated outside and independently of it. This perspective has yielded a number of fine essays. Shahid Amin has documented the ways in which the villagers of Gorakhpur district decoded Congress and Gandhian messages in their own way, rather than on the model of a simple peasant religiosity responding to the sanctified figure of the Mahatma, as party activists assumed. The way in which the figure and message of the Mahatma, particularly the polysemic word 'Swaraj,' were contextualised within the villagers' own popular religious culture, helped give birth to a vision of a millennial world which was their own rather than the Congress's, and which was directly political in intent.[4] In his examination of the Kisan Sabha movement in Awadh over the same period, Gyan Pandey reconstructs both the peasants' appropriation of the image of the Mahatma, and the ways in which they drew upon their own profoundly moral and religious world-view in order to voice their protests against the growing impositions of landlords. This radicalism, culminating in the Eka movement of 1921, was not a product of Congress leadership, but rather of the experience of the peasants themselves: first, of very high rents, debt and severe land shortage in a talukdar-dominated agrarian structure; and second, of the peasant leadership in their encounters with landlords, British officials and the police, whom they came to see as a common enemy. The Congress turned down this radical lead on the ground that it breached national unity. However, Pandey argues, the sort of unity envisioned here was actually of a very specific kind:

> It should be evident that the nature of the Swaraj that eventuated from this struggle would depend very much on the nature of the alliance (the 'unity') that was forged. From this point of view, the Congress' insistence in 1921–2 on a united front of landlords as well as peasants and others, was a statement in favour of the *status quo* and against any radical change in the social set-up when the British finally handed over the reins of power.[5]

The third genre which the contributors have brought under attack is that of conventional Indian Marxist historiography. The perspective of the Subaltern group naturally at once calls into question their relationship with Marxist theory. The argument here, which Partha Chatterjee puts most succinctly, is that the teleologies of Marxist historical writing have acted to empty subaltern movements of their specific types of consciousness and practice, and to see in the history of colonial South Asia only the linear development of class consciousness. For the national–colonial opposition of neo-nationalist historiography, Marxists have substituted that between feudal and bourgeois forces, and read all South Asian history in the same totalising manner.[6] As we shall see, by no means all of the contributors are free from the notion of a progression of consciousness, and a teleology which finds some resistances to be backward and primitive, and hence less congenial material for the historian to work on than those which are advanced along the road to an enlightened awareness of class interest. A number of critics have made the point that this conflicts with the proclaimed interest in the historical specificity of subaltern movements.[7] There is indeed a conflict here, and it would be surprising if there were not; it is a genuine difficulty as to how we may discern, in the consciousness and practice of those we study, processes of unilinear change, real learning experiences gained in the course of struggle and resistance, and how far we should assign all change to the realm of the reversible and contingent. Much the same issues, of the specificity and irreducibility of experience versus the onward movement of class consciousness and struggle, have been fought out in the context of English working class history.[8]

Having looked very briefly at some of the main themes in the series' critique of established historiography, I should now like to ask whether the contributors share some more positive common ground or set of assumptions between them—most obviously, of course, in the significance of the term 'subaltern' itself—or whether a dissatisfaction, for all the difficulties attendant on the task of the iconoclast, is all that unites them. First, however, it would be useful to clarify this question of what we might expect in the way of internal consistency or common ground among the contributors, since this has been a point of criticism already. It would be unhelpful of us to expect either that a project of this duration should not shift and develop in its emphases over time, or that a large body of scholars, intent primarily on the task of deconstruction, should hasten to establish a new uniformity. Quite rightly, the contributors have decided that it is positive and useful to work in some respects within a loose rather than a rigid interpretative framework. As Ranajit Guha puts it, the focus on the subaltern provides only 'a new orientation within which many different styles, interests and discursive modes may find it possible to unite in their rejection of academic élitism.'[9] However, I think that it is legitimate to distinguish between a difference of view or interpretation which is clearly stated and understood in public discussion, and inconsistencies which arise as the product of a failure or confusion in debate, which work to obscure both the issues raised in the series, and our ability to respond critically to them.

For—to return to the question of a set of shared assumptions—my argument here, and it may well seem a presumptuous one, is that underlying and making possible the separate essays in the series is indeed a recognisable theory or progression of ideas. The problem, rather, is that it has been inadequately recognised as such, with two consequences. First, some of the contributors have employed these ideas in an unhelpful and confused manner, and this without any clear discussion which is available to a general readership. Second, there has been something of a confusion in the minds of critics, together with a quite inadequate scrutiny of what is important and distinctive in the broader project. This progression of ideas concerns the category of the subaltern itself, and the way in which it is employed to break up the hegemony of the three modes of interpretation mentioned above. It is certainly true, as Sabyasachi Bhattacharya has remarked, that 'people's history' or 'history from below' has been a category to which historians writing from a very broad range of perspectives—nationalist, liberal, Marxist, Annales school—have laid claim.[10] When, however, the idea of 'history from below' is made to take on the form of a project to 'recover the experience' of those 'hidden from history,' in the phrase made classic in feminist historiography, we move to a very specific and powerful set of assumptions indeed. This is a very important point, both because this is the idiom in which a very great deal of contemporary historical writing concerned with the subordinate and the marginal—feminist and black history, as well as regional projects like *Subaltern Studies*—is cast, and because it is an inadequate understanding of these assumptions which gives rise to the widespread idea that writing in this idiom represents only a very general orientation of interest, rather than any specific notion of how the task of recovering lost or suppressed experience is to be carried out.

The Subaltern contributors would, I think, accept the argument that their own project has been cast in these terms: that they have come together in an effort to recover the experience, the distinctive cultures, traditions, identities and active historical practice of subaltern groups in a wide variety of settings—traditions, cultures and practice which have been lost or hidden by the action of élite historiography. What this asserts, against élite historiography's pretensions to comprehensiveness and universality is, of course, that the history of the people is an unknown quantity, an area of darkness which the dominant modes of historical discourse have failed to penetrate, and which mocks their claims to complete or even partial knowledge. This, the first step in what I have referred to above as a progression of ideas, represents an enormously powerful challenge, precisely because of the overwhelming normative value which the identification with 'the majority,' 'the people,' has assumed in the political and sociological discourses of the twentieth century (of which, of course, the discourse of democracy is only one) and hence in the legitimation of all our cultural and ideological projects. As Jean Baudrillard notes in his provocative commentary on the significance which 'the masses' have taken on in our present political culture: 'They are the leitmotif of every discourse; they are the obsession of every social project.'[11] At the level of our political culture, this consuming ideological imperative makes it intolerable for us to accept publicly that we cannot appropriate the masses to our projects, that there may be only silence where their own authentic voices should be raised in our support: 'This silence is unbearable. It is the unknown of the political equation, the unknown which annuls every political equation. Everybody questions it, but never as silence, always to make it speak.'[12] It is this same value, of course, which allows us to make the term 'élite historiography' itself one of criticism; and which makes that undoubted majority of professional historians who remain preoccupied with élites of various kinds defend this preoccupation not with a frank disavowal of any interest in 'the people,' but with the assertion that it is élites, or those in power, after all, who are most in a position to determine what happens to the people at large, and who therefore remain the best means through which we may understand the changes through which the people must live.

With this reminder of the tremendous ideological significance of an identification with 'the people'—and let us be clear that this remains a matter of the norms of political discourse, rather than of actual historiographical practice—we are in a better position to appreciate the strength of this first step. It is the assertion not just of a space of which dominant historical discourses have failed to take account, but of their fundamental inability to occupy the central ideological ground of our culture. It is this central ground, the masses and the recovery of their own specific and distinctive histories, with all of the legitimating power implied in such a concern, which the Subaltern contributors claim as the hallmark of their project. Their task, and that of all historians who write in the same idiom, thus becomes one of 'filling up': of making an absence into presences, of peopling a vacant space with figures—dissimilar in their humble and work-worn appearance, no doubt, but bearing in these very signs of their origin the marks of a past and a present which is their own. As Partha Chatterjee puts it, 'The task now is to fill up this emptiness, that is, the representation of subaltern consciousness in élitist historiography. It must be given its own specific content with its own history and development. . . . Only then can we recreate not merely a whole aspect of human history whose existence élitist historiography has hithèrto denied, but also the history of the "modern" period, the epoch of capitalism.'[13]

If this is the task, how is it to be carried out? Not, I would argue, in as many ways as there are contributors. Rather, the very notion of the restoration of an original presence suggests—and particularly so where the presence is an 'insubordinate' or resistant one—the means by which it is to be done, and this constitutes our second step. Essentially, this consists in the recuperation of the subaltern as a conscious human subject-agent. We are to restore him, in the classic manner of liberal humanism, as a subject 'in his own right,' by reclaiming for him a history, a mode of consciousness and practice, which are *his own*: which are not bestowed upon him by any élite or external leadership, which have their origins nowhere else but in his own being. We are to recuperate him as an agent, rather than as the helpless victim of impersonal forces, or the blind follower of others, through the recognition of his capacity for purposeful action: for a considerable degree of self-determination in favourable times and, returning to his own inextinguishable subjectivity, possessed at least of his own modes of ideation and practice in unfavourable ones. This, then, I think, is what Gayatri Chakravorty Spivak means when she speaks of the contributors' use of 'a *strategic* use of positivist essentialism in a scrupulously visible political interest.'[14]

Having said that the manner in which the subaltern makes his reappearance through the work of the contributors is in the form of the classic unitary self-constituting subject-agent of liberal humanism, let me at once make three qualifications. The first is that I am not implying by this that any unthinking positivism or empiricism pervades the series. We should see this rather as a strategy although, as I shall argue, it is not completely understood by all those who use it, and its larger significance and, more importantly, its limitations, have yet to receive any proper public discussion. Second, there is some variation in the centrality accorded to this figure. It appears most weakly in the work of Shahid Amin, and particularly in his study of small peasant production of sugarcane in eastern Uttar Pradesh at the turn of the century, whose central focus is on agricultural seasonality, its variance with the economic demands made on the peasantry during the year, and the consequences for peasant indebtedness of these structural mistimings.[15] Yet, I would argue that it remains the dominant trope in the series, precisely because it is very strongly suggested in the project itself of recovering 'their own' history of the subordinate and the marginal. This brings me to my third qualification. I am not here saying that it is always impossible to write about these groups without transforming them into autonomous subject-agents, unitary consciousnesses possessed of their own originary essence, in the manner which we now understand to be the creation, very largely, of Enlightenment humanism's reconstruction of Man. Put on its own like this, I do not believe that any of the contributors would want to espouse an essentialism of this kind. The difficulty, however, is that in the assertion—which is very difficult *not* to make, without having to abandon the strategy altogether—that subordinate groups have a history which is not given to them by élites, but is a history of *their own*, we arrive at a position which requires some subtlety and skill if it is to be held from slipping into an essentialist humanism. This skill will depend in very large part precisely upon our rejection of humanism's obsessive invocation of origins as its ultimate legitimation and guarantee: of the myth, which gives us the idea of the self-constituting subject, that a consciousness or being which has an origin outside itself is no being at all. From such a rejection, we can proceed to the idea that though histories and identities are necessarily constructed and produced from many fragments, fragments which do not contain the signs of any essential belonging inscribed in them, this does not cause the history of the subaltern to dissolve once more into invisibility. This is first, because we apply exactly the same decentring strategies to the monolithic subject-agents of élite historiography; and second, because it is the creative practice of the subaltern which now becomes the focus of our attention, his ability to appropriate and mould cultural materials of almost any provenance to his own purposes, and to discard those, however sacred or apparently an integral part of his being, which no longer serve them.

Skill of this kind, the ability to argue for a distinctiveness of practice without slipping into a metaphysics of presence, is clearly very difficult to achieve, and most of all so where our object is a recovery of presence. Some of the contributors possess this skill in greater proportion than others, but in almost all of them, as we shall see, there appears a persistent wavering or slipping between the two positions, which is the most striking evidence of the tension or difficulty in the common strategy which I have argued to be theirs. It is not only the difficulty of maintaining the first position which should make us hesitate before criticising such an instability. We must also bear in mind the siren attractions of the idea of the self-constituting human subject, in a political culture in which the free and autonomous individual represents the highest value. To lay claim to this highest value for our subaltern peoples represents an overwhelmingly attractive and apparently effective move, creating possibilities for retributive polemic along the lines of primordial being and distinctive identity, which far outstrip any to be had in a nuanced focus upon practice alone. We can be sure, moreover, that none of the genres of dominant historiography, with their own much more towering subject-agents, are about to perform any act of deconstruction upon themselves, thus giving us very little incentive at all to refrain from taking up the same metaphysical weapons in our own cause.

It is also worth noting that very similar dilemmas have beset other projects intent upon restoring the subordinate and the marginal to history. Since the publication of his work on the English working class in 1963, written against what he regarded as a reductive Marxist economism, as well as the silences in official British historiography, Edward Thompson's project has been to rescue the authentic experience of those sections of England's pre-industrial working class absent from official histories, and to employ this recovered experience to show how these groups were able, by recognising their essential identity and interests as a class, to become active historical agents, to exert some control over the conditions of their own existence. The criticisms of Thompson's work, and, by implication, of those of the numerous social historians now writing in the same idiom, range over a set of issues strikingly similar to those raised in the Subaltern project: those of an essentialism arising from the assertion of an irreducibility and autonomy of experience, and a simple-minded voluntarism deriving from the insistence upon a capacity for self-determination.[16] There is another very strong parallel in feminist projects of historical and literary reconstruction. As Toril Moi has pointed out, the framework within which almost all Anglo-American feminist writing in these fields has been cast is that of a search for a history, or a literature, 'of their own:' an idiom which contains within it the suggestion of an original female nature or essence, which will provide a firm ground of truth for those engaged in the search, and a means of testing the authenticity of what they find. Moi notes the undoubted polemical advantages of such a suggestion, but is also very clear as to its ultimate limitations as a strategy for restoring the presence of women to literature or to history.[17]

It will be clear, then, that the progression of ideas which I have argued to underlie, and to give unity and coherence to the Subaltern project, is not without great difficulties of its own, to which I shall return. But what is important to note here is the structure of the strategy which is being pursued, the way in which it challenges prevailing orthodoxies, and its strength and potential in a field in which so much value is vested in the autonomous subject, on the one hand, and 'the masses' or 'the people,' on the other. Given the strength, the possibilities, and the interest of the issues raised in such a strategy, I find two things puzzling. The first is the refusal of the contributors to own to any set of common suppositions beyond a general orientation of interest. Usually one of the most theoretically astute of their number, Partha Chatterjee prefaces his important explanatory essay by denying any fundamental theoretical position in common between the contributors, except for a dissatisfaction with current historiographical orthodoxies.[18] Yet he concludes the essay by making just this point, that a most effective way of breaking up the false ideological totalities of nationalist, colonialist and Marxist historiography is precisely by reopening the question of subaltern consciousness.[19] The second puzzle is the weakness and confusion of much critical response to the project, and in particular the failure of Marxist critics to grasp what is distinctive and important about it. The closest that we come to such a recognition is in the collective review published in *Social Scientist* in 1984, where it is pointed out that the contributors have made of the subaltern a subject-agent, in the manner of bourgeois humanism, which accords ill with the structural and materialist emphases of a proper Marxist historiography. Having made this important identification, however, the authors do not pursue the point about the strategic potential, for histories of the subordinate, of subjectivity in a culture which places such supreme value on it, or of the possibilities of restoring presence without essentialism. Rather, the issue of the subject-agent is brushed aside as an old one, and said to have been resolved conclusively by Louis Althusser in his exchange with John Lewis over the discourse of idealist history.[20] Instead, the contributors are enjoined to take a better account of the familiar preoccupations of Marxist historiography: the structure of agrarian society, the importance of activist leadership, the centrality of the anti-imperialist struggle.

Yet misunderstanding of the contributors' work is not simply the product of insensitivity or careless reading. It arises further when the instability in the argument which I noted above is placed in the context of the juxtaposition or dichotomy between élite and subaltern itself, and the associated notion of the 'autonomy' of the latter's experience. It is this juxtaposition or dichotomy, of course, which not only allows us to think about the subordinate as a kind of category, but which introduces the emphasis upon power and dominance in their mutual relations, which is another distinctive feature of the contributors' work. It is important to clarify the purpose of this dichotomy, the ways in which it may most fruitfully be used, in part because it has been so widely taken to represent what is distinctive about the Subaltern project, and in part because the confusion surrounding it reinforces the sense that the contributors do not have any joint theoretical contribution to make, but are brought together only by a diffuse focus on the heterogeneous and analytically unusable category of the subaltern.

Much criticism has been directed, as we shall see, at the apparent implication of a crude social division between those on top and those underneath. Now the point about the dichotomy, I believe, if it is to be used in any effective way, is that it actually contains two separate propositions, the first of which is prior to the second. The first proposition, which we might call the theoretical one is, as the very generality of the two blocks should indicate, not concerned with categorising actually existing social groups at all, but with making a point about power. This is that what is fundamental to relationships in South Asian society is not negotiation, consensus or common contribution, but domination: exercised over the weak, where possible, without overt conflict, through modes of hegemonic appropriation and legitimation; and where necessary, through actual violence and coercion. It is here that the assertion of subaltern autonomy belongs: as Partha Chatterjee indicates, the purpose of this assertion 'is precisely to conceptualise this domination as a relation of power.'[21] The point of making such a general proposition about power is to undermine the liberal assumption of a plurality in social structures and of consensus in a shared culture which, in different ways, underlies both colonial and nationalist historiographies; but to make this point about power in a way which is not immediately assimilable to an economistic Marxism.

The second proposition, which we might call the substantive one, is that we should seek to understand how different forms of domination have operated in the societies of the subcontinent. The categories which we employ in the actual task of analysis will not be those of monolithic blocks at all, since the existence of such totalities has proved so distorting in the genres of élite historiography. Having made the statement about power and domination, rather, the categories which we must employ to understand their workings must be as multifarious and nuanced as the courses and ligaments through which power itself runs.

The confusion surrounding the dichotomy—a confusion which besets critics and some contributors alike—is that the two propositions are not made explicit and kept separate. Rather, some of the contributors employ the first as the instrument of the second, making the dichotomy itself an instrument for direct application to their historical material, so that élite and subaltern groups are made to appear as distinct social entities. This is, of course, to take the argument of subaltern autonomy quite literally, rather than as making a point about power. It is certainly very easy to see how this might be done, in view of what I have identified as the strategic importance of the statement that the subaltern has a history, an identity and practice, that are *his own*. Yet the result is that the argument degenerates into an unhelpful set of assertions to the effect that subaltern groups generated their own traditions and pursued their political projects quite independently of anyone else, and especially of the Indian National Congress. By no means all of the contributors make such a move, and where it is made it does not always result in this reduction to what is sometimes no more than a set of cliches underlying the empirical material. In particular, I want to distinguish Ranajit Guha's work in the book *Elementary aspects of peasant insurgency* here. Yet the literal interpretation of subaltern autonomy, and the use of the dichotomy itself as an instrument for direct social analysis, appear in the contributions with a troubling frequency. Stephen Henningham's essay on the Quit India campaign in Bihar and eastern Uttar Pradesh places its central emphasis upon '*the revolt's dual quality, whereby it comprised not one but two interacting insurgencies. One insurgency was an élite nationalist*

*uprising of the high caste rich peasants and small landlords who dominated
the Congress. The other insurgency was a subaltern rebellion in which
the initiative belonged to the poor, low caste people of the region.*'[22] Not
only was the initiative all their own, 'achieved in the absence of overall
co-ordination' with the arrest of most leading nationalist activists,[23]
but they also came endowed with their own distinctive modes of
consciousness, 'the subaltern world vision.' Their popular nationalism
was imbued 'with a characteristically subaltern religious consciousness,'
while their entry into political action was distinguished by 'the articulation of a moral justification, in terms of their consciousness, for
acts of physical force.'[24]

In the fourth volume, both Ramachandra Guha and Swapan
Dasgupta take it that the main point of the enterprise should be to
delineate a distinctive area of consciousness and initiative, originating
with the subaltern, as against those of an élite-dominated Congress.
Investigating protest movements against the increasing exactions of
the Forest Department and its officials in the village communities of
British Kumaun at the turn of the century, one of Ramachandra
Guha's main purposes is to demonstrate that these communities
mobilised on their own, on the basis of ancient community solidarities
and sets of values. Not only was Richard Tucker wrong to assume that
these movements were led in any way by nationalist activists from
outside[25] but the values which underlay them were absolutely distinct:
'For the Kumaun peasant the cohesion and collective spirit of the
village community provided the main spring of political action. . . .
Expressed through the medium of popular protest were conflicting
theories and social relationships that virtually amounted to two
world-views.'[26] Swapan Dasgupta's account of Adivasi politics in
Midnapur between 1760 and 1924 sets out to make very similar
points. His aim is to demonstrate the existence of the 'autonomous
political tradition' of the Adivasis of this area.[27] Despite some links
with the local Congress, these communities mobilised themselves
essentially from within: 'Élite politics in Midnapur had thus only a
very tenuous connection with the autonomous mobilisation of this
particular section of the subaltern. Adivasi insurgency belonged on
the whole to another domain of politics.' This mobilisation arose out

of their own original traditions: 'an alternative conception of justice born out of fundamentally different sets of values.'[28] Even Tanika Sarkar, who, as we shall see, displays a very sophisticated sense of the processes of reconstruction and metamorphosis at work in Santal 'tradition,' and of the tension and ambiguity with which these were accompanied, still holds on to a notion of Santal identity as in some sense *originary*. The transformations of that tradition represented, albeit in an ambiguous and uncertain way, 'the Santal's flight from himself'[29] and the symbolic battle to appropriate a mosque, with which Jitu Santal's battle ended, leads her to conclude that 'the Santal thus returned to his indigenous code of belief.'[30]

The difficulty arises in examples such as these, as I have argued, from a tension in the progression of ideas which underlies their accounts and which, insufficiently understood, produces the slide towards essentialism which we see here. It is a similar essentialism which Dipankar Gupta has identified in the work of Ranajit Guha: an 'ethnicised history' in Guha's conception of a primordial and autonomous insurgent peasant tradition running right through Indian history, which implies, in almost Hegelian fashion, that the 'independent organising principle of the insurgent's mind' is what actually moves the historical process forward.[31] Gupta pinpoints exactly what are the historiographical difficulties in this undoubted tendency towards idealism. It shuts off the whole field of external structural interaction and determination, so that 'the potentialities of a movement and its final limits are . . . understood in terms of what the culture allows and not in terms of what the structure forecloses.'[32] This 'culturological' style of explanation, present in the work of some of the contributors, is carried to an extreme in Guha's *Elementary aspects of peasant insurgency*, and renders particularly weak his attempts to document any of the 'real' structures outside the subjective world of the insurgent. Guha explains the failure of peasant movements to spread beyond their own limited territories, for example, in terms of their 'habit of thinking and acting on a small and local scale' rather than considering 'what could have been the structural features of colonial societies, or even of pre-modern societies, which could have accounted for the spatial circumscription of the peasant movements.'[33]

At this level, of course, Gupta is quite right. There is a real historiographical difficulty in this apparent idealism, and in particular in Guha's drive to posit an originary autonomy in the traditions of peasant insurgency. He does at times appear to be approaching a pure Hegelianism, as in his criticism of the way in which, in élite historiography, 'insurgency is regarded as *external* to the peasant's consciousness, and Cause is made to stand in as a phantom surrogate for Reason, the logic of that consciousness.'[34] Yet Gupta does not, it seems to me, grasp that this drive towards the originary is the outcome of a tension in the difficult strategy which underlies the Subaltern project, but sees it only as an old-fashioned idealism which is the product of an uninformed employment of anthropological concepts and methods. The problem with Gupta's reluctance to consider the broader issues which the strategy raises in any other way is not only that he hastens what is intended to be a project of deconstruction and critique too rapidly back to a world of determination with whose deficiencies it is all too familiar. It is also that we are left with the unfortunate, and I think unintended, impression, that the historiographical issue at stake is that of man's freedom as against the determining power of his external world. But this very juxtaposition, of the free man as against the man determined, is itself an idealist conception, in which the mode of existence of the unitary subject-agent is never called into question. Man under this conception can either be free or he can be bound; but in either case, he himself looks very much the same. A Subaltern strategy, reconstructed along the lines I have suggested, might be used to recover the presence of the subordinate without slipping into an essentialism, by revealing that presence to be one constructed and refracted through practice, but no less 'real' for our having said that it does not contain its own origins within itself. Such a strategy would not only be able to subvert the self constituting subject of idealism, but much more subtly and effectively to address the undoubted historiographical problem of determination. Other critics, however—and this seems to me quite understandable, in view of the confusion over the purpose of the dichotomy and the assertion of subaltern autonomy which I have described—have written rather less perceptively than Gupta. In a review of the second volume,

Anand Yang takes its authors to task for not having precisely and rigorously defined the concept of the subaltern as a substantive social category: for their apparent application of the term to anyone and everyone oppressed by the Raj, whereas in actuality very significant differences existed within such an enormous mass of humanity, making the dichotomy quite inadequate as an instrument of social analysis.[35] Of the third volume, Majid Siddiqi asks how the possibility of subordinate groups being exploiters in one context, and exploited in another, can be consonant with any idea of genuine autonomy.[36]

I want now to turn to these same issues in Ranajit Guha's work, where the drive to identify the peasant insurgent as a conscious subject-agent appears to be made, not in any wavering semi-awareness of its significance and consequences, but with great deliberation and purposefulness. For—and this is a passage insufficiently noted by his critics—Guha makes it clear at the start of *Elementary aspects of peasant insurgency* that 'it is rebel consciousness which will be allowed to dominate the present exercise. We want to emphasise its sovereignty, its consistency and its logic in order to compensate for its absence from the literature.'[37] It is clear that Guha construes the category of the subaltern to be a substantive social one. The subaltern classes literally represent '*the demographic difference between the total Indian population and all those whom we have described as the élite.*'[38] The repressiveness of élite historiography, itself generated by the counter-insurgency concerns of the colonial state, consists precisely in its refusal to the peasant of 'recognition as a subject of history, even for a project that was all his own.'[39] The insurgent consciousness or mind of this collective subject-agent, its essential unity and autonomy, and its pervasion of all particular historical forms, are explained with the help of reference to Hegel's *Logic.* The common form of insurgency

is not a generality which is 'something external to, or something in addition to' other features or abstract qualities of insurgency discovered by reflection. On the contrary, 'it is what permeates and includes in it everything particular'—a pervasive theoretical consciousness which gives insurgency its categorical unity.[40]

Yet this deliberate drive towards unity and origins, the prerequisites of humanism's subject-agent, is not without its own tensions and contradictions, not only in the assumptions on which it is made, but in the rich documentation of the insurgent peasant's subjective world which constitutes the main body of the book. The assumptions which underlie it become clearer if we look at Guha's attacks on what he regards as élitist theories of causation. We have already noted his hostility to the way in which 'insurgency is regarded as *external* to the peasant's consciousness.' What he confuses here, it seems to me, is the reduction of insurgent consciousness to its causes, to which he is certainly quite right in objecting, with the matter of externality. His fear seems to be that any suggestion of such an externality, that the peasant does not bear the founding *causes* of his insurgency within his own consciousness, will be enough to empty or extinguish that consciousness, to deny its existence in the manner of élite historiography. Seen from this perspective, his forceful insistence upon humanism's unitary subject-agent in its most extreme form, and his use of Hegelian ideas to make of insurgency a 'mind' which draws all particular historical forms into its own founding unity, become comprehensible. In not seeing beyond humanism's myths of origin to the possibility of a presence without essence, he assumes that the latter alone will be enough to secure the return of the insurgent peasant to history.

A further paradox, and one that is not confined to Guha's work, is that the process by which the insurgent actually arrives at a sense of himself is through negation: as Guha says, 'not by the properties of his own social being, but by a diminution, if not negation, of those of his superiors.'[41] This, more than anything, should suggest that this self was constantly in the process of production, and that, too, mediated through symbols and signs which were external to it, those of élite authority. Within the limits of this contradiction, however, Guha and others have entered and begun to chart what must be a vital area for anyone concerned with relationships of power and the possibilities and limitations of resistance. The idea of 'identity' is itself a highly problematic one, always implying the duplication of an original whose locus and manner of existence remain elusive. Analysis of the process whereby the subject arrives at a sense of 'identity,' and the place of an Otherness in that capacity to identify is, of course, the concern of a very large field of psychoanalytic theorising, as well as having been a central preoccupation of existentialist thought. The insights generated in these two fields have been applied most success-fully to non-Western contexts, to explore the tortuous relationship between the coloniser and his other, the native, between the projection of the former's repressed desire and the latter's dehumanisation in the discourses and forms of knowledge which colonialism produces, by Frantz Fanon and then, more recently, by Edward Said.[42] It hardly needs to be emphasised what an important and complex field is this production of the self in the colonial context, particularly of the self of the colonised. For we have not only the approved selves which the coloniser attempts to produce for the native and to constitute as the sole area of legitimate public reality, but the continual struggle of the colonised to resolve the paradoxes which this displacement and de-humanisation of indigenous processes of identification sets up in his daily existence. Moreover, as Homi Bhabha points out, the desire of the native to supplant the coloniser is not thereby a desire simply to extinguish himself as a slave but, in a splitting of the self always asso-ciated with the dominated in the colonial context as elsewhere, to stand in two places, and 'keeping his place in the slave's avenging anger,' to witness himself triumphant.[43]

The explorations of the theme of negation in the series have much to contribute to this field, and also, I think, something further to glean from it. With the focus on the subaltern's negativity, we include another dimension in the conflicted process of identification under colonialism: that of the subordinate within the ranks of the colonised. The theme of negation runs right through *Elementary aspects*, and Guha draws on a most impressive range of exemplary material to illus-trate the purposefulness and discrimination with which peasants violated the symbols of the dominant, both indigenous and colonial: speech, both verbal and written; bodily gestures and social space, clothing, means of transport, the ostentation of wealth in domesticity.[44] His grasp of the importance of the violation of signs, precisely as a process of identification, is a wonderful antidote to an instrumentalist notion both of the way in which power works upon its object, and of fixed categories of action themselves which are 'symbolic,' as op-posed to real or material. Tanika Sarkar's study of the reconstruction of Santal identity during Jitu Santal's movement draws our attention very importantly to the fact that it was not only through the negation of the signs of élite authority that the Santal moved towards a sense of his own identity. Jitu also expressed a strong hostility and contempt for Muslims and Hindu low castes and untouchables. Thus 'the "other" that defines the subaltern's self-consciousness need not then only be the élite groups exerting dominance; it may equally be the classes and groups that lie even lower in the hierarchy, and the striving to maintain a distance from them may be the most important content of his self-image and self-respect.'[45]

Yet we should note a further point, which needs to be made a little clearer in the contributors' treatment of negation. This is that the insurgent did not invariably wish to destroy the signs of authority, but very often preserved and appropriated them for himself. This was not merely the kind of discrimination between friend and foe which Guha describes, emerging out of the peasant's obscure sense of the real connections of power between the disparate groups who wielded authority over him.[46] Rather, it was the symbols of the latter which were at issue, forming the object alternatively of the peasant's anger, and of his desire: negation took the form of 'the peasants' attempt to destroy or appropriate for themselves the signs of the authority of those who dominate them.'[47] David Arnold records this complex mingling between desire and destructiveness in the *fituris* of the late nineteenth century among the hillmen of Andhra Pradesh, and describes the inversions which it brought about: 'To seize and burn a police station, to brandish weapons or to don the uniforms of the vanquished constables, was a spectacular inversion of the oppression hillmen had so recently suffered: they were on top now, and it was the policemen who begged for their lives to be spared.'[48] 'Inversion' is, of course, the figure which many of the contributors use to describe negativity in action. Yet Arnold's account here gives us something further, a sense of the importance of desire in negativity, of precisely that wish to stand in two places at once, which underlies it and makes it comprehensible. For, as he points out, inversion viewed thus constitutes not only resistance, but the limits of its own particular form, the peasant's 'incapacity for real revolution, that is, structural change.'[49]

For all of Guha's emphasis, quite deliberately made, on the internal world of the subaltern, we should note that he is not content to leave this as an overt idealism. Rather—and here one can only admire his furious pursuit of consistency and comprehensiveness—he brings idealism and materialism together in a wrenching move which eliminates any of the mediations between consciousness and structure which are the stuff of most conventional historical narratives. The polarisation of consciousness between élite and subaltern, and the long history of hostility between them, are nothing other than the reflection of a long-standing divide in the material structures of Indian society itself: between the peasant on the one hand, and the collusive forces of landlord, moneylender and colonial state on the other, who established 'a composite apparatus of dominance' over him.[50] And it is this dominance in the end, it seems, which is the source not only of the ways in which insurgents organise themselves, but of insurgent consciousness itself: 'What the pillars of society fail to grasp is that the organising principle lies in nothing other than their own dominance. For it is the subjection of the rural masses to a common source of exploitation and oppression that makes them rebel even before they learn how to combine in peasant organisations.'[51] Thus, insurgent subjectivity and the determination of material structures of dominance stand mutually opposed, but in a curious disconnection: the latter appearing, in a highly deterministic fashion, responsible not only for the existence, but for the very form of the first, while the former, in its prescribed sovereignty, forbids us to make any such allusion to a cause beyond itself. It is very likely, indeed, that this is precisely the effect Guha intends: contradictory, no doubt, but no more so than much of the historiographical field in which he has to work.

Before leaving this issue of autonomy, I should like to make two further points. The first is that the Althusserian phrase, 'relative autonomy,' taken up by Sumit Sarkar and Partha Chatterjee, among others, as a way of attempting to avoid the implication of an absolute disjunction between the worlds of the élite and the subaltern, seems to me further to confuse the issue.[52] Certainly, we want to find ways of connecting the classes and communities of South Asian society, and the idea of 'relative autonomy' certainly suggests a connectedness, although with an air of analytical power which is quite specious, since its employment to suggest relationships within the social field is quite alien to the purpose for which Althusser developed it, in his suggestion of the modified determining power operating between the three 'instances'—economic, political, ideological–cultural—which compose the social formation, in place of Marxism's conventional base–superstructure model. Implying that it is a modification in the autonomy of the subaltern which is required only serves to reinforce the misconception that it is intended as a substantive social category, rather than a statement about power, and gives us no way out of the essentialism to which such a misconception tends to lead.

The second point is that while I have laid great emphasis on this constitution of the autonomous subject-agent, we should also notice that there is a theme in some of the essays to which several critics have pointed, and which appears to cut across it. This is, as Dipankar Gupta points out in his critique of Guha's work, the imposition of what looks very like the kind of unsophisticated Marxist teleology, assigning value and significance in the extent to which consciousnesses are more or less 'developed' which was supposed to be one of the objects of the Subaltern project's attack.[53] Such a tendency, an attempt to trace a unitary 'learning' process, undoubtedly exists in Guha's work. However, we can hardly accuse him of ignoring in consequence the specificity of the forms of nineteenth-century peasant insurgency, even if he does assign them places on a notional evolutionary curve. As I remarked earlier, moreover, the problem of mapping what on the surface look like quite fundamental transformations of mentality, of noting their origins and their consequences for the peasant in his relationship to the state or to organised religion, without slipping into a rigid teleology or a denial of historical specificity, is a genuine problem for all historians of the recent non-European world and Guha seems to me to have made strenuous efforts to tread between these two.

Less wary contributors do not make this negotiation quite so successfully. In his reconstruction of agrarian protest in twentieth-century Bihar, Arvind Das sees nothing very mysterious or difficult to understand in the nature of peasant consciousness or practice. What peasants want is perfectly clear, and that is land; the problem is whether or not they should seek alliances in the organised political world to try to get it. This seems to me a good example of a large genre of well-intentioned scholarly concern with economic welfare in contemporary India whose unfortunate, and ironically impoverishing assumption is that for the poor of modern India, questions of strategy and instrumentality have succeeded those of culture or value. In Das's case, this is in spite of concerns not reducible in this way, which he himself gives us, such as the Bhojpuri widow whom he quotes as saying that for her the struggle against landlords and police was a matter of dignity or honour.[54] For Das, such concerns, and the peasant's diffusion of energy over a heterogeneous collection of issues, such as exploitation by indigo planters, the unjust settlement of a landed estate, social degradation and low wages, are misguided and regrettable. They lead the peasants 'to ignore the basic question of land distribution, and to take up other, subsidiary issues in its place.'[55] Very interestingly, the subaltern's sense of 'dignity' is something that crops up again in N.K. Chandra's essay on agricultural workers in Burdwan, where the concern is also primarily with 'welfare' questions of wages, working conditions, nutrition and education. Chandra records the growing insistence of labourers that they should be able to eat their meals in their own homes, even if these had actually been prepared in their employers' kitchens. Explained only as the product of 'poverty and a desire to assert their independence' this insight is lost beneath the drive to gather information about the externals of the labourer's existence, on the assumption that he is now the proper subject of the welfare worker and the local activist.[56] Whatever his pressing need for their services, such an assumption is as impoverishing and oppressive in its own way, as the material deprivations of which he is the victim.

Having argued there to be a recognisable strategy underlying the work of the contributors, and identified some of its difficulties, I turn now to its consequences for the treatment of two themes absolutely central to the project: those of domination or hegemony in South Asia, and the nature and possibilities of resistance to it. From the invocation of Gramsci in the category of the subaltern itself, and from the general emphases of the project, we would expect this theme to be one of its greatest strengths. Before we go on to look at this in detail, it is worth reminding ourselves of the formidable Western critique, both of traditional Western philosophy's essentialising search for origins, and of its product in humanism's self-constituting subject, against which this attempt at recuperation of a non-Western subject-agent is made. This critique, which had its most important origins in Marx and Nietzsche, is now, of course, a dominant theme in many fields of theory: perhaps best represented in political theory of a conventional kind by Louis Althusser, and in history and theory of a less easily classifiable sort, in the work of Michel Foucault. There can be little doubt, moreover, that this attack on humanism's subject—encountered in history as the agent who produces it, and of whose experience all history is the continuous expression, in literature, in the notion of the author and his autonomous creativity, and in philosophy, in the assumption of a unitary sovereign consciousness—has been extremely fruitful and liberating. Critics have attempted to dismantle this figure—which is, needless to say, a masculine one—in very varied ways, but all of which recognise in its insistence upon us all as fundamentally free, equal and autonomous selves, a profoundly repressive strategy of power. For the Marxist tradition, Althusser has been most effective in pointing out its consequences, in masking the real constraint and inequality which is at the foundation of capitalist society, and in making 'responsible' for their own history classes whose real power-lessness must forever condemn them to failure within its terms. Marx's theoretical anti-humanism meant

> a refusal to root the explanation of social formations and their history in a concept of man with theoretical pretensions, that is, a concept of man as an *originating subject*. . . . For when you begin with man, you cannot avoid the idealist temptation of believing in the omnipotence of liberty or of creative labour—that is, you simply submit, in all 'freedom', to the omnipotence of the ruling bourgeois ideology, whose function is to mask and to impose, in the illusory shape of man's power of freedom, another power, much more real and much more powerful, that of capitalism.[57]

Yet it is Foucault, of course, who has constructed our most powerful critique here, not only of Man as a universal category, but of the way in which modern societies discipline and subjugate their populations through the production, in the discourses of the human sciences, of norms of thought and behaviour which lay down the sort of subjects that we are, and prescribe to us the law of our being. More than anyone, Foucault has documented the repressiveness of this imposition of 'normality,' with its fastening of subject-natures to us which are ever open to its gaze, and its insistence, both individualising and totalising, upon their fundamental sameness:

> This form of power applies itself to immediate everyday life, which categorises the individual, marks him by his own individuality, imposes a law of truth on him which he must recognise and which others have to recognise in him. It is a form of power which makes individuals subjects. There are two meanings of the word *subject*: subject to someone else by control and dependence, and tied to his own identity by a conscience or self-knowledge. Both meanings suggest a form of power which subjugates and makes subject to.[58]

With Nietzsche, Foucault exposes the obsession with origins which underlies the search for a self-constituting universal human nature, for 'the existence of immobile forms that precede the external world of accident and succession.'[59] With the dissolution of the universal human subject goes also, of course, the seamless narrative movement of history, from the past to our present, which we continually attempt to construct and to recognise ourselves in.

As Rashmi Bhatnagar has very perceptively traced, moreover, these themes in Western critical theory have already borne rich fruit in the attempt to understand the nature of colonial power and the way in which it operated upon its subjects, most of all in the work of Edward Said. This is first in the documentation of the way in which colonised peoples were endowed with identities, made into subjects, in the great scholarly apparatuses, both discursive and institutional, of Orientalism. The second is in the very obsession with origins which these discourses of colonialism, themselves formed around the dominant humanist themes of traditional Western philosophy, unleashed upon their subjects: 'In effect the search for Aryan/Islamic/Semite origins becomes for the colonised people a longing for an impossible purity and a yearning for the fullness of meaning' which is not only fundamentally misguided, but leads, in the Indian context, to revivalism and thence towards communalism.[60]

What are the implications of this fruitfulness, the severity and evidently liberating effects of this critique of the constitutive subject-agent, for what I have identified as the strategy underlying the Subaltern project, and in particular for its potential for our understanding of the themes of domination and resistance? Let us be clear as to the importance of this question: the most fruitful one which the contributors raise for us, and one which is at the heart of all efforts to comprehend not merely the possibilities for resistance within coercive or hegemonic structures, but also the very constitution of those structures themselves, whose power to coerce we can only comprehend as it acts upon its objects. I have argued above that the assumptions underlying the work of the contributors do not consist straightforwardly in the recuperation of the subaltern as subject, but that their very structure, and especially the emphasis, very difficult to avoid making, on the subaltern's action *on his own*, have led many of the contributors towards such an identification, while Guha proceeds very deliberately in this direction. We must examine here, therefore, not only the consequences of such an identification for understanding power and resistance, but whether the strategy itself is the best way to restore the subaltern to history. There is undoubtedly an enormous dilemma here, precisely because of our difficulty in envisaging any other form which such a presence might take except the virile figure of the subject-agent, and in the resulting temptation to appropriate the categories of dominant discourse, in the form of a distinctive subaltern self and tradition.

We should also note that to do this might in its own way become a profoundly authoritarian exercise, and this, ironically, precisely in the framing of a concern to recover subaltern experience itself. For it is this focus on experience in all its authenticity which resolves the problem of how the subaltern is to be 'represented,' in the political as well as the descriptive sense of the term; which enables the contributors to distinguish their project from the master discourses which have failed to make the silence of the subordinate speak, but only enclosed it within a hegemony which may be broken up through the very indication of that fact. Through the restoration of subjectivity and the focus on experience, the conceit is that a textual space has been opened up in which subaltern groups may speak for themselves and present their hidden past in their own distinctive voices, whose authenticity in turn acts as the guarantee of the texts themselves. We recognise that this is a conceit, of course, but it is a very powerful one, and we must ask ourselves whether we are in danger in using it to turn the silence of the subaltern into speech, but to make their words address our own concerns, and to render their figures in our own self image. For my contention here is not only that the recuperation of the subject-agent imposes real limitations on our ability to comprehend the workings of power upon its object, but that its unguarded pursuit produces a diminution in the only constant feature of the subaltern's 'nature' which we can identify with any certainty, which is its alienness from our own. It can become a drive just as Baudrillard says, 'to keep the masses *within reason*,'[61] a joining in that common abhorrence, which marks our own age, that they should remain mute before all our meanings and ideals: 'Everywhere the masses are encouraged to speak, they are urged to live socially, electorally, organisationally, sexually, in participation, in free speech, etc. The spectre must be exorcised, it must pronounce its name.'[62] We will return to this theme in our conclusion, and turn now to examine the contributors' treatment of the themes of power and resistance.

The first difficulty refers to the way in which the contributors represent the collective traditions and cultures of subordinate groups. Dipankar Gupta has already criticised very perceptively the tendency to attribute a timeless primordiality to these: not only in Guha's work, but in, for example, Dipesh Chakrabarty's notion of the 'primordial loyalties' of religion, community, kinship and language which was the 'essence' of the pre-capitalist culture of the Calcutta jute-mill worker,[63] in Sumit Sarkar's assumption of a timelessness in the cultural significance of the figure of the *sannyasi*, or of Stephen Henningham's invocation of the 'traditional consciousness' of the peasant insurgent in Bihar and eastern Uttar Pradesh.[64] This is not merely poor historical or anthropological practice; it undermines just that sense of power which it is the contributors' concern to restore. We can best see how this is so in Partha Chatterjee's notion, developed in essays in the first and second volumes of the series, of a 'peasant-communal ideology.'

This ideology, 'acting as a live force in the consciousness of the peasantry' held the community itself to possess an authority over the land which was prior to that of any single individual, so that legitimate political power was itself 'organised as the authority of the entire collectivity.' These shared values acted above all to mediate the peasant community's relations with the potentially threatening political forces of the world beyond it, through 'norms of reciprocity, formulated in an entire system of religious beliefs—origin myths, sacred histories, legends—which laid down the principles of political ethics and were coded into a series of acts and symbols denoting authority and obedience, benevolence and obligation, or oppression and revolt.'[65] This model of collective political authority holds good for all peasant communities: 'When a community acts collectively, the fundamental political characteristics are the same everywhere.'[66]

The important and deleterious consequence of this portrayal is that it restores, within a redrawn and smaller notion of the collectivity, exactly that impression of unity and consensus, of the absence of relationships of power, which is intended to be the object of attack. The ideology of the collective authority of the peasant community is seen primarily as providing strategies for resistance to external coercion. There is very little sense that the same ideology might be employed within the collectivity, for the suppression of those not counting as the 'individuals' of which Chatterjee speaks: women, untouchables, labourers and so on. Certainly, he says, these bonds of affinity offer 'possibilities of manipulation.' But 'the point which distinguishes the communal mode from other modes or organisations of power is this: here is not a perception of common interests which compels organisation to achieve unity; there is rather the conviction that bonds of affinity *already exist* which then become the natural presupposition for collective action.'[67] Presumably Chatterjee does not wish to imply a perfect equilibrium of material and political forces within any peasant community: in which case, we are entitled to ask, whose conviction is this and how widely is it actually shared as a 'natural' assumption, rather than as a product of anything similar to the calculation of interests and formation of alliances which he regards as the essential feature of the differently constructed realm of 'organised politics.' The point is that if the contributors are to maintain the radical impetus of their emphasis on power, it is vital that it should not be brought to a halt through a static idea of the subaltern collectivity: whether in the shape of this apparently 'natural' community, or in the unitary 'moral economy' of which many contributors speak, or in any other laying down of a preordained subject-position which can stand outside the fluctuations of human existence to impose an order of value or of narrative. I do not mean to imply by this that we should thereby surrender the search for the regularities of practice or the schemes of value through which subordinate groups attempt to bring order and coherence into their existence, but rather that we should not forget that such order can only ever represent the contingent and temporary creation of this practice, a creation capable of being turned to effect in repressive ways within their number, as well as of conducing to their mutual understanding and solidarity. What is interesting, indeed, is that just the same issue, of the attempt to reintroduce homogeneity and consensus within a redrawn idea of an essential collectivity, has arisen in feminist debate. Toril Moi describes how minority feminist groups have forced white heterosexual feminists 'to re-examine their own sometimes totalitarian conception of "woman" as a homogeneous category.' To maintain the radical thrust of feminist criticism, she argues, these groups 'ought to prevent white middle class First World feminists from defining their own preoccupations as *universal* female (or feminist) problems.'[68]

From this strategic weakness in the treatment of power, I come now to the discussion of resistance, and to a difficulty which arises out of the way in which contributors envision and classify fields of activity—the political, the economic, the cultural—symbolic. There has been a criticism of the project, from without as well as within, that the contributors have dwelt largely on moments of overt resistance and revolt.[69] This tendency is, of course, the product of the insistence on agency itself: the demand for a spectacular demonstration of the subaltern's independent will and self-determining power. This means, as has been accepted, that there has been little sustained focus upon the continuities in subaltern culture. The notable exception here would be Gyan Pandey's study of the town of Mubarakpur in eastern Uttar Pradesh, seen through the eyes of two very different chroniclers:

an obscure weaver, Abdul Majid, and the member of a local zamindari family, Ali Hasan. Pandey employs the comparison not only to suggest the differences between what these accounts, and the narratives of official records, identified as 'events,' but to illuminate what was shared between these representatives from very different areas of Muslim society. What emerges most interestingly from both accounts is that although their authors possessed a strong sense of community,

> this consciousness of community was an ambiguous one, straddling as it did the religious fraternity, class, qasba and mohalla. Here, as in Ali Hasan's account, the boundaries shift all the time. It is difficult to translate this consciousness into terms that are readily comprehensible in today's social science—Muslim/Hindu, working class/rentier, urban/rural—or even to argue that a particular context would inevitably activate a particular solidarity. What is clear is that Ali Hasan is quite untroubled by the problems that confound the modern researcher as he moves from one notion of the collective to another through the eighty-nine pages of his manuscript.[70]

Pandey's reference to the habitual dichotomising of conventional social science, and its tendency to obscure the real ambiguity and contingency of the fixed identities for which we continually search, brings our attention to another pressing question in the contributors' treatment of cultural continuities, that of the classifications between fields referred to above. Beneath the tremendous variety in the empirical material upon which the contributors draw, there very frequently appears a quite similar basic model of explanation: a long tradition of exploitation, or a shorter term economic dislocation, which provokes resistance and rebellion; challenges to landlords or the agents of the state, the appropriation or destruction of the signs and instruments of their authority. This action, which is independently generated and pursued, draws on the insurgents' own original culture for its values, its symbols and its means of organising. This is to state the argument as a caricature, of course, but not, I believe, to render it unrecognisable. The central limitation of such a model—a model which is very much the product of the unguarded pursuit of subjectivity and agency— is that it fails adequately to displace familiar classifications of activity— the economic, the political and the cultural—from their familiar and respected roles: roles which, in their insistence on a clear distinction between the material and the ideal, the instrumental and the symbolic, have themselves been a formidable ally in élite historiography's denial of a political significance to a whole range of subaltern activity. In making this criticism, I do not in the least want to suggest that the contributors themselves lack such an awareness of the political: such an awareness is, indeed, one of the hallmarks of the project. The essays display, moreover, a very sharp sense of the employment of symbols, either as negation or as appropriation, as an integral part of political practice. We have already noted Ranajit Guha's treatment of these themes. David Hardiman's study of the drive towards purification and cleanliness which marked the Devi movement in south Gujarat is also exemplary in this respect. Rejecting the depoliticising categories of Sanskritisation or revitalisation, Hardiman is clear that the desire for these symbols of dominance was a desire for power itself: 'The values which the adivasis endorsed were those of the classes which possessed political power. In acting as they did, the adivasis revealed their understanding of the relationship between values and power, for values possess that element of power which permits dominant classes to subjugate subordinate classes, with a minimum use of physical force.'[71]

The point, however, is that where resistance is concerned, the model which I have described above acts as a constraint upon our ability to incorporate into our material just this awareness of the real interpenetration of fields of activity conventionally separated as the instrumental and the symbolic. Tanika Sarkar has called attention to our need 'to be able to explain the attitudes of acceptance and submission which remain as strong if not much stronger than subaltern resistance.'[72] This is undoubtedly true, yet it is not the case that after we have exhausted the overt and violent revolts of the subaltern, all that remains to us is to document his submission. The very problem of the model is its tendency to suppress strategies and efforts at resistance which do not take the masculine form of a full-blooded rebellion by a subject-agent such as it tends to have enshrined within it. To make this point, let us turn to N.K. Chandra's attempts to understand why there has been so little protest amongst agricultural workers in Burdwan, despite the wretchedness of their conditions. Yet the protest which he seeks is of a very conventional 'political' kind: of organised labour, of a vigorous effort at political mobilisation, of a direct blow against the collusion of landlord and state. Yet evidence of resistance, of a kind which this implicit and instrumentalist classification of fields tends to overlook, is present in his own text: as we have already noticed, in the labourer's insistence on eating in his own home, but also in a wonderful description of the labourer and his wife's strategies for resisting conformity to the norm of conscientious worker—a norm, let us note, urged upon them by the local kisan leader and social worker:

> A local worker, according to him, is rather inefficient and tries to take time off on one pretext or another. In the middle of the morning he wants to have a rest of between thirty-five and forty minutes in order to smoke a couple of *bidis* at leisure or go off to drink water. Even when both are supplied to him in the field, his wife may come by on the plea that he must attend to some urgent work at home. Constant supervision is needed to make him work properly. On top of this, barely an hour after he goes out to work, his wife appears almost everyday at the *malik's* residence demanding the daily wages in kind for her man. She keeps waiting and nagging until she gets it, but the *malik's* wife resents it. As soon as she gets the rice, the worker's wife runs down to the field to inform her husband who now slackens his pace. On occasion the latter goes home around ten in the morning to find out if his wife has got the rice.[73]

We seem to be turning here, no doubt, to forms of resistance which are modest in the extreme: inscribed in small everyday acts, made in fields apparently quite disconnected from the political as it is conventionally understood, and as it is unfortunately and, I am sure, unintentionally made to appear in the model referred to above. Yet it is in its own way a series of negations, a refusal of approved forms of behaviour, even if these are made within a coercive framework which is not itself directly challenged. Moreover, we should not allow a desire to see direct or violent challenges to the basic matrix of domination either to lead us to assume that such challenges will always be the most effective means of the latter's subversion, or, indeed, that we should assign significance to the categories of resistance according to a pre-set standard of the spectacular and the successful. For, as Jean

Comaroff has noted of tribal life in another highly coercive political order, 'If we confine our historical scrutiny to revolutionary success, we discount the vast proportion of human social action which is played out on a humbler scale. We also evade, by teleological reasoning, the real questions that remain as to what *are* the transformative motors of history.'[74]

If, therefore, we were to ask whether the focus on the subject-agent and his experience has enabled the series to contribute in any systematic or collective way towards understanding the operation of power on its object in colonial South Asia, the answer would have to be largely in the negative, in spite of the undoubted richness of the specific insights which many essays contain. Certainly, there is no concerted attempt to construct a theory of domination as *hegemony*, as the invocation of Gramsci might have led us to expect, and in this sense the critics Suneet Chopra and Javeed Alam seem to me quite accurate in their observation that the series has not turned out to be a Gramscian project at all.[75] If there is a reason outside the intentions of the contributors for this foreclosure, it seems very likely that it lies precisely in the common slippage which I identified above, towards using the dichotomy itself to supply a ready but crude framework for direct social application. The concepts of power which have actually been developed in the series are fragmentary and somewhat disconnected. I should like to mention two here. The first is Partha Chatterjee's notion of 'modes of power,' developed in his two essays on the Bengal peasantry. This concept, most fully elaborated in the idea of the 'peasant-communal' mode of power, is offered as a means of theorising 'the political instance' in a social formation, or rather, in the transition from one mode of production to another, and he is very explicit about his debt to Althusser here.[76] The concept of 'modes of power' has been the subject of extensive disagreement and, as Chatterjee says, still remains an abstract concept in his work. I shall not discuss this further, therefore, but make just two comments. The first is that we have returned with a vengeance to the world of impersonal structure and external determination. Recalling Althusser's own anti-humanism, it would have been useful if we could have had some overt public discussion of Chatterjee's differences with the humanist strategy of the project at large. The second, as I have indicated above, is that it is very often just this assumption that we can readily identify autonomous—or, in Althusser's phrase, 'relatively autonomous' fields or 'instances': the economic, the political, the ideological–cultural—which has arisen as an impediment to our understanding of the way in which power takes effect: as a play of forces which continually moves across and bursts through our efforts to establish coherent fields of activity. Indeed, such efforts bear an uncomfortable similarity precisely to that conventional division between politics and culture, the instrumental and the symbolic, which operates in society at large, and in élite historiography, to mask the real mobility of power.

The second concept of power employed in the series is that of knowledge, given a field of structure and possibility in the form of discourse: a concept most associated, of course, with Foucault. We would expect that the contributors should be much aware of the potential power of discourses over those about whom they speak, for it is the dismantling of discourse, in the form both of historiography and of the texts produced by colonialism, which constitutes their main aim. Yet there is a problem here, which I believe is insufficiently noted in much contemporary theorising about the power of discourse, which does not find a resolution in the essays which discuss it here. This problem is of describing the process through which knowledge, structured, given legitimacy and a proper field for its operation in discourse, operates upon its objects: those 'subjects' who come within its jurisdiction. Within this analytic mode we frequently make reference to a very similar range of phenomena and processes as are more conventionally classified under the title of ideology. While Foucault's conception has the great advantage of its emphasis upon the material and institutional forms in which discourse is invested, it lacks the first concept's apparatus, well-worn though it is, for theorising or explaining the manner in which it has its effects upon its objects. Of course, almost all contemporary discussion of discourse stresses—and herein lies its appearance of great explanatory power—that it imposes a total milieu, institutional as well as intellectual and informational, to whose hegemonic sway its subjects must inevitably succumb. Colonial power thus derives its strength from two sources: from the material ability to coerce which it brings with it in its armies, and from the Orientalist discourses of its second, shadow army of textual scholars, linguists, historians, anthropologists and so on. Now there can be no doubting the ability of colonial power, documented in Edward Said's classic work, to give material effect to its efforts to structure and provide fields for knowledge, through the establishment of a powerful institutional infrastructure. The problem with the argument as it is more generally employed, rather, is its tendency to assume that discourses have an existence which is prior to, and hence unsullied by, the interventions of those over whom they are to have jurisdiction. Rather, colonialism's discourses came into being as attempts at fields of knowledge precisely as a struggle between at least three parties: the Orientalist scholar, the native informant successful in convincing him of his authority to represent, and those others among the colonised unable to do so, but grievously aware of the potential disadvantages in which this would place them in any future political structure established under the colonial power. This struggle was the site not only of contested understandings, but also of deliberate misrepresentation and manipulation, in which the seemingly omnipotent classifications of the Orientalist were vulnerable to purposeful misconstruction and appropriation to uses which he never intended, precisely because they had incorporated into them the readings and the political concerns of his native informants. It is this sense of mutuality—not as common contribution, but as struggle and contestation—which is missing from much contemporary discussion of discourse, with its assumption that new fields of knowledge had only to be enunciated, for them to élicit mute obedience from those whom they purported to know. It is, indeed, this lack of any exploration of the theme of simultaneity and struggle which is responsible for the criticism most frequently levelled at Foucault's own conception: that it allows no room and no possibility for resistance to the fine meshes of knowledge's disciplinary and normalising power.[77] This is an absence, indeed, which is all the more surprising in view of his own stress on the mutuality, the ever-present possibility of reversal, in the play of power itself between agents.

This is not an issue which is very much illuminated in Bernard

Cohn's study, carried out within an overtly Foucaultian framework, of the 'invasion of an epistemological space' which took place in the Orientalist production of knowledge about Indian law, language and textual traditions.[78] This essay contains a most impressive document-ation of the latter's compilatory and exegetical endeavours, and a wonderfully funny account of European attempts to arm themselves with fragments of the vernacular sharp-edged enough to cut decisively through the soft but treacherous world of Indian servanthood and populace. Yet it seems to me written a little too respectfully in the shadow of its own Foucaultian frame, in its assumption that we can capture a discursive formation before it is markedly affected by those over whom it exerts its power. The Indians, he concludes his study, who 'increasingly became drawn into the process of transformation of their own traditions and modes of thought' were 'far from passive'; but 'the delineation of the cumulative effect of the results of the first half-century of the objectification and reordering through the appli-cation of European scholarly methods on Indian thought and culture is beyond the scope of this essay.'[79]

On the other hand, exactly this struggle and mutuality in the form-ation of knowledge is the subject of Dipesh Chakrabarty's examination of the relationship between the generation of colonial texts—in this case, the Calcutta jute mills' records about its workers—and their eventual contents. Chakrabarty refers to Foucault's point, that authority—in this case, the government of India and the capitalist mill-owners—'operated by forming "a body of knowledge" about its subjects.'[80] Yet as he investigates the symptomatic absences and inac-curacies in the knowledge produced in registers of labourers and their hours of work, in reports on housing, health and educational condi-tions, what is actually most striking is precisely the impotence, in different ways, both of the government of India and of the capitalists themselves, to generate documentation whose classifications and framed intent the objects of its knowledge would respect. Thus, the owners of the jute mills remained largely oblivious to the government's drive to amass information on a scale comparable to the detailed documentation available for the English factory worker, because the primitive nature of the production process itself demanded a constant supply of labour, rather than a stable and trained workforce, whose health and housing might have aroused a more deliberate concern.[81] The capitalists, on the other hand, faced the continual frustration that the information generated within the factories, mostly through factory registers, was always 'corrupted' and inaccurate: because, as Chakrabarty describes, the sardars responsible for maintaining them drew upon pre-capitalist notions of authority and community in their relations with the workforce, which accorded ill with bourgeois standards of legality, factory codes and service rules.[82] The effect of such a contextualisation is to situate the colonial pursuit of knowledge within a process which circumscribes and sets conditions upon it: involving not merely the administrator's effort at control through knowledge, but also material production and the limitations and resistances to such control set up in the practice of its hoped-for objects.

Let us return now to the larger themes and questions under discussion, and to note that while in some respects the strategy for recovery employed in the Subaltern series has been strikingly fruitful, in others, especially the key area of power and resistance, the effect has tended to be one of a slow theoretical paralysis. Is this, then, another irony of history, doubly confirming the appropriative powers of the dominant discourse: that like the subaltern himself, those who set out to restore his presence end only by borrowing the tools of that discourse, tools which serve only to reduplicate the first subjection which they effect, in the realms of critical theory? If this is indeed the case, we should certainly hesitate before accepting Gayatri Chakravorty Spivak's suggestion that the strategy of the Subaltern series 'in claiming a *positive* subject-position for the subaltern might be reinscribed as a strategy for our times.'[83] Nevertheless, this is the vital question which the contributors have raised for us: that of what form the presence of the subaltern might take, if it is not to be that of the autonomous subject-agent.

In speaking of the presence of the subaltern, we are, of course, referring primarily to a presence which is in some sense resistant: which eludes and refuses assimilation into the hegemonic, and so provides our grounds for rejecting élite historiography's insistence that the hegemonic itself is all that really exists within the social order. Our question, therefore, must in part be what kind of presence, what kind of practice, we would be justified in calling a resistant one: what is the best figure for us to cast it in, which will both reflect its fundamental alienness, and yet present it in a form which shows some part of that presence at least to stand outside and momentarily escape the constructions of dominant discourse. Let us note that we are engaged in two parallel projects here, between which there is a significant degree of tension: a tension which raises in the most pressing way the political status of our historical practice. As indeed the contributors have always been clear, theirs is a political project, as are in their different ways the genres of élite historiography. Yet to draw the conclusion, as Ranajit Guha does, that our efforts can be co-terminous with the struggles of the dispossessed, feeding directly into them by making sense of them, seems to me fundamentally misconceived.[84] We may wish in all faith for their freedom from marginality and deprivation, and do our best to cast our insights in a form which they will be able to use. But if we ask ourselves why it is that we attack historiography's dominant discourses, why we seek to find a resistant presence which has not been completely emptied or extinguished by the hegemonic, our answer must surely be that it is in order to envisage a realm of freedom in which we ourselves might speak. This is not to say that our project becomes thereby a private and merely selfish one: it is precisely on the predication of such a realm that we can think of our practice as a provider of insight and clarification. Our political concern is thus differently constructed from that of the subaltern. It contains a contradiction; but in such circumstances our best practice is to let it stand, as indeed Guha himself does in many other cases. To seek ways out of it, back to the realms of the absolute, whether in the form of post-structuralist Critic, or of the historian *engagé*, serves only to reinforce the myth that there can be such a transcendent subject-position. It is this contradiction, containing a conceit of the profession which is very difficult to escape, which means that our desire to find a resistant presence will always be in tension, rather than as we might think convergent with, the need to preserve alienness and difference in the figure of the subaltern himself. It will only be a scrupulous respect for this tension, moreover, which will keep our practice from slipping into what Baudrillard described as the obsessive demand of our political culture: from making the subaltern's voice heard, but construing it in the image of our own.

Let us turn back, then, to that category of the autonomous subject-agent, into which the discourse of liberal humanism invites us to step, under the appearance of that realm of liberty and of the universal, from which the dispossessed of our societies have been excluded, and whose restoration there will signal the end of dispossession. The idea of the self-constituting, self-determining individual, his reason enshrined in his sovereign consciousness, came into its full expression, as Michel Foucault has argued, during the European Enlightenment of the eighteenth century. The same period saw the culmination of another crucial process in the evolution of the modern state: the notional separation from it of 'civil society.' This is the sphere of private interests in general: the family, the church, the institutions of learning, trade unions, the media and cultural life, civic institutions; where the individual may exercise his rights and liberties, free from the immediate authority of the state: an authority which itself receives its legitimacy from its respect for and protection of those rights and liberties. It is Gramsci's distinctive contribution to political theory to have tried to map how this intermediary area between structure and superstructure, rather than the institutions overtly identified with the state alone, provides the terrain where classes contest for power and where hegemony is exercised. This is done most powerfully, in our own society, precisely because of the legitimating power of the sphere of civil society itself, the symbol in all its inviolability of the achievements of the Western political tradition, and what marks its politics off from those still enslaved to the state in its traditional form, or caught up in authoritarian dogma.

Where, in this field of civil society, with its myth of independence and political neutrality, does the figure of the sovereign subject-agent enter? Absolutely centrally, because he is its modal figure. It is for him that it is called into existence to provide the ground on which he realises the central features of his being: his liberty and his rights; in his unique individuality, his happiness; and, most importantly, the fact that he possesses a double existence, one led in the private sphere of his home and his family, his personal interests and his leisure, and the other in the public realm of civil society. For the latter is not, in its overt distinction from the state, thereby relegated to the sphere of the private. On the contrary, precisely because of its power over the state, as the source of the latter's value and its legitimacy, civil society, the well-being and nourishment of its multiplicity of cultural, economic and civic institutions, becomes the focus of public concern *par excellence*; and this, too, in a manner which endows the individual who has, in all legitimacy, his practice and his interest within these institutions, with a public voice, of a different but equally powerful kind from that which he exercises within the overtly political institutions of the state. It seems to me impossible to place too much emphasis on this double characteristic of civil society, its capacity for political legitimation, and the space for public concern and deliberation which it creates, just at that moment when it seems to be distancing itself from the formal political structures of the state. We should not assume, either, that these classifications are now just a matter of the history of political theory. One has only to note the huge critical acclaim and discussion which have surrounded John Rawls's *A theory of justice*, since its publication in 1971—a work which structures itself around a theory of social contract, of rights, liberties and rationality inherent in individuals—to appreciate their continuing centrality to our political culture.[85]

It is through this double characteristic that the marginalisation of the subaltern acquires its particular character, and one that is distinct from what I have tried to suggest is, in the problems of recuperation it faces, a parallel dispossession—that of women. The latter is accomplished, as very many critics have noted, through the assimilation of large areas of female existence and concern into the private sphere of the family, and their exclusion from the field of public political culture in civil society. The subaltern is rendered marginal in quite a different way—in part through his inability, his poverty, his lack of leisure and his inarticulacy, to participate to any significant degree in the public institutions of civil society, with all the particular kinds of power which they confer; but most of all, and least visibly, through his consequently weaker ability to articulate civil society's self-sustaining myth.

If these dispossessions are constructed in different ways, however, surely their resolution will be the same: that of stepping into the realm of civil society as sovereign subject-agent, and into the full enjoyment of its double persona. This is, of course, one of the central conceits of the modern Western state in its dealings in this field: that it has been able to realise and to preserve such a realm of neutral freedom, but that obstacles have arisen in the way of all of its population reaching it. We should also note that this conceit has been reproduced exactly in the impression that feminist issues, or indeed regional concerns such as the Subaltern project, represent essentially *neglected* areas, presently the concern of a worthy minority of historians and critics, but which require only to be restored to the whole for matters to be put right. We might also say that it has been reproduced in the delineation of ex-colonial societies themselves as an area of special interest, which will be ended in their restoration to the proper form and fruits of the modern Western state. Yet, as Sabyasachi Bhattacharya has pointed out, no such proposals can be made without calling into question the structure and limitations of the whole.[86] For the figure of the subject-agent is not a universal, but a highly specific one, whose autonomy and self-determination will always render it unobtainable to all but the privileged. Not only is it unobtainable, but it also mocks the dispossessed, impressing upon them that it is only their shortcomings—their fecklessness as subalterns, their closeness to nature as women, their helpless addiction to authoritarian traditionalism as ex-colonial societies—which prevent them from being welcomed into its own numbers. It is this perspective above all which should make it clear to us that the concern with the subaltern, or indeed with women, is not a special interest. Rather, they provide both the theoretical means, and the historical material, through which we may examine and call into question the very stuff of which civil society is made, to appreciate the strategies of power at work in its most cherished figures and self-images. Thus, the documentation of resistance, and that of a hegemony which does not believe in its own omnipotence, ultimately converge and are part of the same task. Resistance—those moments in which the prizes and incentives of the dominant are refused, held inadequate or simply uncomprehended before the pressure of material want—leads us into the structures and appropriative tactics of the hegemonic itself, to demonstrate both the manner in which it works upon its object, and the limits of its power.

What, however, if hegemony is right to insist on its own omnipotence: if our project, rooted ultimately in our own striving to create an area of freedom in which we might conduct our own practice, is quite misplaced before its ability to appropriate and assimilate all real resistance? We must certainly take account of the argument that a hegemonic culture so conditions and mediates resistance, not only giving it its goals, but even marking its approval on its ends, that its appearance can only be an illusion, which underwrites that culture's own liberal self-image. In denying that this is the case, however, it seems best not to follow Partha Chatterjee when he says that 'the dominant group, in their exercise of domination, do not consume and destroy the dominated classes, for then there would be no relation of power, and hence no domination. For domination to exist, the subaltern classes must necessarily inhabit a domain that is their own, which gives them their identity, where they can exist as a distinct social form.'[87] This is misleading precisely because it rests upon the essentialism which we have noted: the notion that there is something inherently inextinguishable in the very form of the subaltern's own subjectivity. Rejecting the idea of inherent being, we must certainly face the possibility that the subaltern may be subject to such an intensity of ideological and material pressure that his consciousness and practice are indeed completely pervaded and possessed by it. It is possible to find fault with this argument, but on other grounds. This is in its assumption, very similar to what I identified in contemporary discussions of discourse, that the monolith of hegemony *precedes* resistance: that it will always provide the matrix or set the arena in which resistance will have to operate, and from which will spring its moulding power. This, what we might call the Swiss cheese theory of hegemony in its assumption that resistance can only crawl through the holes, is in its own way a myth of origins, for hegemony does not spring fully formed into being to be followed by a resistance which must always operate within its pre-given confines. Rather, we should call to mind Gramsci's own insistence that the hegemonic is the articulation of a number of historic blocks, in the ability of a fundamental class to become, in its awareness that its own corporate interests transcend the purely economic, the spokesman of other, subordinate, groups, and to articulate the latter's overt interests to its own. For Gramsci, the specific moment of the political is enacted precisely on this site: through the struggle, in which, as he calls them, 'philosophies' or 'conceptions of the world' play a vital role, to exert leadership over a variety of groups, and to conform to its sway the institutions of civil society as well as the overtly political ones of the state. Thus each form of the hegemonic comes into existence around diversities of interest and potential sites for resistance which fracture and constrain it even as it exerts its conforming power.

If it is possible to postulate a site for resistance, therefore, this still leaves the larger problem of how we are to configure its presence. Many answers are possible to this question, which is no less than that of attempting to conceive of presence and agency outside the approved categories of our conventional social sciences. We have been given a valuable lead in the work of some of the contributors, in their emphases upon the ambiguous and constructed nature even, indeed, especially, of the most apparently fixed subject-position. My own further emphasis would be that the very dichotomy between domination and resistance, as we currently conceive it, bears all the marks of dominant discourse, in its insistence that resistance itself should necessarily take the virile form of a deliberate and violent onslaught. Rejecting this, we should look for resistances of a different kind: dispersed in fields we do not conventionally associate with the political; residing sometimes in the evasion of norms or the failure to respect ruling standards of conscience and responsibility; sometimes in the furious effort to resolve in ideal or metaphysical terms the contradictions of the subaltern's existence, without addressing their source; sometimes in what looks only like cultural difference. From this perspective, even withdrawal from or simple indifference to the legitimating structures of the political, with their demand for recognition of the values and meanings which they incessantly manufacture, can be construed as a form of resistance. As Baudrillard notes, 'Ordinary life, men in their banality, could well not be the insignificant side of history—better: that withdrawing into the private could well be a direct defiance of the political, a form of actively resisting political manipulation.'[88] These, then, would be forms of resistance more 'feminine' than masculine, those of Chandra's labourer and his wife; which are only half perceived as 'resistance,' but which are not, on the other hand, accepted as matters of personal guilt and failure.

In insisting that what may look like idiosyncracy, passivity and even indifference should be included thus, it is not intended to antagonise those who properly insist on the subaltern's capacity for an acute consciousness of the political. It is only to note that this marks the point where our own political project runs into the subaltern's fundamental otherness, which may render his consciousness of the political in forms alien or even antipathetic to us. Moreover, we should stress that this kind of emphasis does not condemn the subaltern to a half-light of faint understanding and fainter effort, outside the moments of his revolutionary heroism. It is one of the deepest misconstructions of the autonomous subject-agent that its own masculine practice possesses a monopoly, as the term signifies, upon the heroic: that effort and sacrifice are to be found nowhere but in what it holds to be the real sites of political struggle. As Raymond Williams has remarked, 'It is a fact about the modes of domination, that they select from and consequently exclude the full range of human practice. What they exclude may often be seen as the personal or the private, or as the natural or even as the metaphysical. Indeed, it is usually in one or other of these terms that the excluded area is to be expressed, since what the dominant has effectively seized is indeed the ruling definition of the social.'[89] We can comprehend and contest this seizure by noting just this most fundamental and least visible level of its operation: its classification, through this certification of resistances, of the range even of heterodox human practice according to the seemingly universal values of endeavour, courage and sacrifice. Although they are at one level separate tasks, that of contesting this definition, its ruling figure and mystifying conceits, and that of carrying the concern with the subaltern out of the realm of special interests, they surely converge for the present to provide a recognisable and crucially important field of exploration, from whose implications very few of us can afford to remain detached.[90]

NOTES AND REFERENCES

1. Edward Said, 'Orientalism reconsidered,' in Francis Barker *et al, Literature, politics and theory: Papers from the Essex conference* (London: Methuen, 1986), p. 223. The most useful recent statement of the difficulties of representing non-European 'others,' which draws on the themes of post-structuralism, is James Clifford and George Marcus (eds), *Writing culture: The politics and poetics of ethnography* (Berkeley: University of California Press, 1986). Good critical introductions to these themes are Richard Harland, *Superstructuralism: The philosophy of structuralism and post-structuralism* (London: Methuen, 1987) and John Fekete (ed.), *The structural allegory: Reconstructive encounters with the new French thought* (Manchester: Manchester University Press, 1984).

2. For a recent exploration of these arguments, see Hans Medick, ' "Missionaries in the row boat?" Ethnological ways of knowing as a challenge to social history,' in *Comparative Studies in Society and History*, 29, 1, 1987. A provocative argument in favour of the value of ethnographic work for social history within the South Asian context is Nicholas B. Dirks, *The hollow crown: Ethnohistory of an Indian kingdom* (Cambridge: Cambridge University Press, 1987).

3. Ranajit Guha, 'On some aspects of the historiography of colonial India,' *SSI*, 1982, p. 2.

4. Shahid Amin, 'Gandhi as mahatma: Gorakhpur district, eastern U.P., 1921–2, *SSIII*, 1984.

5. Gyan Pandey, 'Peasant revolt and Indian nationalism: The peasant movement in Awadh, 1919–22,' *SSI*, 1982, p. 187.

6. Partha Chatterjee, 'Peasants, politics and historiography: A response,' *Social Scientist*, no. 120, May 1983. This brief note, written in response to a critical review article, written from a Marxist perspective by Javeed Alam, in *Social Scientist*, no. 117, February 1983, is useful for clarifying a number of issues.

7. See, for example, the review article by Dipankar Gupta, 'On altering the ego in peasant history: Paradoxes of the ethnic option,' *Peasant Studies*, vol. 13, no. 1, Fall 1985, p. 15. I thank Majid Siddiqi for bringing this article to my attention.

8. Most notably, of course, in the debates surrounding the work of E.P. Thompson, since his publication of *The making of the English working class*

in 1963, and in his exchanges with British Marxist historians who had drawn on the work of Louis Althusser. See especially E.P. Thompson, *The poverty of theory, and other essays* (London: Merlin, 1978); and the riposte by Perry Anderson, *Arguments within English Marxism* (London: New Left Books, 1979).

9. Ranajit Guha, Preface, *SSII*, 1983.

10. Sabyasachi Bhattacharya, 'History from below,' *Social Scientist*, no. 119, April 1983, p. 6.

11. Jean Baudrillard, *In the shadow of the silent majorities . . . or the end of the social and other essays*, translated by Paul Foss, Paul Patton and John Johnston (New York: Foreign Agents Series, 1983), pp. 48–9.

12. Ibid., p. 29.

13. Partha Chatterjee, 'Peasants, politics and historiography,' p. 62.

14. Gayatri Chakravorty Spivak, 'Discussion: Subaltern studies—Deconstructing historiography,' *SSIV*, 1985, p. 342.

15. Shahid Amin, 'Small peasant commodity production and rural indebtedness: The culture of sugarcane in eastern U.P., *c.* 1880–1920,' *SSI*, 1982.

16. For references to parts of this debate, see footnote 8.

17. Toril Moi, *Sexual/Textual politics: Feminist literary theory* (London: Methuen, 1985). See especially part I, 'Anglo-American feminist criticism.'

18. Partha Chatterjee, 'Peasants, politics and historiography,' p. 58.

19. Ibid., p. 61.

20. See the collective review of *Subaltern Studies II*, in *Social Scientist*, no. 137, October 1984, p. 12.

21. Partha Chatterjee, 'Peasants, politics and historiography,' p. 59.

22. Stephen Henningham, 'Quit India in Bihar and the eastern U.P.: The dual revolt,' *SSII*, 1983, p. 137. The emphasis is the author's.

23. Ibid., p. 149.

24. Ibid., p. 153. See the criticism of this essay in *Social Scientist*, no. 137, October 1984, pp. 23–9.

25. Ramachandra Guha, 'Forestry and social protest in British Kumaun, *c.* 1893–1921,' *SSIV*, 1985, pp. 92–4.

26. Ibid., pp. 99–100.

27. Swapan Dasgupta, 'Adivasi politics in Midnapur, *c.* 1760–1924,' *SSIV*, 1985, p. 102.

28. Ibid., pp. 134–5.

29. Tanika Sarkar, 'Jitu Santal's movement in Malda, 1924–32: A study in tribal protest,' *SSIV*, 1985, p. 154.

30. Ibid., p. 10.

31. Dipankar Gupta, 'On altering the ego in peasant history,' p. 9.

32. Ibid., p. 10.

33. Ibid., p. 13.

34. Ranajit Guha, 'The prose of counter-insurgency,' *SSII*, 1983, p. 3.

35. See the review in *Journal of Asian Studies*, vol. XLV, no. 1, November 1985, p. 178.

36. See the review in *Indian Economic and Social History Review*, vol. 22, no. 1, 1985, p. 94.

37. Ranajit Guha, *Elementary aspects of peasant insurgency in colonial India* (Delhi: Oxford University Press, 1983), p. 13.

38. Ranajit Guha, 'On some aspects of the historiography of colonial India,' p. 8. The emphasis is the author's.

39. Ranajit Guha, *Elementary aspects of peasant insurgency*, p. 3.

40. Ibid., p. 334.

41. Ibid., p. 18.

42. Especially in Fanon's *Black skin, white masks*, translated by C.L. Markman (New York: Grove Press, 1967), and, of course, in Said's *Orientalism* (New York: Pantheon Press, 1978).

43. See his foreword to the new edition of Fanon's *Black skin, white masks* (London: Pluto Press, 1986), pp. xv–xvi.

44. Ranajit Guha, *Elementary aspects of peasant insurgency*, esp. pp. 18–76.

45. Tanika Sarkar, 'Jitu Santal's movement in Malda,' pp. 152–3.

46. Ranajit Guha, *Elementary aspects of peasant insurgency*, pp. 20–8.

47. Ibid., p. 28.

48. David Arnold, 'Rebellious hillmen: The Guden-Rampa risings, 1839–1924,' *SSI*, 1982, p. 131.

49. Ibid., pp. 131–2, footnote 106.

50. Ranajit Guha, *Elementary aspects of peasant insurgency*, p. 8.

51. Ibid., p. 225.

52. Sumit Sarkar, 'The conditions and nature of subaltern militancy: Bengal from swadeshi to non-co-operation, *c.* 1905–22,' *SSIII*, 1984, p. 273; Partha Chatterjee, 'Agrarian relations and communalism in Bengal, 1926–35,' *SSI*, 1982, p. 36.

53. Dipankar Gupta, 'On altering the ego in peasant history,' pp. 15–16.

54. Arvind Das, 'Agrarian change from above and below: Bihar 1947–78,' *SSII*, pp. 225–6.

55. Ibid., p. 226.

56. N.K. Chandra, 'Agricultural workers in Burdwan,' *SSII*, 1983, p. 237.

57. Louis Althusser, 'Is it simple to be a marxist in philosophy?,' in *Essays in self-criticism* (London: New Left Books, 1976), p. 205. The emphasis is the author's.

58. Michel Foucault, 'The subject and power,' in Hubert L. Dreyfus and Paul

Rabinow, *Michel Foucault: Beyond structuralism and hermeneutics* (Harvester Press, 1982), p. 212.

59. Michel Foucault, 'Nietzsche, genealogy and history,' in Paul Rabinow (ed.), *The Foucault reader* (Penguin, 1984), p. 78.

60. Rashmi Bhatnagar, 'Uses and limits of Foucault: A study of the theme of origins in Edward Said's *Orientalism*,' *Social Scientist*, no. 158, July 1986, p. 5.

61. Jean Baudrillard, *In the shadow of the silent majorities*, p. 9.

62. Ibid., pp. 23–4.

63. Dipesh Chakrabarty, 'Conditions of knowledge for working class conditions: Employers, government and the jute workers of Calcutta, 1890–1940,' *SSII*, 1983, p. 308.

64. Dipankar Gupta, 'On altering the ego in peasant history,' pp. 9–12.

65. Partha Chatterjee, 'Agrarian relations and communalism in Bengal, 1926–35,' *SSI*, pp. 12–13, 18.

66. Ibid., p. 35.

67. Partha Chatterjee, 'More on modes of power and the peasantry,' *SSII*, 1983, p. 343. See the exchange between Chatterjee and Sanjay Prasad on these points, in *Social Scientist*, no. 141, February 1985, and no. 151, December 1985.

68. Toril Moi, *Sexual/Textual politics: Feminist literary theory*, p. 86.

69. See, for example, Sumit Sarkar, 'The conditions and nature of subaltern militancy,' pp. 273–4.

70. Gyan Pandey, ' "Encounters and calamities": The history of a north Indian *qasba* in the nineteenth century,' *SSIII*, 1984, p. 269.

71. David Hardiman: 'Adivasi assertion in south Gujarat: The Devi movement of 1922–3,' *SSIII*, 1984, p. 217.

72. Tanika Sarkar, 'Jitu Santal's movement in Malda,' p. 153.

73. N.K. Chandra, 'Agricultural workers in Burdwan,' *SSII*, 1983, p. 250.

74. Jean Comaroff, *Body of power, spirit of resistance: The culture and history of a South African people* (Chicago: University of Chicago Press, 1985), p. 261.

75. See their reviews in *Social Scientist*, no. 111, August 1982, and no. 117, February 1983.

76. Partha Chatterjee, 'Modes of power: Some clarifications,' *Social Scientist*, no. 141, February 1985, pp. 56–7. See also his tribute to Althusser, in the Preface to his *Bengal 1920–1947: The land question*, CSSSH Monograph (Calcutta, 1985), pp. xviii–xxxv.

77. See, for example, Mark Poster, *Foucault, marxism and history: Mode of production versus mode of information* (Cambridge: Polity Press, 1984), pp. 111–15; Mark Philp, 'Michel Foucault,' in Q. Skinner (ed.), *The return*

of grand theory in the human sciences (Cambridge University Press, 1985), p. 79.

78. Bernard S. Cohn, 'The command of language and the language of command,' *SSIV*, 1985, p. 283.

79. Ibid., p. 329.

80. Dipesh Chakrabarty, 'Conditions for knowledge of working class conditions,' p. 262.

81. Ibid., pp. 289–91.

82. Ibid., pp. 294–310.

83. Gayatri Chakravorty Spivak, 'Discussion: Subaltern studies: Deconstructing historiography,' *SSIV*, 1985, p. 345.

84. Ranajit Guha, *Elementary aspects of peasant insurgency*, pp. 336–7.

85. John Rawls, *A theory of justice* (Cambridge, Mass.), 1971.

86. Sabyasachi Bhattacharya, 'History from below,' p. 7.

87. Partha Chatterjee, 'Peasants politics and historiography,' p. 59.

88. Jean Baudrillard, *In the shadow of the silent majorities*, p. 39.

89. Raymond Williams, *Marxism and literature* (Oxford University Press, 1977), p. 125.

90. *Subaltern Studies: Writings on South Asian history and society*. Edited by Ranajit Guha (Delhi: Oxford University Press), vol. I, 1982, pp. viii, 241; vol. II, 1983, pp. x, 358; vol. III, 1984, pp. x, 327; vol. IV, 1985, pp. vi, 383.

The Dis/appearance of Subalterns: A Reading of a Decade of *Subaltern Studies*

JIM MASSELOS

THE FIRST volume of *Subaltern Studies* (*SS*) appeared a decade ago; the sixth (and most recent) volume in 1989 marked a turning point in the series with the retirement of the editor, Ranajit Guha. Over the period most of the members of the core co-operative who managed the editorial functions along with Guha—Shahid Amin, David Arnold, Partha Chatterjee, David Hardiman, Gyan Pandey and Dipesh Chakrabarty—have moved from junior academic positions to senior and influential ones in the profession. The transition for Guha has been even more potent. The dust jacket for the first volume informs us merely that he was on secondment from Sussex University to a Senior Research Fellowship at the Australian National University. By the sixth volume the dust jacket highlights his personal inspiration to, and encouragement 'in seminal ways' of, a considerable number of young historians and the likely persistence of his work 'as writer, thinker and guru.' That there has been considerable impact is demonstrated by the numerous students around the world who now do their research using subaltern modes and perceptions—so many in fact that subaltern insights are becoming clichés and even platitudes. The series has in addition been profoundly influential in sparking off methodological debate around the writing of the history of South Asia, in contributing to wider historiographical concerns as well as in focusing research on specific and relatively neglected areas of South Asia's past.[1] It may even be that the subaltern subject has been lost in the theoretical and methodological structures erected over them and the academic agendas created around them.

That there has been a wide and pervasive influence, direct and indirect, stemming from these six volumes is, I think, undisputable. And understanding of South Asian history is all the better for their appearance. The subaltern approach and *Subaltern Studies* have not only become established over the past decade, they have become establishment. But what is established? At the least a terminology has been given vogue, though the referents are diverse. The use of the term subaltern in the literature on South Asia can now as frequently refer to the six-volume collection of subaltern essays and various additional publications, as to the group of historians who wrote and write for the series, as well as to larger congregations beyond them who adopt the general approach and focus, as much as it refers to the subaltern subject in the historical South Asian past itself and interpretations of subaltern action. The historian is now the subject as much as what is studied.

In what follows I present my readings of the texts about the subalterns. Whether what I say represents what was intended in all their subtlety by those who wrote the essays is irrelevant since what I present is my response to the mass of their words. The corpus is a large one, the six volumes contain slightly under two thousand pages, apart from ancillary discussions which have appeared elsewhere. The contents vary in subject matter, scope, and even conceptual and methodological implication. Some of the essays follow the conventional form of a historian's article in a journal, some are theoretical and conceptual discussions and some are rejoinders to critiques of the series that appeared during the course of publication. By the time of the later volumes the series had virtually become a hard-bound academic journal but one limited by its collective approach to the subaltern writing project. Along other axes, the volumes might equally have been put together differently as volumes around specific themes: tribal history, agrarian social structure, communalism, the mentalité of catastrophe, rumour, and so on. Though the research basis of virtually all articles is impeccable, the essays vary in intellectual quality and skill, in writing and in argument. Many are brilliant and it is a pleasure to read and re-read the volumes, following the tracks of the most gifted of the group, enjoying the precision and insights which they bring to whatever they write. As the series progressed, additional writers were co-opted into the undertaking, gathering in younger scholars (Gautam Bhadra, Swapan Dasgupta, Tanika Sarkar, Ramachandra Guha and others) along with professors like Gayatri Spivak, B.S. Cohn, Veena Das and Sumit Sarkar. It is hard to think of a collection of higher quality, especially given that the excellence is maintained over the span of six volumes. Of course there is considerable variety and even divergences between the writers while some of the writers have developed and matured over the decade. Collectively nevertheless they retain a general convergence and focus.

At the centre of all the words and pages remain the subalterns themselves. Who and what are subalterns? Guha explains the usage of the term in two ways: positively, by outlining who they are; and negatively as a constituent of a binary opposition, by distinguishing what they are not. Guha's initial explanation in the preface of the first volume derives from the *Concise Oxford dictionary* usage: subalterns are those of inferior rank, those subordinate in terms of class, caste, age, gender, and office or in any other way (*SS1*, p. vii). As an opposition they are not those who are dominant, the ruling groups, the élites. Élites, he later explains, may be both foreign (officials, industrialists, etc.) and indigenous (feudal magnates, the industrial and mercantile bourgeoisies, upper Indian bureaucrats etc.). Élites were dispersed and heterogeneous; significantly, their members might at regional and local levels either be part of the élite or, according to circumstance and situation, be classified as subaltern. The apparent illogicality of élite groups not in fact being élite, Guha explains, is determined by criteria of opponent actions, although the confusion surrounding the distinction surfaces in some of the essays throughout the ensuing volumes. The critical test lies in determining in whose interests the apparently élite but really non-élite were acting: as Guha puts it, the test was whether they '*acted in the interests of the latter* [the dominant all-India groups] *and not in conformity to interests corresponding truly to their own social being* (Guha's italics, *SS1*, p. 8).

Introducing a welcome note of empiricism by placing the subaltern project within an apparently scientific, value-free context, Guha insists it is a matter for investigation in specific instances as to whether, given the ambiguous nature of rural social structure, the rural gentry and the lowest strata among them (who ideally should belong to the people), actually so locate themselves according to their actions. For him the criterion is action, activity. But behind that determination is another, the reading into action of interests and the assigning of moral values to certain interests over others. The distinction is subtle and confronts a class/materialist interpretation of vested interests and behaviour patterns. Since élites may behave variously, individuals, people, groups, do not behave or respond automatically in terms of their material interests, sometimes they behave in contradiction to their own social being. Whether they are doing so is determined by the historian in assessing the actions of subalterns. Subalterns, on the other hand, it would seem, behave in terms of their social being; their activity is essentially right and proper; if they do not and if they are not, then they are not subaltern. Conversely, the action of people and groups classified as élites may however be ambiguous. Who determines proper action, who determines that subaltern classification, are the writers of their history, the historian. Moral values hence creep into the empirical weighing of the evidence and information from the past: the subaltern historian becomes an arbiter of values.

There is an associated issue: the approval of action according to social category. Papers in the first volumes analyse the interweavings of action against the British Raj by both subalterns and élites. Even Hardiman, in a not entirely successful attack upon the notion and reality of factions in rural Indian society, notes the existence of class linkages, collaborations between élites and subalterns (*SS1*, p. 231). Stephen Henningham in his account of 'the mass upsurge and its guerilla aftermath' during the Quit India movement in Bihar and eastern Uttar Pradesh sees 'the essential incoherence of the insurrection' as being due to a duality of its components, 'an élite nationalist uprising combined with a subaltern rebellion' (*SS2*, p. 164). Why the one is an uprising and the other a rebellion is unclear, since the characteristic of subalternity, that of action against domination, applies equally to both in their opposition to the Raj. Presumably in terms of the subaltern definitions outlined by Guha both should be subaltern by the very act of opposition to Raj domination, yet the analysis and discussion retain the distinction between the two groups though both are located in what would seem a subaltern role by opposition to the Raj. Group/Class affiliation and consciousness are not then determined by action and through the act of opposition: despite all that is said, the basis of subalternity as presented in the volumes rests first with material determinants of social category and only then with the action and consciousness of that social category. Action is a sign of subalternity as it emerges through the essays in the series but again in the essays it is not a necessary condition of subalternity. Nor, it would seem, is subaltern consciousness itself a determinant in the way it is for aboriginal people in Australia nowadays, though this point is less clear. In these texts, the binary opposition, the starting postulate of the series, thus élides into a ternary interaction between subalterns, Indian élites and Raj élites, triangular confrontations of varied permutations. The subaltern confronts both Indian and British élites in a polarised world, and Indian élites cannot be subalterns in practice in written subaltern history, whatever their opposition to Raj power and despite an application of the words of Guha's definitions.

Though the Raj is necessarily pervasive through the volumes, many of the later essays in fact move the Raj into the far distance: the concern is as often with establishing the junctures between Indian élites and Indian subalterns as it is with the confrontations with the Raj. The élites emerge both as the end of the line of a kind of world systems of power derived from the Raj but also have an autonomous existence of their own in the Indian context—and it is this existence which subaltern historians are concerned with delineating and confronting through the story of subaltern resistance. There is a further implication. Some essays explicitly establish that élites and subalterns have existence independent of the Raj. Subalternity existed before the Raj (see Bhadra's essay on uprisings in Mughal India in *SS2*, pp. 43–59) and after the Raj (see Arvind Das on Bihar after 1947 in *SS2*, pp. 180–227) as therefore do the élites they resisted. Since neither is dependent on the Raj for existence, the Raj is not a necessary precondition for their being, although in specific historical situations the one élite may reinforce the other. Again, it is the ternary nature of the structures of regional power that underpins the various analyses even if the frame of the presentation is the subaltern in the process of resisting.

Guha's critical objective is of course to change focus, to make central the subaltern and subaltern consciousness. The insight of the project is not concern with putative élites but to focus on the subaltern, the '*autonomous* domain' (Guha's italics, *SS1*, p. 4) of the people, to demonstrate they had their own consciousness, their own politics of resistance, their own mobilisations and their own ideologies of opposition. Subaltern mentalité however is the mentalité of the subaltern at the time of opposition, at the moment of their action against domination. They have their own '*autonomous* domain, for it neither originated from élite politics nor did its existence depend on the latter' (Guha in *SS1*, p. 4). By the second volume Guha extends the point: the subaltern is 'the maker of his own history and the architect of his own destiny' (*SS2*, p. vii). The subaltern group are to write that history and oppose élitism through the detailed intensity of their scrutiny of the past record no matter how great the difficulties posed by the recovery of information about the past.

The claim for the need to refocus history writing on sections and groups hitherto ignored is unexceptional. There has of course been a long tradition of studying such groups in European historiography and it is a sad comment on the state of the region's histories that the cry needed to be voiced at all in terms of South Asia. Or that its championing should be seen as being such a blinding light of revelation. Guha's *bête noir*, the dominance of historians concerned with explaining the success of nationalists in taking power from the British, is of course a part explanation as is the parallel dominance of imperial and Wallersteinian economic histories. But there were other historians concerned with oppressed groups before *Subaltern Studies* began appearing and others who were independently making their own paths through such subject matter while it was appearing—Zelliot, Omvedt and O'Hanlon for instance—or with the position of farmers, tenantry and bonded labour in changing agrarian situations (among many, Stokes, Brennan and others) or with crowd studies and violence (including but not only Ian Catanach, Ravinder Kumar, Anand Yang, and Sandria Freitag and others). Surprisingly, it is rare to find reference to any of these or other similarly inclined scholars in the volumes unless it is as objects of attack. Nor, despite the protestations of subaltern writers are subaltern subjects in active protest against the Raj at all new to more conventional Indian histories. They feature in the various commissioned and non-commissioned government and Congress histories and hagiographies of the freedom movement that began appearing from the 1950s. While by their function they privileged the linear story of the Congress battle and Congress victory over the Raj and in this sense fit in with Guha's critique of an interpretative élitist perspective dominance, such histories also have a strong concern with non-élite resistance by those whom the Guha group of historians would classify as subaltern. Such accounts and narratives see any and all opposition to the Raj—uprisings, and rebellions—as resistance much as do the subaltern writers and they create much the same kind of heroes of them. There is of course considerable difference in the technical skill and intellectual thrust of the history they are producing but at the moment the point I am concerned with here is subject matter rather than perceptive history writing. Others also have taken the path of tracing subaltern resistance without of course using subaltern terminology or underlying rationales: not least is historian and anthropologist K.S. Singh's documentary research, participant observation and personal identification with Birsaite Munda codes but there are others also. Additionally, in an early volume Guha notes that radical historians have in fact dealt with such resistance, the example being the Santal rebellion of 1855, but he dismisses that writing: it is a reaction against colonialist historiography, it rearranges events 'along the alternative axis of a protracted campaign for freedom and socialism.' It performs an act of 'appropriation' and by substituting 'an *abstraction* called Worker-and-Peasant, *an ideal rather than the real historical personality of the insurgent*' it mediates the insurgent's consciousness by that of the historian—that is, as Guha explains it, 'of a past consciousness by one conditioned by the present' (Guha's italics throughout, quotations from various places on *SS2*, p. 33). The argument is persuasive particularly when he goes on to argue that distortion is built into historiography and cannot be eliminated; though it is not possible to grasp fully a past consciousness or reconstitute it, it is possible with proper sensitivity and awareness to achieve 'a close approximation' (*SS2*, p. 3).

The issues raised here are central to the endeavours of historians generally as much as they are specific to the subaltern historian's project. In either case they require further consideration. I will try to tease out some of the implications before returning to the general discussion of subalternity.

One part of Guha's argument is based upon empiricism and the proper exercise of the historian's craft. If research is undertaken meticulously and with appropriate sensitivity to the issues on hand, it should be possible to come close to portraying reasonably accurately a past that is alien, foreign and not recoverable. Perfection, though unattainable, is approachable. Perhaps here the driving idea is not dissimilar to the Collingwood act of creative imagination. But Guha continues: when historians use the past to make points in a contemporary polemic then they are not being properly sensitive and the past eludes them. But when they are sensitively attuned then they may come close to past realities. So, attitude of mind and research craft are both necessary. This is of course a proposition that most historians would accept as a basis for their practice in the writing of history. However historians of course live in and are products of their own time, they are never free of their contemporaneity, and the history they create through their writing is the history as seen through their present. Even if they do not consciously fashion the past in terms of the present agenda of their politics, as Guha sees the radical interpretation of the Santal rebellion as doing, historians cannot but display the past in terms of the present in which they are located, the perceptions which they possess, and the currents and ideas with which they intersect. The history historians write is as much the history of themselves as it is the history of the subjects located in the past. Perhaps it is even more so or, if the logic is to be pursued to its conclusion, completely so. Guha and the subaltern historians seem unwilling to move very far with the logic of such an argument, though there are references to their being sensitised by the experience of writing subaltern history. In consequence they see the past differently from other historians and are able to perceive people, events, processes, they would not have seen without the experience of being part of this group. Sumit Sarkar's essay on the Kalki-Avatar of Bikrampur is a superb example of the effect of such sensitising in producing work that might not otherwise have appeared (see footnote 5 of his essay in *SS6*, p. 3). The methodological ambivalence in subaltern writing is that while the group is very much concerned with current political theory, with using research of the past to inform current political and theoretical debate they seem not to consider that such debate affects their constructions of the past; for them, it would seem, it merely heightens their ability to see the past accurately. Here the issue is not merely the simple one of being sensitised differently to events in the past, which is given and accepted, but that overall interpretation, the designing of people as subaltern subjects, is equally affected. It is not only what is perceived but what the subaltern group do with what is perceived that is at issue here. And what they do is derived from their contemporary location and from their underlying agenda in approaching the past.

As to subaltern authors being bound within their own contemporaneity the most extended and subtle expression of the issue occurs in parts of Spivak's major conceptual discussion paper on deconstructing historiography (*SS4*, p. 330–63).[2] She locates the subaltern writers and their project within the mainstream of European intellectual and philosophical thought—the critique of humanism, the group's rethinking of Marx so as to take his thought outside the European provenance of his 'homogeneous internationalism, to the persistent recognition of heterogeneity' (*SS4*, p. 350), as well as within contemporary deconstruction and post-structuralist theory. And in so doing she probes at the creation of the subaltern discursive historiography, the problematics it poses, and examines some of the theoretical consequences.

At one point Spivak seems to take the issue of writing the past in terms of the present a step further by effectively turning it upside down. She argues the subaltern exists through the historian, but additionally so does the historian through the subaltern: 'the discourse of the unified consciousness of the subaltern *must* inhabit the strategy of these historians' (Spivak's italics, *SS4*, p. 349). The point would seem to be not much different structurally from that in the potent opening of Nandy's essay on Gandhi's assassination: 'Every political assassination is a joint communiqué. It is a statement which the assassin and his victim jointly work on and co-author.'[3] Spivak's conclusion to her essay repeats the emphasis on 'the complicity between subject and object of investigation' (*SS4*, p. 363). Perhaps, then, the barrier of the otherness of the alien past is dissipated in the loop of complicity between subject and object, the historian and the past signifier. Their project is the same, and is the product of mutual interaction. This is not to say however that the historian has knowledge of the past: Spivak earlier advises that the reading of a past text must always be 'strategic,' suggesting a reading against the grain that is dependent upon 'practical exigencies.' Her implication as far as the subaltern authors are concerned is that 'it would get the group off the dangerous hook of claiming to establish the truth-knowledge of the subaltern and his consciousness' (*SS4*, p. 356). The theoretical problem of the unknowable and irreproducible past is hence not resolved by a loop of complicity. If the subaltern subject cannot be known by the historian, there cannot be interaction between them: historians do not reproduce the past, they construct their history of the past. In this sense the subaltern is as much the creation of the subaltern historian engaged in a present day strategy just as and as much as writers of the British Raj constructed the lower orders, criminal castes and the like, in terms of their systems of knowledge, the needs of their power and the structures of their domination. The underlying conceptual contradictions—between the not-knowing of past realities and the timebound contemporary producers of history—are not resolved in the Subaltern Series volumes nor do they affect the various papers by lack of resolution.[4] The pragmatics of writing history and concern with subaltern subject matter preclude the group from adopting the solutions followed by Foucault who in his later stages was moving towards an abdication of presenting the oppressed subject ('who could seemingly speak for himself) or of Barthes who moved to autobiography and 'the celebration of the fragment' (*SS4*, p. 347).

On the contrary, in the earlier volumes of the series most of the essays in their praxis operate with fervour in endeavouring to establish the truth-knowledge of the subaltern. In the later volumes when the influence of post-structuralism becomes more evident, there is some change in tenor. Sarkar puts his finger on it but in a considerably less rarefied way than characterises the abstracted and theoretical level of Spivak's discussion. His major concern, he tells us, is not with constructing a narrative of the Rankean past as it really happened but with analysing the representations that surrounded the events around the Kalki-Avatar, with what was remembered or forgotten and why (*SS6*, p. 5). It is in these areas of representation and techniques of analysis that the subaltern writers operate at their most subtle to discover or create their subject.

Their technology of retrieval functions in a number of ways. Some essays work against the grain of the documentation in order to recover subaltern perceptions which are then explicated and analysed. Often this is done by turning colonial observations on their head, by approving what colonial commentators disapproved of, by reversing the emotive connotations of what has been recorded. Notable among such endeavours of retrieval is Arnold's piecing together of famine victims' responses to their situation and of tracing a narrative of how they interpreted their position through analysing their rumours, riots and religious innovations ('Famine in peasant consciousness and peasant action: Madras, 1876–8' in *SS3*, pp. 62–115). Equally perceptive is his similar account of plague responses ('Touching the body: Perspectives on the Indian plague, 1896–1900' in *SS5*, pp. 55–91). Hardiman, apart from significant contributions in earlier volumes on tribal consciousness, has an equally penetrating analysis of the place of alcohol in tribal life which occasionally lapses into a kind of functionalism of explanation ('From custom to crime: The politics of drinking in colonial south Gujarat' in *SS4*, pp. 165–228). Amin's way into the specific subaltern responses towards Gandhi and nationalist politics, into how and why nationalist phenomena were perceived in ways so different by the wider base of society, is to detail rumours and stories current about the Mahatma ('Gandhi as mahatma: Gorakhpur district, eastern UP, 1921–2' in *SS3*, pp. 1–61). Pandey looks at communalism by analysis of rumour and religious perceptions ('Rallying round the cow: Sectarian strife in the Bhojpuri region, *c.* 1888–1917' in *SS2*, pp. 60–129). In a later essay he moves further into perception and representation—into how people saw and read their own history by comparing a local history of a casbah written by a Muslim member of the local élite with how the casbah's history features in British accounts (' "Encounters and calamities": the history of a north Indian *qasba* in the nineteenth century' in *SS3*, pp. 231–70). In his final essay in the series ('The colonial construction of "communalism": British writings on Banaras in the nineteenth century' in *SS6*, pp. 132–68) Pandey examines the creation of a master narrative on riots by tracing how the colonial power, through its accounts and narratives, constructed a discourse of communal riots, creating otherness of perception. His summary of the effect of Raj portrayals points to the reduction of individuality and the delineation of what was to become twentieth-century stereotypical communalism:' "rioting," "bigotry," "criminality" are of a piece—the marks of an inferior people and a people without history. Naturally, even the violence of the subject population is distinguished from the often unacknowledged but, in any case, "controlled," "rational" and "legitimate" violence of the colonial state . . . But the violence of the "native" has other, specifically Oriental characteristics . . .' (*SS6*, p. 168).

Other essays follow a different technical strategy and pursue the subaltern in individual surviving documents by detailed pieces of deconstruction. The emphasis is upon the act of deconstruction and the theoretical imperatives which underpin the technology of the approach. The lead here is again given by Guha, initially with a preliminary foray in the first volume (*SS1*, pp. 1–8) and then with an elaborated discussion in the second volume. With 'The prose of counter-insurgency' (*SS2*, pp. 1–42) Guha brings to Indian studies Roland Barthes's procedures for analysing texts through the semiology of signs. The concern is with signifiers, the words, phrases and contexts used in texts, and with what is signified by them, the deepening levels of implications and connotations. He establishes his point by pondering over two British reports, one of an 1831, the other of an

1855, uprising, and from them argues that the contemporary record is not 'uncontaminated by bias, judgement and opinion' (*SS2*, p. 15), that in fact they represent documents of counter-insurgency. The point is more than effectively made and justifies the complex technology adopted to establish the proof. However, it is surely Barthes's point that all language, that is, all signifiers, have significations, and are therefore, to echo Guha's terminology, contaminated. It is not only the prose of counter-insurgency that is contaminated but all prose. Guha's is nevertheless a brilliant probing into what older-fashioned more conventional historians would call bias in history, and a demonstration of the need to query the source, the creator, of evidence rather than to accept uncritically what the source itself apparently maintains. But in Guha's project the analysis goes further: he locates his deconstructed text within the creation of knowledge and the processes of control by the Raj, the 'complex of coercive intervention . . . with arms and words' that constituted the Raj's 'code of pacification' (*SS2*, p. 15). He poses a subsidiary question: if this was the case with the primary texts, the primary discourse of Empire, was it also the case with the secondary and tertiary discourses, subsequent texts and histories of Empire and even of later Indian commentators? Again, Guha's answer is in the affirmative, and of course, following Barthes, they must be. And, again, they are constructions of insurgency which differ from past reality because of the present concerns of those who created the texts.

In his final essay in the series, 'Dominance without hegemony and its historiography' (*SS6*, pp. 210–309), Guha returns to this kind of point by analysing British histories of India in the eighteenth and nineteenth centuries but does not advance the analytical technology. Nor does Bernard Cohn's 'The command of language and the language of command' (*SS4*, pp. 276–329) add to the methodological debate though it does address the issue of how Raj control of language and education and Raj codification processes around language operated as part of the Raj apparatus of constructing knowledge and power over the subcontinent. The problem with this general approach is that once the basic point is made and accepted, that language reflects power and the systems of knowledge, and that knowledge is determined by the needs of power and is formulated through those needs, then perhaps there is little more to be said. The explanation may become mechanical and deterministic—and even circular. What then becomes the operative question, why power takes the form it does, why knowledge assumes the shape it does is not always answered in ways that permit explanation of the specificity of variant forms of power and knowledge. Because it has happened therefore it is a product of power and that is essentially all that can be said. The explanation ceases to explain and tends towards reflex cliché and dogma.

There is another dimension to the issue of power/knowledge which gets less explicit attention in these volumes. That is, the construction of knowledge and power by the other élite that features in the text, the Indian élites. It features in some of Pandey's work but is more explicitly addressed in Chatterjee's typically thoughtful analyses of the Congress discourse of power and Gandhian theory ('Gandhi and the critique of civil society' in *SS3*, pp. 153–96) and of religion and social structure ('Caste and subaltern consciousness' in *SS6*, pp. 169–209). Against the grain of the author's specific intent some of Guha's final essay ('Dominance without hegemony and its historiography' in *SS6*, pp. 210–309) reads more as exposition of Indian élite strategies of codification and their creation of processual and discursive power/knowledge structures than as explication of the discourse of subalternity.

To return to the technology of the project, Shahid Amin in a essay that is deservedly becoming a classic deconstructs in a different way in his 'Approver's testimony, judicial discourse: The case of Chauri Chaura' (*SS5*, pp. 166–202). His gaze at approver's testimony in court does not focus on the significations and connotations necessarily contained within any written text but sees how being a Crown witness in a trial requires the creation of self-implicating evidence as well as 'evidence' tailored to the needs of prosecution ritual. Distorted and false information is therefore a function of the situation of the approver in court which enables the court/the state to operate as a mechanism of social control by transcreating an initial political action into a criminal act, and thus bring it within the realm of criminal discourse. The approver's is not 'reliable' evidence either for trial purposes (though the courts so utilise it) or for historians without further analysis. Approver's testimony is thus not about the signification of language but of the function for which language and meaning are created and the locale in which this happens. A similar methodological point is made by Guha in his use of a narrative fragment concerning the events surrounding the death of Chandra after a failed abortion ('Chandra's death' in *SS5*, pp. 135–65). Here the recorded direct speech of witnesses in trial processes deprives individuals of their individuality and positions them in stereotypical roles as criminals. Guha shows that what the witnesses say in the record of their direct speech and how they say it, is formed and moulded by the constraints of the legal context in which the actors are placed. The result enables the codification of their activities within legal categorisations and brings them within the purview of punishment. It also, as Guha notes, takes the actors out of history and out of their context and it is this that he attempts to restore. He recontextualises the murder but in doing so places Chandra and her relatives and friends not only in the discourse in which they existed but in the discourse which Guha and his colleagues are establishing in these volumes. She becomes the exemplar of the subaltern condition, and specifically here of a female subalternity which challenges 'the limits of a solidarity that pretends to be neutral to gender' (*SS6*, p. 165). As she moves into a world of female solidarity and opts for the abortion which is to cause her death, the functional and contextual analysis of text, rather than the semiotic, bring us back to the subaltern subject and to the project of the six volumes.

Having written so much about how the subaltern writers achieve their effect throughout the volumes it may seem strange that I come back to the subaltern so late in this review. But what is striking is that throughout the volumes the subaltern subject continually disappears within the historians' subaltern project. Part of that project is methodological and it is that which I have considered hitherto in the discussion. Part of it is conceptual and ideological and part factual and informative. All three inform and illumine one another and each is a necessary part of the whole.

The initial formulation of the project was brilliantly simple though its implications are extraordinarily dense and subtle, a subtlety intensified by the range of different skills and approaches of the various contributors. Subalternity provided a strategy for moving away from the mazes and the dead ends into which rural history had been moving with its intricate analyses of what constituted poor, middle and wealthy peasantry. It confronted a dominant South Asian historiographical mode which focused on the politics of élite nationalism and substituted another modality that drew from the current intellectual contexts and political debates as much as it related to trends in the historiography of areas beyond the subcontinent. The range of referents was already large in the first volumes: Marx, Gramsci, Hobsbawm, E.P. Thompson, James Scott and the like, and it expands as the series progresses to incorporate, as I have noted, deconstruction and postmodern writers, Barthes, a little Foucault and others, while Spivak in her essay promised access to the intellectual Mecca, entry into 'the élite theoretical *ateliers* in France' (*SS4*, p. 363). It is noteworthy however that French historians of mentalité do not feature until late in the series as significant methodological influences, and when they do it is infrequently. The notable exception is Sumit Sarkar whose essays come closest in approach to the mentalité history produced in France and elsewhere.

The intellectual conceiving of the project is linked with the ideological context in which it evolved. The background was the activist world of the late 1960s and early 1970s, the priority of the need for mass political action with the combining of Marxist class theory as reinterpreted through Gramsci and brought into vogue by recent English translations and numerous commentaries. The term subaltern as used in the series derived from Gramsci's use, a usage explained at length in a paper published by Arnold elsewhere.[5] The combining of polarisation and action was part of the praxis and theory of engaged intellectuals of the 1970s in many places, not the least England, India and Australia from which the subaltern writers came. Poulantzas' neo-Marxism with his view of class consciousness as expressed through and in action pointed to one way in which theory was going, while Marxist–Leninist activists in India with their strategy of creating rural polarisation by militant action against local élites pointed to the way in which party cadres were moving. The Marxist–Leninist programme as put out in some of its early polemic is in fact often close to the earliest formulations of the subaltern approach to social analysis.

Given the emphasis on polarisation, the subaltern is located as an independent agent. But while the terminology of subaltern classes derives from Gramsci, another element of Gramsci's thinking, that of the hegemony of the upper classes and its downward thrust, is explicitly denied by the subaltern historians. Hardiman mounts a strong attack on factions, which might otherwise be viewed as the social and political mechanisms through which hegemony operates in an Indian context (*SS1*, pp. 198–232). Ajit K. Chaudhuri's complex discussion paper ('In search of a subaltern Lenin,' *SS5*, pp. 236–51) draws on Lenin and Althusser to consider the ramifications of socialist consciousness as being 'brought from the outside to the working class' (ibid., p. 236) and seems to conclude with an argument for 'the specificity of the worker's rebellion' (ibid., 250) and the lack of interaction— though I should point out I do not find his text particularly lucid. Finally, in the last volume it is Guha who puts the strongest case against hegemony in his 'Dominance without hegemony and its historiography' (*SS6*, pp. 210–309). His case is based upon an analysis of British historiography of India, its assumptions of hegemony and its patent inability to explain what is different about India. He denies the Raj a hegemonic role but is less convincing on the hegemony of Indian élites. I quote part of his otherwise persuasive concluding remarks:

> What is there in the power relations of that rule [British rule in India] which makes the colonial state in our subcontinent so fundamentally different from its architect, the British metropolitan state? Where lies the originality of Indian culture of the colonial era and why does it defy understanding either as a replication of the liberal-bourgeois culture of nineteenth-century Britain or as the mere survival of an antecedent precapitalist culture? And how adequate are representations of that colonial past to any genuine search for any answer to those questions? (*SS6*, p. 308)

By contrast Cohn earlier in his delineation of the reordering and objectifying of Indian thought and culture by European scholarly methods had reached somewhat differing conclusions before moving on to posit a hopeful utopian subaltern future:

> The Indians who increasingly became drawn into the process of transformation of their traditions and modes of thought were, however, far from passive. In the long run the authoritarian control which the British

tried to exercise over new social and material technologies were taken over by Indians and put to purposes which led to the ultimate erosion of British authority. The consciousness of Indians at all levels in society was transformed as they refused to become specimens in a European-controlled museum . . . (*SS4*, p. 329)

While hegemony is explicitly denied in the conceptual discussions in the series, it emerges in the texts of many of the specific essays about subaltern resistance and is centred on discussions of negative consciousness and so on. Even in the quotation from Cohn above, the ultimate erosion of British authority seems to refer to the victory of hegemonised Indian élites over the British and the achievement of their position of domination in post-independence India rather than of subaltern achievement. Others have more detail of the interactions. Chatterjee attempts to handle the issue of caste by considering whether it is autonomous or borrowed, his frame of reference being the subaltern and Indian élites. If it is an ideological system imposed by the super-structure on those below and if it reflects material relations then the explanation is functional, circular—and not useful. If caste represents an Indian form of material relations at the base then caste itself is a material reality rather than an ideology. His solution is to opt for the specificity of different dharmas affected by relations of power, rather than being held together by any single dharma. He denies the Dumontian hierarchy of ideology, sees consciousness alienated from the dominant dharma but 'bound to nothing else than its spirit of resolute negativity.' His conclusion is that 'subaltern consciousness is not merely structure, characterised solely by negativity; it is also history, shaped and developed through a changing process of interaction between the dominant and the subordinate' (*SS6*, p. 206). Here he at least seems to be approaching a modified Gramscian hegemony.

If hegemony is absent as a theoretic of the subaltern universe, so too is Foucault's perception of power. The early Foucault is certainly present: power as represented through control over the body, the containing of the body in delimited, self-contained universes created through changes in and reflecting current discourses of power, the reifying of phenomena in order to establish control. What is absent is his view of power as disaggregated, permeating and pervasive: 'Power must be analysed as something which . . . only functions in the form of a chain . . . Power is employed and exercised through a net-like organisation. And not only do individuals circulate between its threads; they are always in the position of simultaneously undergoing and exercising this power. They are not only its inert or consenting targets; they are always also the elements of its articulation.'[6] Being concerned with opposition, the logic of the strategy of subalternist historiography inhibits acceptance of any such approach.

The subaltern is a creation, a reification of historians. No one in India called themselves subaltern, nor do any of the writers quote Indian terms which were equivalent. The categorisation constructs those who joined in assorted and diverse acts of geographically widely dispersed violent action, it brings them together as subalterns and, increasingly frequently in the later volumes, calls them subaltern classes. There is hence a quasi-Marxist tenor to the perception of subalterns. The frisson is discussed by Marxist writers in the series who try to marry subalternity with class formation through examining the material base of both and through assessment of action as an index of class/subaltern consciousness. The marriage is not entirely successful, or necessary for the formulation of the subaltern concept since the sign of subalternity is resistance and the ideas that go along with that action.

A critical point about subalternism is that it combines polarised social category with the mentality of opposition. The subaltern is presented as the oppressed in the act of protest and with the consciousness of action. Everything is brought together in the moment which combines mental state and action as one. Subaltern consciousness as it emerges in these texts is the consciousness of resistance and in resistance. Such consciousness may contain within it ideas of religion and caste, ideas of status and power but they are all subsumed in the act of protest and opposition to domination. Religion here is a focus for subaltern expression, it has no role otherwise as a set of belief systems which energise people. In this sense, though the volumes are exemplars of mentality, they exemplify, obviously according to the writers, the mentality of subaltern resistance. Though religion and various other underlying structures of social and cultural mentalité are contained within the analyses—and are usually handled with considerable skill and sensitivity—they have a functional role as components of subaltern resistance. They do not feature in their own right in the way they do in mentalité treatments in European historiography. Critical then to the enterprise is the point of opposition, the polarisation inherent in the exercise of power and resistance to power. In praxis, the effect of this is to deprive individuals of presence in the pages of these histories. The statement may seem quixotic and requires further discussion.

What the volumes are about is the reification of a collective personification. They are about the subaltern, subalternism, subalternity, the collective act of resistance, the idea represented by that resistance as it is analysed and explicated by the historian. Though the historians here are meticulous in presenting all the minute detail, the culmination of the determinism of preceding change in material conditions and even in cultural and religious perceptions, all of these are subsumed in the moment and point of opposition. It is not that resistance provides one of the few means available for historians to penetrate into the consciousness of those who leave few records and who do not usually feature in the record, though the group of historians do sometimes use resistance for such retrieval purposes, it is rather that the resistance itself is what the historians are concerned with. It is their subject matter and it is the collective resistance with which they are concerned. Ultimately they make and repeat the same point—which is of course the purpose of the volumes but it is a point that becomes elaborated as being central to history. So it is how changing land and other material determinants affect the collective subaltern, how modes of thought affect the collective group in and at the point of resistance that is important to these historians' narratives. What is presented is continued social warfare. Despite all the narrative of the particularities of change in various variables, what is offered is not processual change but an underlying, consistently similar structure of continued resistance. In these narratives the individual has little place and is presented usually only as the exemplar of resistance. Otherwise there is no space available for the individual. Notable among a handful of other exceptions is Sumit Sarkar's use of the Kalki-Avatar incident to hang a pertinent analysis of social history (*SS6*, pp. 1–53). Although obviously individuals do feature in the accounts they more often than not figure as leaders of subaltern resistance, those thrown up by the event, that is, those who are made significant in and by the event. Thus Bhadra's account of some people involved in the course of the uprising of 1857 is a discussion of local leaders, not of the individuals who constituted their following ('Four rebels of eighteen-fifty-seven' in *SS4*, pp. 229–75). In this sense the subaltern historians despite themselves conform to one of the English meanings of subaltern—a subaltern officer—rather than the meaning prescribed by Guha in his opening definition or that intended by Gramsci where the Italian seems not to have such a variant meaning. Where individuals do feature, as in Guha's 'Chandra's death,' it is in situations where the polarisation is according to the politics of gender and the idea of opposition to dominant élites elides into the contradictions of gender power. Apart from a few other exceptions, the writings of Sumit Sarkar being the most obvious, the texts are about collective approaches and collective attitudes, collective phenomena—to religion, communalism, alcohol, rumour and so on.

Even the moment of resistance is curiously depersonalised in these accounts. Veena Das in the final discussion paper of the series has noted the series brings violence as a key variable to serious consideration but she also notes that the texts avoid crowd studies (*SS6*, p. 321). While the moral economy of the crowd as mediated through Thompson and Scott is certainly present, the crowd study as developed by Rudé, the Tillys and others is far less prominent. The crowd as an active force, and the crowd as composed of individuals and groups, has little place in these studies except when they exemplify the logic of the background causations traced by the historians and when they represent the rightness of the subaltern situation.

Subalterns are curiously elusive in these volumes even if the subaltern is clearly not. The series succeeds spectacularly in making the subaltern the subject of his/her own history. It establishes a change in the focus of writing history dealing with the subcontinent that should endure. Yet does the series succeed in substantiating Guha's initial programme—to demonstrate that the subaltern has autonomy and is the maker of his own history. Though subalternity is about resistance it would seem the subaltern cannot have autonomy since he is located in a universe which he does not control and which he seeks to resist. Likewise he cannot be the maker of his own history since he is part of a context which is not of his own making. Whether as a category he has autonomy within that specific environment may well be the case. His attitudes, ideas, perceptions, behaviours may well be unique to him and his social environment, all of which have their own life and are subject to processes following their own logic but subaltern historians are not concerned with that identity, only with identity expressed through opposition to those outside the category. Whether subalterns can inhabit a domain isolated and cut off from what is happening elsewhere, in the centres of power of various kinds and dimensions is another matter. Their acts of resistance link up with, interact with, intersect with what is happening around them. They are not then autonomous even if the alliances are at the least merely strategic, although some essays present interactions that are more than the merely strategic. Thus Arnold, in writing of an 1879–80 hill rebellion, states it was 'a complex amalgam of élite grievance and subaltern discontent' (*SS1*, p. 126).

Again, as Spivak has noted (*SS4*, p. 333), the Subaltern series accounts are accounts of failure. Failure is not the site of autonomy. And what failure does to consciousness, how it affects resistance is less well delineated, excepting as some essays note, to create a tradition of resistance, to provide the base for further opposition (for example, Ramachandra Guha's conclusion to his essay on forestry and social protest in Kumaun, *SS4*, p. 97). Others, like Arnold, see uprisings over a century as reflecting changes in the social demography of an area and consequent changes in the hillmen's relationship to material conditions (in his 'Rebellious hillmen: the Guden-Rampa risings 1839–1924' in *SS1*, pp. 140–2). One or two writers suggest the opposite, the dispersion and disappearance of resistance (see Hardiman's conclusion to his essay on the Bhils of Eastern Gujarat in *SS5*, p. 54). Is that all that failure does, either create a genealogy or disperse a set of mind for resistance? In either case, the volumes do not fully explore the consequences of failure: they assert the primacy of struggle as a necessary condition of subalternity—a constant of that condition.

If there is a middle-range interpretative question in the series, it is why the subalterns did not come together as a class, why they did not become the makers of a new independent state. It is also part of the underlying political agenda of the series as far as India is concerned. In Guha's words: 'It is the study of this *historic failure of the nation to come to its own . . . it is the study of this failure which constitutes the central problematic of the historiography of colonial India*' (*SS1*, p. 7). If the answer is the nature of power then the subaltern again does not have autonomy, except possibly, as I have suggested, in a limited sense of consciousness contained within the category. But a mentality of resistance, a mindset that is independent, in effect means the perception of power, the nature of power, is altered so it is delimited, no longer representing dominance. The insurrection of a subjugated knowledge, to use Foucault's term, should mean that the conceptualisation of power must also be altered. If the logic of mental perceptions is taken as far as it can go, the subaltern ceases being subaltern, the subject matter of oppression disappears. If the conclusion is unacceptable and the forces of material and conceptual power are reasserted as primary elements, then subaltern autonomy disappears.

In practice in these pages the subaltern does not disappear, even if subalterns do. Instead the subaltern becomes hero. By such reification he (or she or they) serve and satisfy other underlying needs that history writing meets and again the subaltern is apparently appropriated for purposes other than their own. While the quality of the intellectual analysis of virtually all the essays presents the logic of contextual oppression and opposition to that location with analytical rigour of the highest order, there is an underlying emotive content to much of the analysis. Despite the logical form of the presentation, there surfaces from time to time an alternate text which constructs the subaltern within another contextual level, so that the subaltern stands for a different range of associations. In places there is a tendency to romanticise the subaltern in the suffering of oppression or in the failure of resistance, in the impossibility of resistance achieving change. The inexorability of fate, the impossibility of success, is the subject matter of tragedy—and becomes the underlying agenda of these histories. And it is the techniques of analysis of a Hayden White that are required to handle the modalities inherent in the subaltern hero as it gradually emerges in these volumes. The subaltern may be a historical subject but here also becomes a literary object, an objectification of the forces of the classic world working on human destiny. The will and agency of the subaltern is dissipated in the need for epic narrative, in epic portrayal. The tendency is most clearly articulated late in the series, again by Guha. The tenor of subaltern as mood subject, as tragic hero underlines his thoughts on the death of Chandra after her abortion. He sees it as

> indeed a classic instance of choice overruled by necessity—by fate, in short. For Chandra was killed by the very act which was meant to save her from living death in a ghetto of social rejects. Yet here, as in all tragedies, the triumph of fate helped to enhance rather than diminish human dignity . . . (*SS5*, p. 161)

The transition is subtle, from independent agent to objectified hero. Such romantic distancing of the subaltern may in fact explain some of the appeal the series has evoked since its appearance. There is a richness in emotive connotations attaching to the subaltern that seems to be continually growing. It will be interesting to see where the construing of the subaltern will lead in the next decade of the publication of the series, in the years without Guha's inspiration as editor. While the overtly political parameters, the immediate political programmatics, may become less relevant, the subaltern seems likely to fill a role in the historical myth-making of the new Indian state. Subalternity privileges the role of continued dissent and establishes a traditional, legitimated, genealogy of opposition. It provides a consciousness of a past as colonial subjects (the phrase is from Veena Das, *SS6*, p. 310) which eliminates the subordination inherent in other readings of that past, and by prioritising the autonomy of resistance goes far to eliminate the dominator as actor or influential agent. In depicting the subaltern as hero, it establishes a symbol amenable to appropriation by the dominant orders of the new polity, the intellectuals who construct the new knowledge of the state, those who purvey it or turn it into cultural artifacts, and those who use it in their political strategies. The subaltern has value but do subalterns?

Notes and References

1. This essay reviews the first six volumes of the *Subaltern Studies* series. Volumes of this series have been reviewed in virtually all major academic journals concerned with South Asia. Typical of the kind of debate sparked by the series is Rosalind O'Hanlon, 'Recovering the subject: Subaltern studies and histories of resistance in colonial South Asia,' *Modern Asian Studies*, 22, February 1, 1988, pp. 189–224; Burton Stein, 'A decade of historical efflorescence,' *South Asia Research*, 10, November 2, 1990, pp. 125–38; C.A. Bayly, 'Rallying around the subaltern,' *Journal of Peasant Studies*, 16, 1, 1988, pp. 110–20 amongst a host of other reviews.

2. There is also a paper which addresses this problem by Julie Stephens in her extended attempt to bring authorship, contemporaneity, feminist theory and historical writing together. See her 'Feminist fictions: A critique of the category "non-Western woman" in feminist writings on India,' in *SS6*, pp. 92–126. The paper is the object of bitter attack by Susie Tharu (*SS6*, pp. 126–32). These seem to be the only essays in the six volumes which bear a note advising that the concurrence of the editorial team with the views expressed 'may not be presumed' (*SS6*, p. 92, footnote 1).

3. Ashis Nandy, 'Final encounter: The politics of the assassination of Gandhi,' *At the edge of psychology. Essays in politics and culture* (Delhi: Oxford University Press, 1980), p. 71.

4. Sarkar's comment on this issue best sums up the approach: 'Yet total relativism, a complete absorption in the enchantments of a kind of epistemological hall of mirrors, is hardly viable . . . for the discipline of history. The craft does seem to require the construction of narratives of the "as-if-true" kind, constructions which should remain open-ended and which are privileged only within the text the historian is engaged in composing at that moment' (*SS6*, p. 4).

5. David Arnold, 'Gramsci and peasant subalternity in India,' *Journal of Peasant Studies*, 11, 4, 1984, pp. 155–77.

6. Michel Foucault, *Power/Knowledge: Selected interviews and other writings 1972–1977*, ed., Colin Gordon (New York: Pantheon Books, 1980), p. 98.

Situating the Subaltern:
History and Anthropology in the
Subaltern Studies Project*

K. SIVARAMAKRISHNAN

> When one wants to study men . . . one must first learn to look
> into the distance; one must first see difference.
>
> —Jean-Jacques Rousseau

> Culture is the common frontier of anthropology with historio-
> graphy.
>
> —Alfred Kroeber

Introduction: Anthropology and History

A PIONEER OF disciplinary fusion, Bernard Cohn (1987: 44) has persuasively argued that 'one of the primary subject matters of an historical anthropology or anthropological history is . . . the colonial situation.' Not surprisingly new approaches in combining anthropology and history gained prominence and generated theoretical debates, specially in literatures dealing with colonialism and in the

*I am grateful to David Apter, Sugata Bose, Indrani Chatterjee, Joseph Erring-ton, Vinay Gidwani, Ramachandra Guha, Sumit Guha, William Kelly, Yutaka Nagahara, Gyan Prakash, James Scott and Helen Siu for commenting on earlier drafts of this essay. Special thanks go to Daniel Nugent for detailed comments and encouragement.

study of resistance and power (Cohn 1980, 1981; Davis 1981; Darnton 1984; Comaroff and Comaroff 1987, 1991; Dirks 1987; Hunt 1989; Feierman 1990; Sewell 1992). These authors have shared with Cohn the belief that human history has been culturally shaped, a culture that in turn was transformed by historical processes.[1] This has often meant—methodologically speaking—looking for the 'strange and the surprising in the familiar landscape of historical texts' (Davis 1981: 275). Another notable practitioner of anthropological history has remarked in a similar vein, 'the anthropological impulse is chiefly felt not in model building, but in locating new problems, in seeking old problems in new ways, in an emphasis upon norms or value systems and upon rituals, in attention to expressive functions of forms of riot and disturbance, upon symbolic expressions of authority, control and hegemony' (Thompson 1977: 248).

Apart from indicating the importance of studying folklore, music and other oral materials to recover ideologies excluded from the written record, Thompson has consistently insisted on placing such study in the same analytic field as the study of privileged histories, sharing with Cohn (1980: 40) the belief that 'the dispossessed have to be put in the same contextual framework as the élites and ruling groups who are engaged in the maintenance and representation of social orders.' Interestingly, this resonates with Foucault's evaluation of the Enlightenment episteme and the development of representational theories. For instance, Foucault argues the case for the integration of history and ethnology in the following manner:

> It is no doubt difficult to maintain that ethnology has a fundamental relation with historicity since it is traditionally the knowledge we have of people without histories yet ethnology itself is only possible on the basis of a certain situation, of an absolutely singular event which involves not only our historicity but also that of all men who can constitute the object of an ethnology; ethnology has its roots in fact, in a possibility that properly belongs to the history of our culture, even more to its fundamental relation with the whole of history . . . (Foucault 1973: 377)

More recently, drawing on some of the same and other intellectual traditions, Roseberry (1989) has described the concatenation of structure and conjuncture as a constant process. According to him, culture is perennially being shaped, produced, reproduced, and transformed by activity, rather than being something that encapsulates activity until the structure of culture can no longer hold. The dialectics are conveyed pithily when he says:

> Culture is at once socially constituted (it is the product of present and past activity) and socially constitutive (it is part of the meaningful context in which action takes place). (Roseberry 1989: 42)

As he further elucidates, cultural meaning is important because social and political actors, and their actions are formed in part by their pre-existing conceptions of the world and self. Cultural differentiation, social and political inequalities are equally important as they are the substance of the historical formation of anthropological subjects within processes of uneven development (Roseberry 1989). It is significant that despite their dissimilar theoretical origins, both Foucault and Roseberry recommend a historic turn in their respective appeals for a critical ethnology.

The convergent project of history and anthropology can encompass the discussion of state-making processes through contest and cooperation at different levels of society, where the past is recaptured in the present along patterned pathways which are both culturally and politically delineated.[2] The study of colonial encounters can most profitably proceed from such an integrative perspective of history and anthropology. The efficacy of the study would, however, depend on the precise way in which history and culture—as analytical categories and approaches—are brought together in a single conceptual framework. Many of the challenges for such a theoretical and methodological fusion are illuminated by the scholarship of peasant resistance in colonial South Asia. This essay reviews the contribution of Subaltern Studies in responding to these challenges and evaluates the anthropological history they provide through their unique perspective on rural unrest.

Delimitations

In a terse note prefacing the sixth volume in 1989, Ranajit Guha signed off as the editor of the Subaltern Studies series, thus bringing to an end his decade-long and magisterial leadership of the collective.[3] Their accomplishments have been several, but we shall be concerned here primarily with *Subaltern Studies'* sustained attempt to combine history and anthropology which energised and drew upon a larger trend in cultural historical studies in different parts of the world. Commenting on this, a contributor to the seventh volume of *Subaltern Studies* notes, 'Historians have along with other mainstream social scientists, traditionally neglected discourse . . . anthropologists were, by contrast, more attentive to these questions. Consequently, it is not surprising that new forms of history writing for instance *Subaltern Studies* . . . use a great number of the anthropologist's tools' (Kaviraj 1992: 36.49n). Such a reading of anthropology as the study of discourse is selective. Curiously enough, *Subaltern Studies'* engagement with anthropology has always been selective. But this most recent elective affinity has brought subalternists to an intellectual terrain shared by some anthropologists, many literary critics and the project of post-colonial critique that, in the words of Gyan Prakash's (1994: 1475) sympathetic review of *Subaltern Studies*, 'seeks to undo the Eurocentrism produced by the institution of the West's trajectory, its appropriation of the other as history.'

Admittedly, 'anthropology' and 'history' convey widely varying meanings when understood from different perspectives. For our purpose they are taken to represent the antinomious relationship between culture and political economy, ideal and material, consensus and conflict, community and class, that frequently characterise anthropology and history respectively, when stereotypically contrasted. Practitioners in both disciplines have used structural formulations to explain human behaviour and the course of events. But the vital difference often was between teleological historical processes driven by economic and material structures in society as opposed to timeless cultural ones that motivated human agents in cycles of production and reproduction.[4] *Subaltern Studies* resonate with the wider anthropology and history convergence we started with because in their approach, too, these facile oppositions are rendered suspect, interrogated and demonstrated to be theoretically limiting. At the same time we also need to point out some problematic new oppositions that *Subaltern Studies* erect. As Suleri (1992: 11) puts it, the binaristic approach of the subalternists runs the danger of stressing cultural difference and thereby the self–other dichotomy, and thus coming 'perilously close to a political allegorisation of romance.' The question is, why is this important? These binarisms of coloniser–colonised, Western–non-Western, domination–resistance help initiate the analysis of power but also constrain the study of the ways in which power is engaged, contested, deflected and appropriated (Cooper 1994: 1517).

Arguably the main goal of *Subaltern Studies* was to develop a critique of, and an alternative to, the standard nationalist and 'neo-imperialist' history of modern India. Guha (1982: 1–9) succinctly presents the shortcomings of what he calls 'élite historiography.' Methodologically the challenge was to recover the voice of the subaltern.[5] It was here that the *Subaltern Studies* project intersected with some anthropological approaches and their concern to hear the Other speak; to elicit the narrative constructions of identity among subordinated groups in rural society and elucidate the cultural structures mediating and shaping subaltern resistance and protest. This aspect of their work can be summed up in the words of Ana Alonso (1988: 51), who says 'the interpenetration of meaning and memory implies that history and anthropology have a common ground.' Subalternists have also displayed a commitment to documenting the local agency motivating peasant unrest and this again has meant recourse to writing 'history from below' to discover the cultural bases of protest, since political-economic approaches divested the subaltern of agency. In this respect, too, *Subaltern Studies* have turned to anthropology and cultural studies paralleling the work of the Birmingham Centre for Cultural Studies, a luminary of which said 'an interest in history from below has crucial political consequences. It can restore a sense of agency, a sense of the capacity of . . . the repressed' (Hall 1978: 9–10).

Therefore, the subalternist contribution to the convergence of history and anthropology is important. Resorting to anthropology and history from below can recover partial and hidden histories but it is not enough to juxtapose these fugitive accounts with master narratives and their exalted claims to total knowledge. The subaltern story may lose its punch if not situated in context. Comaroff and

Comaroff (1992: 17) stress this very point when they say 'improperly contextualised, the stories of ordinary people . . . stand in danger of remaining just that: stories. To become something more these . . . have to be situated in wider worlds of power and meaning that give them life.'

To clarify, let us consider the related issue of studying rural resistance and protest. It has aptly been remarked that scholars associated with *Subaltern Studies* have 'been instrumental in bringing the study of resistance on the Indian sub-continent to center-stage in historical work' (Haynes and Prakash 1992: 7). They have explored a wide range of issues hitherto neglected in South Asia as forms of popular protest—communal disturbances, grain riots, uprisings of hill peoples, small-scale peasant insurgencies and struggles over forest rights. In doing so, *Subaltern Studies* have not only uncovered new arenas of contest and a new level of analysis but have also brought into relief the limitation of frameworks confined to the study of resistance. *Subaltern Studies* have defined a subaltern consciousness separate from hegemonic cultural forms, and rooted in myth, religion and magical belief, that was realised in the practice of rural resistance. *Subaltern Studies* thereby infused anthropology into social history. However, these scholars authored a unique and somewhat flawed anthropological history by conceiving the subaltern ideology in what may be characterised as Lévi-Straussian terms.[6] Any binaristic mode of analysis is somewhat reminiscent of Lévi-Strauss and structured oppositions. But more particularly, in contributions discussing the creation and expression of subaltern consciousness, the subalternists treat myths and religiosity as indexical of a subaltern ontology that only surfaces at specific moments to reveal an underlying structural pattern that was distinctively is own.[7] These moments are defined by their confrontationist nature, by their explosive character. We are then faced with an opposition between resistance and power, a disjunction between subaltern protest and élite politics.

Through an examination of the subalternist project we can proceed to an alternative framework that would place 'all forms of resistance within the ordinary life of power . . . where social structure appears as a constellation of contradictory and contestatory processes' and would argue that 'neither domination nor resistance is autonomous; the two are so entangled that it becomes difficult to analyze one without discussing the other' (Haynes and Prakash 1992: 2–3). But unravelling the subalternist project is a complicated business, since the corpus itself is highly diverse. We have perforce to select a few salient categories (like subalternity itself) and expose the genealogical connections to anthropological/cultural theory and literature, illustrating thereby the manner in which the subalternists have drafted their version of anthropological history. In doing so it seems appropriate to briefly outline the central claims of the subalternist project, its origins in the Gramscian notion of the subaltern peasantry and review the major achievements and critiques of the corpus. We will trace the movement of subaltern historiography from its inspiration by Gramsci, through the involvement with structural modes of cultural analysis and engagement with Foucault and his conception of power, where anthropology and history converge to yield a unified approach. In what is probably the clearest formulation of the project in Foucauldian terms, Guha (1987b: xx) wrote, 'anthropological history will develop a study of political culture, a culture of power relations, constructed by the interaction of coloniser and colonised . . . it follows therefore, that according to this approach the interpenetration of power and knowledge constitutes the very fabric of colonialism.'

Subaltern Studies—The Project and Its Existing Critique

Originating in a critique of all metanarratives of Indian historiography—nationalist, Marxist and revisionist (Cambridge school and others that discounted the effects of colonialism)—*Subaltern Studies* repudiated the 'privileged themes of global capitalist modernisation and focused instead off-centre on what those themes exclude: histories of the subordinate whose identity . . . resides in difference' (O'Hanlon and Washbrook 1992: 143). According to them, neocolonialist, nationalist and Marxist historiography attributes the making of the Indian nation and the development of national consciousness to processes of élite conflict and élite response to the stimulus of political and cultural institutions, opportunities and resources provided by colonial rule (Guha 1982: 1–3). This historiography failed because it did not comprehend the internal dynamic of the mass movements studied.

Responding to the work of Alavi (1973) and others, Marxist historians have scoured the countryside in quest of incipient class conflict and the revolutionary peasant. Some of them recognised the economic differentiation that occurred in the nineteenth century which weakened the concept of peasant homogeneity.[8] However, even as these later Marxists delved into particular regional histories they continued searching for organisational features in social movements that mediated between peasant protest and larger counter-hegemonic discourses like omnibus nationalism (Dhanagare 1983, Prakash 1985). As a result, the symbolic materials generated in the struggles organised by Mahatma Gandhi, to take but one example, were never analysed in terms of their incorporation into peasant ideology. *Subaltern Studies* rightly came out against such divestiture of the consciousness of peasantries. In a series of studies they sought to rectify this omission (Guha 1983, Amin 1984, Chatterjee 1984, Sarkar 1984, Hardiman 1987, Guha 1989).

Another contention of *Subaltern Studies* is that all preceding forms of historiography have excluded the rebel as the conscious subject of his own history, incorporating him only as a contingent element in another history of the march of British imperium or Indian socialism respectively. Hence all the rich material of myths, rituals, rumours, hopes for a Golden Age and fears of an imminent end to the world, all of which speaks of the self-alienation of the rebel, was wasted on sterile discourse looking for a grand design (Guha 1983). In recovering subaltern subjectivity by paying attention to precisely those materials that élite historiography has shunned, subalternists contend that Asia's underclasses 'regularly generated' their own forms of social action . . . and possessed an insurgent consciousness' (Haynes and Prakash 1992: 7). *Subaltern Studies*, therefore, dispute the validity of factional analysis. An early and seminal essay, for example, contends that the Great Indian Faction is in fact a myth, an artifact of liberal social science (Hardiman 1982). This critique is directed against the

'Cambridge School' of historians led by Anil Seal, who in the 1960s and 1970s argued that the dynamic of action in the rise of Indian nationalism was factional rather than class-based politics—Indians primarily responding to opportunities for office created by the colonial government.

Such a metropolis-centred approach was complemented in rural India by Eric Stokes (1978, 1986). While heralding the return of the peasant to South Asian history, Stokes wrote regional accounts of rural revolt in terms of supra-regional kinship affiliations and embattled high-caste rentiers.[9] The emphasis was on the vertical integration of struggles through caste, clan and patron–client ties by which local politics were drawn into the national mainstream (Mukherjee 1970, Charlesworth 1978, Fisher 1978).[10] In contrast, the subalternists hold that there is an autonomous domain of peasant politics exemplified by peasant insurgency, where there was a common notion of resistance to élite domination that resulted in a horizontal integration of subaltern groups in the said domain as opposed to a vertical integration into élite politics through factions, caste, clan and patron–client relationships (Guha 1982: 3–4). More importantly, *Subaltern Studies* tried to extract the subaltern consciousness through novel use of historical sources as a prelude to establishing the subaltern as the agent of historical change. This effort evoked the compliment 'perhaps for the first time since colonisation Indians are showing signs of reappropriating the capacity to represent themselves' (Inden 1986: 445). It also represented a significant divergence from the Gramscian idea of the subaltern, since for him subaltern groups could not by definition possess autonomy (Arnold 1984).

The concept of subalternity itself is explicitly derived from Gramsci for whom the peasantry was a live force. He recommended close examination of the subaltern consciousness of peasantries revealed in popular belief and folklore (Arnold 1984). Describing subaltern common sense, Gramsci (1971: 325–6), wrote, 'It is a conception that even in the brain of one individual is fragmentary . . . in keeping with the social position of the masses whose philosophy it is.' Gramsci also describes the peasant ideology as emerging from contingent construction bundling together different ideas in bizarre combination. There is a curious resemblance in this formulation to the *bricoleur* of Lévi-Strauss.

The programme of research Gramsci urged was based on a belief that if the historical record were more complete, greater consistency, cohesion and political consciousness might be found in the subaltern classes. *Subaltern Studies* clearly set out with this agenda for South Asia. The idea was not to suggest a two-fold simplification of social hierarchy, but rather to retain in the analysis of peasant protest the essential character of domination and subordination permeating power relationships and evoke the conflict and contradiction found within actual historical situations. Guha (1982: 5, 8) points out that the diversity of social composition of subaltern groups as well as the ambiguities inherent in the concept as applied to India, cannot be forgotten. The category has been used to describe tribals (*adivasi*), low-caste agricultural labourers, sharecroppers, smallholder peasants, artisans, shepherds and migrant labour working in plantations and mines. *Subaltern Studies* thus accomplished a substantial qualification of Gramsci's concept by 'showing the extent to which peasant politics possessed autonomy within . . . encompassing structures of subordination' (Arnold 1984: 169). Which brings us to a more explicit consideration of the existing critique of their work.

One limitation of the method was almost immediately realised by Sarkar (1984) who refers to the preoccupation in *Subaltern Studies* with conflict, violence and confrontation, to the exclusion of both periods of collaboration and quiet resistance in everyday forms.[11] This deficiency is partly rectified in a study by Guha (1987a) who deconstructs the judicial record of a murder trial involving Chandra (a Bagdi low-caste woman in Bengal), her attempted abortion, subsequent death and the prosecution of the village medicine man. He exposes the network of solidarity and fear through which male patriarchy and dominance both leaves its imprint and is eluded in Chandra's death. The subaltern discourse he recovers for history is the evidence given (rather denied) by the women complicit in Chandra's futile attempt to avoid disgrace and excommunication. In death she escaped the sanctions institutionalised convergently by the social system and the juridical one.

There is in Guha's carefully crafted study a keen awareness of domination within kinship networks ostensibly functional and benign, as well as documentation of a mode of resistance that is effective precisely because it was carried out in the external form of compliance. But taking careful account of subaltern initiative in the context of local power relations threatens to dissipate the notion of subaltern unity. As Mallon (1994: 1511) points out, 'Complicity, hierarchy and surveillance within subaltern communities . . . makes clear that no subaltern identity can be pure and transparent, most subalterns are both dominated and dominating subjects.' Ortner (1995) adds that these insights, offered repeatedly by structural Marxism and feminist studies in their different ways, by and large elude *Subaltern Studies*.

The most valuable lesson of the subaltern method, however, remains its focus on the particular forms of subaltern subjectivity, experience and agency. This privileging of marginal discourses and their autonomous construction has been called 'a strategic use of positivist essentialism in a scrupulously visible political interest' (Spivak 1985: 342). In that respect, *Subaltern Studies* deny the structural unity of systems of domination that are attributed to universalistic processes of capitalism (Prakash 1992).[12] But this move to construct an autonomous domain of subaltern politics and ideology also attracted some of the most acute criticism. Pointing to a fundamental contradiction within a project that set out to assail dominant historiography for its conceit of universalising narratives and then created its own universal redemptive categories, O'Hanlon (1988: 191) wrote: 'The figure of the subaltern as self-originating, self-determining, in possession of a sovereign consciousness as defined is to readmit through the back door the classic figure of Western humanism—the rational human subject. The valuable insights that the subaltern method provided into modes of power and élite discourse were blurred in this account by a failure to decentre the monolithic subject-agents of élite historiography and a refusal to acknowledge the creative practice of the subaltern, namely, an ability to appropriate and mould cultural materials of any provenance while discarding those materials—however apparently sacred or integral to an essential subaltern being—that serve little purpose. In this respect *Subaltern Studies* created new foundational categories (Prakash 1990b).

These contradictions were produced in part by the rich tensions within the collective and its programme, and they surfaced with the increased attention paid to the study of power. As Gyan Prakash notes, subaltern agency was doubly besieged. First, as he says, these scholars failed to recognise fully that the subalterns' resistance did not simply oppose power but was also constituted by it.' Second, recovery of the subaltern subject also became difficult given the use by *Subaltern Studies* of 'anti-humanist structuralist and post-structuralist theory' (Prakash 1994: 1480). Ranajit Guha in particular drew explicitly on Saussure, Lévi-Strauss, Jakobson, Barthes and Foucault. This clearly negated the possibility of agency and subaltern autonomy. With the diffusion of the Foucaultian mode of analysis through the later subalternist work, and the discovery of omniscient power relationships, both analytic binarisms of the sort referred to earlier, and the self-constituting subjectivity of the subaltern became increasingly problematic to sustain in *Subaltern Studies*. Mallon (1994: 1497–1506) effectively traces this tension and its outcomes. Described by Mallon (1994: 1506) as the rift between a 'narrowly post-modern literary interest in documents as constructed text . . . (and) . . . reading documents as windows . . . on peoples' lives,' the contrary pulls within *Subaltern Studies* mirror the divisions within anthropology and its crisis of method as they unfolded in the wake of the onslaught from Clifford (1988) and the contributions to Clifford and Marcus (1986). Productive or not, these tensions between 'real social history' and the study of 'discursive effects' caused at lease one subalternist evaluated in this essay to dissociate from the group (see Ramachandra Guha 1991).

Another problem is the heterogeneous category of the subaltern, which is difficult to deploy analytically. The purpose of introducing the category was two-fold: first, to highlight the fundamental nature of relations of power and domination in South Asian history and society, as opposed to pluralistic explanations of negotiation and consensual conflict resolution; second, to provide a rubric within which nuanced categories could be developed for specific cases. Instead certain subalternists, particularly those dealing with peasant movements in *adivasi* areas (cf. Guha 1983, Dasgupta 1985, Sarkar 1985) have mechanistically applied the categories of élite and subaltern to their material, without attending to the actual power relations they were intended to signify or examining the historical formation of important sociological categories like tribe and caste, shifting cultivator, pastoralist, labourer, petty peasant producer and so on. Hence the various complaints that *Subaltern Studies* downgrade class (Brass 1991: 179); and that by avoiding, erasing and silencing much in the historical record, subalternists distil a vagueness into the peasant category that reeks of bad historical sociology (Ludden 1993: 4–5).[13]

Again, still on the topic of the nebulous and confusing constitution of subalternity, paradoxes revealed in *Elementary Aspects of peasant insurgency* are troublesome, as when Guha (1983: 18) says, 'the insurgent arrives at a sense of himself not by properties of his own social being 'but by diminution, if not negation of those of his superiors.' The theme of negation runs right through his book, as Guha draws on an impressive range of exemplary material to illustrate the purposive and discriminating way peasants violated symbols of domination, both indigenous and colonial; in speech and text; in bodily gesture and social space; clothing and ornamentation. This should suggest that the subaltern self was constantly in the process of production, mediated through symbols and processes both internal and external to the subaltern's moral and physical domain.

We must, in addition, be dissatisfied with the way *Subaltern Studies* treat collective traditions and cultures of subordinate groups. As a mentality or ideology, subalternity is defined in terms that are ahistorical, emphasise internal consensus within subaltern groups and utilise unreconstructed notions of primordial loyalties.[14] Frequently, while the accounts are historical in the sense of being chronological constructions, subaltern consciousness is treated as strangely static, transported through time unchanged. For example, Ramachandra Guha (1989) fails to problematise the ecological consciousness of the Chipko agitators; this even while the book contains material suggesting contentious construction of the ideology of protest by women, men, villagers and leaders. Their ideology is then seen as somehow reproducing a traditional conservationist ethic rooted in the notion of self-governing egalitarian village communities which bridges the historical time gap between the Chipko movement of the 1970s and its colonial precursors. The deleterious consequence of this portrayal is that 'it restores within a redrawn and smaller notion of the collective exactly that notion of unity . . . of the absence of the relations of power, which is the subject of attack' (O'Hanlon 1988: 212). History is here simplified by reified culture into oppositional dyads where idyllic past may be counterpoised to turbulent present or unified subaltern groups lined up against monolithic élites.[15]

In another case, Dasgupta (1985) discusses subaltern politics in Midnapore, West Bengal, India. He characterises the struggle over forest rights as one where *adivasis* (indigenes) resent the sudden curtailment of their earlier unfettered use of forests. In a recent essay, the stalwart agrarian historian of Bengal has cautioned against such easy conflation of peasant and tribal societies in eastern India (Chaudhuri 1993: 67–8). My own research in Midnapore suggests that the post-land settlement conflicts over forest rights in that district were part of a more processual renegotiation of rights between landlords and peasantries, who were both *adivasi* and non-*adivasi*. This process was inflected by changing agricultural regimes, altering representations of forests, and a colonial state committed to fixing through the documentation project flexible arrangements prevalent in forest use and management. The point is that a shared moral economy is itself a contingent historical creation, which is modulated and contested, promoting both internal solidarity within groups and hostility across them.[16] The subaltern may be used as a purely contrastive category, but to have force it must itself be critically disassembled. How subaltern groups as political coalitions achieve temporary unity in any struggle is a process that *Subaltern Studies* often take for granted rather than as a subject of inquiry. As Ortner (1995: 179) astutely indicated, 'the lack of an adequate sense of prior and ongoing politics among subalterns must inevitably contribute to an inadequate analysis of resistance itself.'

Given all that has been recapitulated in preceding paragraphs, evaluations of subalternity and its deployment in South Asian history, despite their wide range and impressive depth, have not really addressed a significant aspect of *Subaltern Studies*, which is to tease out an anthropological history of South Asia by critical analysis of peasant protest and agrarian struggles. Recent surveys have stressed the interdisciplinarity of *Subaltern Studies* (cf. Prakash 1994, Ortner 1995). But what has not been done is to track this interdisciplinarity, the movement between changing genres of anthropology and the implications of *Subaltern Studies*' greater affinity to literary studies in the recent past. Any assessment of this aspect of their scholarship has to interrogate the manner in which they deal with issues like subaltern religiosity, the construction of subaltern culture in myth, narrative and discourse, and subaltern conceptions of community, resistance and power. We would have to examine the anthropological theories drawn upon to recover the subaltern culture central to their historiography. In the following sections, therefore, we shall unpack the idea of subaltern culture and its genealogy.

Subaltern Religion, Semiotics and the Symbolic Structures of Action

Ranajit Guha criticises bourgeois Indian nationalism for failing to take into account the different needs of the subaltern classes, but takes the central issue for modern Indian history to be the 'historic failure of the nation to come into its own' (Guha 1982: 7).[17] Subalternity is thus constructed in opposition to élite nationalism in a binarism that seeks to use culture to repudiate history. Chakrabarty (1992: 8) acknowledges this and admits that subalternists adopt models of symbolic inversion when he says 'as in the practice of the insurgent peasants of colonial India, the first step in a critical effort must arise from a gesture of inversion.' In this sense, subalternists theory returns in its formulation of the concept of ideology, to a deliberation over the relation between representation and praxis that engaged Ricoeur in his lectures on ideology and utopia (Ricoeur 1986). Building a framework juxtaposing ideology and utopia facilitates for Ricoeur the elaboration of symbolic structures of action and the description of the effects of economic forces in a behavioural frame, emphasising real people under definite conditions. Thus Ricoeur, by placing together the symbolic mediation of action and the determinate context of history, is attempting a fusion of Marx and Geertz. Representation and praxis are analogous to Ricoeur's discussion of ideology and utopia because they contain the common theme of what Spivak (1988) characterises as cognitive failure.

What is striking in this strongly dialectical model, is the complete absence of any conception of inequality and therefore interpretation of social texts is defended by Ricoeur (1986: 77) by saying 'there is a language of real life that exists before all distortions, a symbolic structure of action that is absolutely primitive and ineluctable.' There is persistent recourse in much of the *Subaltern Studies* work to what can be termed a Ricoeur–Geertz model for elaborating the symbolic structure and mediation of action.[18] For example, Arnold, writing about the *fituris* in the Gudem-Rampa hills of Andhra Pradesh, argues that sacrifice of policemen captured in the *fituris* to the goddess Malveli was adivasi reassertion, the re-emergence of an essential tribal inversionary discourse, rooted in a ritual of human sacrifice suppressed by the British in the 1860s (Arnold 1982: 97). Similarly, through inter-textual analysis of English and Hindi language newspaper accounts of Gandhi's visit to Gorakhpur in 1921–2, during the Non-Cooperation Movement, Shahid Amin proposes an interpretation of Mahatma myths prevalent in the area as *they were decoded* by the subaltern peasantry. He says, 'In the spring of 1921 when all was charged with magic, any mental or physical affliction suffered by persons found guilty of violating panchayat decisions adopted in Gorakhpur villages in the *Mahatma's* name was often perceived as evidence of Gandhi's extraordinary powers, indeed as something providential and supernatural' (Amin 1984: 9).

As long as the dialogic–dialectic tension between ideology and utopia that is central to Ricoeur is considered in a framework of power, the analysis is persuasive. But in the urge to establish inversionary discourses of protest on an independent footing, subalternists lapse into structuralist abstraction and decontextualisation that weakens their case. This argument will be made more transparent in our discussion of subaltern religiosity and the manner in which *Subaltern*

Studies treats myth and narrative. For many of the writers of the school, the rejection of economistic approaches (Marxist and nationalist) and 'double market place analysis' (Cambridge School) is based on identifying an essential character to the religiosity of the subaltern groups that defined and articulated their inversionary discourse. Thus in saying 'certain recurrent patterns do emerge, whether we study mass participation of a national issue or a communal riot or a caste movement,' Sarkar (1984: 277) argues for the existence of a popular mentality as a structural formation in the Lévi-Straussian sense of an implicit, perhaps largely unconscious logical system lying beneath the surface of myths, beliefs, values and activities (Lévi-Strauss 1963; Leach 1976).[19]

In support of his argument Sarkar (1984) harnesses the Non-Cooperation and Khilafat movements of 1921–2 in Bengal where subaltern militancy was manifest in *hat* looting, jail breaks and such violent forms not sanctioned by the Gandhian centre.[20] In Chittagong there was widespread violation of forest law, with a ten-day permission to collect building materials after the cyclone of 1921 extended indefinitely by popular action, and eight out of twelve forest offices burnt. These outbursts by villagers continued long after the Congress party had called off the Non-Cooperation Movement in February 1922. Describing the wave of looting fish ponds and deliberate violation of restrictions on forest use in the Midnapore district of Bengal, Sarkar (1984) points out that the movement was rooted in the resentment engendered by the Midnapore Zamindari Company and the construction of railways that impinged on Santhal use of the forest, but were activated by the memory of a recent Santhal past when jungles were open and ponds freely available for fishing.

This collective mentality favours subaltern militancy when the contingent political conditions are perceived as a period of breakdown in structures of hegemony and coercion. Such evaluation of circumstances and hence opportunities uses as its raw material rumours, contingent events and norms of resistance inculcated by the Gandhian movement. However, in Sarkar's version, the actual subaltern outburst is mediated by the 'magico-religious character of peasant society . . . untouched by creeds of secular progress' (Sarkar 1984: 308–9).[21] For

Subaltern Studies the very nature of peasant ideology and consciousness is religious. 'Religion provides an ontology, an epistemology, as well as a practical code of ethics, including political ethics. When the subalterns act politically, the symbolic meaning of particular acts—their signification—must be found in religious terms' (Chatterjee 1982: 32).[22] This fundamentally religious ideology of peasant action is described in another work of the subaltern school by Hardiman (1987: 1) on the Devi movement in Western India, an *adivasi* assertion built on the worship of goddess Salabai, 'who came from the mountains, and expressed her demands through spirit mediums . . . holding red cloth in their hands they (media) began to shake their heads and soon were in a state of trance. Then as if reading from their cloth they pronounced the commands of the Devi.'

This message of vegetarianism, abstinence, and cleanliness is neither attributable, according to him, to the uplifting contact of social reform as Nationalist accounts have it, nor a product of autochthonous primitivity. As Hardiman (1987) shows, *adivasis* have cultivated land in diverse ways, engaged in extensive economic interchange with other ethnic groups and shared religious belief and practice with caste peasantries. Both groups believed that nature was controlled by various deities and spirits that had to be propitiated by ceremonial rites. In many cases the supernatural forces were localised, though there was a tendency among caste peasants to give Brahmanical names to the deities. The key factor that left the stamp of subaltern autonomy on the movement was that ordinary *adivasi* peasants were the medium for Devi, challenging the traditional role of *bhagats* (medicine men) and their ritual prerogative in this respect, something that caused them (the *bhagats*) to view the movement with suspicion.[23] The credibility of these ordinary mediums stemmed not from the traditional legitimacy of their agency but the combination of traditional forms of revealing divine wisdom with their compelling eloquence and clarity rendered all the more remarkable by their erudite exegesis of exalted philosophical ideas, despite complete illiteracy. Hardiman's fine study to some extent escapes the criticism by Ortner (1995: 181) that subaltern religiosity is discussed as a diffuse consciousness, but remains attached to a conception of subaltern religiosity as essentially the manifestation of mentalité, and not constructed in social practice. The study of subaltern culture through the strange (diabolic realm, ecstatic narration, devil pacts) slides easily into assumptions about uniformity in beliefs, when in fact the lack of such uniformity reveals more about peasant ideology and politics (Edelman 1994: 61).

Myth, Narrative and the Discursive Constitution of Subaltern Culture

Through such inspired narration, as that of the bhagats of the Devi movement, subaltern consciousness is found to reveal underlying structures of meaning. This is an uncanny throwback to Lévi-Strauss who when analysing the story of Asdiwal says, 'abandoning the search for a constantly accurate picture of ethnographic reality in the myth, we gain on occasions, a means of reaching unconscious categories' (Lévi-Strauss 1963: 173). To him the operational value of myth is that its specific pattern is timeless, and therefore denies that the content could be contingent.[24] Such patterns of elucidation, as we have seen, at times informed the way subalternists deal with religion and continue to be apparent as they move through mythological and mythic material in trying to reconstitute subaltern subjective consciousness and culture as an alternate and free standing discourse on their condition. In this respect *Subaltern Studies* seem to stand uneasily between the 'invention of tradition' argument which basically says that culture is the organisation of the past in terms of the present; and the historical anthropology of Sahlins (1985: 155) who says that 'culture is the organisation of the current situation in the terms of the past.' They then fail to specify the way in which past and the present are interpenetrated in the constitution of culture.[25]

The rebellious activities described by Guha (1983) are of moments suffused with insurgent consciousness. These activities are immersed in myth and ritual, in generating a force that would turn the world upside down. Subaltern identity rests not only in the perception of collective grievance but in the practice of collective violence, thus authoring a violent narrative of protest that serves to enlarge the collective memory of subaltern defiance of domination by inscribing new episodes into their mythology of resistance. It is clear from a careful reading of Guha (1983) that he is unable to posit the emergence of class identity and moves therefore to uncover ideational structures and modes of thought drawing on religion, myth and ritual that coalesced a motley collection of subalterns into a cohesive fighting unit.[26]

In most accounts, the construction of oppositional discourses by the subalterns seemed to follow a pattern of storytelling that created a logical sequence of myth and magic that recounted the loss of patrimony, the struggle for recovery and the powerful intermediation of inspired leadership at crucial junctures, marking conjunction or intersection with other movements, particularly Gandhian peasant uprisings. In their adoption of vegetarianism and personal purification programmes, both the Devi movement and Chipko were adapting Gandhian reformism to their cause. Hardiman (1987) has described the adoption of vegetarianism, temperance and cleanliness by poor tribal peasants in the Devi movement, interlocking with both socioeconomic changes in Western India in the early decades of the twentieth century and their transformation of cultural categories which were at once historical and contemporary in their emerging consciousness.

The use of religion and other large mythic structures was often innovative, when subalterns creatively used the *bricolage* at their disposal to suit particular moments of resistance. The Chipko agitation reached out to overarching Hindu belief when readings of the *Gita* in the forest marked protest against green felling. This was crucial in deterring non-local labourers used by timber contractors from participating in continued felling. Equally, the act of tree hugging by women—the traditional controllers of the hearth—was aimed at striking a chord in a shared subsistence ethic that transcended differences of territory, gender and caste. Religion was important precisely because it developed syncretic forms using adivasi rites and Hinduism. In the same fashion, fifty years earlier, the incorporation of adivasi religious sites into the Koya and Bagata pantheon became important to the rebellious hillmen Arnold (1982) writes about, to demonstrate autochthonous origins for their faith.

Citing Lévi-Strauss (1972), Arnold (1982: 16–17) does argue that religion and myth are not devices by which tribesmen and peasants repudiate reality; rather, they provide structures for comprehending the immediate reality and responding to it. In the Gudem-Rampa case, religion was used to express dissatisfaction with subjugation and frame the terms of deliverance within a known model that provided symbolic capital to counteract the superior control of economic capital by their oppressors. Travelling ecclesiastes (sivasaris) moved through the region, with the prophecy in 1886 of one Bodadu that God had ordained a successful *fituri* (rebellion). This was rendered authentic by the encounter of Bodadu with the five pandavas (the redemptive brotherhood of the *Mahabharata* epic in the Hindu tradition) in the jungle, a symbolic mediation of local and national culture that was politically expedient for integrating hillmen with supporters in the plain (Arnold 1982). Later Rama Raju, a Telugu Kshatriya leader of the agitation against forest reservation, gained authority among local inhabitants through his knowledge of astrology and medicine, which gave him magical powers in the eyes of the hillmen. However, by advocating temperance and *khadi* (homespun cloth), he also strategically allied with Gandhian politics (Arnold 1982).

Clearly then we have to be wary of treating the symbolic aspects of these movements too rigidly or in isolation from the material conditions under which religion and mythic narratives were deployed. Too assiduous a search for an untainted subaltern culture can occlude recognition of the economy as a system of calculation, competition and exploitation, constantly negotiated by relentlessly strategising individuals and interested actors, pursuing their own subjective ends to the maintenance of social structures (Bourdieu 1977, DiMaggio 1979).[27] However, *Subaltern Studies* do not much heed the strictures of practice theory, a problem that arises not only from the hypostatic ideational models but more significantly from their non-romantic conception of the subaltern. The Other observed as separate and knowable through representation is a notion that has endured in anthropology. Even Geertz's (1976) essay on the native's point of view is driven by the same logic, and we could well translate 'what the native perceives with' as the indigenous cultural system understood in its own terms.

From Mythic Structures of Knowledge
to the Neo-romantic Subaltern

According to Richard Shweder the urge to make a methodological break placed the anthropologists he calls the 'romantic rebels' on an epistemological fault line. 'A central tenet of the romanticist view holds that ideas and practices have their foundation in neither logic nor empirical science, that ideas and practices fall beyond the scope of deductive and inductive reason, that they are neither rational nor irrational but rather nonrational' (Shweder 1984: 28). Drawing on this flawed tradition *Subaltern Studies* formulate the notion that archetypical subalterns like the tribal and scheduled castes inhabit cultural worlds founded on mythic structures. The pedigree for such construction of tribal social consciousness, especially, can be traced to the ethnographic research conducted between the wars, principally by Verrier Elwin and Furer-Haimendorf.[28] The colonial ethnographies of these authors and other administrator-anthropologists like Archer, Carstairs, Grigson and Bradley-Birt are admirable for their detailed documentation of tribal culture, but certainly must be regarded as the Orientalist corpus pertaining to Indian tribes.[29]

Starting out in central India, Elwin entered the tribal world thorough poetry and comparative religion, a predilection rooted in his Oxford training in English literature, a fascination for the Romantic poets, and subsequent training as a Protestant theologian. He writes:

> when I first went to live in the tribal hills of India, with my Wordsworth, my T.S. Eliot, my Blake and Shakespeare burning like torches in my little mud house, it was natural that I look around me for poetry. And I soon found it, for among these gentle and romantic tribal people poetry jumps out at you . . . I found the people talked poetry. An old woman talks of a fire as a flower blossoming on a dry tree, of an umbrella as a peacock with one leg. (Elwin 1964: 143)

Not surprisingly Elwin's first ethnography was of the Baiga, a central Indian tribe that personified for him the kingly type. They were the magicians and medicine men, who mediated between other tribes and their gods, of all tribes he knew the ones most possessed by their myths (Elwin 1939). He had earlier prepared the companion book *Songs of the forest* (Hivale and Elwin 1935), and thereafter a systematic collection of myths, folktales and poetry of central and east Indian tribes like the Gonds, Agaria, Bhils, Mundas, Bondos; Elwin initiated what became a veritable deluge of ethnographic work that illuminated tribal society through its mythology and fine arts. In the same vein, Christoph von Furer-Haimendorf, the other prolific and peripatetic chronicler of tribal society from the period between the two world wars wrote, 'Every aspect of Gond culture is rooted in mythology which provides a reason for most ritual action and sanctions and norms regulating tribal life' (Fürer-Haimendorf 1990: 76).[30]

Such a formulation of tribal culture enters *Subaltern Studies* as a powerful discursive formation underpinning the construction of the subaltern mentalité as something non-rational and hence structurally separated from the 'big traditions' of resistance crafted in turn from the interaction of 'big traditions' of culture with Western liberal-rational philosophy.[31] In this process we can detect a movement away from the situated character of folklore analysis that Gramsci, the original mentor of *Subaltern Studies*, had in fact recommended:

> Folklore should instead be studied as a 'conception of the world and life' implicit to a large extent in determinate (in time and space) strata of society and in opposition (also for the most part implicit, mechanical and objective) to 'official' conceptions of the world (or in a broader sense, the conceptions of the cultural parts of historically determinate societies) that have succeeded one another in the historical process . . . This conception of the world is not elaborated and systematic because by definition the people (the sum total of the instrumental and subaltern classes of every form of society that has so far existed) cannot possess conceptions which are elaborated, systematic and politically organized in their albeit contradictory development. It is, rather, many-sided—not only because it includes different and juxtaposed elements but *also because it is stratified* [emphasis added]—if indeed, one should not speak of a confused agglomerate of fragments of all the conceptions of the world and life that have succeeded one another in history [Gramsci 1985: 189].

The point being adumbrated can be illustrated by the manner in which *Subaltern Studies* analyse subaltern readings of Gandhian political culture for their own causes. Tracing the treatment of such material through different phases of the *Subaltern Studies* project, we can notice the movement from Lévi-Strauss to Ricoeur–Geertz (culture as text and neo-romanticism) to early glimpses of Foucault. For Sarkar (1984), rumours about Gandhi in Bengal fell into three categories.

1. Those presenting episodic evidence of Gandhi as miracle worker, an avatar who breaks with impunity the laws of nature. The myth of Gandhi magically breaking the locks on his jail cell and walking out parallels the legend of Lord Krishna in the *Bhagavatham*—born in prison, using his supernatural powers as Vishnu avatar to escape with his parents. While Sarkar (1984) notes but does not problematise this miscegenation of mythic traditions, in a sense he remains within the dominant anthropological discourse about tribal mythology as something that originated separately and yet at times paralleled neigbouring Hindu cosmology.[32]
2. Others promoting the belief that emulating his practice, like donning the Gandhi cap, would provide immunity from bullets and turn bombs to water.
3. Those engendering millenarian faith in miraculous total transformation or reversal of the social conditions obtaining, rather than invoking support for reformism or issue-based politics.

The ritual obligations entailed by such emerging myths were vegetarianism, abstention and self-purification, strengthened by stories such as the one told about the Brahmin Congress leader who embraced mehtars, doms and chamars (all scavenging and untouchable castes) when they practised *shuddhi* (purification).[33] In this connection another subalternist stresses the polysemic nature of mahatma myths and rumours about Gandhi, sparking a many-sided response to the political culture he was articulating. Thus commenting on the rise of cow protection societies and the greater interest in caste Hindu ritual observance, Amin (1984: 13) points out 'the very act of self-purification on the part of the ritually impure amounted to a reversal of the signs of subordination.'[34]

Guha (1989) provides material about the way Chipko leaders similarly originated in the Sarvodaya and liquor abolition agitations and frequently resorted to reading of the *Bhagavad Gita* in the forests to hark back to the writing of all major scripture of the Hindu tradition in the forests, recalling Gandhi's slogan of restoring Ram Rajya. Thus *Subaltern Studies* located the association of Gandhi with the supernatural bases of power in primordial belief, within a discourse that linked peasant politics to Gandhian nationalism not in terms of Congress platform but through peasant perception of a cosmology of redemptive change. By examining various stories that were recounted in vernacular press and which contributed to the spread of Gandhi's rumoured miraculous powers (*pratap*), Amin (1984: 48) shows 'these stories indicate how ideas about Gandhi's *pratap* . . . derived from popular Hindu belief and practices and the material culture of the peasantry.'

In another study systematically linking cultural values to power, Chatterjee (1983) has perceptively highlighted the constraining influences of such adaptation of hegemonic discourse, both religious and political, on the particular movement. It is nevertheless interesting to see the bricolage of myths and legends surrounding Gandhi becoming a text without an author in the Barthesian sense (Barthes 1977). This even as they gain authenticity by attribution specifically to the Mahatma, because that brings us to the narrative technique by which myth is ordered into a powerful logic of explanation and strategy. For instance, Sunderlal Bahuguna, the leader of the Chipko movement builds the narrative of the expropriation of the village forests by the state on recurrent symbols of government trucks ferrying out harvested timber, as well as on specific major events like the great flood of 1970, to link these images to the material reality of soil erosion, loss of agricultural productivity and the growing paucity of clean water in hill villages of Uttarakhand (Guha 1989).

Particularly in the work of Chatterjee, Amin and Ranajit Guha the transition to a more Foucaultian understanding of power leads to insightful essays in *Subaltern Studies*.[35] As this happens a tension is noticeable between the timeless subaltern mentality and the ambivalent mixture of lower caste traditions and Hindu cosmologies, all of which are thrown into the grab-bag of subaltern culture. Such discursively constituted culture displaces the binarisms of process–structure, high–low, subaltern–élite that through the influence of Hegel, Gramsci and

Lévi-Strauss endured in the way subalternity was conceptualised by *Subaltern Studies*.[36] Examining one such central antimony of the subaltern project, that of class and community in subaltern culture, will lead us to some concluding remarks on the shift in subalternist focus onto dominant discourses and the transformed fusion of history, anthropology and literary criticism in *Subaltern Studies*.

Subaltern Culture and Insufficient Classness

We have noted the manner in which the central problematic of Indian historiography was defined by Ranajit Guha as the failure of the bourgeoisie and the working class to achieve a successful bourgeois democratic revolution (Guha and Spivak 1988: 43). Subaltern autonomy was thus defined as emerging from the aborted class division of Indian society, and seen to reside in a sense of community. Chakrabarty (1992) describes this as permitting the conception of original idioms of struggle in a 'non-modern' sphere. Spivak (1988: 288) divides this feeling of community into public and family domains. Having described a distinctive religiosity or mythic universe as constitutive of subaltern consciousness, *Subaltern Studies* approach the question of collective action by the subaltern with some circumspection. Instrumentality and intention reveal no straightforward relationship. Considering the need to locate the concept of subalternity within theories of social organisation, some of the scholars have argued that class may happen, but cannot be presumed to exist in the nature of this identity.

In a style akin to Thompson's (1965, 1978), Sen (1987: 205) says, 'some men may as the result of common experiences feel and articulate the identity of interests between themselves, and as against interests of other . . .' According to his argument, the historical processes of colonial India were marked by an admixture of pre-capitalist relations. The nature of power, exploitation and popular resistance was not therefore amenable to adequate understanding in terms of clearly enunciated class categories. Clear patterns of social differentiation did not develop, providing the subalterns with space to show independent initiative even as such initiative remained fragmented and distant from organised or formal political society. Once again, the centrality of capitalist modernisation to the colonial transformation of Indian society was challenged. This notwithstanding recent work emerging from the Cambridge school that presents the eighteenth century as a period that threw up distinctive and ultimately transient structures of class on the basis of which colonial rule was initially established (O'Hanlon and Washbrook 1992).[37]

The insufficiency of classness has led several of the studies to emphasise community consciousness (Arnold 1982, Bhadra 1985, Chatterjee 1984).[38] Subaltern consciousness sought the sense of community as paradise lost, placing its faith in eschatological prophecy and the magical elimination of powerful enemies (Guha 1983, Sen 1987). This notion of community is frequently based on an insider–outsider dichotomy that is strongly linked to the territoriality of the subaltern subjective consciousness. For example, Arnold (1982: 89) says, 'The inhabitants of hill the tracts were opposed to outsiders who threatened their territory and their customary ways of life. The outsiders were of several kinds—British colonial administrators, their Indian troops, police and civilian subordinates, Telugu traders and contractors moving up from the coastal plain. But this diversity did not weaken the hillman's conviction that they conspired together and had a mutual interest in oppressing and exploiting him.' Such tight conflation of notions of space and place, is then used to argue that subaltern communities were knit into a peasant society comprising a self-sufficient economy, shared religious-beliefs and the even-handed experience of power and land control through institutions like the *muttadari* system in the Gudem-Rampa case. Arnold (1982) is clearly indebted to the colonial ethnography of Fürer-Haimendorf (1945), for his understanding of the tribal agricultural system and cosmology. This is highly problematic, since he then carries into his subaltern category the neo-romantic idealisation of undifferentiated tribal society that informed the Elwin–Fürer-Haimendorf genre of anthropology. More generally, such a treatment reveals a conceptual framework that Bakhtin called the chronotope, 'an intrinsic connectedness of time and space' (Bakhtin 1981: 84). Subalterns are more credibly perceived as marginal people, and as Gupta and Ferguson (1992: 7–8) suggest, 'the fiction of cultures as discrete . . . occupying discrete spaces becomes implausible for those who inhabit borderlands . . . instead of assuming the autonomy of the primeval community we need to examine how it was formed as a community out of the interconnected space that already existed. Colonialism then, represented the displacement of one form of interconnection by another.' Community thus has to be seen as a constructed entity, a sense of place that is contingent and negotiated (Cohen 1985).

While they principally stress autonomous construction of this consciousness and the political discourse generated from it, *Subaltern Studies* also contain cases where this community consciousness interacted with élite movements. For instance the Gauraksha (cow protection) agitation in north India and Jitu Santhal's *bidroha* in Malda (Bengal) were critically influenced by purificatory cults in Hinduism and the Gandhian struggle (Pandey 1983, Sarkar 1985). Thus this analysis presages and makes possible the analysis of state and élite political forms, the substance of hegemonic discourse, in a setting of interaction and structuring. The historical impossibility of a complete subaltern cultural autonomy is best read from the evidence of all the occasions when the project of subaltern community was appropriated by élite projects of nation-state building. The development of capitalism everywhere articulated unevenly with race, ethnicity and gender making insufficient classness a problem everywhere, albeit with different effects. On the one hand, as Chakrabarty (1992: 18) puts it, 'colonial India is replete with instances where Indians arrogated subjecthood to themselves precisely by mobilising . . . sometimes on behalf of the modernizing project of nationalism, devices of collective memory that were both antihistorical and antimodern.' On the other hand, as elucidated by Pandey (1990) in his book on communalism in India, the urge for community does not necessarily require a non-hierarchical material base, but finds its material in the world of political discourse, arising in relation to and in conflict with the liberal modernising discourse of individual rights and the secular state.

Thus getting away from the binarism that the subaltern method ultimately leaves us with requires recovery of the hidden transcript,

as Scott (1990) calls it, without slipping into essentialism and by revealing such latent ideology also as something constructed and refracted
through practice (Bourdieu 1977). This would allow a subtle and effective addressal of the problem of historical determination without
speaking only of what culture allows or what structure forecloses.
Widening the definition of resistance is certainly a necessary first step
as Comaroff (1985) and Scott (1985) have shown. Going further
would call for the treatment of resistance as an index of power and
thereby exploring the dialectical relationship between stratified discourses of protest and the multivocal discourses of rule. There are
several advantages to doing this. First, we could avoid mis-attributing
particular forms of consciousness and politics to acts of resistance.
Second, we can detect historical shifts in configurations of power
(Abu-Lughod 1990).

Conclusion

At several places in this essay, we have noted the definite move within
Subaltern Studies towards studying power as opposed to an earlier
focus on overt resistance or revolt. Recognising this realignment of
agenda, Gyan Prakash (1994: 1481) says, 'this perspective, amplified
since *Subaltern Studies III* identifies subalternity as a position of critique, as a recalcitrant difference that arises not outside but inside élite
discourses to exert pressures on forces and forms that subordinate it.'
Reformulating the subaltern concept in this fashion certainly strips
the subaltern of an independent existence, and invokes this entity as
a shadowy figure imagined in the 'subterfuges and stereotypes' of
dominant discourses. Later in the same appreciation of *Subaltern
Studies*, Gyan Prakash (1994: 1483–6) acknowledges that the Foucaultian turn has brought subalternists into a literary criticism mode of
analysing colonialism as a text, and its power as a diffuse force running
through the whole social body.

This raises the question, are not *Subaltern Studies* moving from a
diffuse notion of resistance to a miasmic description of power that
removes it from the world of production and experience? If the subaltern subject is fragmented and the outcome of several post-colonial

displacements, are we left with a worthwhile concept of subalternity? What was most appealing about the *Subaltern Studies* project as initiated, was the search for human agency among the relatively powerless groups in society, the move to restore dignity and purpose to the actions of the anonymous poor peasantry in colonised worlds. As this essay has demonstrated, this laudable project was predicated on the drafting of a new anthropological history of colonialism, peasant movements and the study of resistance. In the process the effort got mired in anthropologies inimical to the exposition of subaltern agency. Part of the problem was the creation of new binarisms in place of old ones interrogated, and the reification of power as a result.

A welcome return to the careful study of power applied a corrective to these trends in *Subaltern Studies*, but to resort to an overarching and pervasive conceptualisation of power in Foucaultian terms follows him in locating power as the transcendent subject; a curious inversion for those would earlier install the irreducible subaltern's resistance as such a transcendent subject.[39] To some extent these transformations in *Subaltern Studies* and their coincidence with post-colonial criticism adhere to the new agendas recommended by Cohn and Dirks (1988: 227) for historical anthropologies of culture, when they suggest we must link histories of power to anthropology, by studying 'how culture is produced, controlled, transformed and reproduced, both through small-scale networks and the legitimation project of the state.' But an emphasis on the social production of power that such an approach must entail is lost. Scholars assessing Foucault and *Subaltern Studies* have suggested several reasons for this loss; Ortner (1995) simply refers to this phenomenon as ethnographic refusal to reconcile socially constructed subjectivity with human agency.

In a similar vein, Mallon points out that by giving up local history and theorising at the level of grand generalities (cf. Guha 1989, 1992), subalternists analyse power in a way that does not raise the spectre of disunited subalterns. Others, in recent *Subaltern Studies* confine their discussion of subalternity to one version, usually that of élite groups within a subaltern community, a strategy that in the case of Skaria (1999) and Hardiman (1993) allows them to treat Bhil chieftains as subalterns and their discourse as the authentic voice of Dangi subalternity. While these approaches resurrect, albeit in a modified form the autonomous subaltern, they also remain limited by the diffuse notion of power derived from Foucault (Cooper 1994: 1533). The problem is that Foucault's notion of power and discourses can be aspatial, which means it deals poorly with multiple levels of identity and community in real social space (Sangren 1995: 16–17).

In contrast, power needs to be located in the spatial and temporal realities of social activities, and this requires a disaggregation and examination of the processes through which it is produced, exercised, limited and appropriated (Sangren 1995: 26; Cooper 1994: 1533). This requires a pluralisation of the colonial situation concept, as Stocking (1991: 5) suggests. In the colonies surveillance, control and the narrowing of the boundaries of political discourse was concentrated spatially and socially and by not discussing these patterns, we could miss the implications of the limits of coercion or fail to recognise the possibilities stemming from partial and contradictory hegemonic projects (Cooper 1994: 1531). One way to proceed is to examine the everyday forms of power, to describe the ambivalences, contradictions, tragedies and ironies that attend it, and do so in particular locations, situating subaltern and élite in regional histories.[40] Parallel unpackings of subaltern cultures and the processes of state-making are called for, in short a revalidation of history and anthropology as fieldwork, informed by the insights of textual analysis. After all, an interdisciplinarity predicated on the combination of history and anthropology, challenges us to study structures and discourses without closing out the possibility of agency. *Subaltern Studies* amply reveal the difficulties and attractions of such an ambitious project.

NOTES

1. Cohn (1981: 73) defines historical anthropology in the following words, '[it] will be the delineation of cultures, the locating of these in historical time through the study of events which affect and transform structures, and the explanation of the consequences of these transformations.'

2. The combination of culture, history and political economy at various levels in state formation through negotiation and contest is well brought out in recent historical ethnography in the work of Kelly (1985), Mintz (1985), Sider (1986), Siu (1989), Feierman (1990), and Prakash (1990a).

3. Volumes VII (Chatterjee and Pandey 1992) and VIII (Arnold and Hardiman 1993) have been published since. Volume IX is forthcoming this year. This review deals with selected propositions and concepts clearly articulated in the volumes edited by Guha. This has partly to do with the changing character of the interdisciplinarity displayed in *Subaltern Studies*, and the more recent tendency to affiliate with post-colonial criticism, 'arising in the interstices of disciplines of power/knowledge that it critiques' (Prakash 1994: 1476).

4. Such reformulation of the culture concept through historicalisation and politicisation, through vigorous debate within anthropology, has been comprehensively discussed by Dirks, Eley and Ortner (1994: 3–46).

5. Such an assertion raises the sticky question of who is the subaltern. As we shall see later, the contributions to *Subaltern Studies* have no simple classificatory scheme in response to this question. What they consistently do, however, is destabilise grand modes of production narratives and invest this subaltern actor with historical agency (Spivak 1988).

6. I refer here, among other things, to the distinction Lévi-Strauss drew between anthropology and history when speaking of their complementary perspectives. He wrote, 'History organises its data in relation to conscious expressions of social life, while anthropology proceeds by examining the unconscious foundations' (Lévi-Strauss 1949: 18).

7. One of the major contributors to *Subaltern Studies* has opined, 'Ranajit Guha has demonstrated the historian of the subaltern classes needs in particular to know the methods and concerns of structural anthropology and semiology in order to decode the underlying meanings of subaltern actions and beliefs' (Arnold 1984: 168). Also see Sarkar (1984: 275–80) for a discussion of subaltern ideology as a logical system submerged below myth. Arnold (1982: 16–17), explicitly cites *The Savage Mind* and argues that myth and religion provide structures for comprehending reality and serve as a means to frame the articulation of liberatory ideas in known models.

8. For a detailed discussion of the debate regarding class differentiation of peasantries in South Asia in the colonial period, with specific reference to eastern India, see Prakash (1990a) and Sivaramakrishnan (1992).

9. Stokes himself continued to emphasise regional particularities and remained wary of overarching approaches that used categories like rich peasants, or traditional aristocracy. In the final analysis, we may discern in his work a unifying ecological theory. For the Marxist/nationalist critique of Stokes and the underestimation of colonialism in his and similar explanations of economic change in the British period, see Habib (1985).

10. An internal revision has emerged among English scholars, some of them trained in Cambridge, who have dug deep into seventeenth-century South

Asian history to recover processes of early capitalist development in the continent before its colonial subjugation, arguing thus a material base to political struggles of collaboration, co-option and contest that marked nineteenth- and twentieth-century struggles over the formation of a nationalist state (Bayly 1983, 1988; Washbrook 1988).

11. The best exposition of everyday protest and its significance may be found in Scott (1985) and also the work of Adas (1981, 1986). In a recent response to a growing trend in this direction a subalternist scholar suggests the greater salience of the moment of violence and its capacity to illuminate more of a problem, even while constituting 'our sense of community, our communities and our history' (Pandey 1992: 41).

12. Spivak (1988: 8–9) makes a similar point when speaking of subaltern successes arising from the failure of their political struggles.

13. In what is probably the most recent Marxist attack on *Subaltern Studies*, Brass (1991: 180) identifies the subaltern as an anti-socialist and neo-populist category chiefly defined by the agrarian petty bourgeoisie, or the much-maligned middle peasant of earlier peasant studies debates.

14. This can be seen in the notion of community discussed by Chatterjee (1982), Chakrabarty (1984) in his treatment of caste as a source of allegiance among jute mill workers, and Sumit Sarkar's ideas about shared structures of religiosity discussed in this essay.

15. A fuller treatment of such idealised opposition in the context of environmental politics in India can be found in Sivaramakrishnan (1995).

16. See for instance the excellent discussion of the modern construction of Hinduism drawing on pre-colonial and Orientalist texts, in the historical processes of colonialism and nationalism by Thapar (1989).

17. In a recent article, Chakrabarty (1992) has reiterated that this assertion continues to define the abiding concerns of the *Subaltern Studies* collective.

18. Culture as a symbolic code, deeply embedded in the psyche, is central to the Geertzian argument in his 1964 essay, 'Ideology as cultural system,' in David Apter (ed.), *Ideology and discontent*, Glencoe, Ill.: The Free Press; and his earlier essay, 'Ethos, worldview and the analysis of sacred symbols,' which first appeared in 1957 in *The Antioch Review*. This piece also elaborates the notion of culture as a hierarchical symbolic structure used to interpret reality. Both are reprinted with other essays that collectively constitute a Geertzian theory of semiosis in Geertz (1973).

19. This is Lévi-Strauss in his most Saussurean mode, treating myth as cultural code, synchronic, abstractable from context and fully comprehensible in terms of its internal structure and relationship of parts to whole (Saussure 1966: 1–125).

20. *Hat* is a Bengali term for local village or small town markets, usually held on a specific day of the week.

21. The importance of historical contingency to the argument is evident from Sarkar's description of the way widespread violation of forest laws restricting collection of building materials in Chittagong erupted into burning of forest offices in the aftermath of the Non-Cooperation Movement in 1921–2, but by the same token, similar evidence seems to erode the plausibility of his structuralist formulations as determinant of forms of protest.

22. For the direct influence of Gramsci on this proposition, compare with his statement that religion was for the subalterns 'a specific way of rationalizing the world and life providing the general framework for political activity' (Gramsci 1971: 337).

23. Thus Hardiman refutes the Adasian logic of messianic movements which necessarily originate with a prophetic leader (Adas 1987). Also see the classic account of messianic movements in India by Fuchs (1965) that categorised them in fourteen ways.

24. 'The criterion of validity (of myth) is not found among the elements of history . . . mythological patterns have to an extreme degree the character of absolute objects' (Lévi-Strauss 1983: 13).

25. For illustration of this argument through ethnographic example, see Friedman (1992: 196), who rightly states that the realisation of myth in practice 'may occur in specific circumstances where an emergent social identity manifests itself via the display of mythical models. Such circumstances occur at certain moments in the course of social movements, but they are always dependent on a prior mythologisation of the present.' For fine discussions of the politics whereby past struggles penetrate issues through the interaction of popular and élite cultures, see Alonso (1988), Nugent and Alonso (1994).

26. More recently, Bhadra (1989: 90) has argued that subaltern consciousness can be read from élite discourse, not because of hermeneutic possibilities, but because exchange and sharing of ideas occurs across classes. At this point the category subaltern is becoming porous and osmotic, a redefinition that seems credible but also undermines the neat binarisms that characterised the earlier formulations of Guha (1982, 1983).

27. I am not suggesting here that Bourdieu's Kabyle study provides a universal theory about strategising individuals. The emphasis is more on culture in the making through practice, what he has called regulated improvisation. Intent forms an element of such creative practice especially among those who are relatively powerless in terms of formal social and political institutions. What we need to be cautious about is the relationship between intent and effects.

28. Recently, Guha and Gadgil (1989: 34n) have acknowledged the debt of their work to Elwin and Furer-Haimendorf, and called for the treatment of their ethnographic writings as 'primary sources' on tribal culture. Considering the colonial context of their production and the structural-functional/

romanticist anthropological theories in which they were steeped, it seems highly problematic to dissociate these texts from the process of producing colonial knowledge, and hence their implication in power relations that were highly complex. I have elaborated elsewhere on the several strands of colonial ethnography and how they may be used in studying the state (see Sivaramakrishnan 1993).

29. Said (1979) has vigorously exposed the implication of Orientalism in colonial rule by identifying the tropes of reification and denigration underlying much cultural anthropology and area studies (Dirks: forthcoming). The significance of Said is his casting into suspicion all forms of dichotomisation of the relationship between different cultures, and the possibility this afforded for the constitution of the West in potentially hegemonic terms (Clifford 1988). The most prominent way in which Orientalism emerged in India was the displacement of human agency in Indological discourse, not onto a reified state or market, but onto a substantialised caste. The representations of India as a civilisation dominated by caste, as a theocracy in which Brahmans, priests and ascetics, and a principle of purity or hierarchy takes precedence over kings, the state, and the principle of secular power are legion (Inden 1986). For the discussion of caste as a contested political social category that was spiritualised by Indologists, Weber and structural anthropologists, see Dirks (1987, 1989) and Cohn (1987: 136–71).

30. This of course is a restatement, in a reminiscent genre, of the ethnographic conclusions from the original monograph on the Raj Gonds (Fürer-Haimendorf 1948). See also the work of W.G. Archer, especially his work on Oraon folk poetry and the more substantial ethnography of the Santhals of Bengal (Archer 1974), which is predicated on the study of Santhal poetry. Archer went on to write numerous monographs on middle and north Indian art and sculpture.

31. As Chris Gill (1993) shows in a fine examination of Paul Friedrich and his classic study of agrarian revolt in Mexico, similar romanticism, privileging a vision of inviolable community and independent community, produced in Friedrich's case a narrative that the principal actors in his story themselves seemed sceptical of. Similarly, even the sophisticated study by Comaroff and Comaroff (1991) makes an argument for the colonisation of African consciousness based on a prior notion of fundamental difference. Thus, as Eric Gable (1995: 254) suggests, the colonial encounter is used to cleave two world-views apart, and 'the new historical anthropology recreates the geography on which colonial anthropology depended.'

32. For explicit statements of such parallelisms in the development of mythic tradition, see Elwin (1964).

33. We should treat vegetarianism and such syncretic practices as rituals of protest, because they engender through collective performance the counter-hegemonic ideology, through appropriations from the hegemonic (Dirks 1992: 217–20). See also Comaroff (1985) for a similar argument based on a practice theory orientation.

34. More detailed discussion of the widespread adoption of vegetarianism, abstention and other Sanskritising practices by low-caste sweepers, washermen and barbers in north India focused around the cow protection movement as it arose in the context of *shuddhi* (purification) and the struggle to evolve political symbols from hegemonic religious discourse can be found in Pandey (1983) and Freitag (1980).

35. See the article by Bernard Cohn (1985) on the language of command which contextualises power relationships through the examination of institutions and technologies through which colonial power reached into a region or a social stratum. Cohn thus provides the lead within *Subaltern Studies* for a widening of focus that by initiating the careful analysis of colonial discourse, has become more common now.

36. I am indebted to Gyan Prakash (personal communication) for this insight.

37. Notably Bayly (1983, 1988) and the Brenner debate (Aston and Philpin 1985) have explored the wider non-Western relations of production and social formation, while trying to break down East–West dichotomies by examining indigenous capitalist forms and their associated military and mercantile institutions.

38. The concept of community often borders on the undifferentiated and static notion of otherness developed in Orientalism, especially where the borrowings from cultural anthropology are uncritical. For a fuller critique of this problematic use of the community idea, in the context of merging history and anthropology for studying South Asia, see Dirks (forthcoming).

39. For a detailed discussion of how Foucault ultimately arrives at power as the primary productive force in society, thereby disarticulating it from agency or subjectivity, see Sangren (1995).

40. For a fine recent example of such an approach, see several essays in Joseph and Nugent (1994).

REFERENCES

Abu-Lughod, Lila, 1990, 'The romance of resistance: Tracing transformations of power through Bedouin women,' *American Ethnologist,* 17(1): 41–55.

Adas, Michael, 1981, 'From avoidance to confrontation: Peasant protest in pre-colonial and colonial South Asia,' *Comparative Studies in Society and History,* 23(2): 217–47.

————, 1986, 'From footdragging to flight: The evasive history of peasant avoidance protest in South and South-east Asia,' *Journal of Peasant Studies*, 13(2): 64–86.

————, 1987, *Prophets of rebellion: Millenarian protest movements against the European colonial order*, Cambridge: CUP.

Alavi, Hamza, 1973, 'Peasant classes and primordial loyalties,' *Journal of Peasant Studies*, 1(1): 23–62.

Alonso, Ana Maria, 1988, 'The effects of truth: Re-presentations of the past and the imagining of community,' *Journal of H.S.*, 1(1): 33–57.

Amin, Shahid, 1984, 'Gandhi as Mahatma: Gorakhpur district, eastern Uttar Pradesh, 1921–2,' *Subaltern Studies*, 3, Delhi: OUP.

Archer, William G., 1974, *The hill of flutes: Life, love and poetry in tribal India, A portrait of the Santals*, Pittsburgh: University of Pittsburgh Press.

Arnold, David, 1982, 'Rebellious hillmen: The Gudem-Rampa rebellions (1829–1914),' *Subaltern Studies*, 1, Delhi: OUP.

————, 1984, 'Gramsci and peasant subalternity in India,' *Journal of Peasant Studies*, 11(4): 155–77.

Arnold, David and Hardiman, David (eds), 1993, *Subaltern Studies*, 8, Delhi: OUP.

Aston, T.S. and Philpin, C.H.E. (eds), 1985, *The Brenner debate*, Cambridge: CUP.

Bakhtin, Mikhail M., 1981, 'Forms of time and of the chronotype in the novel,' in Michael Holquist (ed.), *The dialogic imagination: Four essays by Bakhtin*, Austin: University of Texas Press.

Bayly, Chris A., 1983, *Rulers, townsmen and bazaars: North Indian society during the British expansion*, Cambridge: CUP.

————, 1988, *Indian society and the making of the British empire*, Cambridge: CUP.

Barthes, Roland, 1977, 'Introduction to the structural analysis of narratives,' in Stephen Heath (ed.), *Image-music-text*, New York: Hill and Wang.

Bhadra, Gautam, 1985, 'Four rebels of 1857,' *Subaltern Studies*, 4, Delhi: OUP.

————, 1989, 'The mentality of subalternity: Kantanama or Rajadharma,' *Subaltern Studies*, 6, Delhi: OUP.

Bourdieu, Pierre, 1977, *Outline of a theory of practice*, Cambridge: CUP.

Brass, Tom, 1991, 'Moral economists, subalterns, new social movements and the (re-)emergence of a (post-)modernised (middle) peasant,' *Journal of Peasant Studies*, 19: 173–205.

Chakrabarty, Dipesh, 1983, 'Conditions of knowledge for working class conditions: Employers, government and the jute workers of Calcutta, 1890–1940,' *Subaltern Studies*, 3, Delhi: OUP.

————, 1992, 'Postcoloniality and the artifice of history: Who speaks for "Indian" pasts?' *Representations*, 37: 1–26.

Charlesworth, Neil, 1978, 'Rich peasants and poor peasants in late nineteenth-century Maharashtra,' in Clive Dewey and A.G. Hopkins (eds), *The imperial impact: Studies in the economic history of Asia and Africa*, London: The Athlone Press.

Chatterjee, Partha, 1982, 'Agrarian relations and communalism in Bengal,' *Subaltern Studies*, 1, Delhi: OUP.

————, 1983, 'More on modes of power and the peasantry,' *Subaltern Studies*, 2, Delhi: OUP.

————, 1984, 'Gandhi and the critique of civil society,' *Subaltern Studies*, 3, Delhi: OUP.

Chatterjee, Partha and Pandey, Gyanendra (eds), 1992, *Subaltern Studies*, 7, Delhi: OUP.

Chaudhuri, Binay Bhushan, 1993, 'Tribal society in transition: Eastern India, 1757–1920,' in Mushirul Hasan and Narayani Gupta (eds), *India's colonial encounter: Essay in memory of Eric Stokes*, Delhi: Manohar.

Clifford, James, 1988, *The predicament of culture: Twentieth-century ethnography, literature and art*, Cambridge: Harvard University Press.

Clifford, James and Marcus, George, 1986, *Writing culture: The politics and poetics of ethnography*, Berkeley: University of California Press.

Cohen, A., 1985, *The symbolic construction of community*, New York: Tavistock.

Cohn, Bernard S., 1980, 'History and anthropology: The state of play,' *Comparative Studies in Society and History*, 22: 198–221.

————, 1981, 'History and anthropology: Towards a rapprochement?' *Journal of Interdisciplinary History*, 12(2): 227–52.

————, 1985, 'The command of language and the language of command,' *Subaltern Studies*, 4, Delhi: OUP.

————, 1987, *An anthropologist among the historians and other essays*, Delhi: OUP.

Cohn, Bernard and Dirks, Nicholas, 1988, 'Beyond the fringe: The nation-state, colonialism and the technologies of power,' *Journal of H.S.*, 1(2): 224–9.

Comaroff, Jean, 1985, *Body of power, spirit of resistance: The culture and history of a South African people*, Chicago: University of Chicago Press.

Comaroff, Jean and Comaroff, John, 1987, 'The madman and the migrant: Work and labor in the historical consciousness of a South African people,' *American Ethnologist*, 14(2): 191–209.

————, 1991, *Of revelation and revolution: Christianity, colonialism and consciousness in South Africa*, vol. 1, Chicago: University of Chicago Press.

————, 1992, *Ethnography and the historical imagination*, Boulder: Westview Press.

Cooper, Frederick, 1994, 'Conflict and connection: Rethinking African history,' *American Historical Review*, 99(5): 1516–45.

Darnton, Robert, 1984, *The great cat massacre and other episodes in French cultural history*, New York: Basic Books.

Dasgupta, Swapan, 1985, 'Adivasi politics in Midnapur,' *Subaltern Studies*, 4, Delhi: OUP.

Davis, Natalie, 1981, 'The possibilities of the past,' *Journal of Interdisciplinary History*, 12(20): 267–76.

Dhanagare, D.N., 1983, *Peasant movements in India, 1920–1950*, Delhi: OUP.

Dimaggio, Paul, 1979, 'Review essay on Pierre Bourdieu,' *American Journal of S.*, 84(6): 1460–73.

Dirks, Nicholas B., 1987, *The hollow crown: Ethnohistory of an Indian little kingdom*, Cambridge: CUP.

————, 1989, 'The invention of caste: Civil society in colonial India,' *Social Analysis*, Special Issue, 42–52.

————, 1992, 'Ritual and resistance: Subversion as social fact,' in Douglas Haynes and Gyan Prakash (eds), *Contesting power: Resistance and everyday social relations in South Asia*, Berkeley: University of California Press.

————, Forthcoming, 'Is vice versa: Historical anthropologist and anthropological histories,' in Terence McDonald (ed.), *The historic turn in the human sciences*, Ann Arbor: University of Michigan Press.

Edelman, Marc, 1994, 'Landlords and the devil: Class, ethnic, and gender dimensions of Central American peasant narratives,' *Cultural Anthropology*, 9(1): 58–93.

Elwin, Verrier, 1939, *The Baiga*, London: John Murray.

————, 1964, *The tribal world of Verrier Elwin*, Delhi: OUP.

Feierman, Steven, 1990, *Peasant intellectuals: Anthropology and history in Tanzania*, Madison: University of Wisconsin Press.

Fisher, Michael, 1978, 'Planters and peasants: The ecological context of agrarian unrest in the indigo plantations of north Bihar, 1820–1920,' in Clive Dewey and A.G. Hopkins (eds), *The imperial impact: Studies in the economic history of Africa and India*, London: The Athlone Press.

Foucault, Michel, 1973, *The order of things: An archaeology of the human sciences*, New York: Vintage.

Friedman, Jonathan, 1992: 'Myth, history and political identity,' *Cultural Anthropology*, 7(2): 194–210.

Freitag, Sandria B., 1980, 'Sacred symbols as mobilizing ideology: The north Indian search for a Hindu community,' *Comparative Studies in Society and History*, 22: 597–625.

Fuchs, Stephen, 1965, *Rebellious prophets: A study of messianic movements in Indian religion*, Bombay: Asia.

Gable, Eric, 1995, 'The decoloniztation of consciousness: Local sceptics and the will to be modern in a West African village,' *American Ethnologist*, 22(2): 242–57.

Geertz, Clifford, 1973, *The interpretation of cultures*, New York: Basic Books.

————, 1976, 'From the native's point of view: On the nature of anthropological understanding,' in K.H. Basso and H.A. Selby (eds), *Meaning in anthropology*, Albuquerque: University of New Mexico Press.

Gill, Chris, 1993, 'Wresting memory from the violence of the present: Rape, martyrdom and double narrative in Paul Friedrich's agrarian revolt in a Mexican village,' *Journal of H.S.*, 6(4): 30–53.

Gramsci, Antonio, 1971, *Selections from the prison notebooks*, London: Lawrence and Wishart.

————, 1985, *Selections from cultural writings*, Cambridge: Harvard University Press.

Guha, Ramachandra, 1989, *The unquiet woods: Ecological change and peasant resistance in the Himalaya*, Delhi: OUP.

————, 1991, 'Review of *Subaltern Studies* 5 and 6, *Indian Economic and Social History Review*, 28(1): 116–19.

Guha, Ramachandra and Madhav Gadgil, 1989, 'State forestry and social conflict in British India: A study of the ecological bases of agrarian protest,' *Past and Present*, 123: 141–77.

Guha, Ranajit (ed.), 1982–9, *Subaltern Studies: Writings on South Asian history and society*, 1–6, Delhi: OUP.

————, 1982, 'The prose of counter-insurgency,' *Subaltern Studies*, 1, Delhi: OUP.

————, 1983, *Elementary aspects of peasant insurgency in colonial India*, Delhi: OUP.

————, 1987a, 'Chandra's death,' *Subaltern Studies*, 5, Delhi: OUP.

————, 1987b, 'Preface,' in Bernard Cohn, *An anthropologist among the historians and other essays*, Delhi: OUP.

————, 1989, 'Dominance without hegemony and its historiography,' *Subaltern Studies*, 6, Delhi: OUP.

————, 1992, 'Discipline and mobilise,' *Subaltern Studies*, 7, Delhi: OUP.

Guha, Ranajit and Spivak, Gayatri Chakravorty, 1988, 'Introduction,' *Selected Subaltern Studies*, Delhi: OUP.

Gupta, Akhil and Ferguson, James, 1992: 'Beyond "culture:" Space, identity and the politics of difference,' *Cultural Anthropology*, 7(1): 6–21.

Habib, Irfan, 1985, 'Studying a colonial economy without studying colonialism,' *Modern Asian Studies*, 19(3): 355–81.

Hall, Stuart, 1978, 'Marxism and culture,' *Radical Historical Review*, 18: 5–14.

Hardiman, David, 1982, 'The Indian faction: A political theory examined,' *Subaltern Studies*, 1, Delhi: OUP.

———, 1987, *The coming of the Devi: Adivasi assertion in Western India*, Delhi: OUP.

———, 1993, 'Power in the Dangs, 1820–1920,' *Subaltern Studies*, 8, Delhi: OUP.

Haynes, Douglas and Prakash, Gyan, 1992, 'Introduction: The entanglement of power and resistance,' in Douglas Haynes and Gyan Prakash (eds), *Contesting power: Resistance and everyday social relations in South Asia*, Berkeley: University of California Press.

Hivale, Shamrao and Elwin, Verrier, 1935, *Songs of the forest*, London: Allen and Unwin.

Hunt, Lynn (ed.), 1989, *The new cultural history*, Berkeley: University of California Press.

Inden, Ronald, 1986, 'Orientalist constructions of India,' *Modern Asian Studies*, 20(3): 401–46.

Joseph, Gilbert and Nugent, Daniel (eds), 1994, *Everyday forms of state formation: Revolution and the negotiation of rule in modern Mexico*, Durham: Duke University Press.

Kelly, William W., 1985, *Deference and defiance in nineteenth-century Japan*, Princeton: Princeton University Press.

Kaviraj, Sudipta, 1992, 'The imaginary institution of India,' *Subaltern Studies*, 7, Delhi: OUP.

Leach, Edmond, 1976, *Claude Lévi-Strauss*, London: Penguin.

Lévi-Strauss, Claude, 1963 (1949), 'Introduction: History and anthropology,' in *Structural anthropology*, New York: Anchor.

———, 1963, *Structural anthropology*, Boston: Beacon Press.

———, 1972, *The savage mind*, London: Weidenfeld and Nicolson.

———, 1983, *The raw and the cooked*, Chicago: Chicago University Press.

Ludden, David, 1993, 'Subalterns and others, in the agrarian history of South Asia,' Yale University, December 1993.

Mallon, Florencia, 1994, 'The promise and dilemmas of Subaltern Studies: Perspectives from Latin American history,' *American Historical Review*, 99(5): 1491–1515.

Mintz, Sidney, 1985, *Sweetness and power: The place of sugar in modern history*, New York: Penguin.

Mukherjee, S.N., 1970, 'Class, caste and politics in Calcutta,' in Edmund Leach and S.N. Mukherjee (eds), *Élites in South Asia*, Cambridge: CUP.

Nugent, Daniel and Alonso, Ana Maria, 1994, 'Multiple selective traditions in agrarian reform and agrarian struggle: Popular culture and state formation in the ejido of Namiquipa,' in Gilbert Joseph and Daniel Nugent (eds), *Everyday forms of state formation: Revolution and the negotiation of rule in modern Mexico*, Durham: Duke University Press.

O'Hanlon, Rosalind, 1988, 'Recovering the subject: Subaltern Studies and histories of resistance in colonial South Asia,' *Modern Asian Studies*, 22(1): 189–224.

O'Hanlon, Rosalind and Washbrook, David, 1992, 'After Orientalism: Culture, criticism, and politics in the third world,' *Comparative Studies in Society and History*, 34(1): 141–67.

Pandey, Gyanendra, 1983, 'Rallying around the cow: Sectarian strife in the Bhojpur region, 1888–1917,' *Subaltern Studies*, 2, Delhi: OUP.

———, 1990, *The construction of communalism in colonial North India*, Delhi: OUP.

———, 1992: 'In defense of the fragment: Writing about Hindu–Muslim riots in India today,' *Representations*, 37: 27–55.

Ortner, Sherry, 1995, 'Resistance and the problem of ethnographic refusal,' *Comparative Studies in Society and History*, 37(1): 173–93.

Prakash, Gyan 1990a, *Bonded histories: Genealogies of labour servitude in colonial India*, Cambridge: CUP.

———, 1990b, 'Writing post-Orientalist histories of the third world: Perspectives from Indian historiography,' *Comparative Studies in Society and History*, 32(3): 383–408.

———, 1992, 'Can the "subaltern" ride: A reply to O'Hanlon and Washbrook,' *Comparative Studies in Society and History*, 34(1): 168–84.

———, 1994, '*Subaltern Studies* as postcolonial criticism,' *American Historical Review*, 99(5): 1475–90.

Prakash, Sri, 1985, 'Models of peasant differentiation and aspects of agrarian economy in colonial India,' *Modern Asian Studies*, 19(3): 549–71.

Ricoeur, Paul, 1986, *Lectures on ideology and utopia*, G.H. Taylor (ed.), New York: Columbia University Press.

Roseberry, William, 1989, *Anthropologies and histories: Essays in culture, history and political economy*, New Brunswick: Rutgers University Press.

Sahlins, Marshall, 1985, *Islands of history*, Chicago: University of Chicago Press.

Said, Edward, 1979, *Orientalism*, New York: Vintage.

Sangren, Steven, 1995, 'Power against ideology: A critique of Focaultian usage,' *Cultural Anthropology*, 10(1): 3–40.

Sarkar, Sumit, 1984, 'The conditions and nature of subaltern militancy: Bengal from swadeshi to non-cooperation,' *Subaltern Studies*, 3, Delhi: OUP.

Sarkar, Tanika, 1985, 'Jitu Santhal's movement in Malda,' *Subaltern Studies*, 4, Delhi: OUP.

Saussure, Ferdinand de, 1966, *Course in general linguistics*, New York: McGraw Hill.

Sen, Asok, 1987, '*Subaltern Studies*: Capital class and community,' *Subaltern Studies*, 5, Delhi: OUP.

Scott, James C., 1985, *Weapons of the weak: Everyday forms of peasant resistance*, New Haven: Yale University Press.

———, 1990, *Domination and the art of resistance: Hidden transcripts*, New Haven: Yale University Press.

Sewell, William H., 1992, 'A theory of structure: Duality, agency and transformation,' *American Journal of Science*, 98: 1–29.

Shweder, Richard A., 1984, 'Anthropology's romantic rebellion against the enlightenment, or, there is more to thinking than reason and evidence,' in R.A. Shweder and R.A. Levine (eds), *Culture theory: Essays on mind, self and emotion*, Cambridge: CUP.

Sider, Gerald, 1986, *Culture and class in anthropology and history: A Newfoundland illustration*, Cambridge: CUP.

Siu, Helen F., 1989, *Agents and victims in South China: Accomplices in rural revolt*, New Haven: Yale University Press.

Sivaramakrishnan, K., 1992, 'Persistent élites and social change: Agrarian relations in colonial Bengal, 1750–1950,' *Yale Graduate Journal of Anthropology*, 4: 1–15.

———, 1993, 'Unpacking colonial discourse: Notes on using the anthropology of tribal India for an ethnography of the state,' *Yale Graduate Journal of Anthropology*, 5: 57–68.

———, 1995. 'Colonialism and forestry in India: Imagining the past in present politics,' *Comparative Studies in Society and History*, 37(1): 3–40.

Skaria, Ajay, 1999, 'Writing, orality and power in the Dangs, Western India, 1800s–1920s,' *Subaltern Studies*, 9, Delhi: OUP.

Spivak, Gayatri C., 1985, 'Subaltern Studies: Deconstructing historiography,' *Subaltern Studies*, 4, Delhi: OUP.

———, 1988, 'Can the subaltern speak?' in Cary Nelson and Lawrence Grossberg (eds), *Marxism and the interpretation of culture*, Urbana: University of Illinois Press.

Stocking, George, 1991, 'Introduction,' in George Stocking (ed.), *Colonial situations: Essays on the contextualisation of ethnographic knowledge*, History of anthropology, vol. 7, Madison: University of Wisconsin Press.

Stokes, Eric P., 1978, *The peasant and the Raj: Studies in agrarian society and peasant rebellion in colonial India*, Cambridge: CUP.

———, 1986, *The peasant armed*, Oxford: Clarendon Press.

Suleri, Sara, 1992: *The rhetoric of English India,* Chicago: University. of Chicago Press.

Thapar, Romila, 1989, 'Imagined religious communities: Ancient history and the modern search for Hindu identity,' *Modern Asian Studies,* 23(2): 209–31.

Thompson, Edward P., 1965, *The making of the English working class,* London: Pelican.

———, 1977, 'Folklore, anthropology and social history,' *Indian Historical Review.*

———, 1978, 'Eighteenth-century English society: Class struggle without class,' *Social History,* 3(2): 133–65.

von Furer-Haimendorf, Christopher, 1945, *The Reddis of the Bison Hills: A study in acculturation,* London: Macmillan.

———, 1948, *The Raj Gonds of Adilabad,* London: Macmillan.

———, 1990, *Life among Indian tribes: The autobiography of an anthropologist,* New York: OUP.

Washbrook, David, 1988, 'Progress and problems: South Asian economic and social history, 1720–1860,' *Modern Asian Studies,* 22(1): 57–96.

CHAPTER II. 4

Conflict and Connection: Rethinking Colonial African History*

FREDERICK COOPER

T HIS ESSAY is part of an effort to bring historiographies of Africa, Latin America, and Asia—with their particular scholarly traditions, insights, and blind spots—into relationship with each other, avoiding the assumption that interaction simply means borrowing from apparently more 'developed' historiographies. South–South intellectual exchange is not new. The earliest attempts by African intellectuals to confront the issues of colonialism and racism, beginning in the nineteenth century, entailed contacts forged with Americans of African descent and later with anti-colonial leaders from Asia and the Caribbean. Later still, the limitations of anti-colonial ideologies and of nationalism were analysed in Africa with the help of arguments originating with Latin American dependency theorists.

The Subaltern Studies group has had a particularly empowering effect on the scholarship of once-colonised regions, for it has put the process of making history into the picture. While striving to recover

* I am grateful for the criticisms and advice of Shiva Balaghi, Keith Breckenridge, Jane Burbank, Catherine Burns, David William Cohen, Fernando Coronil, Mamadou Diouf, Nicholas B. Dirks, Prasenjit Duara, Dorothy Hodgson, Florencia E. Mallon, Mohamed Mbodj, Gyan Prakash, Timothy Scarnecchia, Julie Skurskie, John Soluri, Ann Stoler, Kerry Ward, and Luise White.

the lives of people forgotten in narratives of global exploitation and national mobilisaton, this collective of historians has called into question the very narratives themselves, indeed, the source material, theoretical frameworks, and subject-position of historians. The 'subalternity of non-Western histories' as much as the subalternity of social groups within those histories has been uncovered. Those histories exist in the shadow of Europe not solely because of colonisation's powerful intrusion into other continents but because Europe's self-perceived movement towards state-building, capitalist development, and modernity marked and still mark a vision of historical progress against which African, Asian, or Latin American history appears as 'failure': of the 'nation to come to its own,' of the 'bourgeoisie as well as of the working class to lead.'[1]

In these pages, I will take advantage of the emphases in the essays of Gyan Prakash and Florencia Mallon to take a somewhat different tack. They have explained the contributions of Subaltern Studies to a wider historiography, and they bring out the important tension in its writings between efforts to recover the history and the agency of the subaltern and to analyse the discursive production of the subaltern, how colonial categories of knowledge flattened the multi-sided experiences of people in colonies into such a category. I want to explore the ways—with parallels and differences—in which historians of Africa have confronted the experience of colonial rule. To the African historian, the value of Indian historiography is not that our colleagues offer readymade solutions to our problems but that all of us are engaged in different ways with closely related debates.[2] Both historiographies wrestle with—but do not quite escape—the dichotomous vision characteristic of colonial ideologies, originating in the opposition of civilised coloniser and primitive colonised. The risk is that in exploring the colonial binarism one reproduces it, either by new variations of the dichotomy (modern versus traditional) or by inversion (the destructive imperialist versus the sustaining community of the victims). The difficulty is to confront the power behind European expansion without assuming it was all-determining and to probe the clash of different forms of social organisation without treating them as self-contained and autonomous. The binaries of coloniser–colonised,

Western–non-Western, and domination–resistance begin as useful devices for opening up questions of power but end up constraining the search for precise ways in which power is deployed and the ways in which power is engaged, contested, deflected, and appropriated.

With Africa's independence, historians were strongly moved to find a domain that could be defined as both unambiguously African and resistant to imperialism. In the historiography of Subaltern Studies, the clarity of such categories is questioned, but they keep coming back in the very concept of the subaltern and in Ranajit Guha's insistence that one can examine the 'autonomous' domain of the subaltern and reveal people acting 'on their own.'[3] Guha, like many African historians, wants his subalterns to have a rich and complex consciousness, to exercise autonomous agency, and yet to remain in the category of subaltern, and he wants colonialism to remain resolutely colonial, despite the contradictions of its modernising projects and its insistence on maintaining boundaries, despite its interventionist power being rendered contingent by the actions of subalterns.[4] Colonial discourse, Subaltern Studies rightly points out, has tried to contain its oppositions—whether in the form of its 'liberal' ideas of self-determination or the 'irrational' actions of 'primitive' people— within its own categories. How far colonial discourse could actually contain its challenges and tensions remains in question.

The Subaltern Studies group has turned what could be yet another exercise in Western self-indulgence—endless critiques of modernity, of the universalising pretensions of Western discourse—into something more valuable because it insists that the subject-positions of colonised people that European teleologies obscure should not simply be allowed to dissolve. While profiting from the insights of Subaltern Studies to re-examine work in African colonial history, I also hope to push back the dualisms that are coming in the rear door in both historiographies. African historians' use of the concept of 'resistance' is generally less subtle, less dialectic, less self-questioning than Indian historians' deployment of the idea of subaltern agency, yet both concepts risk flattening the complex lives of people living in colonies and underestimate the possibility that African or Indian action might actually alter the boundaries of subordination within a seemingly powerful colonial regime. The critique of modernity has its own dangers, as Dipesh Chakrabarty recognises in warning that too simple a rejection could be 'politically suicidal.'[5] One can agree with Guha and his colleagues that Marxist master narratives of relentless capitalist advance are yet another form of Western teleology—as are nationalist metanarratives of the triumphal takeover of the nation-state—yet historians should not deprive themselves of the analytical tools necessary to study capitalism and its effects around the world—in all their complexity, contingency, and limitations. Nor should the recognition of the violence and oppression within the generalisation of the nation-state model around the world blind us to the potential for violence and oppression that lies in other social formations. I am also trying to push capital and the state back in, making them the object of an analysis more nuanced and interactive than attacks on metanarrative and modernity.

There are reasons for different emphases in the historiographies of the two continents. Subaltern Studies emerged in the 1980s, nearly forty years after India's independence, as a critique of an established nationalist interpretation of history, as well as of 'progressive' arguments, whether liberal or Marxist. Africa's independence movements are more recent, their histories only beginning to be written. Africans' and Africanists' disillusionment with the fruits of independence in the 1970s took the form of an emphasis on the external determinants of economic and social problems, and hence a look towards Latin American dependency theory. Most important of all have been the obstacles to the density of debate possible in India: the catastrophic economic situation Africa faced, particularly since the 1980s, and the harsh material conditions in which African scholars and educational and cultural institutions function.[6]

Different experiences give rise to different initial assumptions. The category of subaltern is an intuitively attractive point of departure for South Asianists, given the widely shared perception of social distinction in India as long-lasting, coercive, and sharply delineated, even when scholars put the bases of social distinction in question. Recent generations of African scholars have witnessed—and often been part of—a moment, perhaps not to be repeated, of considerable mobility and category jumping, reflecting the sudden expansion of education systems in the 1950s, the post-Second World War export boom, the precipitous Africanisation of the civil service, and the rapid development by African rulers of clientage networks and distributional politics. Whereas many scholars have been trying to pull apart and examine the idea of an essential 'India,' others have felt they had to put together 'Africa' in the face of general perceptions of everlasting and immutable division. Subaltern Studies' critique of ways in which a nationalist state picks up the controlling project of a colonial state gives rise to sympathetic echoes among Africans and Africanists—disillusioned with post-independence states—but also to a measure of scepticism about conceivable alternatives, given bitter experience, as in contemporary Somalia, with what 'communities' can do to one another when a state loses its controlling capabilities in the age of automatic weapons.[7]

What follows is a consideration of African historiography, stressing the connections between the 'resistance' model that was crucial to its development and the new scholarship on colonialism. Both concepts, I argue, should be further scrutinised. Politics in a colony should not be reduced to anti-colonial politics or to nationalism: the 'imagined communities' Africans saw were both smaller and larger than the nation, sometimes in creative tension with each other, sometimes in repressive antagonism.

The burst of colonial liberations that followed Ghana's independence in 1957 led Africanists to project backward the idea of the nation. The new states of Africa needed something around which diverse peoples could build a sense of commonality. Africa scholars, as one acute observer put it, acted like the 'Committee of Concerned Scholars for a Free Africa.'[8] The first generation of historians of Africa, seeking to differentiate themselves from imperial historians, were eager to find a truly African history.

African resistance to European conquest and colonisation both ratified the integrity of pre-colonial polities and structures (themselves a major topic) and provided a link between them and the nationalist challenge to colonial rule. Resistance was the key plot element in a continuous narrative of African history. Terence Ranger argued specifically for a connection between 'primary resistance movements' in the early days of colonisation and 'modern mass nationalism.' Early resistance implied mobilisation across a wider network of affiliation than kinship units or 'tribes' provided, and this enlargement of scale created a basis for subsequent movements. In a detailed study of a revolt in Southern Rhodesia, Ranger pointed to the role of spirit mediums in mobilising rebels across a large region and providing a coherent framework for the resistance.[9]

While analyses such as these attempted an Africa-centred perspective, they paradoxically centred European colonialism as the issue that really mattered in the twentieth century.[10] An apparently populist rhetoric concealed the privileging of African élites—in the 1960s as much as the 1890s—by virtue of their anti-colonialism and downplayed tensions and inequalities within African societies. Sensitive to these historiographical issues, Ranger himself stepped away from the linearity of his earlier argument and advocated a more multivalent and nuanced approach to African political mobilisation.[11] Nonetheless, studies within the resistance framework conclusively showed that colonial conquests and heavy-handed interventions into African life were vigorously challenged, that guerrilla warfare within decentralised polities was as important as the fielding of armies by African states, that women as well as men engaged in acts of resistance, and that individual action—moving away from the tax collector or labour recruiter, ignoring orders, speaking insolently, and criticising the claims of missionaries, doctors, and educators—complemented collective actions.[12]

For the authors of the UNESCO history of Africa (a collective series intended to reflect the first generations of post-independence African and Africanist scholarship), the key issue of the early colonial era was the defence of sovereignty. Adu Boahen, the editor of the relevant volume, saw African societies in the late nineteenth century as dynamic, moving towards a form of modernity that retained sovereignty but selectively engaged with European commerce, religion, and education. The dynamism of African societies before colonisation is no longer in question, but Boahen's conception grants Western modernity too much power—particularly in its emphasis on the strength of the state as a marker of political progress and a unit for social advancement—while it fails to address the contradictions stemming from specific social structures within Africa. Boahen has little to say about Africans who conquered other Africans or about the slave-owners in coastal Dahomey or Sahelian Sokoto or island Zanzibar who made other Africans bear the burden of expanding commerce. Sovereignty was not the only issue facing Africans, and the European invasions entered a long and complex process of state-building and oppression, of production and exploitation, as well as a history of small-scale producers and merchants for whom the overseas connection offered opportunities they did not want to give up and oppressions they wanted to contest.[13]

Here, I will break the linearity of the discussion of the historiography itself for a moment and point to another pioneering approach. In 1956, K. Onwuka Dike, generally regarded as the first African to become a professional African historian, authored *Trade and politics in the Niger Delta*, seeking to make a decisive break with the imperial historians who had been his mentors and to write history from an African perspective. His book is less remarkable for the new sources it used than for the matter-of-fact way in which it analysed interaction. Africans do not appear in this text as either resistors or collaborators in the face of European involvement in the Delta; Europeans, indeed, appear as actors in the universe of different actors within the region, all trying to work with the opportunities and constraints of overseas trade and regional political structure. Dike knew what the Delta traders could not—that the European traders' metropolitan connections would one day break the framework of interaction—but he nonetheless provided an account of African agency intersecting with European in a crucial moment of history.[14]

Resistance had a special power in the two decades after Dike's study appeared. Scholars and journalists wanting to make the world aware of anti-colonial movements in Africa—Thomas Hodgkin and Basil Davidson the most knowledgeable among them—sought to show the complex roots of political mobilisation, from Africa's own traditions of rule to memories of battles against foreign conquerors, to religious and labour movements that provided an experience of organisation culminating in the development of nationalist political parties.[15] Dike's own project took on a nationalist bent as well: the 'Ibadan' school emphasised the integrity of pre-colonial African societies, which sometimes appeared as precedents for independent Africa. J.F. Ade Ajayi termed colonialism an 'episode in African history,' a break in the otherwise continuous exercise of African political agency.[16] What was most neglected was colonial rule itself: to my cohort in graduate school (1969–74), studying pre-colonial history or resistance constituted genuine African history, but bringing a similar specificity of inquiry to that which was being resisted risked having one's project labelled as a throwback to imperial history.

Questionings of the nationalist metanarrative came from two generations of African scholars. B.A. Ogot, the senior historian of Kenya, in an eassy of 1972 on the 'Loyalist crowd' in Mau Mau, pointed out that the violent conflicts of the 1950s could not be reduced to a simple morality play: both sides had their moral visions, their moral discourses. The 'Loyalists' saw themselves as engaged in a defence of a way of life in which Christianity, education, and investment in small farms were the means to progress. Colonial policy could be contested within limits, but to the Loyalists the young rebels were violating Kikuyu traditions of respect for elders and threatening the community.[17] Some twenty years later and across the continent, Mamadou Diouf published a book that debunked Senegal's basic myth of resistance, the battle of Lat Dior and his Wolof kingdom against the French. Lat Dior, Diouf argued, was defending 'the privileges of the ruling class and the traditional field in which it exercised its exploitation' as much as sovereignty. His study entailed a complex enactment with how power was mobilised and contested within Africa and the extent to which the long-term French presence first made the emergence of a Lat Dior possible and then rendered the continued existence of this sort of polity impossible.[18]

The metanarrative of nationalist victory—and many of the tales of 'resistance'—have most often been told as stories of men, with a rather macho air to the narrating of confrontation. Women's history, to a significant extent, began by arguing that 'women could do it, too' or by adding African patriarchy to the colonial object of resistance. As historians increasingly showed that economic and social activity was defined, contested, and redefined in terms of gender, the gendered nature of politics needed to be examined as well.[19] The contestation of gender roles within the Mau Mau movement is being explored by Cora Ann Presley, Luise White, and Tabitha Kanogo, while Timothy Scarnecchia shows the masculinisation of African politics in the 1950s in Harare. Housing regulations that effectively disallowed women access to residential space except through a man meant that women on their own were by definition outside the law, and they were driven into certain niches in the unofficial economy. For a time, such women worked with a male-led union-cum-political movement to challenge the way the state defined and constrained urban women. The movement failed; and, when nationalists later began to challenge the colonial state in other ways, their quest to balance respectability against the movement's need to recruit migrant male labourers meant that they, too, treated such women as dangerous and disruptive. Nationalism in the 1950s explicitly constructed itself in masculine— as much as class—terms, leaving aside its own more ambiguous history.[20]

Apartheid in South Africa affected women in particular ways: through male-only labour compounds, the policing of migration, the feminisation of rural poverty, and a complex hierarchy of residential rights that divided black workers and families. Protest was thus also shaped by gender. Women led bus boycotts and demonstrations against the application of pass laws to women. A strong and sustained series of women's protest movements in the Herschel district of Cape Province reflected the circumstances of women in the context of increasing male out-migration, but the more formally organised Industrial and Commercial Workers' Union largely shunted women aside.[21]

The heroic narrative fell victim not only to wise elders and young scholars with new questions but also to continuing crises in Africa itself. African novelists were the first intellectuals to bring before a wide public inside and outside the African continent profound questions about the corruption within post-colonial governments and the extent to which external domination persisted.[22] Growing disillusionment made increasingly attractive the theories of 'underdevelopment,' which located the poverty and weakness of 'peripheral' societies not in the colonial situation but in the more long-term process of domination within a capitalist world system. The debate that dependency theory unleashed had the beneficial effect of legitimising among African intellectuals the notion that theoretical propositions were not mere impositions of Western models on a unique Africa but offered ways of understanding the predicament Africa shared with other parts of what had come to be called the 'Third World.' The direct link in bringing dependency theory to Africa from Latin America was Walter Rodney, a Guyanese of African descent, instrumental in founding the 'Dar es Salaam' school of radical African history.[23] It may be that an engaged expatriate was better positioned than were Tanzanians to open the challenge to nationalist conventions, the tragic counterpart to this being Rodney's assassination after his return to Guyana and the detention, in their own country, of several Kenyan historians who had questioned reigning myths.

The issues opened by dependency theorists prompted an increasing interest in Marxist theory among Africanists and Africans in the 1970s and opened the possibility of a dialogue across the continents.[24] Ironically, dependency theory emphasised common subordination and gave little place to African or Latin American agency. Certain Marxist approaches assumed the dominance of capitalism, although a useful contribution of African history to Marxist theory would be to point to the limits capital encountered in trying to tame Africa's labour power.[25] More recently, post-structuralist theory has turned towards an examination of discourse and modes of representation—including the scholar's own—but often at the cost of surrendering the tools with which to undertake studies of global power and exploitation. For all the critique and counter-critique among these approaches, there has been a certain facility with which historians outside the African continent have slid from one paradigm to another, post-Marxism and post-structuralism embodying this tendency in their very labels. To many American or European scholars, insisting that Africa had a history—irrespective of what one said about it—was evidence of a progressive bent; African history was subaltern studies by default.[26]

The notable exception to this observation comes from the part of Africa that did not fit into the 1960s' narrative of liberation from white rule, South Africa. My cohort of graduate students in the United States felt that the history of South Africa was not African enough.[27] South African expatriates contributed the most in the 1970s to the focus on that region, and as they did one of the sharpest theoretical divides opened up: a 'liberal' view that stressed African initiative and Afro-European interaction stymied by the rigid racism of Afrikaners versus a 'radical' paradigm that saw South African racism as itself a consequence of the way in which capitalism emerged in the late nineteenth and early twentieth century. Within the 'radical' approach, one branch tended towards a structuralist conception of an unfolding logic of capital determining South African history, but another looked directly to the inspiration of European and American social historians to uncover the ways in which Africans carried out their struggles and forged community as well as class.[28] South African historians shared some of the 'history from the bottom up' concerns with Subaltern Studies but generally not their conception of the subaltern's autonomy. Charles van Onselen has most sharply described the element of shared culture across racial divisions and antagonisms within poor farming communities, and likewise the efforts of diverse and changing groups of blacks and whites to make their way in the rough world of urbanising Johannesburg.[29] The most interesting autonomist argument—independent of Subaltern Studies—comes from Keletso Atkins's analysis of a distinctly African work culture, although her point is that this work culture influenced and constrained the apparently dominant work culture of developing capitalism.[30] South African history in the 1970s and 1980s was thus distinguished by a focused debate—only occasionally engaging the historiography of the rest of Africa—over race, class, and capital. In the 1990s, poststructuralist questionings of the categories and narratives of Marxist history have been strongly resisted in South Africa by those who insist that here, at least, the lines of power and exploitation are clear.[31] This is a useful debate and another instance of the 'irresolvable and fertile tensions' between different conceptions of history, theory, and political activism that Florencia Mallon stresses in her contribution to the *Forum*. It also opens opportunities for engagement with the issues being raised by Subaltern Studies.

Over the past several years, a new colonial history has emerged, in dialogue with anthropology and literary studies and ranging over many areas of the world.[32] Anthropologists questioned past and current modes of ethnographic inquiry, suggesting the need for a more contextual and historical examination of the apparatus that collected and classified knowledge of Africa or Asia.[33] Literary critics began to study the politics of representations and the process by which the assertion within European discourse of a sense of national or continental identity depended on inscribing 'otherness' on non-European populations.[34] Both scholarly traditions encouraged an examination of the categories and tropes through which the Africa of explorers, missionaries, settlers, scientists, doctors, and officials was symbolically ordered into the grid of 'tribe' and 'tradition.' Historians explored how censuses defined or reified such categories as caste, how medicine defined susceptibility to disease in racial or cultural terms, how colonial architecture inscribed modernity onto the built environment while appropriating a distilled traditionalism to its own purposes, and how missionaries sought to 'colonise minds' by forging an individual capable of thinking about his or her personal salvation, separated from the collective ethos of the community.[35] The Subaltern Studies group took the further step of asking whether categories of colonial knowledge set the terms in which oppositional movements could function and in which colonialism itself could be critiqued.[36]

This trend has opened up possibilities of seeing how deeply colonies were woven into what it meant to be European and how elusive—and difficult to police—was the boundary between colonisers and colonised.[37] It is nonetheless open to the danger of reading a generalised 'coloniality' from particular texts, abstracting what went on in colonies from local contexts and contradictory and conflictual global processes.[38] Even as subtle and interactive an argument as Homi Bhabha's treatment of mimicry, in which the colonised person's acting as if 'white but not quite' destabilises the coloniser's view of boundaries and control, relies on detaching the dyad of coloniser–colonised from anything either subject might be engaged in except their mutual confrontation.[39]

It is far from clear what Africans thought about the symbolic structure of colonial power or the identities being inscribed on them. The cultural edifice of the West could be taken apart brick by brick and parts of it used to shape quite different cultural visions.[40] Piecing together such processes is one of the most promising endeavours being undertaken by innovative scholars. A scholarly trend that began from the opposition of 'self' and 'other' has thus ended up confronting the artificiality of such dichotomies and the complex *bricolage* with which Africans in colonies put together practices and beliefs.[41]

The problem of recovering such histories while understanding how colonial documents construct their own versions of them has been the focus of thoughtful reflections by Ranajit Guha.[42] At first glance, these contributions may appear to the African historian more as sound practice than a methodological breakthrough. African historians cut their teeth in the 1960s on the assertion that colonial sources distorted history, and they saw the use of oral sources—as well as reading colonial documents against the grain—as putting themselves on the path to people's history. But Africa scholars put more emphasis on showing that Africans had a history than on asking how Africans' history-making was implicated in establishing or contesting power.[43] Guha and his colleagues, facing the rich but problematic corpus of Indian colonial documents, have provoked a useful discussion over the conceptual difficulties in the attempt to recover consciousness and memory outside of a literate élite—and the ultimate impossibility of true knowledge across the barriers of class and colonialism—while African historians have tried to see how far one could push with nondocumentary sources. There is room here for exchange across differing perspectives, although Gayatri Chakravorty Spivak's rhetorical question 'Can the subaltern speak?' may tempt the historian struggling for his or her modest insights to ask in return, 'Can the theorist listen?'[44]

Recognition of the much greater power of the Europeans in the colonial encounter does not negate the importance of African agency in determining the shape the encounter took. While the conquerors could concentrate military force to defeat African armies, 'pacify' villages, or slaughter rebels, the routinisation of power demanded alliances with local authority figures, be they lineage heads or recently defeated kings. A careful reading of colonial narratives suggests a certain pathos: the civilising mission did not end up with the conversion of Africa to Christianity or the generalisation of market relations throughout the continent, and colonial writing instead celebrated victories against 'barbarous practices' and 'mad mullahs.' Colonial violence, in such a situation, became 'acts of trespass,' vivid and often brutal demonstrations distinguishable for what they could violate more than what they could transform.[45]

The economic geography of colonisation is as uneven as the geography of power. Colonial powers established islands of cash crop production and mining surrounded by vast labour catchment areas in which coercion and, as time went on, lack of alternatives were necessary to extract labourers. To a significant extent, the wage labour force that capital could use—whatever the wishes of employers—was largely male and transitory, in large measure because Africans were seeking to incorporate periods of wage labour into their lives even as capital was trying to subordinate African economies.[46] It took the wealth and power of South Africa—where a racialised version of 'primitive accumulation' took place through the relative density of white settlement, the impetus of gold mining after the 1880s, and the agency of the state—for labour power to be detached from its social roots. Even in South Africa, the struggle over how, where, and under what conditions Africans could actually be made to work never quite ended.[47] Elsewhere, some of the greatest success stories of colonial economies came about through African agency: the vast expansion of cocoa production in the Gold Coast at the turn of the century, Nigeria from the 1920s, and the Ivory Coast from the 1940s was the work of smallholders and did not depend on colonial initiatives. Cash cropping was neither a colonial imposition nor an unmediated African response to price incentives; it gave rise, in certain places, to accumulation without producing a bourgeoisie. This is the kind of history that Subaltern Studies scholars want to have told, a history that breaks out of the moulds of European modernity and Afro-Asiatic stasis, yet these farmers' experience cannot easily be contained within a notion of subalternity.[48]

The juxtaposition of a disruptive but concentrated colonising presence and a large and unevenly controlled 'bush' had paradoxical consequences: fostering episodic exercises of collective punishment or direct coercion against unwilling workers or cultivators on whom the effects of routinised discipline had not been successfully projected;[49] making the boundaries of African communities more rigid and their 'customary law' more categorical than in days before colonial 'progress;'[50] marginalising educated and Christian Africans as the colonising apparatus assumed control and established alliances with 'traditional' leaders;[51] fostering commercial linkages that enabled Africans who adapted to them to acquire collective resources that later enabled them to resist pressures to enter wage labour;[52] expanding an ill-controlled urban economy that offered opportunities for casual labourers, itinerant hawkers, criminal entrepreneurs, and providers of service to a migrant, largely male African working class, thus creating alternatives (for women as well as men) to the roles into which colonial regimes wished to cast people;[53] and creating space for missionary-educated Africans to reject mission communities in favour of secular roles in a colonial bureaucracy or to transform Christian teaching into critiques of colonial rule.[54]

This is not just an argument about African 'adaptation' or 'resistance' to colonial initiatives. Rather, it is an argument that policy and ideology also reflected European adaptation (and resistance) to the initiatives of the colonised. This notion extends to the periodisation of colonial history: Imperial conquerors began by thinking they could remake African society and rationalise the exploitation of the continent; by the Second World War, they were largely frustrated in such endeavours and began to make—through policies of 'indirect rule' and 'association'—their failures sound like a policy of conserving African society and culture; by the late 1930s, the imagined Africa of 'tribes' was proving unable to contain the tensions unleashed by the much more complex patterns of economic change; in the late 1930s and 1940s, Great Britain and France tried to re-seize the initiative through a programme of economic and social development; Africans political parties, trade unions, and rural organisers turned the development initiative into a claim for social and political rights, effective enough for the abdication of power and responsibility to become increasingly attractive in London and Paris; most recently, the tendency of

Western powers to write off Africa as a continent of disasters and bad government is a sign that the development framework still has not pushed Africa into the role of a quiet and productive junior partner in the world market.[55]

Ranajit Guha has characterised colonisation as dominance without hegemony, a direct contradiction of the trends in metropoles to envelop the exercise of power under universal social practices and norms.[56] The claim of a colonial government to rule a distinct people denied the universality of market relations, revealed the limits to capitalism's progressive thrust, and led colonial regimes to seek legitimacy by hitching themselves to indigenous notions of authority and obedience. Nationalists, seeking to displace colonial rulers without undermining their own authority, continued to practice dominance without hegemony.

The distinction between capitalist universality and colonial particularism is a compelling one, but Guha does not get to the bottom of it. He misses the implications of the limits of coercion, and he underplays the dynamic possibilities stemming from the partial and contradictory hegemonic projects that colonial rulers attempted: the disputes within colonising populations and metropolitan élites over different visions of colonial rule and the space that efforts to articulate hegemony opened up for contestation among the colonised. He implicitly draws a contrast between colonial dominance and metropolitan hegemony that the exclusions and violences of twentieth-century Europe belie. Guha's insight, however, offers an opportunity to explore the tensions of particularism and universality within colonies themselves and in a dynamic interconnection of colony and metropole. As I will argue below, the inability of colonial regimes to establish and maintain 'dominance' amid the uneven effects of capitalism led them to deploy the 'universalistic' conceptions of social engineering developed in Europe, only to find that their own hopes for the success of such technologies required giving up the beliefs about Africa on which a sense of 'dominance' depended.[57]

The incompleteness of capitalist transformation in a colonial context has been a major theme of Subaltern Studies, but the tensions of colonialism in a capitalist context are equally important to analyse.

Just as elusive are the conceptual categories with which scholars try to understand the movements that have challenged colonial and capitalist power in Africa, Asia, and Latin America.

At one level, the concept of resistance is generally accepted and unproblematic. In the clash of African and colonial armies, individual acts of disobedience or flight, and the elaboration of powerful arguments for liberation, colonial rule has been continually and severely challenged. But much of the resistance literature is written as if the 'R' were capitalised. What is being resisted is not necessarily clear, and 'colonialism' sometimes appears as a force whose nature and implications do not have to be unpacked. The concept of resistance can be expanded so broadly that it denies any other kind of life to the people doing the resisting. Significant as resistance might be, Resistance is a concept that may narrow our understanding of African history rather than expand it.

Scholars have their reasons for taking an expansive view. Little actions can add up to something big: desertion from labour contracts, petty acts of defiance of white officials or their African subalterns, illegal enterprises in colonial cities, alternative religious communities— all these may subvert a regime that proclaimed both its power and its righteousness, raise the confidence of people in the idea that colonial power can be countered, and forge a general spirit conducive to mobilisation across a variety of social differences. The problem is to link the potential with the dynamics of a political process, and this problem requires careful analysis rather than teleology. It is facile to make causal generalisations across diverse circumstances, as Donald Crummey does in proclaiming, 'Most popular violence is a response to state or ruling-class violence,' and it is questionable to link all acts of assertion with a military metaphor, as James Scott does in terming them 'weapons of the weak.'[58]

Foucault saw resistance as constitutive of power and power of resistance; he denied that there was a 'single locus of great Refusal.' He found 'mobile and transitory points of resistance, producing cleavages in a society that shifts about, fracturing unities and effecting regroupings.' Although 'strategic codification' of those points can make for revolution, such a process cannot be assumed, and his stress was on the continual reconfiguration of both power and resistance.[59] In the current atmosphere of post-colonial pessimism, such an idea resonates: even the counter-hegemonic discourses of the colonial era and the subversions of European notions of modernity become enmeshed in concepts—the nation-state most prominent among them—that re-deploy ideas of surveillance, control, and development within post-independence politics, fracturing and producing unities and reconfiguring resistances. In such a light, Subaltern Studies scholars have scrutinised the reconfiguration of power-resistance at the moment of nationalist victory.[60]

The difficulty with the Foucaultian pairing of power and resistance lies in Foucault's treatment of power as 'capillary,' as diffused throughout society. However much surveillance, control, and the narrowing of the boundaries of political discourse were a part of Europe in its supposedly democratising era, power in colonial societies was more arterial than capillary—concentrated spatially and socially, not very nourishing beyond such domains, and in need of a pump to push it from moment to moment and place to place.[61] This should be a theoretical rallying point for historians: they have the tools (and often the inclination) to analyse in specific situations how power is constituted, aggregated, contested, and limited, going beyond the post-structuralist tendency to find power diffused in 'modernity,' 'the post-Enlightenment era,' or 'Western discourse.'

The resistance concept suffers from the diffuseness with which the object of resistance is analysed, as well as from what Sherry Ortner calls 'thinness.' The dyad of resistor–oppressor is isolated from its context; struggle within the colonised population—over class, age, gender, or other inequalities—is 'sanitised'; the texture of people's lives is lost; and complex strategies of coping, of seizing niches within changing economies, of multi-sided engagement with forces inside and outside the community, are narrowed into a single framework.[62]

Some of the best recent work in African history discards the categories of resistors and collaborators and starts with the question of how 'rural people saw their circumstances, made their choices, and constructed their ideas about the larger society.'[63] The relationship of gender issues and colonisation, for example, emerges in a complex way from the studies of Elias Mandala and Elizabeth Schmidt. Before the conquest, women had once exercised considerable control over farming and the crops they produced, but the expanding slave trade made women vulnerable to kidnapping or to the control of their would-be protectors. Colonial rule—the decline of warfare and increased possibilities for cash cropping—for a time gave women space to reassert power within domestic economies, but the subsequent decline of village agriculture and the increasing importance of labour migration made women increasingly dependent on men's fortunes.[64] Luise White, meanwhile, has shown that women sometimes seized niches in the expanding and ill-organised urban economy, as prostitutes and landlords, providing cheap services to male migrant labourers. White's study points up the basic ambiguity in colonial relationships: her women were both subverting the cultural project of colonialism and subsidising the economic one. Officials were indeed confused, in some contexts willing to let women furnish low-cost services, in others afraid that women's knowledge of urban society and their social networks were reproducing the wrong kind of African working class.[65]

The complexities of engagement and autonomy surface again and again. Karen Fields' analysis of Watchtower in Central Africa reveals a substantial refashioning of Christian doctrines in relation to the local power structure and labour migration. What made Watchtower subversive in official eyes was not that it encouraged active 'resistance' but that it defined a moral community in which the structures, notably chieftaincy, painfully elaborated by the colonial regime became irrelevant.[66] Did such processes contribute in the long run—as the secular Africanists of the 1960s thought they would—to a coming together of diverse strands of African thought and practice that rejected colonial rule in its entirety? Or did such movements go off in their own direction, as likely to clash with secular nationalisms as to assist their assault on the colonial state?

I am arguing here for the complexity of engagement of Africans with imported institutions and constructs, as opposed to James Scott's emphasis on a 'hidden transcript' among colonised people that develops among them only to burst forth into a 'public transcript' in moments of confrontation.[67] My approach also differs from Ranajit Guha's quest to explore the 'autonomous' domain of the subaltern, although the complex and varied practice of historians in the Subaltern Studies collective, more so than the manifestos, is filled with stories of engagement.[68]

In discussing labour, as Dipesh Chakrabarty points out, the historian can usefully invoke general theories about 'abstract labour,' a set of relationships characteristic of capitalism, while preserving a notion of 'real labour,' located in his case in the systems of authority and client-age of Bengali villages and the power structure of colonial India.[69] In my own research on Africa in the era of decolonisation, I examine both the tensions between African labour movements whose demands are shared around the capitalist world—wages, family welfare, security, and working conditions—and whose rhetoric invoked the universality of wage labour through a demand for equal pay for equal work, and a political movement focusing on self-determination for all Africans.[70] Ironically, the wave of strikers and general strikes in French and British Africa from the mid-1930s into the 1950s drew on the integration of workers into a wider population—which provided food to sustain strikes and at times brought about generalised urban mobilisation—yet the workers' demands distanced them from that population.

Colonial regimes sought to regain the initiative through 'stabilisation,' to form the poorly differentiated, ill-paid population that moved in and out of urban jobs into a compact body of men attached to their employment. They wanted employers to pay workers enough to bring families to the city so that the new generation of workers would be properly socialised to industrial life and separated from the perceived backwardness of village Africa. The dynamic of the situation lay in the fact that trade unions were able to capitalise on this yearning for predictability, order, and productivity—on officials' hope that Western models of the workplace and industrial relations might actually function in Africa—to pose their demands in ways officials found difficult to reject out of hand. Unions seized the developmentalist rhetoric of post-war imperialism and turned it into claims to entitlements, even as officials began to concede that a unionised workforce might aid stabilisation.[71]

By the mid-1950s, colonial regimes feared that their development initiatives were being undermined by rising labour costs, and they began to pull back from their own universalising stance. They realised that conceding African politicians a modest measure of power in colonial governments would force them to weigh the cost of labour against the territorial budget. A national reference point now seemed less threatening economically than a universalistic one. This time, colonial officials guessed right, for nationalist leaders, granted limited territorial authority, quickly set about disciplining African labour movements in the name of a single-minded focus on a national unity defined by the political party.

One can read the actions of labour movements in French and British Africa as one example among many of African militance or as an instance of the universal struggle of the working class or as the successful co-optation of an unquiet section of the African population into a set of structures and normalising practices derived from Europe. All three readings have some truth, but the important point is their dynamic relationship: labour movements both brought material benefits to a specific class of people and opened new possibilities for other sorts of actions, which themselves might have mobilising or normalising consequences. In this period, labour had a window of opportunity it lacked before and lost afterward, facing a colonial regime invested in a tenuous development initiative and fearing the mobilisation of an unpredictable mass. The tension between the demands of labour and efforts to forge unity against the colonial state was often a creative one—except in the too-common instance in which party élites fearful of organised challenges and insistent on the supremacy of the national struggle moved to deny the tension and suppress such movements.

Rural mobilisation, which was sometimes led by 'organic intellectuals' emerging from a peasant milieu, also developed in alliance and tension with movements led by Western-educated people from towns and constituted a challenge to the tyranny of colonial agricultural officers with their ideas of scientific agriculture. Rural political discourse sometimes focused on the integrity and health of the local community, and it also deployed the transcendent languages of self-determination, Christianity, or Garveyism. But, as Norma Kriger has shown, the connections of cultivators with the commercial economy and the state were so varied and complex that 'polarising society along racial lines' was difficult for radical movements to accomplish.[72]

Whether nationalist movements by themselves were strong enough to overthrow colonial rule is unclear, but a variety of social movements from labour unions to anticonservation movements disrupted the economic project of post-war colonialism while discrediting its hegemonic project. Unable to get the Africa they wanted, European powers began to think more seriously about the Africa they had. Empire became vulnerable to another of bourgeois Europe's contradictory tendencies: the calculation of economic interest. By the mid-1950s, France and Great Britain were adding up the costs and benefits of colonial rule more carefully than ever before and coming up with negative numbers.[73]

To the extent—never complete—that issue-specific or localised movements came together in the 1940s and 1950s, the threads also came apart, leaving the unsolved problems of the colonial era to new governments and a tenuously constituted political arena. It is to the problem of framing the national question in relation to other political questions that I now turn.

From the cauldron of politics in the 1950s and 1960s, nation-states emerged across the African continent. Benedict Anderson's conception of the nation as an imagined community should be set against two related notions: the nation was not the only unit that people imagined,[74] and the predominance of the nation-state in post-1960 Africa resulted not from the exclusive focus of African imaginations on the nation but from the fact that the nation was imaginable to colonial rulers as well.[75] Pan-Africanism—embracing the diaspora as well as the continent—had once been the focus of imagination more than the units that eventually became states, but pan-Africanist possibilities were written out of the decolonisation bargains.[76] Regional federation, though once a basis of French administration and of the mobilisation of trade unions and political parties, fell victim to a French programme of 'territorialisation' and to the interests in territorial institutions that the partial devolution of power to individual colonies gave African politicians.[77] At the same time, linguistic and ethnic groups were denied a legitimate place in politics—which did not prevent them from becoming even more salient and more sharply demarcated in post-colonial politics—and the menace of 'tribalism' was used by governing élites to try to eliminate many sorts of subnational politics.[78] In the confrontations of the 1950s, colonial states used violence to exclude certain options, for example, the explicit leftism and the premature (in official eyes) claims to independence of the Union des Populations du Camaroun or the anti-modern radicalism of Mau Mau rebels in Kenya.[79] Imperial bureaucrats, however, gave up aspects of their own imaginings: the idea that social and economic change could be directly controlled by those who claimed already to have arrived was lost in the struggles over decolonisation.[80] Where the imagination of anti-colonial intellectuals in Africa and imperial bureaucrats overlapped was in the formal apparatus of the nation-state, the institutions and symbols contained within territorial borders.[81]

Pan-Africanism actually pre-dated nationalism—defined, as it should be, as a movement to claim the nation-state.[82] Leading intellectuals, notably Léopold Senghor, navigated the perspectives of Pan-Africanism, nationalism, and a desire for social and economic reform in complex ways: Senghor's 'négritude' embraced essentialist notions of African culture yet inverted the valuation placed on them, erasing difference and eliminating conflict within an idealised Africa. Senghor was just as brilliant at analysing and working through the specific social structures of his own Senegal: a Christian politician with a political machine based on Muslim brotherhoods, a poet who expressed his ideas of Africa through the French language, a man who defended Africa from a seat in the French legislature, a romantic defender of African village life who after independence sought to use trade and aid to transform an African nation. Living these complexities entailed pain and difficulty, but there is no indication that Senghor—or the many others navigating similar currents—experienced them as personally destabilising, as intellectually contradictory, or as threatening to his sense of cultural integrity: *in between* is as much a place to be at home as any other.[83] The implications for the historian are crucial:

we must analyse the culture of politics and the politics of culture by constantly shifting the scale of analysis from the most spatially specific (the politics of the clan or the village) to the most spatially diffuse (transatlantic racial politics) and examine the originality and power of political thought by what it appropriated and transformed from its entire range of influences and connections.[84]

The triumph of nationalist movements appears less as a linear progression than as a conjuncture, and the success of African political parties less a question of a singular mobilisation in the name of the nation than of coalition building, the forging of clientage networks, and machine politics. For a time, nationalist parties made the colonial state appear to be the central obstacle facing diverse sorts of social movements, from labour to anti-conservation to regional movements. Coalition politics may not have been the stuff of revolutionary drama, but it was often conducted with enthusiasm and idealism. The give-and-take of this era forced—and allowed—colonial governments to make a necessary imaginative leap themselves. They came to envision a world that they no longer ruled but that they thought could function along principles they understood: through state institutions, by Western-educated élites, in the interest of progress and modernity, through integration with global markets and international organisations. British archives, notably, disclose that top echelons of government wanted to believe all this but were not quite convinced. A non-hostile post-colonial relationship was the best they thought they could achieve.[85] In the process, they could eliminate some enemies, but in other cases the one-time Apostles of Disorder—Kwame Nkrumah, Jomo Kenyatta, Nnamdi Azikiwe—were remade in the colonial imagination into the Men of Moderation and Modernity.[86]

Some of the best recent studies of post-Second World War politics focus not on the parties that took over the state but on Asante nationalism in the Gold Coast (thrust aside by Nkrumah's quest for a unitary Ghana), on the guerrilla movement of the Cameroon, which the French successfully marginalised and destroyed, on the rural people who were caught in the middle of guerrilla–government warfare in Zimbabwe, and on the squatters who fought the hardest, suffered the most, and won the least in the violent decolonisation of Kenya.[87] The nationalist parties paid a price for their conjunctural coalitions: the social struggles they tried to attach to their cause remained unresolved. As Aristide Zolberg first showed in 1966, the public's nationalist sentiment was actually quite thin. Attempts at building national institutions were inevitably read as building up particularistic interests: for the leader's tribe, for his class, for his clientele, for himself. New states, taking on a transformative project at which European powers had failed, were politically fragile and ideologically brittle, their insistence on unity for the nation and development denying legitimacy to the social movements out of which political mobilisation had often been achieved.[88]

The idea of the nation, as Benedict Anderson stressed, emerged in a particular historical context, when the circuits along which creole élites (starting in Latin America) moved and built their careers began to exclude the metropole and focus on the colonial capital and when print capitalism provided a medium to establish a bounded identity.[89] Europe learned to imagine the nation from the tensions that emerged within its old empires and passed the imaginative possibility along to its new colonial conquests. Partha Chatterjee reluctantly grants Anderson a point: the kind of politics that eventually took over colonial states was this nation-centred one, focused on the European-defined boundaries and institutions, on notions of progress shaped by capitalism and European social thought. The idea of 'reason' through which nationalists critiqued colonialism arrived in the colonies wed to capitalism and colonialism. In making claims on colonial powers, nationalists became caught up in the colonial regimes' categories; nationalism was a 'derivative discourse.' Chatterjee finds possibilities for 'a "modern" national culture that is nevertheless not Western' but locates them in a spiritual domain set outside economy and statecraft.[90] The Indian élite, drawing its power both from notions of caste and communalism rigidified by British rule and from its immersion in colonial commerce, was willing neither to undertake a drastic assault on the Indian past nor to repudiate those elements of the colonial present from which it benefited. Chatterjee, following Antonio Gramsci, identifies élite nationalism as a 'war of position,' an effort to change society bit by bit, rather than a more radical 'war of movement.' At some moments, more radical appeals—notably those of Mohandas

Gandhi himself—were necessary to widen the mobilisation of the Indian National Congress; but, as victory came into sight, the Congress leadership's immersion in the economic, political, and ideological structures of the Indian state marginalised alternative visions. The institutions of state and the goal of state-directed development were only a part of Indian politics in the twentieth century, but they were the politics that triumphed.[91]

Both Anderson and Chatterjee do more than take the nation and nationalism from the realm of 'natural' sentiment to social construct;[92] they do so in a way grounded in material conditions and aspirations of certain social groups, in the life trajectories of those who imagined the nation, in the networks of intellectuals and political leaders, in the ways in which ideas were circulated. The 'state' should be examined with the same care as the 'nation'—its institutions and rhetorics carefully scrutinised.[93] One can agree up to a point with Anthony D. Smith that particular qualities of the colonial state—'gubernatorial, territorial, bureaucratic, paternalist-educational, caste-like'—were carried over to post-colonial states, yet African rulers gave their own meanings to institutions they took over, adapting them to patrimonial social structures and complex modes of representing power.[94]

To historicise the nation-state is not, however, to postulate that it is Africa's 'curse,' as Basil Davidson called it. One should not assume the innocence or autonomy of community or 'civil society' any more than that of the nation, and the articulation between state and social units within and beyond it is where analysis should focus. The 'national order of things' should neither be taken as natural nor dismissed as an artificial imposition on Africa. State and nation need to be examined in relation to diasporic communities, to the migratory circuits around which many people organise their lives, to the structures and rules—from market transactions to factory discipline—that also cross borders, and to the cleavages that exist within borders and at times both destroy and remake the nation-state.[95]

In concluding this discussion, I turn to a view of colonialism and re-sistance that in the recent past would have been a likely starting point: Frantz Fanon. The West Indian psychiatrist and intellectual who devoted much of his life to Algeria and was read as a voice of the 'African Revolution' epitomises the anti-imperialist who crosses borders. His view of violence negating the psychological power of colonialism captured the imagination of other African intellectuals and, above all, those in the West who did not have to face the consequences of that violence.[96]

Fanon was no nationalist. For him, nationalism was a bourgeois ideology, espoused by those who wanted to step into the colonial structure rather than turn that structure upside down. Nor was Fanon a racialist: he criticised 'négritude' and saw no solace in the sharing of a mythic black identity, opposing a universalistic notion of liberation to arguments about authenticity or cultural autonomy. Fanon's future came out of the struggle itself: ' "The last shall be first and the first last." Decolonisation is the putting into practice of this sentence.'[97]

Yet Fanon was also denying colonised people any history but that of oppression, any ambiguity to the ways they might confront and appropriate the intrusions of colonisers. Instead, he provided a sociological determinism: the petty bourgeoisie was absorbed in mimicking the culture of the coloniser and was best understood in terms of psychopathology;[98] the working class had become a labour aristocracy intent only on capturing the privileges of white workers; the peasantry and the lumpen proletariat, by contrast, were the true liberationists, the last who would become first. The categories were actually colonial ones, and the irony of Fanon's fervent argument was that it allowed— by its inversionary logic—France to define the present and future of people in colonies.[99]

Fanon's reduction of ideology and political strategy to traits of social groups in effect created purge categories: the organised worker or the petty bourgeois, like the kulak of the Stalinist Soviet Union, was a traitor by definition. And the singularity with which the 'anti-colonial' eclipsed all other notions of affiliation or common interest implied post-colonial uniformity as much as anti-colonial unity.

Some African leaders were saying exactly that. Sékou Touré, one of Africa's most notable radical nationalists, himself once a trade unionist, spoke on the eve of his assuming power in Guinea of the new imperatives of African rule. Trade unions were 'a tool' that should be changed when it got dull; striking against the 'organisms of colonialism' had been a legitimate action, but a strike 'directed against an African Government' was now 'historically unthinkable,' and the labour movement was 'obligated to reconvert itself to remain in the same line of emancipation' as the government.[100] Sékou Touré was to practice what he preached by destroying the autonomy of the trade union movement and jailing much of its leadership. Other once-autonomous, once-activist organisations were similarly destroyed, co-opted, or marginalised in many African countries.[101] There were, of course, complex questions to be faced about the role of unions, of regionally or ethnically based associations, of representatives of farmers, traders, and other economic interests in post-colonial polities, as well as questions of allocating more resources to groups that had fared well or badly under colonial rule. But Sékou Touré was not issuing an invitation to a debate. Nor were his fellow leaders who made the national ideal compulsory, via such devices as one-party states and such ideological constructs as Mobutu's *authenticité* or Kenyatta's *harambee* (pulling together).[102] The last were now declared to be first. The others deserved to be last.

This is not to deny Fanon's critique of the self-serving nationalists of his day or the appeal of his call for a liberation that overrode national or racial chauvinisms. The issue is one of facing consequences. The casting out of all but the True Anti-colonialist from the political arena and the reduction of entire categories of people to class enemies gave an exhilarating legitimacy to state projects, which were often deflected into less liberationist goals than Fanon had in mind. Enthusiasms for projects of state-building, modernisation, and development, in the name of the market or of socialism or of good governance, have consequences, too. Those who find in notions of 'community' or 'new social movements' a welcome antidote to one sort of oppression need to worry about the other forms of oppression that lie within them. For the historian, searching for those historical actors who found the true path is a less fruitful task than studying different paths into engagement with colonisation as well as the tensions between different sorts of liberations, between local mobilisation and state institutions, between cultural assertion and cultural interaction.

For the historian who seeks to learn what can be learned about the lives that African workers or market women lived day by day, the

Manichean world of Frantz Fanon is no more revealing than a colonial bureaucrat's insistence that such people stood at the divide between African backwardness and Western modernity or a nationalist's dichotomy between an authentic community and an imposed Westernisation.[103] The Guinean port worker was not just seeking European wages or fighting colonialism: he may also have used his job for a colonial firm to seek autonomy from his father, just as his wife may well have been acting within the urban commercial sector to attain a measure of autonomy from him. As a trade unionist, he drew on organisational forms and institutional legitimacy from the French model of industrial relations, but union and political activities also drew on and contributed to webs of affiliation, languages of solidarity, and a range of cultural institutions that colonial officials did not understand and could not adequately monitor. The worker and the market seller were remaking institutions and their meanings even as they used them.

The concept of subalternity also does not categorise the lived experience of such people, but Subaltern Studies historians are not saying that it should. Their emphasis is on the tension between such experiences and the historical process that generates the categories of knowledge themselves. The tension defines a valuable entry point for probing colonial experiences and an essential reminder of the scholar's inability to escape the implications of the material and cultural power that Europe exercised overseas. Yet, as we look ever more deeply into the contested spaces of colonial politics, we would do well to look beyond the notion of subalternity—and conceptions of colonialism that assume its ability to coerce, co-opt, and categorise challenges into its own structure of power and ideology—in order to pry apart further the ways in which power was constituted and contested. The violence of colonisers was no less violent for the narrowness of its range and the limits of its transformative efficacy, and the totalising arrogance of modernising ideologies is not diminished by the fact that Africans often disassembled them and created something else. But if 'subalterns' are to be seen as vital parts of history, the possibility, at least, that the very meanings of domination and subalternity could be undermined should be kept open. And if, at the same time, we are to follow the call of Chatterjee and Chakrabarty to 'provincialise' European history—to subject its universalising claims to historical examination rather than use them as measures of other people's histories—we should move beyond treating modernity, liberalism, citizenship, or bourgeois equality as if they were fixed and self-contained doctrines unaffected by the appropriations and reformulations given to them by processes of political mobilisation in Asia, Africa, or Europe itself.[104]

Nationalism, meanwhile, can be explored in tension with a range of social movements, and, as with the colonisation process, the ability of nationalist parties to subsume other sorts of mobilisations under its roof should be seen as contingent and partial. The forms of power in Africa after decolonisation—the institutions through which it is exercised and the idioms in which it is represented—reflect not so much the all-consuming thrust of the national order of things but the fragilities, the compromises, and the violences of insecure leaders that emerged in the process of ending colonial rule.

In Africa, the encounters of the past are very much part of the present. Africa still faces the problems of building networks and institutions capable of permitting wide dialogue and common action among people with diverse pasts, of struggling against and engaging with the structures of power in the world today. Africa's crisis derives from a complex history that demands a complex analysis: a simultaneous awareness of how colonial regimes exercised power and the limits of that power, an appreciation of the intensity with which that power was confronted and the diversity of futures that people sought for themselves, an understanding of how and why some of those futures were excluded from the realm of the politically feasible, and an openness to possibilities for the future that can be imagined today.

NOTES AND REFERENCES

1. Dipesh Chakrabarty, 'Post-coloniality and the artifice of history: Who speaks for "Indian" pasts?' *Representations*, 37 (1992), 19; Ranajit Guha, 'On some aspects of the historiography of colonial India,' in Ranajit Guha and Gayatri Chakravorty Spivak, eds, *Selected Subaltern Studies* (New York, 1988), p. 43.
2. An example of useful debate is that between Gyan Prakash—arguing for an 'antifoundationalist' history of the Third World—and Rosalind

O'Hanlon and David Washbrook—arguing that such an approach disabled the historian from analysing the global process of capitalist development. Their debate is notable not only for the intelligence and civility with which it was carried out but for the fact that both sides have a point. Gyan Prakash, 'Writing post-Orientalist histories of the third world: Perspectives from Indian historiography,' Rosalind O'Hanlon and David Washbrook, 'After Orientalism: Culture, criticism, and politics in the third world,' Gyan Prakash, 'Can the 'subaltern' ride? A reply to O'Hanlon and Washbrook,' *Comparative Studies in Society and History*, 32 (1990): 383–408; 34 (1992): 141–67, 168–84.

3. Guha, 'On some aspects,' pp. 39, 40. Guha admits that élite and subaltern worlds were not isolated from each other but insists that they represent 'dichotomies,' p. 42. In practice, he complicates the dichotomy, and as Gyan Prakash points out in his essay in this issue, other Subaltern Studies historians, including Gyanendra Pandey and Shahid Amin, have complicated it further with subtle analyses of the relationship of élite and peasant movements, of local and national politics. See also the critical essay by Rosalind O'Hanlon, 'Recovering the subject: *Subaltern Studies* and histories of resistance in colonial South Asia,' *Modern Asian Studies*, 22 (1988): 189–224.

4. Gayatri Chakravorty Spivak, 'Subaltern Studies: Deconstructing historiography,' in Guha and Spivak, *Selected Subaltern Studies*, p. 15, questions the subject-position into which the category of 'subaltern' drives colonised peoples but accepts that such a concept nonetheless represents a 'strategic' essentialism—a useful device to open up a politically vital question. The question is whether the essentialism might outlive the strategy.

5. Chakrabarty, 'Post-coloniality and the artifice of history,' 23.

6. In the decade after independence, Africa-based historians and social scientists made a strong effort to found journals and hold congresses. Their drive has been impossible to sustain. Besides Africa's size and linguistic diversity, the economic crisis of the 1980s has had disastrous consequences for universities and other institutions (the Dakar-based consortium, CODESRIA, being the most notable effort to reverse this trend) and has led to considerable intellectual out-migration. Conditions worsened just when a younger generation of scholars, some of them trained in Africa itself, were injecting new ideas and questions into scholarship. The recent 'structural adjustment programmes' imposed on Africa by outside lending institutions—forcing governments to cut services—do not consider that a vibrant and critical intellectual life helps to distinguish a creative society from one incapable of adjusting its structures. Differential access to the resources for research, publishing, and scholarly interchange is probably the single most important

way in which scholars based in Africa are distinguished from those in the United States or Europe.

7. Although Subaltern Studies is increasingly mentioned by Africanists, the only sustained effort I know of both to use and critique this body of literature is Terence Ranger, 'Subaltern Studies and "social history," ' *Southern African Review of Books* (February–May 1990): 8–10; and Terence Ranger, 'Power, religion and community: The Matobo case,' in Partha Chatterjee and Gyanendra Pandey, eds, *Subaltern Studies VII* (Delhi, 1993), pp. 221–46.

8. John Lonsdale, 'States and social processes in Africa: A historiographical survey,' *African Studies Review*, 24, no. 2/3 (1981): 143.

9. Terence Ranger, 'Connexions between "primary resistance" movements and modern mass nationalism in East and Central Africa,' *Journal of African History*, 9 (1968): 437–53, 631–41; Ranger, *Revolt in Southern Rhodesia, 1896–1897* (London, 1967). Similarly, John Iliffe showed that a major rebellion in German East Africa followed lines of religious cults across ethnic boundaries. The revolt—though brutally repressed—caused Germany to alter its colonial policy. 'The organisation of the Maji Maji rebellion,' *Journal of African History*, 8 (1967): 485–512. In a more recent context, David Lan found spirit mediums mobilising peasants in the guerrilla war against the white regime in Rhodesia in the 1970s. Lan, *Guns and rain: Guerrillas and spirit mediums in Zimbabwe* (Berkeley, California, 1985).

10. Specific questions have been raised as well, mainly about the importance of spirit mediums in the southern Rhodesian revolt and the extent to which the revolt's organisation went beyond the pre-colonial Shona polity. David Beach, ' "Chimurenga:" The Shona rising of 1896–7,' *Journal of African History*, 20 (1979): 395–420; Julian Cobbing, 'The absent priesthood: Another look at the Rhodesian risings of 1896–7,' *Journal of African History*, 18 (1977): 61–84.

11. Terence Ranger, 'Religious movements and politics in sub-Saharan Africa,' *African Studies Review*, 29 (1986): 1–69. For a comprehensive review of recent literature on the rural dimension of these issues, see Allen Isaacman, 'Peasants and rural social protest in Africa,' in Frederick Cooper, Allen Isaacman, Florencia Mallon, William Roseberry, and Steve J. Stern, *Confronting historical paradigms: Peasants, labour, and the capitalist world system in Africa and Latin America* (Madison, Wisconsin, 1993).

12. See, for example, Allen F. Isaacman, *The tradition of resistance in Mozambique: Anti-colonial activity in the Zembesi Valley, 1850–1921* (Berkeley, California, 1976); Timothy C. Weiskel, *French colonial rule and the Baule peoples: Resistance and collaboration, 1889–1911* (London, 1980); Yves Person, *Samori: Une révolution dyula*, 3 vols (Dakar, 1968–75). The resistance

model is alive and well in such studies as John Lamphear, *The scattering time: Turkana responses to colonial rule* (Oxford, 1992); and Les Switzer, *Power and resistance in an African society: The Ciskei Xhosa and the making of South Africa* (Madison, Wisconsin, 1993). There is something in the choice of the word 'resistance'—as opposed to alternatives such as 'liberation' or 'emancipation'—that fits the mood of many Western leftists: identification with the heroic but vain defence of community against intrusion. Jan Nederveen Pieterse, 'Emancipations, modern and post-modern,' *Development and Change*, 23 (1992): 5–41.

13. A. Adu Boahen, 'Africa and the colonial challenge,' in A. Adu Boahen, ed., *Africa under colonial domination, 1880–1935* (Berkeley, California, 1985), 1–18. The seven chapters that follow contain 'African initiatives and resistance' in their titles. For a fuller exposition of Boahen's views, see A. Adu Boahen, *African perspectives on colonialism* (Baltimore, Md., 1987). For an interpretation of the same era that stresses the cleavages within Africa, see John Lonsdale, 'The European scramble and conquest in African history,' in Roland Oliver and G.N. Sanderson, eds, *Cambridge history of Africa*, vol. 6: *From 1870 to 1905* (Cambridge, 1985), pp. 680–766.

14. K. Onwuka Dike, *Trade and politics in the Niger delta 1830–1855: An introduction to the economic and political history of Nigeria* (Oxford, 1956). Dike did mention the importance of oral sources, but they informed his interpretation rather than provided evidence to be cited. In its time, the book derived much of its legitimacy from its scrupulous use of conventional archival material. The francophone African equivalent of Dike's book, also keeping its distance from nationalist historiography and focusing on Afro-European interaction, is Abdoulaye Ly, *La compagnie du Sénégal* (Paris, 1958).

15. Thomas Hodgkin, *Nationalism in colonial Africa* (London, 1956); Basil Davidson, *The liberation of Guinea: Aspects of an African revolution* (Harmondsworth, 1969); Davidson, *In the eye of the storm: Angola's people* (Harmondsworth, 1972); Davidson, 'African peasants and revolution,' *Journal of Peasant Studies*, 1 (1974): 269–91.

16. J.F. Ade Ajayi, 'The continuity of African institutions under colonialism,' in Terence O. Ranger, ed., *Emerging themes in African history* (London, 1968), pp. 189–200. The francophone equivalent is 'colonial parenthesis.' See Marc H. Piault, ed., *La colonisation: Rupture ou parenthèse?* (Paris, 1987).

17. B.A. Ogot, 'Revolt of the elders: An anatomy of the loyalist crowd in the Mau Mau uprising,' in B.A. Ogot, ed., *Hadith 4* (Nairobi, 1972), pp. 134–48. The moral complexity of Mau Mau was also addressed in the early novels of Ngugi wa Thiong'o, particularly *A grain of wheat* (London,

1967). Some of the issues of Kikuyu discourse first raised by Ogot have been pursued in a stimulating fashion by Bruce Berman and John Lonsdale, *Unhappy valley: Conflict in Kenya and Africa,* Book 2: *Violence and ethnicity* (London, 1992).

18. Mamadou Diouf, *Le Kajoor aux XIX siècle: Pouvoir ceddo et conquête coloniale* (Paris, 1990), p. 283. Diouf's efforts got him into a confrontation with Lat Dior's descendants, in which Diouf stood his ground. Martin Klein, 'The Development of Senegalese Historiography,' in Bogumil Jewsiewicki and David Newbury, eds, *African Historiographies: What history for which Africa?* (Beverly Hills, California, 1986), pp. 222–3. One should also note the more sweeping attacks on nationalist historiographies (as practised by African and non-African scholars alike), in Arnold J. Temu and Bonaventure Swai, *Historians and Africanist history: A critique* (London, 1981).

19. On the evolution and accomplishments of the field, see Nancy Rose Hunt, 'Placing African women's history and locating gender,' *Signs,* 14 (1989): pp. 359–79; and Susan Geiger, 'Women and African nationalism,' *Journal of Women's History,* 2 (1990): p. 227–44.

20. Luise White, 'Separating the men from the boys: Constructions of gender, sexuality and terrorism in Central Kenya, 1939–59,' *International Journal of African Historical Studies,* 23 (1990): 1–27; Cora Ann Presley, *Kikuyu women, the Mau Mau rebellion, and social change in Kenya* (Boulder, Colo., 1992); and Tabitha Kanogo, *Crossing boundaries: African women's experience in colonial Kenya,* forthcoming; Timothy Scarnecchia, 'The politics of gender and class in the creation of African communities, Salisbury, Rhodesia, 1937–57' (Ph.D. dissertation, University of Michigan, 1993). Norma J. Kriger writes of gender—as well as age—cleavages in *Zimbabwe's guerrilla war: Peasant voices* (Cambridge, 1992).

21. Julia Wells, 'We have done with pleading: The women's 1913 anti-pass campaign,' *History Workshop Topic Series 3* (Johannesburg, 1991); Cherryl Walker, *Women and resistance in South Africa* (London, 1982); William Beinart, '*Amafelandawonye* (the Die-Hards): Popular protest and women's movements in Herschel District in the 1920s,' in William Beinart and Colin Bundy, *Hidden struggles in rural South Africa: Politics and popular movements in the Transkei and Eastern Cape, 1890–1930* (Berkeley, California, 1987), pp. 22–69; Helen Bradford, *A taste of freedom: The ICU in rural South Africa, 1924–1930* (New Haven, Connecticut, 1987); Belinda Bozzoli, *Women of Phokeng: Consciousness, life strategy, and migrancy in South Africa, 1900–1983* (Portsmouth, New Haven, 1991).

22. See above all the depiction of the highs and lows of Ghana's independence in Ayi Kwei Armah, *The beautyful ones are not yet born: A novel* (Boston,

1968). One can also contrast Chinua Achebe's novel of European conquest, *Things fall apart* (New York, 1959), with his sarcastic novel of post-independence moral decay, *Man of the people* (New York, 1966), but Achebe's work is much more complex than a romanticisation of pre-conquest Africa, and indeed both novels portray masculine power in telling ways.

23. Walter Rodney, *How Europe underdeveloped Africa* (London, 1972).

24. Florencia Mallon, 'Dialogues among the fragments: Retrospect and prospect,' in Cooper, *et al.*, *Confronting historical paradigms*, pp. 371–404.

25. The power of the capitalist world system has not so much been its capacity to call into being new structures that maximise the extraction of commodities or surplus value as its global flexibility in finding alternatives to areas it could not rigorously exploit and, ideologically, to marginalise and demean the people it could not incorporate. This theme is explored in Frederick Cooper, 'Africa and the world economy,' in Cooper, *et. al.*, *Confronting historical paradigms*, pp. 84–204.

26. The ethical conundrums of radical scholarship have been probed in Bogumil Jewsiewicki, 'African historical studies: Academic knowledge as "usable past" and radical scholarship,' *African Studies Review*, 32, no. 3 (1989): 1–76.

27. My former adviser remembers student fashions at the time much the same way. Leonard M. Thompson, 'The study of South African history in the United States,' *International Journal of African Historical Studies*, 25 (1992): 27–8.

28. The relevant literature here is now vast. The battle lines were first drawn in reviews of the pioneering 'liberal' text, Monica Wilson and Leonard Thompson, eds, *The Oxford history of South Africa*, 2 vols (New York, 1969–71). Early structuralist arguments are Frederick A. Johnstone, *Class, race, and gold* (London, 1976); and Harold Wolpe, 'Capitalism and cheap labour power in South Africa: From segregation to apartheid,' *Economy and Society*, 1 (1972): 425–56; whereas the social history school may be seen in Charles van Onselen; *Studies in the social and economic history of the Witwatersrand*, 1886–1914, 2 vols (London, 1982).

29. Charles van Onselen, 'Race and class in the South African countryside: Cultural osmosis and social relations in the sharecropping economy of the South-Western Transvaal 1990–50,' *AHR*, 95 (February 1990): 99–123; and *Studies*. For another complicated history of how ties of class and gender sometimes crossed racial frontiers—and sometimes did not—see Iris Berger, *Threads of solidarity: Women in South African industry, 1900–1980* (Bloomington: Ind., 1992). On the complexities of politics, see Shula Marks, *The*

ambiguities of dependence in South Africa: Class, nationalism, and the state in twentieth-century Natal (Baltimore, Md., 1986).

30. Kelesto E. Atkins, *The moon is dead! Give us our money!: The cultural origins of an African work ethic, Natal, South Africa, 1843–1900* (Portsmouth, New Haven, 1993).

31. I witnessed the debate at the June 1993 symposium of the Johannesburg History Workshop, whose title, 'Work, class, and culture,' specifies the categories in contention. For a history influenced by post-structuralism, see Clifton Crais, *White supremacy and black resistance in pre-industrial South Africa: The making of the colonial order in the Eastern Cape, 1770–1865* (Cambridge, 1992).

32. See Frederick Cooper and Ann Stoler, 'Tensions of empire: Colonial control and visions of rule,' *American Ethnologist*, 16 (1989): 609–21, and the essays that follow; and Nicholas B. Dirks, ed., *Colonialism and culture* (Ann Arbor, Michigan, 1992).

33. Talal Asad, ed., *Anthropology and the colonial encounter* (London, 1973); James Clifford and George E. Marcus, eds, *Writing culture: The poetics and politics of ethnography* (Berkeley, California, 1986); George W. Stocking, Jr., *Colonial situations: Essays on the contextualisation of ethnographic knowledge* (Madison, Wisconsin, 1991).

34. The pioneering text is Edward W. Said, *Orientalism* (New York, 1978); and a more recent example is Mary Louise Pratt, *Imperial eyes: Travel writing and transculturation* (London, 1992).

35. Bernard S. Cohn, 'The census, social structure and objectification in South Asia,' in Cohn, *An anthropologist among the historians and other essays* (Delhi, 1987), pp. 224–54; Randall M. Packard, 'The "healthy reserve" and the "dressed native:" Discourses on black health and the language of legitimation in South Africa,' *American Ethnologist*, 16 (1989): 686–703; Megan Vaughan, *Curing their ills: Colonial power and African illness* (Cambridge, 1991); David Arnold, *Colonising the body: State medicine and epidemic disease in nineteenth-century India* (Berkeley: California, 1993); Jean Comaroff and John Comaroff, *Of revelation and revolution*, vol. 1: *Christianity, colonialism and consciousness in South Africa* (Chicago, 1991); T.O. Beidelman, *Colonial evangelism: A socio-historical study of an East African mission at the grassroots* (Bloomington, Ind., 1982); Gwendolyn Wright, *The politics of design in French colonial urbanism* (Chicago, 1991).

36. Ranajit Guha, 'The prose of counter-insurgency,' and Dipesh Chakrabarty, 'Conditions for knowledge of working-class conditions: Employers, government and the jute workers of Calcutta, 1890–1940,' in Guha and Spivak, *Selected Subaltern Studies*, pp. 45–84, 179–232. See also Partha

Chatterjee, *Nationalist thought and the colonial world: A derivative discourse?* (London, 1986).

37. Ann Stoler, 'Sexual affronts and racial frontiers: European identities and the cultural politics of exclusion in Southeast Asia,' *Comparative Studies in Society and History*, 34 (1992): 514–51.

38. Literary scholars, among whom the terms post-colonialmoment, post-colonial discourse, post-colonialism, and post-coloniality arose, are not unaware of the problems with them, as one can see in the papers 'On "post-colonial discourse," ' edited by Tejumola Olaniyan and published in *Calaloo*, 16 (1993): 743–1033, or the telling critique of Anne McClintock, 'The angel of progress: Pitfalls of the term "post-colonialism," ' *Social Text*, 31–2 (1990): 84–98. How 'post' the 'post-colonial' world is one question; aother is whether the histories of all parts of the world that experienced colonial rule can be reduced to that one essence. The adjective 'colonial,' minus 'isms' or 'itys,' has the virtue of being a native category, a term by which Europeans described what they were about. It described a project that was simultaneously incorporative and differentiating: the extension of power to areas whose people were regarded as distinct in such a manner that distinction was reproduced. The 'ism' makes 'colonial' an explicitly political issue, and in the twentieth century 'colonialism' was most often used by critics to demarcate a set of ideologies and practices they wanted to remove from the body politic; the word has the value and the inadequacies of most polemicising terms. What the 'ity' gives in return for its homogenising and essentialising quality is not so clear.

39. Homi Bhabha, 'Of mimicry and man: The ambivalence of colonial discourse,' October, 3–4 (1985), 125–33.

40. The growth of messianic Christian cults, with the message of missionaries turned upside down, is only one example of this process. When Jean-Pierre Chrétien uses the words 'mutations,' 'adaptations,' 'reinterpretations,' 'reconstructions,' 'crystallisations,' and 'inventions' to describe the dynamics of African religions and their interactions with Christianity and Islam, he at least makes clear that there is a complex problem of analysis here. Chrétien, 'Introduction,' *L'invention religieuse en Afrique: Histoire et religion en Afrique noire* (Paris, 1993), 9. See also Achille Mbembe, *Afriques indociles: Christianisme, pouvoir et état en société post-coloniale* (Paris, 1988).

41. Achille Mbembe, 'Domaines de la nuit et autorité onirique dans les maquis du Sud-Cameroun (1955–8),' *Journal of African History*, 32 (1991): 89–122; Luise White, 'Cars out of place: Vampires, technology, and labour in East and Central Africa,' *Representations*, 43 (1993): 27–50; David William Cohen and E.S. Atieno-Odhiambo, *Burying SM: The politics of*

knowledge and sociology of power in Africa (Portsmouth, New Haven, 1992); Leroy Vail and Landeg White, 'Forms of resistance: Songs and perceptions of power in colonial Mozambique,' *AHR*, 88 (October 1983): 883–919. One can also learn a great deal from older anthropological literatures on witchcraft eradication movements, possession cults, and religious movements, as well as from philosophy, literary studies, and intellectual history, including Kwame Anthony Appiah, *In my father's house: Africa in the philosophy of culture* (New York, 1992); V.Y. Mudimbe, *The invention of Africa: Gnosis, philosophy, and the order of knowledge* (Bloomington, Ind., 1988); Christopher L. Miller, *Theories of Africans: Francophone literature and anthropology in Africa* (Chicago, 1990). The concept of *bricolage* was deployed effectively in Jean Comaroff, *Body of power, spirit of resistance: The culture and history of a South African people* (Chicago, 1985), although within a resistance framework that is less persuasive.

42. Guha, 'Prose of counter-insurgency.'

43. Such questions as what made narratives credible, what was remembered and what forgotten, how written and oral texts derived authority from each other have been receiving increasing attention. The starting point for rigorous analysis of African oral sources was Jan Vansina, *Oral tradition: A study in historical methodology*, H.M Wright, trans. (Chicago, 1965); and an important example of analysing the implications of the production of history is David William Cohen, *The combing of history* (Chicago, 1994).

44. Gayatri Chakravorty Spivak, 'Can the subaltern speak?' in Cary Nelson and Lawrence Grossberg, eds, *Marxism and the interpretation of culture* (Urbana, Ill., 1988), pp. 271–313; Benita Parry, 'Problems in current theories of colonial discourse,' *Oxford Literary Review*, 9 (1987): 27–58. Fernando Coronil argues that Spivak pushes the subaltern 'outside the realm of political exchange,' beyond relationships, and he posits instead that 'subalternity is a relational and relative concept.' Coronil, 'Listening to the subaltern: The poetics of neocolonial states,' *Poetics Today*, 15 (1994). Likewise, Mallon, in this issue, wants to restore plural voices and multiple subject-positions to the subaltern. All these scholars want to complicate and enrich their subalterns but still keep them subaltern.

45. I am following the insightful argument of David Edwards, 'Mad mullahs and Englishmen: Discourse in the colonial encounter,' *Comparative Studies in Society and History*, 31 (1989): 649–70. The colonial assault on 'barbarous practices' has been most fully explored in the case of slavery, where colonial regimes focused on the symbol of African backwardness and often shrank before the complexities of what slavery actually meant in its context. See Richard Roberts and Suzanne Miers, eds, *The end of slavery in Africa*

(Madison: Wisconsin, 1988); Frederick Cooper, *From slaves to squatters: Plantation labour and agriculture in Zanzibar and Coastal Kenya, 1890–1925* (New Haven: Connecticut, 1980); and Paul E. Lovejoy and Jan S. Hogendorn, *Slow death for slavery: The course of abolition in northern Nigeria, 1897–1936* (Cambridge, 1993). Gyan Prakash shows how a British government effort to focus narrowly on slavery in India avoided more difficult questions of how inequality and exploitation were constituted; Prakash, *Bonded histories: Genealogies of labour servitude in colonial India* (Cambridge, 1990).

46. The gender implications of this are discussed with particular effectiveness in Elias Mandala, *Work and control in a peasant economy: A history of the Lower Tchiri Valley in Malawi, 1859–1960* (Madison, Wisconsin, 1990); and Elizabeth Schmidt, *Peasants, traders, and wives: Shona women in the history of Zimbabwe, 1870–1939* (Portsmouth, New Haven, 1992).

47. Atkins, *The moon is dead!*; William Beinart, *The political economy of Pondoland, 1860–1930* (Cambridge, 1982); William H. Worger, *South Africa's city of diamonds: Mine workers and monopoly capitalism in Kimberley, 1867–1895* (New Haven: Connecticut, 1987).

48. Some scholars have tried to preserve monolithic views of a colonial economy or peripheral capitalism by confining these experiences to categories such as 'coerced cash crop producers' (which is simply wrong) or 'disguised proletarians' (which devoids the concept of proletarian of any meaning). See critical surveys in Cooper, 'Africa and the world economy'; Isaacman, 'Peasants and rural social protest in Africa.' David Ludden argues that in India, capitalism also had a varied impact, and examples of mobility and accumulation among relatively poor or middling cultivators need to be set alongside sharply exploitative systems of labour and tenancy, a process he believes makes the category of subaltern overly rigid. Ludden, 'Subalterns and others, or competing colonial histories of agrarian India,' paper for Workshop on 'Historicising development,' Emory University, December 1993, pp. 10–12.

49. Colonial violence—the most obvious feature of colonial rule—is inadequately studied, largely because anti-colonial intellectuals portrayed it as ubiquitous while apologists saw it as incidental, whereas it was above all *located* and often all the more brutal for its limitations. See William Beinart, 'Political and collective violence in Southern African historiography,' *Journal of Southern African Studies*, 18 (1992): 453–86.

50. Martin Chanock, *Law, custom, and social order: The colonial experience in Malawi and Zambia* (Cambridge, 1985); Kristin Mann and Richard Roberts, eds, *Law in colonial Africa* (Portsmouth, New Haven, 1991);

Terence Ranger, 'The invention of tradition in colonial Africa,' in Eric Hobsbawm and Terence Ranger, eds, *The invention of tradition* (Cambridge, 1983), pp. 211–62.

51. Two pioneering studies are J.F.A. Ajayi, *Christian missions in Nigeria, 1841–1891: The making of a new élite* (Evanston, Ill., 1965); and Margaret Priestley, *West African trade and coast society: A family study* (London, 1969).

52. For bibliography on labour history, see Bill Freund, *The African worker* (Cambridge, 1988).

53. Luise White, *The comforts of home: Prostitution in colonial Nairobi* (Chicago, 1990); Claire Robertson, *Sharing the same bowl?: A socioeconomic history of women and class in Accra, Ghana* (Bloomington, Ind., 1984).

54. Beidelman, *Colonial evangelism*; Comaroff and Comaroff, *Of revelation and revolution*.

55. The early periodisation of colonial policy given here emerges in the case of British and French West Africa as described by Anne Phillips, *The enigma of colonialism: British policy in West Africa* (London, 1989); and Alice Conklin, 'A mission to civilise: Ideology and imperialism in French West Africa 1895-1930' (Ph.D. dissertation, Princeton University, 1989); while I have argued along these lines for East Africa in *From slaves to squatters*; and *On the African waterfront: Urban disorder and the transformation of work in colonial Mombasa* (New Haven, Connecticut, 1987); and in current research on the colonial development initiative.

56. Ranajit Guha, 'Dominance without hegemony and its historiography,' in Ranajit Guha, ed., *Subaltern Studies VI: Writings on South Asian history and society* (Delhi, 1989), pp. 210–309. For a quite different perspective on the contradictions of imperialism in a bourgeois world, see Bernard Semmel, *The liberal ideal and the demons of empire: Theories of imperialism from Adam Smith to Lenin* (Baltimore, Md., 1993).

57. Similarly, the failure of French efforts to contain colonial challenges in the 1940s by extending to colonial subjects a form of citizenship in Greater France eventually led—as many of those ex-citizens migrated from colony to metropole—to pressures that threaten the definition of citizenship in France itself and the universalistic logic of French political ideology. Rogers Brubaker, *Citizenship and nationhood in France and Germany* (Cambridge, Mass., 1992). For the case that the structure of power and the forms of exclusions in modern metropolitan societies were shaped in relation to colonisation, see Ann Stoler, *Race and the education of desire: A colonial reading of Foucault's history of sexuality* (Durham, N.C., forthcoming).

58. Donald Crummey, 'Introduction: "The great beast," ' in Crummey, ed.,

Banditry, rebellion, and social protest in Africa (London, 1986), p. 1; James C. Scott, *Weapons of the weak: Everyday forms of peasant resistance* (New Haven, Connecticut, 1985). Crummey tries to get beyond the assimilation of popular violence to anti-colonial resistance by arguing that pre-colonial regimes were resisted too, but he ends up treating in this context 'the agent of oppression' (p. 21) in an even more abstract manner than was colonialsim when seen as the object of African resistance.

59. Michel Foucault, *The history of sexuality*, vol. 1: *An introduction*, Robert Hurley, trans. (New York, 1978), pp. 95–6.

60. Chatterjee, *Nationalist thought and the colonial world*; Douglas Haynes and Gyan Prakash, 'Introduction: The entanglement of power and resistance,' in Haynes and Prakash, eds, *Contesting power: Resistance and everyday social relations in South Asia* (Berkeley, California, 1991), pp. 1–22.

61. Megan Vaughan points out that surveillance and control in metropolitan societies addressed the individual, whereas colonial power tended to address collectivities. Her latter point has some validity (less in relation to the developmentalism of the 1940s than the control mechanisms of 'indirect rule' in the 1920s and 1930s), but the Euro-African dichotomy is too stark. Vaughan, *Curing their ills*, pp. 8–12. Even after formal decolonisation, global power remains arterial—even aortic—rather than capillary, given the immense power of the World Bank and the International Monetary Fund over decision-making by African states.

62. Sherry Ortner, 'Resistance: Some theoretical problems in anthropological history and historical anthropology,' in Terence McDonald, ed., *The historic turn in the human sciences* (Ann Arbor, Mich., forthcoming).

63. Beinart and Bundy, *Hidden struggles in rural South Africa*, p. 31.

64. Mandala, *Work and control*; Schmidt, *Peasants, traders, and wives*.

65. White, *Comforts of home*.

66. Karen E. Fields, *Revival and rebellion in colonial Central Africa* (Princeton, N.J., 1985).

67. James C. Scott, *Domination and the arts of resistance: Hidden transcripts* (New Haven, Connecticut, 1990). Scott is vague in specifying the domain to which his arguments apply, eliding slavery and colonialism and taking examples from a wide array of cases as if the particular structures of power in each were of little consequence.

68. Subaltern Studies historians have, for example, studied communalism as a colonial category of description, as a nationalist category to be used as a foil against the Indian nation, and as a shifting, manipulated, and contested category of popular action; wage labour appears as a universal construct and as particular lived experience; and Gandhi is shown to imply very different meanings within the Indian National Congress and local contexts.

Gyanendra Pandey, *The construction of communalism in colonial North India* (Delhi, 1990); Dipesh Chakrabarty, *Rethinking working-class history: Bengal 1890–1940* (Princeton, N.J., 1989); Shahid Amin, 'Gandhi as mahatma,' in Guha and Spivak, *Selected Subaltern Studies*, pp. 288–350. See also the discussion of these issues in O'Hanlon, 'Recovering the subject.'

69. Dipesh Chakrabarty, 'Marx after Marxism: History, subalternity and difference,' *Meanjin*, 52 (1993): 421–34; and Chakrabarty, *Rethinking working-class history*.

70. Labour was a numerically small category but an extremely influential one, because the very narrowness of colonial commercial, mining, and industrial channels meant that a small group—in a position to use face-to-face relations to organise—could disrupt the entire import-export economy; in the post-Second World War era, rising prices for African commodities and the colonial development initiative (combined with inflationary pressures on workers) shaped a favourable conjuncture for labour activism. This section is based on Frederick Cooper, *Decolonisation and African society: The labour question in French and British Africa*, forthcoming.

71. The leaders of African political parties were not necessarily sympathetic to strikers or labour movements. In the strike that contributed most to the myth of labour as the spearhead of nationalism—the great French West African railway strike of 1947–8—the region's leading politicians were notably diffident about taking up the workers' cause, and some of them worked to betray it. Workers' demands for equality within the French labour system had an ambiguous relationship to anti-colonial politics. The myth is most clearly developed in the novel of Sembene Ousmane, *God's bits of wood*, Francis Price, trans. (London, 1962).

72. Beinart and Bundy, *Hidden struggle*, esp. pp. 31–7; Steven Feierman, *Peasant intellectuals: Anthropology and history in Tanzania* (Madison, Wisconsin, 1990); Richard Grove, 'Colonial conservation, ecological hegemony and popular resistance: Towards a global synthesis,' in John M. MacKenzie, ed., *Imperialism and the natural world* (Manchester, 1990); Kriger, *Zimbabwe's guerilla war*, p. 157. Kriger is critical of the view that a particular kind of politics flowed from the very existence of a peasantry, as argued in Terence Ranger, *Peasant consciousness and guerilla war in Zimbabwe* (Berkeley, California, 1985).

73. The most persuasive account so far of the calculations that ended a colonial empire is Jacques Marseille, *Empire colonial et capitalisme francais: Histoire d'un divorce* (Paris, 1984), but his resolutely metropolitan focus does not allow him to explain the factors within colonies that raised the costs and diminished the benefits. In the British case, see Prime Minister Macmillan's

call for an explicit cost–benefit analysis of each colony, in Prime Minister's Minute, January 28, 1957, CAB 134/155, Public Record Office, London. Portugal, economically weaker, fell back on its empire and sought to extract more from it, exacerbating conflict even as the international climate turned Portugal from a laggard but acceptable colonial partner to a pariah. Settler colonists fought even longer.

74. A notorious instance of scholarly hubris is Fredric Jameson's insistence that the literature of Third World people—oppressed as they were by imperialism—was supposed to consist of 'national allegories.' He was duly rebuked for the presumption of his telling oppressed people that they could only write about their oppression and could only feel themselves oppressed in national terms. Fredric Jameson, 'Third world literature in the era of multinational capitalism,' *Social Text*, 15 (1986): 65–88, 69 quoted; Aijaz Ahmad, 'Jameson's rhetoric of otherness and the "national allegory," ' *Social Text*, 17 (1987): 3–25.

75. Benedict Anderson, *Imagined communities: Reflections on the origin and spread of nationalism*, rev. edn (London, 1991).

76. J. Ayodele Langley, *Pan-Africanism and nationalism in West Africa, 1900–1945: A study in ideology and social classes* (Oxford, 1973). An intriguing but vain attempt by a leading intellectual at the moment of independence to turn an argument about the historical unity of Africa into a case for a continent-wide federal system is Cheikh Anta Diop, *Les fondements culturels, techniques et industriels d'un futur état fédéral d'Afrique noire* (Paris, 1960). The concept of 'Africa' itself is a tricky one, and as Kwame Anthony Appiah argues, seeing Africa as an entity risked engaging in the kind of racial essentialising that leaders such as W.E.B. Du Bois were intent on combating. He insists that 'Africa' should be defined not by some kind of racial or cultural authenticity but by looking at the history of struggle itself: how slavery and colonisation defined Africans and how Africans turned this imposed definition into something positive. Appiah, *In my father's house*. See also Mudimbe, *Invention of Africa*, and, for an Indian parallel, Sudipta Kaviraj, 'The imaginary institution of India,' in Chatterjee and Pandey, *Subaltern Studies VII*, pp. 1–39.

77. Territorialisation was more than a divide-and-rule strategy aimed at African political movements. It was also an attempt to break away from the notion, much invoked by African unions, that government wages and benefits throughout Greater France should be equalised across the races. By giving African politicians authority over budgets at the territorial level, the policy made government wage policy beholden to the territorial taxpayer. Territorialisation in 1956 had powerful incentives attached to it—a genuine

devolution of power to elected officials within each colony. Although some officials tried to revive federation, each had to look first to his own electoral base—and the wealthiest territory, the Ivory Coast, stood to gain the most by keeping its resources within is borders. Federation became politically impossible to revive. William J. Foltz, *From French West Africa to the Mali federation* (New Haven, Connecticut, 1965). A post-independence attempt to build federation in former British East Africa also failed. Joseph S. Nye, Jr., *Pan-Africanism and East African integration* (Cambridge, Mass., 1965).

78. Pandey's study, *The construction of communalism in colonial North India*, has echoes in colonial and post-colonial Africa: nationalists took over from colonial officials the idea that religious and communal movements were 'irrational' and legitimised only 'the mass of the people mobilised into a new national community' (p. 254). Some of the same rhetoric was also used to delegitimise movements, including labour, that were secular and 'modern' yet limited to particular segments of the national community.

79. Richard A. Joesph, *Radical nationalism in Cameroun: Social origins of the U.P.C. rebellion* (Oxford, 1977); Achille Mbembe, *La naissance du maquis dans le Sud-Cameroun: Histoires d'indisciplines (1920–1960)* (Paris, 1993); Berman and Lonsdale, *Unhappy valley*.

80. I do not accept the argument made by Ronald Robinson and others that in the British case, a clear plan to devolve power was developed prior to the rise of nationalist movements and that these movements—the consequence rather than the cause of British policy—did no more than speed up a previously conceived policy. This 'Whig' interpretation, as John Darwin calls it, misses the extent to which urban and rural movements—not specifically nationalist—destabilised colonial regimes' sense of control, pushed them to emphasise their own developmentalist objectives while trying to play down what was 'colonial' about colonial authority, and later helped to reveal that the developmental initiatives would themselves generate conflict more than alleviate it. Ronald Robinson, 'Andrew Cohen and the transfer of power in tropical Africa, 1940–51,' in W.H. Morris-Jones and Georges Fischer, eds, *Decolonisation and after: The British and French experience* (London, 1980), pp. 50–72; John Darwin, 'British decolonisation since 1945: A pattern or a puzzle?' *Journal of Imperial and Commonwealth Studies*, 12 (1984): 187–209.

81. Dipesh Chakrabarty argues that 'what European imperialism and third-world nationalisms have achieved together' is 'universalisation of the nation-state as the most desirable form of political community.' Chakrabarty, 'Post-coloniality and the artifice of history,' p. 19. Some argue that, given the internal weakness of Third World states, it is their insertion into

international relations that preserves them. Robert H. Jackson, *Quasi-states: Sovereignty, international relations, and the third world* (Cambridge, 1990).

82. Such definitions have been controversial for decades, since James Coleman insisted on limiting 'nationalist' to movements specifically directed at assuming power within a nation-state. Thomas Hodgkin wanted nationalism to include all anti-colonial protests and ideologies. Hodgkin's notion is really a definition of political action and barely allows a political movement in a colony to be anything but nationalist. The words mean more if nationalism is viewed as only one of many possibilities for politics. James S. Coleman, 'Nationalism in tropical Africa,' *American Political Science Review*, 48 (1954): 404–26; Hodgkin, *Nationalism*, p. 23.

83. Janet G. Vaillant, *Black, French, and African: A life of Léopold Sédar Senghor* (Cambridge: Mass., 1990); Appiah, *In my father's house*; Mudimbe, *Invention of Africa*; Miller, *Theories of Africans*.

84. On this last point, see Edward Said's impassioned defence of colonial and ex-colonial intellectuals' engagement with European literature and culture as well as his critique of nationalist thought. Said, *Culture and imperialism* (New York, 1993).

85. Note by the Secretaries, 'Future constitutional development in the colonies,' May 30, 1957, CP (O) 5, C AB 134/1551, Memorandum by the Secretary of State, 'Nigeria,' C 57 (120), May 14, 1957, CAB 129/87, Memorandum by the Secretary of State, 'Future policy in East Africa,' CPC (59) 2, April 14, 1959, CAB 134/1558, Public Record Office.

86. Joseph, *Radical nationalism*; Mbembe, *Naissance du maquis*. Such remaking of political figures is not unique to Africa: Yassar Arafat seems to be the latest beneficiary.

87. Jean Marie Allman, *The quills of the porcupine; Asante nationalism in an emergent Ghana* (Madison, Wisconsin, 1993); Mbembe, *Naissance du maquis*; Kriger, *Zimbabwe's guerrilla war*; Tabitha M. Kanogo, *Squatters and the roots of Mau Mau, 1905–1963* (London, 1987).

88. Aristide Zolberg, *Creating political order: The party-states of West Africa* (Chicago, 1966).

89. There is a problem in Anderson's argument about creole nationalism that is related to the issue raised here: the claim of élites to transcend social divisions. As Julie Skurskie argues, the politics of the creole élite were not so much inclusive—trying to cut across, co-opt, and minimalise conflict in the name of the nation—as exclusive, violently defining racial and cultural groups out of the nation. Skurskie, 'The ambiguities of authenticity in Latin America: *Dona Barbara* and the construction of national identity,' *Poetics Today*, 15 (1994).

90. Chatterjee, *Nationalist thought and the colonial world*; Partha Chatterjee, *The nation and its fragments: Colonial and post-colonial histories* (Princeton, N.J., 1993), p. 6. Chatterjee is only opening the door on what is likely to be a long and useful debate over the interrelation of economic/political and domestic/spiritual domains. See also Karen Tranberg Hansen, ed., *African encounters with domesticity* (New Brunswick, N.J., 1992); and Dipesh Chakrabarty, 'The difference-deferral of (a) colonial modernity: Public debates on domesticity in British Bengal,' *History Workshop*, 36 (1993): 1–34.

91. See also David Ludden, 'India's development regime,' in Dirks, *Culture and colonialism*, pp. 247–88.

92. The construction argument is often made. See, for example, Homi K. Bhabha, ed., *Nation and narration* (London, 1990).

93. One subject into which this kind of inquiry has begun is health. A Subaltern Studies historian (Arnold, *Colonising the body*) has done a pioneering study on India, and state and health have been studied perceptively by Vaughan, *Curing their ills*, and Packard, ' "Healthy reserve" and the "dressed native." '

94. Anthony D. Smith, *State and nation in the third world: The Western state and African nationalism* (Brighton, 1983), p. 56. As in my study of labour, one can examine in many domains how institutions (trade unions, industrial relations boards) of specifically European origin—but discussed by officials as if universal—were used by Africans in particular ways, while they, too, made claims to universality to serve their ends. On modes of exercising and representing power in Africa, see Jean-François Bayart, *L'état en Afrique: La politique du ventre* (Paris, 1989); and the controversy unleashed in *Public Culture*, 5, 1 (1992), by an article by Achille Mbembe, 'The banality of power and the aesthetics of vulgarity in the post-colony,' *Public Culture*, 4, 2 (1992): 1–30.

95. Basil Davidson, *The black man's burden: Africa and the curse of the nation-state* (New York, 1993); Pieter Boele van Hensbroek, 'Cursing the nation-state,' *Transition*, 61 (1993): 114–21; Liisa Malkki, 'National geographic: The rooting of peoples and the territorialisation of national identity among scholars and refugees,' *Cultural Anthropology*, 7 (1992): 24–44; Akhil Gupta, 'The song of the nonaligned world: Transnational identities and the reinscription of space in late capitalism,' ibid., 63–79.

96. Recent entries on Fanon—commenting on the other entries—are Cedric Robinson, 'The appropriation of Frantz Fanon,' *Race and Class*, 15 (1993): 79–91; Henry Louis Gates, Jr., 'Critical Fanonism,' *Critical Inquiry*, 17 (1991): 457–70; and a particularly critical discussion in Miller, *Theories of Africans*, pp. 45–62.

97. Frantz Fanon, *The wretched of the earth*, Constance Farrington, trans. (New York, 1966), p. 30. See also Frantz Fanon, *Black skin, white masks*, Charles Lam Markmann, trans. (New York, 1967), pp. 226–9. Said, *Imperialism and culture*, pp. 267–70, finds Fanon a useful ally in his critique of nationalism. Fanon did not seek to build a 'true Algeria' embodying some national essence but rather a society emancipated of its colonial oppression. Yet, in his own way, Fanon isolates the 'true anti-colonialist' from history and experience, turning impure categories into criteria for exclusion from the liberation project. I use the word 'true' in the ironic sense applied to the other side of colonial divide by Herman Lebovics, *True France: The wars over cultural identity, 1900–1945* (Ithaca: New York, 1992).

98. Fanon's psychologising of the colonial situation—and other versions of this enterprise—strike me as deeply flawed, a too-easy transposition of issues of state sovereignty to personal autonomy, abstracted from the multi-dimensional contexts in which personalities are actually shaped. A more recent and sophisticated attempt to address issues of personality and colonisation, not wholly convincing, is Ashis Nandy, *The intimate enemy: Loss and recovery of self under colonialism* (Delhi, 1983). There were colonialist versions of the psychologising argument, too, eliding individual and collective psychologies, claiming that Africans were unable to stand up to the pressures of modernisation or move between different social universes. The most notorious instance is J.C. Carothers, *The psychology of Mau Mau* (Nairobi, 1954).

99. 'The colonial world is a Manichean world,' wrote Fanon (*Wretched*, 33), apparently not realising how much deeper he was in that world than the people about whom and in whose cause he wrote.

100. Exposé de M. le Vice Président Sékou Touré à l'occasion de la conférence du 2 février 1958 avec les résponsables syndicaux et délégués du personnel RDA, 'Le RDA et l'action syndicale dans la nouvelle situation politiques des T.O.M.' PDG (9)/dossier 7, Centre de Recherche et de Documentation Africaine, Paris. His minister of labour, Camara Bengaly, insisted that unions must become 'the precious collaborators' of an African government and abandon their sectional claims: 'Any conception of trade unionism contrary to this orientation must be discarded, and courageously fought in order to be eliminated definitively.' Speech in name of Council of Government of Guinea to Congrès Constutatif de l'UGTAN, Conakry, May 23–25, 1958, sous-dossier UGTAN, K 421 (165), Archives du Sénégal.

101. A Guinean intellectual's conclusion on Sékou Touré is well expressed in the title of his book: *Ibrahima Baba Kaké, Sékou Touré: Le héros et le tyran* (Paris, 1987). See also Claude Rivière, 'Lutte ouvrière et phenomenè syndical en Guinée,' *Cultures et Développement*, 7 (1975): 53–83.

102. One should not assume that post-colonial African states were uniformly authoritarian or that an authoritarian state could not in many ways be a weak state. For one of the first critiques of the brittleness of African regimes and the ideological moves by which contestation was delegitimised, see Zolberg, *Creating political order*. My argument parallels Chatterjee's view of the 'plural development of social identities' emerging from struggles with the colonial state 'that were violently disrupted by the political history of the post-colonial state seeking to replicate the modular forms of the modern nation-state.' Chatterjee, *The nation and its fragments*, p. 156.

103. On the dualism of late colonial conceptions of society, see Cooper, *Decolonisation and African society*.

104. Chatterjee, *The nation and its fragments*, pp. 237–8; Chakrabarty, 'Postcoloniality and the artifice of history,' p. 20. The 'provincialising' argument is a very good one, but it implies a detailed and nuanced engagement with the vagaries of European history. The argument is weakened when it slips into blanket dismissals of liberalism or assumptions that bourgeois equality is an unchanging construct. See Chakrabarty, pp. 20–1; Chatterjee, p. 198.

Subaltern Studies: Radical History in the Metaphoric Mode

Henry Schwarz

The history of subaltern groups is necessarily fragmented and episodic. There undoubtedly does exist a tendency to (at least provisional stages of) unification in the historical activity of these groups, but this tendency is continually interrupted by the activity of the ruling groups; it therefore can only be demonstrated when an historical cycle is completed and this cycle culminates in a success. Subaltern groups are always subject to the activity of ruling groups, even when they rebel and rise up; only 'permanent' victory breaks their subordination, and that not immediately.

—Antonio Gramsci, *Selections from the prison notebooks*

. . . The critique is by its very nature still rather precocious, incomplete and generally endowed with all the immaturity of a thing in its formative stages. But it is this very want of maturity that drives the critique audaciously, if not prudently in every instance, to probe those fundamental contradictions of the existing system which prefigure its demise.

—Ranajit Guha, 'Dominance without hegemony
and its historiography'

WHEN VIEWED from the perspective of 1970s' history, two distinct strands of a solution to the dilemma of colonial middle-class consciousness can be seen to have emerged in recent years. One strand sinks more deeply into the 'collaborationist' middle-class consciousness that Barun De so roundly castigated in the early 1970s and that Marxist historians had decried since at least the mid-1930s, hoping to see in it an enabling duplicity that might offer an opening for criticism. The second strand attempts to bypass the bourgeois delusions of the cultural heritage by 'sinking into the subaltern.' Both are necessarily related. The latter takes its name from *Subaltern Studies*, a series of publications edited by Ranajit Guha beginning in 1982.[1]

Opening the subaltern perspective can be described as the invention of a break through the impasse confronted by middle-class consciousness. I will limit my comments here to Guha's contributions, which should not be taken as representative of the group's varied researches (he has been its major theorist, but never a programmatic voice), but which are characteristic of the spirit animating the formation of the *Subaltern Studies* project. I do so since, in my opinion, Guha more than any of the other contributors to the series maintains the strongest links with the specific traditions of cultural history writing in modern Bengal, even as his call for a new historiography declares itself a radical break from the past. This closeness to the object of inquiry is what charges his statements with their characteristic flamboyance; in their radicalness they can be seen as closing a chapter in Bengali cultural history. To this end, I read his substantial oeuvre synchronically, for while various interests brought to the *Subaltern* project have necessarily changed its direction, I feel that Guha's work possesses an internal consistency whose basic problematic has remained coherent over two decades. I will argue that the *Subaltern* project does not so much uncover a new object for history writing as show us how history is written, and in the process it attempts to pay the debt to Europe that has always been seen as the nemesis of writing cultural history in colonial India.

As we saw in Guha's earlier analysis of *Nildarpan*, by the mid-1970s the renaissance legacy had been substantially revised, and its greatest achievements could now be seen as expressing a duplicitous class interest. This ambivalence, tragic because unavoidable, marked even the most complex and beautiful expressions with the guilt of betrayal. *Subaltern Studies* attempts to rewrite the history of colonial and post-colonial India by resetting the parameters of historiography itself. It hopes to short-circuit the logic of complicity between indigenous and colonial élites by setting out to find a new object (of desire?): now not a nationalist or ethnic identity, and far less a civilisational advance up the evolutionary scale, but rather a field of heterogeneous forces that either resisted the 'official' nationalism of the Congress or had no access to the symbolic discourses of nation forming.[2] The impact of this 'field' on the anti-colonial movement has never been accurately registered in either colonialist or nationalist history writing. Perhaps its telling will unlock new dimensions of the Indian reality.

The field is described in the project's opening manifesto as the '*politics of the people.* For parallel to the domain of élite politics there existed throughout the colonial period in India another domain of Indian politics in which the principal actors . . . were the subaltern classes and groups constituting the mass of the labouring population and the intermediate strata in town and country, that is, the people. This was an *autonomous* domain, for it neither originated from élite politics nor did its existence depend on the latter.'[3] Guha is clearly appropriating a narrow definition of 'subalternity' here, at variance with the earlier usage we had see in Barun De, for whom the term designated the 'subordinate' middle class. This shift in valence of the term partially reflects an evolution within Indian historiography's understanding of the work of Antonio Gramsci, whose writings were introduced to Bengali historians through the teaching of Susobhan Sarkar in the late 1950s, contemporaneous with their first English translation.[4] In more recent uses of the term, 'subaltern' seems to have returned to its earlier broad strokes, as when Partha Chatterjee wrote in 1994 of middle-class subordination as 'the subalternity of an élite.'[5] A first, cursory understanding of the term subaltern should therefore alert us to a certain mobility in its usage.

Guha's definition explicitly attempted to return to the original Gramscian perspective, in which 'subaltern' designated the lower strata of an underdeveloped society lacking in 'naturally' revolutionary classes. For Gramsci, the term subaltern, used interchangeably with 'popular classes' or 'masses' described the inferior social positions of a small industrial and agricultural proletariat subsisting alongside a massive peasantry, all of whom were 'left out' of the historic formation of the Italian state in 1870. The risorgimento was a 'revolution without a revolution,' or a 'passive revolution' that captured state power for the moderate bourgeoisie through the exercise of hegemony, 'intellectual and moral leadership' over the policies of the weak opposition parties, rather than by winning the allegiance of the people.[6] Far from the assertion of a popular, 'national' will, the Italian state was formed by men who 'were not capable of leading the people, were not capable of arousing their enthusiasm and their passion. . . . They said that they were aiming at the creation of a modern State in Italy, and they in fact produced a bastard. They aimed at stimulating the formation of an extensive and energetic ruling class, and they did not succeed; at integrating the people into the framework of the new State, and they did not succeed.' The consequences of that failure were 'a paltry political life . . . the fundamental and endemic rebelliousness of the Italian popular classes, the narrow and stunted existence of a sceptical and cowardly ruling stratum . . . and . . . the sullen passivity of the great mass of the people. . . . They made the people-nation into an instrument, into an object, they degraded it.'[7] Crucially, Gramsci notices that in Italy the subaltern strata 'are not unified and cannot unite until they are able to become a "State." ' Thus 'the historian must record, and discover the causes of, the line of development towards integral autonomy, starting from the most primitive phases; he must note . . . every assertion of an independent will and its efforts to break with those above it and to unite with those of others in its class.'[8] In developing a movement to unseat the hegemonic bourgeoisie, 'every trace of independent initiative on the part of subaltern groups should therefore be of incalculable value for the integral historian.'[9]

In India, where power has historically been consolidated by a minority at the top, and where even the colonial bourgeoisie that led the freedom movement numbered a mere fraction of the total population, the lower strata are immense and extremely heterogeneous. Were they to come to account in any representative reckoning of the populace, they could exert on the democratic process an influence of catastrophic proportions. The existence of such immense and highly diversified subaltern strata within the post-colonial state, prevented from forming adequate political coalitions that might include them in the processes of state power, obviously casts severe doubts upon the representational validity of the state and raises provocative questions about the eventual destiny of 'the people.' For the study of history, it is clear that any understanding of anti-colonialism as a mass movement must come to terms with this overwhelming majority of lower-strata agents, who were selectively mobilised for nationalist agitation but did not participate in the ideological and practical debates of élite leadership.[10]

In an interesting move, Guha's massive study of peasant revolt under the Raj, *Elementary aspects of peasant insurgency in colonial India*, attempts to analyse subaltern consciousness in what he calls its ' "pure" state, before the politics of nationalism and socialism begin to penetrate the countryside on a significant scale.'[11] In focusing on this 'pure state,' Guha hopes to isolate the 'general form' of the 'theoretical consciousness' of the subaltern, a consciousness in which conservative and radical tendencies battle each other 'in order to arrive,' as Gramsci puts it, 'at the working out at a higher level of one's own conception of reality,' that is to say, free and independent.[12] Guha finds that this consciousness in its 'pure state' consistently struggled against itself to assert its radical side, most successfully when it expressed itself in rebellion. Rebellion signified the true vocation of the peasant: to end his oppression and assert his independence by turning things upside down. This did not necessarily mean that peasant rebellion needed to manifest itself as systematic, long term, or horizontally based to be conscious of the forces that denied the peasant freedom; but rebellion did indicate a basic 'political character' at the heart of subaltern identity.

Guha's great contribution is having restored to history the record of 110 peasant rebellions spanning 117 years of British occupation, a history that at once counters British assertions that they ruled the subcontinent by consent as well as Orientalist visions of India as the land of tranquillity. The subaltern identity was 'political' inasmuch as 'the existing power nexus had to be turned on its head as a necessary condition for the address of any particular grievance (*EAP*, 8). British power permeated every level of rural structure under which the peasant laboured, and the rebellions thus translated back in every case to a social arrangement in which the Raj could be seen to play some determining part. This link of peasant rebellion to colonial power situates it as a counter-tradition to the nationalist freedom struggle, the failures of which had been amply detailed by the previous generation. Perhaps by virtue of their very exclusion from élite politics, the subaltern strata escaped the immense resources of middle-class bad faith exposed by the 1970s historiography. Guha's overriding preoccupation is to challenge the vocation of mainstream historiography, which has consistently misrepresented the middle class as speaking for the Indian nation. 'We want to emphasize [subaltern consciousness's] sovereignty, its consistency and its logic in order to compensate for its absence from the literature on the subject' (*EAP*, 13).

In this context it is tempting to read Guha's 'On some aspects of the historiography of colonial India' in the first volume of *Subaltern Studies* as a manifesto explicitly arising from the impasse of the 1970s. In this inaugural statement he tends to separate élite and subaltern realms into mutually repelling existences, defying Gramsci's emphasis on the necessary interrelation between them. Gramsci insists that subalterns must 'attempt . . . to influence the programs of these [dominant] formations in order to press claims of their own,' making the history of subaltern groups 'intertwined with that of civil society and thereby with the history of State and groups of States.' Gramsci clearly states that the history of subaltern organisation 'can only be demonstrated when . . . this cycle culminates in a success,' that is, in revolution.[13] He is far too sceptical of the power of history writing, which is by definition always in the service of the state, to believe that subaltern experience or 'consciousness' can be adequately represented by a state whose very survival depends on repressing such consciousness. 'Only "permanent" victory breaks their subordination.' Is *Subaltern Studies* in fact premature?

Guha claims that 'the experience of exploitation and labour endowed [subaltern] politics with many idioms, norms and values which put it in a category *apart* from élite politics' ('OSA,' 5, my emphasis), and 'there were vast areas in the life and consciousness of the people which were *never integrated* into their [élite] hegemony' ('OSA,' 5–6, my emphasis). He thus implies that a truly alternative historiography can be written of subaltern existence that does not rely on the colonial or national state for its characteristic forms. In fact, as he asserts in a later essay, the pre-colonial Indian reality persisted throughout the British period as a 'distinct paradigm' with only tenuous translations of the dominant idioms of English rule penetrating its exterior, thus reducing all British representations of the 'Indian reality' to the thinnest veneer ('DWH,' 232–70). In stressing the radical difference, if not complete alterity, of subaltern politics, Guha stretches Gramsci's term here, if he is borrowing it at all. Though he fully admits it is not the case that 'these two domains were hermetically sealed off from each other and there was no contact between them' ('OSA,' 6), he does imply that subaltern consciousness was unpredictable and imminent, characterised far more than bourgeois nationalism by a tendency to accelerate into revolt, and thus properly unrepresentable in the sober annals of respectable history writing. Subaltern consciousness was so volatile that, once aroused, it terrified even nationalist leaders with the threat of 'things getting out of control.' As such, 'pure' subaltern consciousness remained outside the capacity of mainstream historiography ('the history of States') to record it with any accuracy. Far more frequently, élite historiography is charged with recording the suppression of peasant revolts, writing the subaltern out of its history. Élite nationalism and its historiography are characterised by a 'relatively greater reliance on the colonial adaptations of British parliamentary institutions' and are 'more legalistic and constitutionalist in orientation . . . more cautious and controlled' ('OSA,' 4–5). By separating the spontaneity and volatility of subaltern politics from the parliamentary decorum of both the national freedom struggle and its historiography, Guha implicitly unseats the claims to legitimacy of both the independent Indian state and mainstream academic history writing. 'The prose of counter-insurgency' provides a textbook example of how the tools of literary criticism can be used to unravel the truth-claims of historical discourse and restore the subaltern as agent of his own history.[14]

The reasoning seems as much theoretical as practical. The independent Indian state is the last and most dramatic legacy left over from colonial rule; it stands as the living testimony of the Raj's influence on the constitutional forms of life in post-colonial India. Yet according to Guha the independent Indian state, like the Raj, exercises a 'dominance without hegemony' in its replication of European forms of law and politics, a replication that neither sufficiently considers the specific nature of Indian reality nor adapts its principles of representation to fit that reality. Combined with the uneasiness towards the cultural legacy that the 1970s' historiography revealed, *Subaltern Studies* begins to appear as an attempt within the realm of disciplinary historiography to counteract the negative effects of previous efforts at representing the complexity of Indian life in the name of something else—the people, the nation, the culture, the state. Cambridge historians of the post-independence era had repeated this gesture with disastrous results. Anil Seal, for one, had claimed that independence was a mere outgrowth of imperial governance: 'The British built the framework; the Indians fitted into it' ('DWH,' 295). This to Guha is a mere continuation of James Mill's early colonialist plan of writing Indian history as 'an interesting portion of the British History.' Subaltern historiography, by contrast, will escape the falsity of such élitist forms of representation by self-consciously measuring the distance between the official forms of history writing and the inscrutable objects they claim to represent.

To do this, it is crucial that subaltern historiography restore an 'outside' to what has previously passed for 'the Indian reality.' For if the bestowal of colonial ideology onto the subject population was indeed as partial as Guha claims, vast territories of incomprehension must exist alongside the English-educated upper crust that were never incorporated into the patterns of dominance and were therefore unrecognisable as forms of conscious thought. These territories could include knowledges, practices, traditions, and techniques having the ability to resist, subvert—or just ignore—the intrusion of Eurocentric modes of governance and representation. The immediate problem for the academic historian is to find the calling of solidarity that can place him, as a member of the élite camp, within this circle of erstwhile compatriots. Methodologically, it would be both too easy and too politically disabling to simply reject the tools of European history, partial as they are, as has been done as much in certain strains of Afrocentrism as in Indian revivalist movements.[15] Instead, Guha turns to a Western Marxist tradition indelibly coloured by Hegel to uncover the historical 'difference' between the consciousness of dominator and dominated. 'Where then does criticism come from? *From outside the universe of dominance which provides the critique of its object, indeed from another and historically antagonistic universe . . .*' ('DWH,' 220, emphasis in original). 'It must begin, in short, by situating itself outside the universe of liberal discourse' ('DWH,' 228–9). Subaltern historiography must do both: it must relocate the subaltern as a site of energy oppositional to both colonialist and nationalist projects of domination, and it must resituate the practice of historiography as one that 'takes sides' with this subaltern project, rewriting what has passed for knowledge. It is both a discovery and a reorientation, an operation which, by demanding a new object of knowledge, will re-organise the practices through which the object is studied. 'The task of historiography is to interpret the past in order to help in changing the world and such a change involves a radical transformation in consciousness' (*EAP*, 336). Whose consciousness?

If Guha's manifesto polemically overstates the alterity of the category 'subaltern,' at least in relation to Gramsci, it does so within a methodological self-consciousness that recognises a pressing need to begin this rewriting immediately. Definitions may be seen as part of an overall strategy. 'On some aspects of the historiography of colonial India' opens with the declaration. 'The historiography of Indian nationalism has for a long time been dominated by élitism—colonialist élitism and bourgeois-nationalist élitism' ('OSA,' 1). In his contribution to *Subaltern Studies II* the following year, Guha asserted that even the contemporary Indian historians who displayed sympathy for sub-altern actors were enmeshed in the colonialist mindset of 'tertiary discourse,' a form of writing that denied the subaltern its agency and thus participated in a form of neocolonialist 'counter-insurgency.' 'It is still trapped in the paradigm which inspired the ideologically contrary, because colonialist, discourse of the primary and secondary types. It follows, in each case, from a refusal to acknowledge the insurgent as the subject of his own history. . . . Tertiary discourse, even of the radical kind, has thus distanced itself from the prose of counter-insurgency only by a declaration of sentiment so far. It has still to go a long way before it can prove that the insurgent can rely on its performance to recover his place in history' ('PCI,' 38–40).

How can the subaltern ever rely on historiography to 'recover his place in history?' As Gramsci attested, the recovery of subaltern agency within the discourse of history would pose a fundamental challenge to both the historical tradition and the state; indeed its writing can occur only when the 'cycle is completed . . . [and] "permanent" victory breaks their subordination.' Guha's admission that the *Subaltern* 'critique . . . is still rather precocious' strikes one as utterly honest in this context, and one must search for logics that explain its continued audacity. If subaltern history will not bring down the state overnight, it may be capable of illuminating the insufficiency and arbitrariness of the state's historiographical tradition up to now, and of instilling an awareness that new tools of practical research and theoretical analysis are needed.

How far can we go in acknowledging this claim? Subaltern historians clearly continue to practice something that looks like 'history,' and they do it, moreover, by drawing on many of the great European traditions of historical method as well as on archives held in the service of the state. And Guha's claims to have discovered history's 'outside' are not unproblematic. Beyond the 'pure state' of the theoretical consciousness examined in *Elementary aspects*, the actual definition of 'subaltern' given in *Subaltern Studies I* deserves closer scrutiny. At the end of Guha's lead essay an appended note defines the terms 'élite,' 'people,' and 'subaltern.' Here Guha unambiguously, though somewhat elliptically, states that subaltern is a situational term, in contrast to its earlier alterity. It is used synonymously with the term 'people,' and the two are defined by their 'difference' from the élite. 'The social groups and elements included in this category represent *the demographic difference between the total Indian population and all those whom we have described as the "élite"* '('OSA,' 8, emphasis in original). In deciding on the specificity of this 'difference,' the historian must determine when particular groups or elements are acting '*in conformity to interests corresponding truly to their own social being*' ('OSA,' 8, emphasis in original). Élites acting in their own interests are fairly easy to identify; more ambiguous are members of inferior social strata acting in the interests of the élite. Still more ambiguous are those fallen from grace—the 'lesser rural gentry, impoverished landlords, rich peasants and upper middle peasants who "naturally" ranked among the "people" and the "subaltern" ' ('OSA,' 8)—the proliferating scare quotes seem significant—who did *not* act in proper conformity to their social being at all times. Finally, subalterns really seem subalterns for themselves only when their actions correspond 'truly to their social being,' and thus only when they act antagonistically towards their oppressors. Is the term 'subaltern' then reserved for the lower classes only when they are insurgent, or does it cover larger sections of the population when *they* rise up, as did the middle and élite classes in 1942 and 1946? 'In spite of such diversity one of its [subaltern activity's] invariant features was a notion of resistance to élite domination' ('OSA,' 5). A subaltern seems most properly a subaltern when he or she is in rebellion, and one must decide when this rebellion is directed against élite domination, as opposed to local grievances, to determine its ultimate consciousness. Determining this difference poses a fundamental choice for the historian, one that will declare whether his or her work will escape the complicity of tertiary discourse: 'It is up to the historian to sort out on the basis of a close and judicious reading of his evidence' ('OSA,' 8). It is the historian who is the final arbiter of 'social being' and the 'truthfulness' of the actions that conform to it or not.

Similar perceptions of the arbitrary and constructed nature of the historical enterprise colour post-modern historiography in the West, but it is somewhat jarring to hear this assertion made in relation to both the earthiness of its subject matter and the assertions of authenticity—'pure form' 'corresponding truly to their social being'— that accompany it. In this respect I think it is a mistake to characterise *Subaltern Studies* as a wholesale rejection of Western Enlightenment Reason along with British historiography, as some reviewers have done. Instead, it seems more correct to characterise it as a strong rereading of Hegel—of whom Alexandre Kojève would be one precursor—rather than an outright denunciation of Reason as such. Guha's emphasis throughout is on the historic failure of the British to perform up to their stated rational ideals, a failure that extended from economics to general improvement, education to historiography. Far from rejecting Enlightenment categories, Guha resolutely challenges the claims of British rule to have measured up to its proclaimed liberal ends. He locates the misery of the colonial situation in this practical failure rather than in any more philosophical deficiency of Reason itself.

Needless to say, the definitional slippage in the term 'subaltern' alerts us to a theoretical error in the valuation by the historian of the 'true' or 'proper' consciousness of the subaltern. It is one thing to return historiographical authority to the Indian historian, but something different to insist on the purity of the object that the historian is called upon to judge. This circularity, which informs Guha's methodological procedure in *Elementary aspects* as well, can be charted as follows: subaltern consciousness has never been accurately recorded by élite historians; subalterns themselves do not leave historical records that could be admitted as new evidence to the historical record; any search for subaltern consciousness must be an interested interpretation by historians committed to its recovery, and must be limited to correcting the inaccurate records of their predecessors. Thus a 'proper' subaltern historiography is a logical impossibility, since subaltern consciousness in itself can be retrieved neither through existing accounts nor through previously unexamined records. Any account of such indecorous people acting 'properly,' '*in conformity to interests corresponding truly to their social being,*' must be a self-conscious fiction, since neither accurate observers nor recorded statements accord with what is imputed to be the 'true social being' of the subaltern. Thus if a separate and autonomous subaltern domain can be said to be retrievable to history, its only necessary condition is its 'antagonism' to the realm of the élite, since neither articulated utterance nor accurate interpretation of historical records can mark its appearance.

In the tenaciously dialectical spirit of the argument, the subaltern becomes everything that élite discourse is not: its Other. Guha does not press this point far enough: if the subaltern is truly history's Other, then it cannot by definition be 'included' within history's discourse. Or rather history can never speak its 'proper' name; subalternity can be felt only through its symptoms as they arise in history's discourse and disturb its smooth appearance. These symptoms are then subject to all the misapprehensions, contradictions, and mistaken identities of dreams. No 'true' identity can be apprehended in the mirror; as Lacan reminds us, the specular image of the 'I' is both fiction and asymptote, a condition of partiality that will remain 'irreducible,' 'whatever the success of the dialectical syntheses by which he must resolve as *I* his discordance with his own reality.'[16]

With such constraints acting on the recovery of an authentic subaltern consciousness, the only task that can be left for historians is to read mainstream history in a new way, searching out oppositional moments from the textual record and interpreting them anew. Chatterjee is thus surely right in calling Guha's method of retrieving subaltern consciousness a 'mirror image' of the counter-insurgent documents used to suppress it, a 'paradigmatic form' rather than a '*history* of this consciousness as a movement of self-transformation.'[17] As such, as Lévi-Strauss commented on his own structural method, it is a 'myth of mythology'; subaltern historiography is the 'myth' about an object, subaltern consciousness, itself unknowable outside the immediate context of its articulation.[18] While Guha's formal dexterity in rereading the documents of counter-insurgency is impressive and provocative, as he displays to great effect in 'The prose of counter-insurgency' and 'Chandra's death,'[19] it remains by necessity a far cry from recovering an authentically *historical* subaltern voice from the ashes of time. Having revealed the very nature of middle-class ideology to be mythological, is Guha here trumping his earlier work? Is *Subaltern Studies* actually the myth of middle-class mythology? *Nildarpan* attempted to identify the urban middle class as protectors of the rural peasantry, compatriots in colonial oppression. Does *Subaltern Studies* identify the radical historian as the true agent of subaltern consciousness?

If the project seemed somewhat theoretically idealist from the start, perhaps its very existence, however feasible in the long term, could generate certain immediate benefits. Sumit Sarkar commented on the project's ambiguities in his contribution to *Subaltern Studies III* (1984), in an essay which, from almost the beginnings of the project, began to push its theoretical limits to extremes. As a historian Sarkar found that 'a serious problem in some "subaltern" writing has been the tendency to concentrate on moments of conflict to the exclusion of much longer time-spans of subordination or collaboration.'[20] He suggested that documents of subaltern antagonism do not unambiguously reveal subaltern 'participation in anti-imperialist struggle.' In fact, in the Bengal countryside from 1905 to 1922, mobilisations around local grievances such as banning cow slaughter or contesting price hikes were far more common than overt acts of resistance to British rule. The relation between subaltern activity and anti-colonialism is extremely detailed: 'One does not automatically lead to the other without a variety of complex mediations in which the specific socio-economic structure of a region, historical traditions, efforts at mobilisation by the élite . . . and British strategies all play a part' ('CNS,' 276). Nonetheless, Sarkar claimed that he could deduce a 'collective mentality underlying apparently very different forms of popular militancy in the period under study. Certain recurrent patterns do seem to emerge. . . . Something like a very tentative "structure" of popular militancy can be reconstructed in the Lévi-Straussian sense of an implicit, perhaps largely unconscious logical system lying beneath the surface of myths, beliefs, values, and activities' ('CNS,' 277).

Whether in deference to the spirit of the project as a whole or through a kind of oblique criticism that takes its references for granted, Sarkar refrained from taking the next decisive critical step towards Guha's manifesto. He could well have done it through his allusion to Lévi-Strauss, had he followed his own reference and considered the famous and devastating rejoinder to the French anthropologist written by Jacques Derrida in 1967.[21] Briefly, Derrida called into question the concept of structure altogether as a legitimate organising tool for the social sciences, illustrating how all structures depended on a paradoxical point or 'center' which served both to ground the structure and to permit the infinite play of its elements. Lévi-Strauss, by positing a 'reference myth' from the Bororo people of Brazil as the centre of his structure of primitive mythology, showed how all subsequent variants of the myth served to emphasise its same basic features. Rather than take the regional or chronological differences of the myths into account as illustrations of variation between the people who told them or in the social contexts of their telling, Lévi-Strauss hoped to illustrate the parameters of a coherent *pensée sauvage* common to all primitive peoples and every bit as logical and orderly as that of the European engineer.

But by assuming that every variant of a myth contributed to the overall structure of this 'savage mind,' Lévi-Strauss committed two fundamental errors. The first error was in assuming the principle of totalisation: that his system could account for any further variants that should arise. This assumption logically demanded that all myths function in essentially the same way, which undercut his assertion that variation was significant in itself. The second error was the inverse of totalisation: empiricism. If the centrality of the reference myth was to be proved by the manifestation of its structure in all subsequent variations, then all the variants must be collected. One deviant example would be enough to bring the structure crashing down. Derrida thus showed that the very positing of a central reference myth was an illusion presupposed by the decision to analyse it structurally. The centre of any structure is in fact *outside* the structure; it is the point that 'escapes the structurality of the structure,' and as such is both arbitrary and theological: arbitrary because the supposed centrality of the ur-myth was in fact decided at random by the researcher; theological since its very positing would govern the subsequent shape of the structure itself, like the God of Christian cosmology. Not itself subject to the rules of the structure it governs, the centre is a site of endless deferral rather than the locus of a stable presence. Derrida calls the entire history of Western philosophy the 'history of such substitutions of the center.' For a project committed to the 'science of the concrete,' as was Lévi-Strauss's, this observation seriously undermined its claims to accuracy. One centre could be substituted for another without altering the structure; and this quality revealed the nature of the stable centre to be its very opposite: play.

Similar charges could be levelled at a 'structure' of subaltern consciousness. Not all popular militancy could be considered as acting in conformity to its true social being. Was there never any collaboration between peasantry and reactionary forces? If subaltern insurgency always acted 'in conformity to interests corresponding truly to [its] social being,' then how could the sheer quantity of this interest possibly have been resisted by the élite? Why hadn't it snowballed? Could the very 'centre' of Guha's structure, the proposition that subalterns rebelled against oppression, be substituted for another, equally verified by empirical observation—that they didn't?

In his essay, Sarkar refrained from recalling this already-classic challenge to the concept of structure, and one wonders if the hesitation—like that of the editors of *Selected Subaltern Studies* in choosing not to reprint Sarkar's essay in their introductory selection—is intentional and in some sense permissive.[22] On the one hand, both the theoretical and practical ambiguities in Guha's definitions are troubling and have troubled the subsequent history of the collective, although probably no more so than in other 'history from below' movements.[23] On the other hand, the rhetorical force of recovering 'people's history' in the context of decolonisation is persuasive. Even if subaltern consciousness as theorised here is finally unrecoverable in fact, it remains a crucial utopian aspiration for a fully decolonised historiography, and should be pursued to the point where its very non-attainment begins to stretch the bounds of 'acceptable' history. Élite nationalist leaders well understood the rhetorical value of popular history when they recorded their own versions of the freedom struggle as rebuttals to the official British story and encountered censorship and repression in the process. Nationalist autobiography is replete with references to the mobilisation of the masses in the cause of de-colonisation, and today 'common sense' says that Gandhi and other élite leaders in India were solicited organically by an upsurge of the popular will. That assumption, however historically inaccurate, lent tremendous moral force to the élite's demand for a self-governing state.

Subaltern Studies does posit a large-scale resistance to domination on the part of the peasantry, but it parts company with nationalist history in refusing to interpret this resistance as directed solely or even predominantly against the colonial rulers. Subaltern insurgency, in its proper relation of antagonism, could just as surely be directed against the nationalist leadership as it was towards local landlords, tax collectors, health inspectors, schoolteachers, and other forms of authority that impinged upon its autonomy. The question then becomes one of *specific* antagonism: does the historian define 'correct' subaltern behaviour by its causes or by its effects? Does 'true accordance with social being' describe *any* resistance to oppression or only those with some consciousness of establishing an alternate social order outside colonial or nationalist rule? Guha asserts that the structure of subaltern rebellion is politically conscious: 'Insurgency . . . was a motivated and conscious undertaking on the part of the rural masses' ('PCI,' 2). Yet this assertion cannot unearth a more recognisable 'history,' based on records or other facts, of wide-scale organisations to support its claim. Structure becomes more determining than historical fact; the structure of subaltern consciousness in its pure state in essence overdetermines the historical record and, if it can be accepted, must be accepted as the radical failure of previous historiography to have recorded its appearance.

Guha claims that in its paradigmatic form subaltern consciousness is in fact organised and 'political,' but this organisation shows no lasting traits that could be extrapolated into an actually existing historical movement, or what Gramsci termed a 'historic bloc.' Javeed Alam noted this seeming contradiction in his review of *Subaltern Studies I*. 'Can autonomy be equated with episodic actions, whatever be the sources or motivational mainsprings of action? . . . In none of these studies do we find any evidence from which it could be inferred that the domain of peasant politics had come to acquire the character of a stable condition that defines the availability of concrete options and choices for these classes or strata in a long term sense.'[24] Guha emphasises that the paradigm of authority and rebellion reappears 'cyclically over the centuries' rather than as a continuous or teleological development (*EAP*, 335). Yet the question remains: if the possibility of peasant insurgency remains merely imminent or cyclical, how does that affect the rewriting of history?

To Gramsci, the Italian peasantry clearly lacked any sense of organised leadership and required intervention from intellectuals to provide it: 'Given the dispersal and the isolation of the rural population and hence the difficulty of welding it into solid organisations, it is best to start the movement from the intellectual groups.'[25] Guha's peasants, by contrast, seem to possess a pure, antagonistic consciousness that defies homogeneous leadership, yet unites them on the basis of this common consciousness. In *Elementary aspects*, their territoriality is overcome by its negation, the ability to define one's identity by what it is not. All outsiders come to symbolise potential sources of disturbance which generate common, if unconnected, forms of resistance.[26] Guha's strategic use of Gramsci thus results in both a contraction and an inflation of the term subaltern. In its contracted form, on the one hand, it seems to confine the definition of subaltern to a perpetual mobilisation against the dominant groups in society. Although *Elementary aspects* is a monumental contribution to the study of this sort of underclass revolt, a great mass of additional scholarship will be needed to challenge the prevailing view of Indian passivity. Far more prevalent in the existing historiography is Marx's view, famously indigenised by D.D. Kosambi, that India has remained a country of torpor, inactivity, and 'the idiocy of village life.'[27] When joined by such an authoritative and committed voice as Sarkar's, the reminder that collaboration as much as resistance characterised the *longue durée* is well taken.

On the other hand, in its inflationary form antagonistic behaviour can lift great masses of mid-strata actors into the properly subaltern realm of 'conformity to interests corresponding truly to their own social being.' Against this backdrop of rural mobilisation, two dimensions of middle-class consciousness emerge more vividly. The first is the almost complete neglect, as evidenced in their historiography, by urban élites of the realities of rural India. The second is the striking juxtaposition of the interests of the colonial élite and those of the masses. Subalterns acting truly are capable of intense and far-reaching rebellions. But 'élite subalterns' acting untruly can be revealed with greater accuracy to be a failed bourgeoisie incapable of exercising hegemony over the masses it claims to speak for. In fact, this may be the real object of the theorisation of the subaltern as 'outside.' Even as the outside is unapproachable in theory, its postulation as a utopian impulse drives the inside to come to terms with it, to confront its lack of revolutionary conviction as the experience of defeat in opposition to the 'true' revolutionary consciousness of the authentic, imagined, subaltern.[28] If 'subaltern' is just a transposition of 'subordinated,' as it seems to be when applied to the colonial middle class, then the mildness of middle-class nationalism pales in comparison to the glorious spontaneity of its rebellious countrymen. Is subaltern, in short, a sociological category or an attitude? Indeed, the project's subsequent publications indicate a shift from studies of agrarian relations, rebellious

hillmen, and peasant revolt to imaginary institutions, urban domesticity, and the disciplinary practices of élite mobilisation.[29] Perhaps the
concept of the subaltern is, finally, a provocation, a theoretical fiction
designed to prod the middle class into awareness of its own historic
complicity in disciplining the masses it could never learn to represent.

We have seen how the floating, situational definition of subaltern
as antagonist can result in a rather static binary. In fact, in *Elementary
aspects* Guha begins with an epigraph from Buddhist scripture that
indigenises the famous Hegelian dialectic of lordship and bondage,
a marvellous simplification of struggle in a country divided not only
by class but by caste, foreign occupation, religion, gender, region, and
numerous other factors. Guha's epigraph records the Buddha exclaim-
ing in amazement to his disciple Assalayana, 'Have you heard that in
Yona and Kamboja . . . there are only two varnas [castes], the master
and the slave? And that having been a master one becomes a slave;
having been a slave one becomes a master?'[30] As they both know, this
simplification of antagonism into master and slave is impossibly
idealistic. But the reduction of the multiplicities of struggle serves a
strategic purpose: by rewriting resistance in absolute terms, it seriously
challenges the legitimacy of élite dominance. This subjects all its ideologies of caste, religion, and obligation, as well as its historiographical
records, to serious doubt. In the specific context of India, this was
above all a pragmatic, short-term strategy, subsequently outgrown.
Partha Chatterjee concurs: 'The point, therefore, is no longer one of
simply demarcating and identifying the two domains in their sepa-
rateness, *which is what was required in order first to break down the
totalising claims of a nationalist historiography.* Now the task is to trace
in their mutually conditioned historicities the specific forms that have
appeared, on the one hand, in the domain defined by the hegemonic
project of nationalist modernity, and on the other, in the numerous
fragmented resistances to that normalising project.'[31]

II

Guha's work goes on to complicate this dichotomous view of resistance.
But in terms of the first few volumes of *Subaltern Studies* it is possible
to see the positing of a static binary—however questionable—as a

necessary first step. The Indian middle classes achieved independence at the expense of their underclass compatriots. The exploits of middle-class leaders are well researched, but the story of their collaboration with English power and their betrayal of the immense and heterogeneous underclass remains untold. Subaltern consciousness is predicated as autonomous in order to deduce the possibility of an 'outside' from that of middle-class collaboration. By doing so, a new Indian culture will spring into view: not the canonised cultural heritage, but the culture that resisted all forms of domination through the long night of foreign occupation. The emancipated bourgeoisie has its national hero in the figure of Gandhi. But as Ajit K. Chaudhury observes, up to *Subaltern Studies V* (1987) there is a profound 'silence in subaltern studies: Lenin.'[32] It is a silence in name only; the entire project points towards an overlooked vanguard party without being able to name it as such. Without historical records that could prove the existence of the Indian Lenin, radical historiography becomes the agent for releasing the full potential of popular mobilisation. History may not necessarily *find* something new, but it will *do* something new: it will rewrite its past from a perspective never before considered, and in the process it will revolutionise that story. If the search for the 'outside' is a structuralist fiction, pursuing it a certain way may serve to reorganise the procedures of the inside—an inside-out revolution. The subaltern thus becomes a technique more than an object, a 'perspective,' as Veena Das has framed it, more than a person.[33]

Guha's impatience is directed towards his contemporary Indian colleagues, but the real antagonist can be seen as the whole disciplinary apparatus of 'élite historiography,' running from early colonial records and memoirs to administrative accounts right through indigenous nationalist and explicitly leftist histories. None of these representational vehicles has so far produced an 'Indian historiography of India.' The methods of narrative analysis he explicates in two articles in particular, 'The prose of counter-insurgency' and 'Chandra's death,' and which he uses to unseat the truth-claims of previous appropriations of this material, could equally well be turned upon any truth-claims, including his own. Guha seems so aware of this danger, however, that his appeals to the alternate truths revealed through his methodology must be placed in quotations. The 'truth' produced by subaltern readings will be the self-conscious production of 'truth-effects.' Historiography as a discipline is to be understood as a class-bound exercise in self-legitimation; nonetheless, it is immensely important as the tool—along with literature—that 'helped the bourgeoisie to change or at least significantly to modify the world according to its class interests in the period of its ascendancy, and since then to consolidate and perpetuate its dominance' ('DWH,' 215). This proposes a dual stance on the nature of historiographical inquiry: retaining the strategic strength of history as a discipline which arose, along with the bourgeoisie, with the division of knowledges in the European universities of the late eighteenth century; and at the same time usurping the claims of European historiography to be the objective, legitimate custodian of *global* history, replacing them with the greater verisimilitude of marginal knowledges uniquely available from the perspective of the subordinated. Coming as they do from history's 'outside,' these knowledges may well be expressed in forms more closely allied to the 'story' that lies at the etymological root of 'history.' Subaltern historiography will replace liberal/colonist historiography as the authentic utterance of the colonised Indian people. Having lost its formal tools of legitimation, the bourgeoisie will wither away.

This self-consuming rhetorical strategy, combined with the ambiguous definition of subalternity and the immediacy of Guha's political demands, allows me to proceed with a reading of *Subaltern Studies* somewhat against the grain of its stated intentions. Rather than accuse his theoretical statements of idealising subaltern politics as a space sealed off from and therefore uncontaminated by élite nationalism, I find it more pertinent to read Guha's texts as a methodological autocritique directed at displacing the authority of the accepted traditions of both indigenous and foreign historical discourse. Guha's rewriting of Indian history is double edged. The point is not to speak for or in place of the subaltern—that project's disastrous history is certainly not to be repeated—nor is the point to achieve the impossible ideal of allowing an unmediated subaltern voice to speak through the historian's work. Rather, much closer to Gramsci, the historical activity is being reconceived as a *transactional* project in which the traditions of acceptable history writing are transformed by the objects they wish to represent. 'Élitist historiography should be resolutely fought by developing an *alternative discourse* based on the . . . recognition of the co-existence and interaction of the élite and subaltern domains of politics' ('OSA,' 7, my emphasis). An alternative discourse is not necessarily a diametrically opposed one, although at times, to be sure, Guha's rhetoric can lead one to believe that the historian is uniquely positioned to reclaim such an unmediated subaltern consciousness. Frequent mentions of 'truth,' 'reality,' 'restoration,' and 'reclamation' mark this project as a redemptive one that will restore misrepresented accounts to some version of a historical 'real,' but the juxtaposition of such claims against theoretical tools for de-realising their effects leave their 'real' status ambivalent. I would argue that the postulation of the subaltern can be seen as the blind spot that undercuts *any* historiography's claims to representational validity. Serious reflection on the possibilities of identifying subaltern consciousness will necessarily challenge the social status of the observer; this will entail a new self-consciousness about the practice of historical studies in general.

The seeming paradox between observer and observed is amply illustrated in 'The prose of counter-insurgency,' the methodological blueprint that claims to restore subaltern agency by debunking its prior historical inscriptions.

> But however noble the cause of an instrument of such appropriation, it leads to the mediation of the insurgent's consciousness by the historian's— that is, of a past consciousness by one conditioned by the present. The distortion which follows necessarily and inevitably from this process is a function of that hiatus between event-time and discourse-time which makes the verbal representation of the past less than accurate in the best of cases. . . . There is nothing that historiography can do to eliminate such distortion altogether, for the latter is built into its optics. What it can do, however, is to acknowledge such distortion as parametric—as a datum which determines the form of the exercise itself, and to stop pretending that it can *fully* grasp a past consciousness and reconstitute it. Then and only then might the distance between the latter and the historian's perception of it be reduced significantly enough to amount to a close approximation which is the best one could hope for. ('PCI,' 33)

'The best one could hope for.' Had these words remained firmly in view, much spurious searching after authentic voices could have been avoided. Subaltern consciousness is always mediated by the historian.

The point is not to retrieve the subaltern, but to bring the historian closer to the realisation of the inherent fictionality of his work.

The essential difference between *Subaltern Studies* and earlier Marxist approaches to Indian history (even when that historiography looked to 'the people') is in the mediatory concepts associated with the historical activity itself. What sets *Subaltern Studies* apart from the self-professed and often idealised populism of early Indian Marxism is its interrogation of the complex mediating apparatus between the recorder of an event, who is by definition a member of the élite camp, and the object of inquiry, the 'autonomous,' 'heterogeneous,' and 'spontaneous' subaltern insurgent. Far from claiming the subaltern as an unambiguous or clearly knowable object of history to be objectively recorded by the historian, *Subaltern Studies* problematises the very act of doing history. Subaltern methodology seems as much an analytical tool for debunking inaccurate truth-claims as one designed to produce new narratives about 'what happened in the past.' It is a quintessential *bricolage*: borrowing from literary criticism and taking the historical text as its object, or approaching a cultural or interpretive anthropology when it turns to kinship structures and rituals in order to interpret in a new way a particular event recorded in official historical sources such as court records or administrator's diaries, Guha's procedures relentlessly resituate events within a thick description that restores their contextual immediacy.

But this new context is no more 'true' than any other narrative choice; the high methodological claim for this procedure is often that by dismantling and reaggregating the biased methods and materials of the coloniser's accounts covering a particular event, the contemporary historian can 'reclaim the document for history' ('CD,' 135). But what *is* history? As opposed to the colonial judicial discourse examined in 'Chandra's death,' for instance, we find that a definition of 'history' emerges only in opposition to the procedures of the law. Turning an event into a legal case involves 'detaching an experience from its living context and setting it up as an empty positivity outside history. It is a process intended to take out of these statements all that stands for empathy and pity and leave nothing to show for their content except the dry bones of a deixis—the "then" and "there" of a "crime" ' ('CD,'

140). The work of 'history,' by contrast, is to restore 'empathy and pity' to this 'dry' account, contextualising the story within new borders that make it a 'tragedy' of 'women's solidarity and its limitation' ('CD,' 165). Guha recreates, far from a 'true' story, a context for Chandra's grim fate that is designed to 'heighten its drama' ('CD,' 148). By illustrating the process through which historical accounts are constructed, all prior historical work is exposed as the cobbling together of data and context to produce an effect of authenticity. Partha Chatterjee write, with some irony, 'The project then is to claim for us, the once-colonised, our freedom of the imagination.'[34] Guha provides the tools both to free the imagination from colonial appropriation and to begin interpreting this freedom once it has been won.

I have three points in conclusion. First, by exposing 'the possibility of the impossible' in recovering subaltern consciousness as the locus of an authentic imaginary, the *Subaltern Studies* project reminds us that *all* identities are imaginary and that there can be no going back to some nostalgic point of origins, no pre-linguistic stability before the signifier, no 'subaltern' before its inscription in the texts of counter-insurgency. This is quite different from claiming that the subaltern as such does not exist empirically on the ground. The scandalous fact exposed by *Subaltern Studies* is that this existence has escaped historical narration. This theoretical/practical point as much ensures the longevity of history as a disciplinary procedure as it debunks the authority of its practice. Rather than a mere objective recorder, the historian simultaneously serves as recorder, scribe, translator, and inventor.

Second is the related practical point that since there is no subaltern consciousness before its articulation, and since illiterate insurgents keep few records of their activities, the search for subaltern consciousness can only be continued by rethinking what constitutes a text. Veena Das offers a pointed practical agenda when she writes: 'It is not that non-official sources are not abundant or not easily accessible, but rather that the legitimacy of those who are producing these materials needs to be recognised by official history.'[35] This redefinition of legitimate sources challenges both the reliance on written (mainly British) documents on subaltern activity up to now and the related rules and norms of academic history writing as a discipline. If the subaltern is to speak, it is high time that speaking subjects were introduced as evidence, and not solely in the coerced forms in which their 'statements' appear on the peripheries of essays.[36] Opening the disciplinary bounds of history to other forms of textual production through which the 'subaltern-effect' can be read would necessarily ally it with what passes as 'cultural studies' in the US academy today: unstable combinations of literary analysis, anthropological description, gender marking, sociological conditions of production and reception, and the mediation of all these forms that makes the practice of history extremely risky business—and all the more worth doing.

Finally, we turn to the dimension of power. Let us assume for heuristic purposes that a subaltern consciousness, in whatever form, can be recovered from the historical record. If we do so, the Freudian dilemma of transference returns with a vengeance. In its most limited form, transference signals the analysand's active participation in producing the narrative he or she thinks the analyst wants to hear.[37] If the subaltern is interviewed in its position 'as subaltern,' that is, in relation to an élite historian, what is to prevent him or her from telling a story he or she might think will satisfy the customer? That possibility should be entertained in the most positive light: subalterns can actually write their own histories outside the conventions of acceptable historiographical style. In the other direction, counter-transference designates the possibility that the historian-analyst will tend to speak in the place of the analysand, preinterpreting historical meaning from an always already occupied position of mastery. By displacing the class categories of Marxist historiography in order to examine the autonomous space of subaltern insurgency, the largest claim of Guha's project aims at an analysis without transference, a history that would let the subaltern speak in full self-possession of his or her words. As Freud himself argued, such a relationship, if possible, would form the analytic ideal. If the symptom rather than the analysand could speak up, what would it say? But we know this is impossible for two reasons: the analysand cannot fully possess his consciousness, neither for himself nor for others, and the analyst is in no position to do anything about it. So what if the subaltern speaks? The real point is that the symptom is speaking all the time, but it is easier to repress than to redress it. Or, as perhaps in the case of the larger utopian desire that the *Subaltern* project attempts to articulate, many may hear the symptom speaking but very few do anything about it. The bottom line, as always, is the power of any imagined historiography to effect social change.

Guha suggests, however—and this I would argue is the necessary and insurmountable challenge of the *Subaltern Studies* project as a whole—that such a historiography is possible. It intends to produce not merely a popular history but an Indian history, one better adapted to the totality of Indian social and political life, by which is meant not only the two or so per cent of ruling élites who have traditionally made history, but the vast and uncharted multitudes who possess the potential, if heard, to liberate India from the ideological hangovers of colonial rule and post-colonial corruption by exposing the immense realm of the 'un-said' of everyday life. According to Guha, the call for 'an Indian historiography of India' that originated with Bankimchandra Chatterjee in the late nineteenth century 'amounted to nothing less than challenging Britain's right to rule India. In other words, *no historiography of colonial India would be truly Indian except as a critique of the very fundamentals of the constitutive power relationship of colonialism itself.*[38] By implication, the new historiography of *Subaltern Studies* amounts to a continued critique of the textual power relationships of a neocolonialist project of knowledge, challenging the standards of acceptable historiography. Yet it must practice history in order to change it; as did the European bourgeoisie, so must the decolonised radical historian: 'Historiography [is] one of the two principle instruments—the other being literature—which would . . . be put to use' in reclaiming the Indian past. To my mind, this insistence on practice largely reclaims the project from the various criticisms charging it with a philosophic idealisation of the subaltern as a Rousseauist subject in nature, or with post-structuralist overtones to debunk the authority of Western Reason as a whole. Gayatri Spivak registers this positive ambivalence when she asserts that the project is *self-consciously* metaphysical, enacting a 'strategic essentialism' whereby the movement to 'retrieve the subaltern consciousness [is] the attempt to undo a massive historiographical metalepsis and "situate" the effect of the subject as subaltern . . . in a scrupulously visible political interest.'[39] I find it indicative of the moment at which subaltern historiography emerged that it should serve as an example of what Spivak terms 'affirmative deconstruction' while its practitioners could resist being recast in the language of post-modernism: using 'the force of anti-humanism . . . even as they share its constitutive paradox: that the essentialising moment, the object of their criticism, is irreducible.'[40]

Must this declaration of fictionality—parametric distortion, strategic essentialism—mark the larger claims of the project as mythopoetic? Recalling Derrida's critique of Lévi-Strauss, are we indeed in the hands of a methodology that declares its referential value as a conscious falsehood, and thus in an area of irresponsibility? Certainly not. In the larger institutional framework of Indian academic history, which has struggled mightily for fifty years to deliver the event of Indian independence to its nationalist élites, the eruption of the rebellious peasant as the covert agent of independence represents the unthinkable. It is a 'terrifying form of monstrosity,'[41] a possibility that something new and unseen, but something that has secretly conditioned all the visible actions of history past, will emerge as the hidden organisational principle of the present.

III

The radical implications of Guha's positions become even clearer when juxtaposed with White's account of the acceptable modes of history writing in the West. Indeed, this most linguistically conscious of Indian historians embodies a tropological configuration seemingly of his own ingenious design, just as much as the subaltern is designed to boondoggle any conception of an acceptable subject of history. Essentially writing in the metaphoric mode (according to White's schema), Guha uses a romantic emplotment (as did Dinesh Sen) to describe the fall from grace of native culture under the pressure of British rule, and just as surely envisions its comic redemption from that fallen state—a movement traced at least in part by the *Subaltern*

Studies' emphasis on recuperating an Indian history. This movement is explicitly Hegelian, as Guha repeatedly asserts in his references to the tragic, immediate perspective of the bondsman set within the macrocosmically comic drama of self-consciousness it promotes.

This fundamentally romantic emplotment is placed within a narrative argument that we have not yet had occasion to study in this survey, an argument I would term formist, as opposed to the more classically mechanist modes of the earlier Marxists. The formist mode, according to White, aims at 'the identification of the unique characteristics of objects inhabiting the historical field. . . . The task of historical explanation is to dispel the apprehension of those similarities that appear to be shared by all objects.'[42] This is clearly in keeping with the motivation to restore historical specificity to the subaltern consciousness, and the meticulous correction of the errors of both nationalist and Cambridge School historians that native élites spoke for the nation. Finally, the important difference separating Guha's project from the nineteenth-century European discourses of a Michelet or Tocqueville (who in White's scheme would be the historical precursors to this narrative alignment of formist argument with romantic emplotment) is the strong ideological assertion of radicalism—the view that the goals of the reforming critique are *imminent,* as opposed to the anarchism of Michelet in which the fallen state of man is redeemed in a remote and inaccessible temporal dimension, or the liberalism of de Tocqueville which projected 'a minimal but hopeful freedom for his heirs.'[43]

The tropological figure of metaphor mediates between these seemingly incommensurable oppositions by asserting a figurative similarity between two objects, despite the obvious differences between them. Metaphor thus *combines* qualities of distinct objects without reducing or negating them. Guha implies that the standard forms of colonial historiography have tended to negate the specificity of the Indian reality or to reduce it to a mere epiphenomenon of English history. The synecdochic and metonymic modes of this type of history remain blind to their objects, instead producing self-referential autobiographies of colonial or élite power. Instead, Guha would restore the Indian reality to the status of a discrete or autonomous object similar to but distinct from élite power, 'intertwined' with it, as Gramsci said, but not smothered by it.

Such a conception of the historical field has direct repercussions for the notion that British power was exercised as a hegemony, or rule by consent. The concept of hegemony, which has often been used to describe the durability of British power in India, is to Guha a deeply troubled one. It is not historically possible to locate any rule by consent in either the colonial or nationalist periods ('DWH,' 229–32). Indian politics was instead, he argues, always a highly differentiated and fluid terrain in which control repeatedly broke down and had to be adjusted periodically, from place to place, more often by force than through agreement. Consent among the subject population to the intentions of government was never achieved on the order of the historic coming-to-consciousness of the European bourgeoisie. The use of the concept of hegemony in the Indian context is inappropriate because of the socio-economic structure of colonialism, which itself caused the failure of British capital in India to aspire to 'the *ideal* of capital's striving towards self-realisation' ('DWH,' 228), its 'universalist tendency' of subjecting all 'pre-capitalist relations in material and spiritual life sufficiently enough to enable the bourgeoisie to speak for all of that society as it had done in its historic incarnations in England in 1648 and in France in 1789' ('DWH,' 228). Ironic in terms of British claims to have ruled the subcontinent by consent, it was probably largely due to British economic policy itself that capital never acquired the momentum that might have resulted in a hegemonic form of politics in the colony. Instead, planned underdevelopment, perpetuated through an asphyxiating system of land rents and forced deindustrialisation, allowed India to maintain the unique mixture of pre-capitalist, proto-capitalist, and imperialist relations of production that effectively rendered the populace ungovernable from the point of view of liberal bourgeois politics. To invoke a distinction made by Benedict Anderson, the English government in India promoted a form of official nationalism through their history writing, a form of representation not duplicated but appropriated by the Indian nationalist élite. No compensatory popular nationalism emerged in India as it did from the combination of print capitalism, languages of power, and the imagined communities that demanded territorial sovereignty from the late seventeenth to late nineteenth centuries in Europe and the American colonies.[44]

Rather, what the British and later the nationalist élite achieved was a 'dominance without hegemony.' A properly Indian historiography is outlined in Guha's essay as a full-scale totalisation of nineteenth-century social and political ideology, conceived as an 'organic composition of power.' The essay's most important moves are to (1) break up the myth of British hegemony over the social and political life of colonial India, and (2) restore the self-directedness of both collaboration and resistance among the natives by nominalising their distinct idioms. To this end, Guha offers a schematic breakdown of the 'General Configuration of Power.' The relationship between the two terms 'Dominance' and 'Subordination' is 'determined and indeed constituted by a pair of interacting elements—Dominance by Coercion and Persuasion, and Subordination by Collaboration and Resistance' ('DWH,' 229). By interrogating the colonial system of power in this way, Guha finds that hegemony simply was not operative as 'a condition of Dominance, such that . . . Persuasion outweigh[ed] Coercion' ('DWH,' 231). Rather, for every term employed in the British vocabulary of persuasion, a native idiom existed that transported the intended meaning of the word and its associated concepts into a similar but crucially different semantic constellation. This two-paradigm model is fundamentally metaphoric.

Thus, for the British notion of order, which evolved with 'the dialectical shift as colonialism outgrew its predatory, mercantilist beginnings to graduate to a more systematic, imperial career' ('DWH,' 234), the subject-population understood the indigenous concept of *Danda*, 'an ensemble of power, authority and punishment' ('DWH,' 238) it had inherited through the *shastras* from the Laws of Manu. British ideology met a readymade native concept of 'order' and obedience that allowed the subordinate population to understand and comply with government—to a degree. Similarly, the colonial idiom of improvement, which embodied the benign aspect of British stewardship, or persuasion—in Western-style education, patronage of the arts, missionary activity, Orientalist projects, paternalistic attitudes towards the peasantry, tenancy legislation, standardisation of weights and measures, legal prohibition of 'barbaric customs,' and so on—was appropriated differentially by the native élite. When the concept of improvement was taken up in reformist projects, it was often referred to an ancient Indian correlate in the concept of *dharma*, 'virtue, the moral duty.' '. . . [I]t was to Dharma that the indigenous élite turned in order to justify and explain the initiatives by which they hoped to make their subordinates relate to them as non-antagonistically as possible' ('DWH,' 244).

In the notion of collaboration or obedience, a utilitarian principle by which it was maintained that the 'subjects owed their loyalty to the government for the sake of their own happiness' ('DWH,' 249), the traditional concept of *Bhakti* could be referred to. 'All the collaborationist moments of subordination in our thinking and practice during the colonial period were linked by *Bhakti* to an inert mass of feudal culture which had been reproducing loyalism and depositing it in every kind of power relation for centuries before the British conquest' ('DWH,' 257). Finally, resistance or rightful dissent was met by the native counterpart of dharmic protest. Rightful dissent had obviously enjoyed special prestige as one of the ideological triumphs of the bourgeois revolution, and was subsequently codified in theoretical statements on natural law and inalienable rights from Locke to the utilitarians. The concept of dharma differed fundamentally from that of the liberal notion of right, however, in that it included no semblance of a contract between the ruler and the ruled, and no notion of citizenship or individual right; the ruler himself was responsible for the protection of his subjects, and indeed, 'the king's failure in his protective function amounts to the most serious violation of dharma, and leads to the destruction both of himself and his subjects' ('DWH,' 268). No less an authority than the *Mahabharata* advises the latter to abandon a bad king 'like a leaky boat on the sea' ('DWH,' 268). Dharmic protest, though deriving from the pre-colonial past, erupted throughout the colonial period. Rightful dissent against British authority was tolerated and even encouraged by the government in many of the institutions that grew up to channel it—petitions, letters to government officials, angry editorials, and even the Indian National Congress, which after 1885 became the central organisation for the expression of dissent within an officially approved form. But rightful dissent was evidently misplaced in a social context having no equivalent notion of right. 'Dharmic Protest remained, therefore, as one of the most incalculable factors of politics under colonial rule' ('DWH,' 269), inspiring fear even in native nationalist leaders, who treated with dread the prospect of things getting out of control. Its outbreak was particularly manifested in subaltern consciousness, where 'the official mind went on, throughout the entire period, to misread and misrepresent' it ('DWH,' 269). Nationalist leaders never 'came to terms with subaltern resistance in its dharmic idiom. The volatility of the latter was something which no liberal-Hindu or liberal-nationalist formula could fully comprehend' ('DWH,' 269).

The mediation of native idioms did little to ensure direct communication, much less compliance, between colonial authority and the Indian masses. In this regard, Guha's conception of metaphor could be termed post-structuralist, in that it denies the formal adequacy between tenor and vehicle that is conveyed by more traditional accounts of the tropes. Rather, the non-fit between Indian concepts of government and the discourse of colonialism helped foster an immense domain of subordination without consent, 'the *co-existence of two paradigms as the determinant of political culture*' ('DWH,' 272, emphasis in original) characterising the entire colonial period. The imperative to recover an 'Indian historiography,' then, entails raising and revealing the native 'paradigm,' which has perpetually lain unrecognised beneath a veneer of historiographical appropriations, whether by outright colonialists or by the well-intentioned heirs of colonialist thought. This assertion of the hidden existence of a plane of native discourse alongside the discourse of the coloniser is essentially metaphorical. It asserts that the ultimate value of the history of the colonised is fully equal to the history of the coloniser, that these two domains occupy an object–object relationship with no sense of inferiority or negation implied between them. Nor are they seen to share the same essence. The relationship between the two planes of discourse is therefore figurative, but not mimetic: one misrepresents the other, but without replacing it. The failure of colonial historiography has been its fundamental misrecognition of the distinct elements of native culture, representing the Other as simply a manifestation of itself. Ironically, the Indian paradigm then forms the Other of any imported historiographical élitism, colonialist or nationalist. Only through the radical assertion of the metaphoric value of native culture would it be possible to comprehensively explore the ironies that constituted the intellectual world of the *bhadralok*, to see the composition of colonial middle-class identity not as a mere repetition and derivation of the 'world-historical' European bourgeoisie, but as its own distinct formation. Though Guha nowhere explicitly states this, his argument implies that élite nationalism and its historiography are really the inscription of the Other of itself; wherever it writes itself it misrecognises the Other it claims to represent. Where can we look for a historiographical recovery of this otherness? If not precisely in the 'subaltern,' then perhaps in the double consciousness of the colonial middle class itself.

NOTES AND REFERENCES

1. Ranajit Guha, ed., *Subaltern Studies: Writings on South Asian history and society, I–VI* (Delhi: Oxford University Press, 1982–90). Eight volumes have been published up to 1996; at least two more are in production. A compilation volume intended to popularise the group's work for the US audience was brought out in 1988, with a foreword by Edward Said and an editor's note and introduction by Gayatri Chakravorty Spivak. Ranajit Guha and Gayatri Chakravorty Spivak, eds, *Selected Subaltern Studies* (New York: Oxford University Press, 1988).

I should note that it is not my intention to summarise or review the group's work here. Review articles include Javeed Alam, 'Peasantry, politics and historiography: Critique of new trend in relation to Marxism,' *Social Scientist*, 117 (February 1983): 43–54; Sangeeta Singh, *et al.*, 'Subaltern Studies II: A review article,' *Social Scientist*, 137 (October 1984): 3–41; Rosalind O'Hanlon, 'Recovering the subject: *Subaltern Studies* and histories of resistance in colonial South Asia,' *Modern Asian Studies*, 22, 1 (1988): 189–224. Also see Gyan Prakash, 'Writing post-Orientalist histories in the third world: Perspectives from Indian historiography,' *Comparative Studies in Society and History*, 32, 2 (April 1990): 383–408; 'Post-colonial criticism and Indian historiography,' *Social Text*, 31/32 (1992): 8–19; 'Subaltern Studies as post-colonial criticism,' *American Historical Review* (December 1994): 1475–90. Prakash has been challenged by Rosalind O'Hanlon and David Washbrook, 'After Orientalism: Culture, criticism, and politics in the third world,' *Comparative Studies in Society and History*, 34, 1 (January 1992): 141–67. His reply, 'Can the Subaltern ride? A reply to O'Hanlon and Washbrook,' appears in the same issue.

2. The formulation is Spivak's. See 'Negotiating the structure of violence: A conversation with Gayatri Chakravorty Spivak,' in *The post-colonial critic*, ed., Sarah Harasym (London: Routledge, 1990).

3. Ranajit Guha, 'On some aspects of the historiography of colonial India,' in *Subaltern Studies I: Writings on South Asian history and society*, ed. Ranajit Guha (Delhi: Oxford University Press, 1982), p. 4, emphasis in original. Further references to 'OSA' in the text are given by page number.

4. Susobhan Sarkar's essay 'The thought of Gramsci' was published in 1968. Its first line reads 'The name of Antonio Gramsci as a foremost Marxist leader reached our country barely a decade back.' *Towards Marx* (Calcutta: Papyrus, 1983), p. 97. Louis Marks translated and edited *The modern prince and other essays* (London: Lawrence and Wishart, 1957).

5. Partha Chatterjee, *The nation and its fragments*, p. 37.

6. Antonio Gramsci, *Selections from the prison notebooks*, ed. and trans. Quentin Hoare and Geoffrey Nowell Smith (New York: International Publishers, 1971), p. 59.

7. Gramsci, *Selections*, p. 90.

8. Ibid., p. 52.

9. Ibid., p. 55.

10. Guha, 'Discipline and mobilise,' in *Subaltern Studies VII: Writings on South Asian history and society*, ed. Partha Chatterjee and Gyanendra Pandey (Delhi: Oxford University Press, 1993), pp. 69–120.

11. Guha, *Elementary aspects of peasant insurgency in colonial India* (Delhi: Oxford University Press, 1983), p. 13. Further references to *EAP* in the text are given by page number.

12. Gramsci, *Selections*, p. 333.

13. Ibid., pp. 52, 54–5.

14. Ranajit Guha, 'The prose of counter-insurgency,' in *Subaltern Studies II: Writings on South Asian History and Society*, ed. Ranajit Guha (Delhi: Oxford University Press, 1983), pp. 1–42. Further references to 'PCI' in the text are given by page number.

15. See, for example, the work of the Institute for the Rewriting of Indian History, a neo-Vedic group that attempts to restore the primacy of Sanskrit learning and an undiluted allegiance to Hindu 'scripture.'

16. Jacques Lacan, *Ecrits: A selection*, trans. Alan Sheridan (New York: Norton, 1977), p. 2.

17. Partha Chatterjee, *The nation and its fragments*, pp. 162–4.

18. Lévi-Strauss, *The raw and the cooked,* p. 12.

19. Guha, 'Chandra's death,' *Subaltern Studies V,* ed. Ranajit Guha (Delhi: Oxford University Press, 1988), pp. 135–65. Further references to 'CD' in the text are given by page number.

20. Sumit Sarkar, 'The conditions and nature of subaltern militancy: Bengal from swadeshi to Non-Cooperation, *c.* 1905–22,' in *Subaltern Studies III,* ed. Ranajit Guha (Delhi: Oxford University Press, 1984), p. 273. Further references to 'CNS' in the text are given by page number.

21. Jacques Derrida, 'Structure, sign, and play in the discourse of the human sciences,' in *Writing and difference,* trans. Alan Bass (Chicago: University of Chicago Press, 1978), pp. 278–94.

22. Spivak, 'Editor's Note,' *Selected Subaltern Studies,* p. xi.

23. For some of the promises and dilemmas of this form of history, see Gregor McLennan, *Marxism and the methodologies of history* (New York: Verso, 1981), pp. 112–28. A recent essay of Sarkar's poses similar challenges to what he calls the 'Saidian framework' of subsequent subaltern work. 'Orientalism Revisited: Saidian frameworks in the writings of modern Indian history,' *Oxford Literary Review,* 16, 1–2 (1994): 205–24.

24. Alam, 'Peasantry,' p. 47.

25. Gramsci, *Selections,* p. 75.

26. Guha, *Elementary aspects,* pp. 278–332.

27. D.D. Kosambi, *The culture and civilisation of ancient India in historical outline* (New Delhi: Vikas, 1970). Also see Gramsci, *Further selections from the prison notebooks,* ed. and trans. Derek Boothman (Minneapolis: University of Minnesota Press, 1995), pp. 118–24.

28. For a broader discussion of utopian thinking in India and the third world, see Ashis Nandy, *Traditions, tyranny, and utopias: Essays in the politics of awareness* (Delhi: Oxford University Press, 1987). Fredric Jameson has offered the most persuasive arguments for the 'necessity' of utopian thinking in general. See especially *The political unconscious,* pp. 281–300; *Marxism and form: Twentieth-century dialectical theories of literature* (Princeton, NJ: Princeton University Press, 1971), pp. 116–59; *The ideologies of theory: Essays, 1971–1986,* vol. 2, *The syntax of history,* pp. 75–102.

29. This assertion comes from a comparison of the contents of *Subaltern Studies I* and *VII.*

30. Guha, epigraph to *Elementary aspects.*

31. Partha Chatterjee, *The nation and its fragments,* p. 13, my emphasis.

32. Ajit K. Chaudhury, 'Discussion: In search of a subaltern Lenin,' in *Subaltern Studies V,* ed. Ranajit Guha, p. 236.

33. Veena Das, 'Subaltern as perspective,' in *Subaltern Studies VI,* ed. Ranajit Guha, pp. 310–24.

34. Partha Chatterjee, *The nation and its fragments*, p. 13.

35. Das, 'Subaltern as perspective,' p. 324.

36. Upendra Baxi has commented on this peripheralisation of witnesses in ' "The state's emissary": The place of law in Subaltern Studies,' in *Subaltern Studies VII*, ed. Ranajit Guha, pp. 247–64.

37. J. Laplanche and J.B. Pontalis, *The language of psycho-analysis*, trans. Donald Nicholson-Smith (New York: W.W. Norton, 1973), pp. 455–62.

38. Guha, *An Indian historiography*, p. 50, emphasis in original.

39. Spivak, 'Subaltern Studies: Deconstructing historiography,' in *Subaltern Studies IV*, pp. 341–2.

40. Spivak, 'Subaltern Studies,' p. 342.

41. Derrida, *Writing and difference*, p. 293.

42. White, *Metahistory and difference*, p. 293.

43. Ibid., p. 229.

44. Anderson, *Imagined communities*, esp. pp. 83–111. One of the most convincing studies of the display of English official nationalism in India is Bernard S. Cohn, 'Representing authority in Victorian India,' in *The invention of tradition*, eds Eric Hobsbawm and Terence Ranger (Cambridge: Cambridge University Press, 1983), pp. 165–209.

PART III

Later Critiques in India

K. BALAGOPAL

'Drought and TADA in Adilabad,' in *Economic and Political Weekly*, 24, 47
(November 25, 1989), 2587–91

VINAY BAHL

'Relevance (or Irrelevance) of Subaltern Studies,'
Economic and Political Weekly, 32, 23
(June 7–13, 1997), 1333–44

SUMIT SARKAR

'The Decline of the Subaltern in Subaltern Studies,'
in *Writing Social History*,
Delhi: Oxford University Press, India (1997),
pp. 82–108

Drought and TADA
in Adilabad

K. Balagopal

T HERE IS a half an hour yet for the district courts complex of Adilabad to open. The wide and clean road—roads are usually wide and clean in drought-hit areas, for land has no premium and there is no water to make mud—running past the courts and out of the town is just now coming to life. A stray lawyer or two, starched and black-coated, walks into the court compound, bearing an unaccustomed air of dignity with some difficulty. Opposite the compound the tea-stalls have already come alive with the clatter of china and court gossip. The purveyor of the gossip—whether *mujrim, munshi* or middleman—wears the air of casual cynicism that affects all places that are visited by people in distress: courts, hospitals and jails, to wit. A certain moral stink envelops the court; it is just now gathering, and will reach a depressing intensity by about midday.

But in the meanwhile, there is a clean young man—by his looks a tribal—coming along the road walking beside a bullock cart laden with wood. One calls it a cart for want of a better word, just as one calls them bullocks for want of a better word. The cart has the tiniest of wheels and the barest of frames, and the bullocks look like mere calves. Since no more elaborate contraption than this cart would make it over the undulating land to the godforsaken Gond hamlet to which it is no doubt destined, the cart could be called 'appropriate technology' (though, on second thoughts, one is bound to ask *what* it is appropriate for, as there is no earthly reason why the terrain should forever remain so uneven and impassable), but there is nothing appropriate about the bullocks: they are merely underfed.

Just as the tribal and his cart come into the shadow of justice, there is a shout from the left and a middle-aged man rushes at him from a bylane. He is slight and awkwardly built but the tribal cringes before him and stops in his tracks. The man goes up to him, and they have an argument. As the curious bystanders near the tea-stalls look on, the argument ends quickly, with the man hitting the tribal across the face and detaching the bullocks. The cart keels forward and the wood it is carrying tumbles onto the road. The tribal looks miserable, and the man who has hit him ties the animals to a pole and walks triumphantly to the tea-stall. Unbidden, he explains his behaviour to the people gathered there. He speaks the gutter Urdu that is the language of street brawls in the erstwhile dominions of the Nizam of Hyderabad. It transpires that he is a petty trader, a Marwari no doubt but a poor one for all that, and he has newly entered this business of buying up plough-cattle from the tribals and renting them out again on an annual basis. How foolish of the tribals to allow such a business, comments a lawyer's *munshi*, whose *paan*-stained lips give him a look of wisdom; no doubt it would be a foolish thing to allow in normal circumstances, assents the trader, but last year was not a normal one. There was a near-total failure of both the *kharif* and the *rabi* crops, for as you all know it rained too much in the first season and not at all in the second, and soon the peasants—especially the tribals, many of whom do not have title deeds for the land they cultivate and therefore cannot raise loans from banks—were close to starvation. They started selling their plough-bullocks at the weekly fair. The Jainur fair soon started looking like an exclusive cattle fair. A man needs a moral reason for doing selfish things, as we all know, and so the tribals would say they are selling the cattle because there is no fodder to feed them with, but in reality the selfish fellows are selling the dumb animals so that they can feed themselves. At this point a dhoti-clad listener, a litigant by his looks, interferes to say that all this nonsense about starvation is so much hot air because the government is supplying rice to the poor at Rs 2 per kg, or has this Marwari not heard of the scheme that has made NTR famous all over the land? The others look suspiciously at the litigant's yellow shirt, and one of them answers that to buy NTR's rice you must have the right amount of money at the right time, neither of which is easy for the poor. When the dealer has stocks you don't have the money, and when you manage to gather enough money the dealer says there are no stocks. That is really why the tribals are selling their cattle; to make NTR's scheme operational.

That is all very well, but what does the Marwari do with the cattle—does he buy up the tribals' land too for the cattle to plough? No, this Marwari has not yet acquired land (others have), nor does he sell the bullocks to anybody else. He has discovered a more lucrative business, which has become quite popular this year. The tribals who have sold the bullocks to feed themselves want them back now that it is monsoon time; and since their need is desperate the traders are now dictating the terms. Instead of selling the bullocks back they are renting them out on an annual basis. The rate? Well, to tell a lie would give displeasure to the gods, so the trader confesses that he charges an annual rent of Rs 400 or more for a pair of bullocks that he has bought for Rs 500. He takes the rent in advance, for these fellows who look so innocent are capable of bluffing you out of your own home, and if you don't collect in advance, you don't collect, ever. A nice business, murmurs an envious listener; yes says the Marwari, the gods have been kind to him. After a while somebody asks what was the meaning of the recent scene, pointing in explanation to the tribal crouching by the roadside opposite the tea-stall. Here the trader's tone becomes almost piteous with injured righteousness. That ingrate you see there is a Gond son-of-a-dog from Tiriani, he says. Three months ago he sold his cattle at the Jainur fair and fattened himself and his bitch of a wife on rice, ghee and curds. Now the monsoons are close at hand, there is a film of cloud in the sky and a strong breeze blowing across the land, and he again wants bullocks to plough his fields. He comes begging, with tears in his eyes, for a pair of bullocks—nice strong animals they are, as you can see—and promises to pay the rent in a week's time. Now, continues the trader, one has always been kind-hearted to a fault, it is a congenital trait, and anyway, my brethren, this world is such an unkind place, if one man does not help another in need, where would we all be? And so he gave the tribal son-of-a-dog the pair of bullocks on the agreement that he would pay Rs 400 in a week's time. A week passes by, two weeks pass by, and the third is drawing to a close, but there is no sign of the dog. Just as the honest trader is contemplating a police complaint he spies him quite by accident now. He has harnessed the animals to a cart—the perfidious liar, he said he wanted them to plough land—and with your own eyes you saw that he was smuggling wood and sneaking out of the town. A fair-minded listener interjects at this point that you do not smuggle wood *out of* the town, it should be the other way round, but the trader's sense of injury is too intense for mere reason. Ignoring the interference the trader continues his narration. He stopped the wretch and demanded an explanation; and do you know what he replies, that arrogant so-and-so? He says his land does not grow a crop in one week; it takes time for the seed to be sown, to sprout, become a plant, and bear a crop—as if one did not know all that. And he even adds—here the good trader is livid with anger—that his land is not like a Marwari who lends to one man now and one man then so that there is always some crop coming home. That, of course, was when he hit the fellow across the face, detached the bullocks, and tied them to the pole.

But by this time the listeners have lost interest in this conflict.

The district of Adilabad has been constantly in the news in Andhra Pradesh these days. There has been news about tribal youth picked up from their villages and shot dead by the police (and described as 'unidentified Naxalites killed in encounters); news about Naxalites laying land mines and blowing up police jeeps; news about Telugu Desam Party leaders going on hunger strike demanding an end to fake 'encounter' killings; and news about raids by starved tribals upon the houses and shops of traders and moneylenders living in towns and big villages, raids of the kind that historians have found fascinating material for spinning theories about popular struggles and popular consciousness. The first raid took place at the village of Pembi in Khanapur taluk on October 3, 1988; and after that there have been raids at Penchikalapeta, Thosham, Jainath, Talamaddi, Rajura and Dandepalli, as well as a few other places across the border, in Maharashtra. In each incident, about 200 to 300 tribals, accompanied by armed Naxalites, have raided the houses of moneylenders and taken away money as well as some of the pawned articles; they have raided the shops of grain dealers and taken away rice and *jowar* to be eaten and sown; and they have also generally broken into the houses and shops of traders of all varieties and taken away money, clothes, jewellery, anything they could lay their hands on.

The background to these raids is the unusually severe failure of crops last year. In a year when the rains were reportedly good (in terms of total precipitation), and in a district which is ringed on three sides by the Godavari and its tributaries—the Pranahita, Penganga, Swarna and Kadem rivers—there is nothing 'natural' about such a failure, but the failure was very real nevertheless. Forty-five out of the 52 *mandals* in the district were declared drought-affected by the government; the district collector reported partial failure of the *kharif* crop (cotton, paddy, *jowar* and pulses) and total failure of the *rabi* crop (mainly *jowar*, pulses and sesamum). The district collector's estimate of crop loss is Rs 36.92 crore, but since crop loss is defined as the shortfall in the yield of the crop that is sown, this does not reflect what the peasants themselves would regard as the actual loss. The actual loss should take into account what is not sown at all, which can be considerable in conditions of continuing crop failure. *Rabi* sowing, for instance, was about 40 per cent below normal in the district last year, though *kharif* sowing was almost normal. For the peasant, this represents a very real loss of income, though official statistics never include it.

The crop failure was due to a peculiar combination of torrential rains in the southwest monsoon and practically no rains in the northeast monsoon. The unceasing rains of the first monsoon flooded the lands, washed away soil and breached tanks. This is one of the problems concerning which nothing has ever been done anywhere in the country, let alone a neglected district like Adilabad. With proper management of land and water sources, heavy rains—at least up to a point—can be a boon, but today they are a disaster. Cultivators in the plains region of eastern and southern Adilabad saw the village tanks breach one by one. The location and construction of irrigation tanks is such that five or six of them form a complex, with the overflow from those located upland flowing into those located below. This structural convenience leads to a cascade effect when the upper tank breaches: the suddenly released water washes off the surrounding soil and rushes into the tanks below, and not only do the tanks below also breach, but the land all round is spoilt. The uplands are denuded of soil and the lowlands become a dumping ground for loose soil. By the time the rains stop the tanks are empty and the land is barren.

But the worst affected were the undulating highlands of the northern part of Adilabad, especially the north-central region consisting of the revenue *mandals* of Jainur, Sirpur, Narnur and Tiriani, which together cover a compact plateau located towards the north of the roadside village of Indravelli where the police fired upon a large gathering of tribals in April 1981. There are neither irrigation tanks nor wells here; the terrain is uneven and forested, and the population is largely tribal. Unevenness of the terrain is no reason why the region has remained unirrigated, for such a terrain offers good scope for minor irrigation projects, and the tribals themselves will point out to a number of locations where water from forest streams can be trapped to irrigate a couple of hundred acres or more, but the government has never shown serious interest in exploiting such possibilities. Irrigation in the whole of Adilabad remains at the low figure of 9.2 per cent of cultivable land (the state's average is about 34 per cent), and most of it is in the south and west, which are watered by tanks, wells, and irrigation projects on the Kadem, Swarna and Godavari rivers.

And so when the skies started belching water, the peasants of the north-central *mandals* just watched helplessly as the uneven terrain got water-logged; the rich 'black cotton' soil of the district makes it impossible to work in such conditions, even to the extent of removing the weeds that grow fast in the rains. The new shoots of *jowar*, cotton and *asmaan tari* (rain-fed paddy) drowned easily in the floods. It rained for weeks without end, but in the beginning the peasants were not altogether disheartened; let the rains stop and we will sow again and get a good crop with the moisture retained by the soil, they thought. The rains did stop, but once they stopped, they stopped so completely that the soil—apart from that which was anyway denuded—lost moisture fast, and the freshly sown crop withered in the sun. There was not a drop of rain in November and December—the active months for the northeast monsoon—and the crop failure was total.

Very soon the people of the area were driven to the verge of starvation. Very little non-agricultural work is available after the close of the summer season. In summer the people pick *tendu* leaves in the forest, an activity available for two months a year; it pays reasonably well now, thanks to the sustained struggles conducted with the encouragement of the CPI-ML groups. The piece-rate for the picking of *tendu* leaf has increased more than six-fold in the last decade and a half all over the Godavari valley region. But with the coming of the rains there is no more picking of *tendu* leaf. The other source of non-agricultural work—laying of roads—is another activity that comes to an end with the coming of the rains. Normally it would not have mattered that these avenues of work are closed but with the sudden and near-total crop failure the lack of other work became a serious matter. There was a considerable amount of migration to far-off areas—the coal mines of the Singareni Collieries Company in eastern Adilabad, the canal-irrigated southern talukas where assured irrigation made the *rabi* crop possible, the coal mines and the thermal power plant in Karimnagar, etc. The non-tribal poor and the more mobile among the tribals like the Lambadas migrated in proportionately large numbers, whereas the more backward and less mobile among the tribals, the Gonds and Kolams, migrated in smaller numbers. For those who stayed behind there were only two sources of succour: the forests and the moneylenders. From the forests they knew how to obtain food of various types and other produce which they could exchange against food. From the moneylenders, who gave them crop loans every season at the rate of 50 paise per rupee per cropping season—amounting to an annual interest of 100 per cent—they hoped to get some consumption loan to tide over the difficult days.

The forests did not disappoint them but the moneylenders did. Giving a crop loan is one thing in a region where cotton is an important crop that occupies 21 per cent of the cultivated area (nearly double the area under paddy and almost half that under *jowar*, the staple cereal); the methods of cultivation remain what they were when the crop was first introduced to the area, and so the yield they get is hardly one-fourth of what the cotton cultivators of the coastal districts like Guntur get, but nevertheless for a moneylender a cash crop is a cash crop. And so every season the tribals borrow working capital from them at an annual interest of 100 per cent and repay it at the end of the season. The loan is usually given in the form of foodgrains and seed, at a time when their price is high, but the repayment must be made in cash, for the price of grain declines after harvest time. The moneylenders are mostly Marwaris, Telugu Komatis and a few Muslims, all of them grain merchants, cotton dealers or landlords. They live in the *mandal* headquarters towns or in big villages. Often it happens that a tribal defaults too often and becomes irredeemably indebted; he does not then become a bonded labourer, for as long as there is some forest left to be cleared and cultivated—whatever the consequences—a tribal will never bond himself the way a harijan in a village would. So what normally happens is that once the accumulated debt exceeds the value of the articles pawned, the tribal gives up his land to the moneylender, though of course there may not be any recorded transfer, first because the tribals themselves frequently do not have title deeds for the land they cultivate, and second because the law does not allow transfer of land from a tribal to a non-tribal in a scheduled area. Many of the moneylenders have become quite big landlords owning 70 to 80 acres of land in the process.

In other words, Adilabad is more like a historical record left over from the nineteenth century than anything that belongs to the late twentieth century. At least so far as the tribal–moneylender relation goes.

When the crops failed so badly last year the tribals thought they would raise a loan from the moneylenders to see them through until the next monsoon. But the moneylenders were not willing. Lending working capital for a cash crop is one thing, but giving a consumption loan in a drought year to a people whose rate of saving even in a normal year is not such as to enthuse any pawnbroker is a different thing altogether. And so they refused bluntly. This angered the tribals a lot, for they had never defaulted in the past, and moreover the moneylenders were still in possession of many of their valuables, pawned against previous loans. They regarded the refusal as a betrayal of trust, a breach of obligation. They were, in the words of the subaltern historian David Hardiman writing on the 'Bhils and shahukars of Eastern Gujarat' (*Subaltern Studies V*), 'morally outraged.'

But if one is not constrained by the usual subaltern scholars' hostility towards any objective assessment of popular consciousness, one will see that the question of 'moral outrage' is quite a complex one. Granting for a moment (but only for a moment) that mere starvation has never led to a rebellion and that people have rebelled only when they are morally outraged by the violation of what they understand as social obligations, what is really involved here is the *legitimacy of rebellion*, which is neither an immutable absolute, nor is it determined autonomously in popular consciousness by the way the oppressed masses relate to the situation of oppression.

Every unequal relation, every relation of domination, is a relation of tension. The very fact that it comes into being and reproduces itself implies the generation and internalisation on both sides of a *certain common morality* that legitimises the domination, while at the same time conceding something to the oppressed in the form of a line of demarcation beyond which the domination is regarded as 'excessive' and is condemned. This is not an equilibrium 'moral code' consisting of 'certain expectations' generated by the 'balance of power' or 'the *status quo* of the moment'; even if we concede Hardiman's contention that the Bhils and Shahukars of eastern Gujarat constituted 'two systems of social organisation and morality interacting and coming into occasional conflict with each other,' rather than two social classes *within* a single social organisation, the concluding tag that neither exercised 'moral hegemony' over the other is more a presumption than an inference. On the contrary, a relation of domination cannot reproduce itself except under the umbrella of a hegemonic ideology, including a hegemonic morality.

It is true that this legitimising morality is not a one-point ideology that forms the sum and substance of the consciousness of the masses, and to the extent that hasty Marxist exposition has tended to treat it as such, the subaltern scholars' criticism is justified (though even so one cannot avoid the feeling that their polemics are as laboured as their research is meticulous). But the internalisation, the legitimacy, is very real, and it is the moral standard which measures and certifies the legitimacy of the social behaviour of either party. This standard, which is the common social conscience of the oppressor and the oppressed, is *itself an aspect of domination*. When the people are outraged at the breach of what they regard as a norm or obligation, they are not reacting from the standpoint of a moral code defined by their way of relating to the unequal relation, but from the standpoint of this social conscience. There is no 'autonomous and undominated region' of popular consciousness, as Partha Chatterjee (who distinguishes himself among the subaltern theoreticians by a laudable desire to make himself intelligible to ordinary mortals) would have us believe. Popular consciousness and the consciousness of the masses are not two separate entities, two separate ways of looking at the relation; they form an unbroken continuum, the *totality of which* is enveloped and penetrated by the hegemonic morality. The values and ideas generated by the material life of the masses are at every point coloured by the values and ideas—the 'ideology'—of what these scholars call the 'élite.' Talk to the tribals suffering from drought, and they will give you their analysis and evaluation, their facts and their myths, their reason and unreason, and go on *without any break* to Brahmanical notions of the inferiority of jungle-folk, and the ideology of bureaucratic patronage summed up by the term scheduled tribe. To break this continuum and separate the ideas of the masses from the ideology of the ruling classes requires struggle and political intervention—not necessarily from outside but not always from within either—but such a development through struggle is precisely what is denied in the notion of an autonomous and undominated region supposedly always present in the consciousness of the masses.

The legitimising morality, for the reason that it is legitimising the domination of the oppressors and therefore has to accommodate the resentment of the oppressed, has perforce to define a perimeter beyond which the behaviour of the oppressors becomes 'outrageous' and the rebellion of the oppressed becomes socially legitimate. The neglected wife is expected to suffer the neglect silently, but it will be understood if she rebels when he starts bringing the other woman home. This perimeter, this dividing line between what is legitimate and what is not in the behaviour of either class, is a product of the state of the struggle between the oppressor and the oppressed. In taking this struggle forward the role of political leadership—whether that is provided by advanced elements of the oppressed classes who are able to perceive that what is 'moral' merely legitimises domination, or by dissident elements of the dominant classes who are alienated from their class by their sensitivity or their private neurosis; or by the cultural influence of a different society—is crucial. That leadership can popularise, spread, and thereby *legitimise* the notion of struggle against oppression itself, and not just against the breach of norms that are sanctioned by the oppressors. The annulment of the perimeter of moral legitimacy, and the definition of a new dividing line that has a lower level of tolerance of injustice, usually takes place hand in hand with the coming together in political solidarity of diverse individuals of the oppressed groups. To describe this annulment as an advance in consciousness will be decried by the subaltern scholars as an élitism that 'seeks to be a judge of what is best for the lower classes' (David Hardiman, op. cit.), but it *is* an advance in the precise sense that it is able to see evil in domination itself, and not in some outrageous consequence of domination. The fact that the lack of a 'strictly scientific-rationalist outlook' did not prevent the Bhils—and has not prevented any oppressed group anywhere—from rebelling need not lead us to the meaningless conclusion that a 'scientific-rationalist' understanding could (not) have served (the people) better.' And once the advance in consciousness takes place, mere inequality or oppression can make them rebel. Perhaps, on second thoughts, more food riots have taken place because of mere hunger than David Hardiman would like to believe.

Coming back to Adilabad 1988–9, it is not very easy to predict whether the tribals would have attacked moneylenders if they had not had the benefit of Naxalite leadership. The difficulty in understanding popular consciousness even in face-to-face conversation (let alone by reading official post-mortem reports) is that it expresses itself in socially legitimate terms, especially when talking to government officials, visiting scholars, civil liberties activists, or a court of law. And government officials writing reports on riots are also likely to find extenuating circumstances—if at all—within the framework of the socially legitimate, if not as a matter of prudence then because that is their own social morality. The ease with which the subaltern scholars have assumed that they have no methodological difficulties in understanding popular consciousness is a little baffling even to one who is not a professional historian. When poor people in a village beat up a landlord, they usually have a hundred reasons for doing so, but when they are questioned they usually lay stress on acts like molestation of poor women, for such acts are objects of social opprobrium. Scholars then go on to conclude that there is no land question or class hatred but only 'honour' involved in the struggle. The fact that every act of rebellion is a penal offence makes the appeal to the prevailing social conscience even more imperative. If a labourer who has beaten up the master tells the inspector who has arrested him that he committed the crime because the master would not give him leave of absence to go to a fair or attend a wedding, the inspector is likely to beat him up and deliver a lecture in the bargain on how such laziness on the part of the labouring classes is destroying the nation's economy; but if he says he wanted leave to attend his father's funeral, the inspector—if at all he is convinced—is likely to be more lenient. And what applies to the severity of the inspector's reaction applies also to the sympathy the judicial magistrate will later on show when the case comes up for trial. The penal institutions are permeated by the ideology of the legitimate, and rebellions are punished as much for their illegitimacy as for their lawlessness.

For the tribals of Adilabad who have looted traders and money-lenders, living as they do in an 'extremist-infested' area where there was one 'encounter' killing every week last year, the need to find a 'legitimate' reason for the crimes they have committed is much more serious. It is not a matter of deliberate hypocrisy or sensible policy, but a matter of locating their class interest as far as possible within the framework of the norms of social morality. They certainly *do* feel outraged that though they have never defaulted on their debts without paying the penalty and more, the moneylenders have now refused to come to their rescue in a time of crisis. But more importantly they know that this is an argument that will strike a chord of sympathy in the heart of the inquisitive journalist, the visiting scholar or the government official; and may help to soften the ire of the policeman. When one talks to the tribals they begin with this argument. As you go on conversing and slowly reveal that there is something slightly wrong with your own notions of morality, they open up bit by bit. The younger or the more audacious will suddenly ask why the traders grow rich without toiling one bit but the tribal who toils all day starves; why some people should have so much land and others none; why the non-tribal settlers get title deeds for their land so easily so that they can borrow from the banks but the tribals have to run to the moneylenders; why it is not called theft or dacoity if the money-lender collects double the loan amount at the end of the year, but it is called theft and dacoity if the tribals take back what was originally theirs. At this point the elder and the more conservative among them are visibly upset by the trend of reasoning. They react sharply and ask the impetuous ones to keep quiet; there is no point—they say—in lamenting the obvious. That is how things are, because that is how they were meant to be. This is the voice of the dominant morality, but the younger ones are not silenced. Their anger leaves the accepted moral code way behind and becomes distinctly seditious. What amount and intensity of 'reading' of commissioners' and collectors' reports on riots and famines can reveal this illegitimate dimension of popular consciousness is a point well worth pondering.

However all that may be, the Gonds, Kolams and Lambadas of Adilabad started attacking traders and moneylenders by October 1988, and kept up the attacks right down to this monsoon. The unhelpful attitude of the moneylenders, and the lack of any drought-relief activity undertaken by the government, forced them to depend upon forest produce by the time winter set in last year. They were soon living on mahua flowers, bamboo-rice, and poisonous tubers. Mahua is consumed in many forms, and bamboo-rice makes a tolerable cereal, but the tubers require so much effort to rid them of the poison that the very fact that the tribals bother to collect, cook and consume them indicates the desperate straits the drought has reduced them to. Here is a description of the collection and preparation of the tubers, published in a booklet issued by the Girijan Rytu Coolie Sangham (Tribal Peasant and Agricultural Labourers Association):

'These tubers, called by the name *matigadda* (gadda is Telugu for tuber) are not cultivated. They are found wild in the forests. The wild animals, especially pigs, dig them up and eat them. There are six varieties of this *mati* tuber: *kehekka mati, noska mati, kirsi mati, tetre mati, bondi mati* and *nul mati*. The first two of the six are the most widely available, but unfortunately they are the poisonous varieties. The other four are not poisonous but they are not widely found.

'A wife-and-husband team can collect about one or two kgs if they search and dig a whole day. The tubers must then be cut into fine pieces and washed in flowing water for three days. Then they have to be boiled seven times. With each boiling some of the poison leaves the tubers and enters the water. The water must be thrown out and the tubers boiled again. After boiling seven times, the tubers must be washed in cold water and then boiled a last time. The whole process takes about five or six days. Only then the tubers become edible.'

After so much treatment, it is unlikely that there will be any nourishment left in the food!

If such were the straits the men and women were driven to, one need not describe the travails of the animals. Selling them in the weekly fair rid the tribals of the burden of animals they could not feed, and at the same time put in their hands some money to buy food for themselves. Whether, in such a situation, they would themselves have thought of raiding the shops and houses of moneylenders and traders is a doubtful point, for there is no record in recent history of the Gonds of Adilabad ever having undertaken such adventures, but as it happens they were not left to their devices.

As this year's monsoon came near, the attacks on traders and moneylenders became more frequent for at least two reasons: one, that with the need to prepare their lands for the *kharif* crop they could not any longer find the time to search the forests for mahua flower and tubers; and two, that they needed *jowar* seed to sow the crop, and the easiest way of procuring it was to steal it from the traders. The announcement by the Integrated Tribal Development Agency

(ITDA) that *jowar* seed would be supplied on loan came very late, well after many of the raids had already taken place, perhaps *because* the raids had taken place. (This is no reflection on the personal integrity of the officers who staff the ITDA, some of whom are the best administrative personnel the state has.)

And then the police moved in. The state government may take its own time to react to ITDA's distress signals, and under the head of relief, may grant only Rs 45 lakh against the district collector's demand of Rs 43 crore, but there is neither such tardiness nor any shortage of funds when it comes to the reaction of the police. The police moved in fast and started arresting hundreds of tribals under the Terrorist and Disruptive Activities (Prevention) Act (TADA). About 160 tribals were arrested in connection with the Dandepalli raid alone, from the villages of Jainur, Narnur, Sirpur and Tiriani *mandals*. The total arrests under TADA in connection with these raids must be about 600. They were all lodged in the far-off prisons of Nizamabad and Warangal (there is no proper prison in Adilabad), and were put to tremendous hardship in getting bail. Many of them are yet to get bail. As it was nearing monsoon time this year by the time most of the arrests were made, they lost the few crucial weeks when the ploughing of the land and sowing takes place. If they lost last year's crop because of drought, they are likely to lose this *kharif* season's crop because of TADA. In consequence that legislative monstrosity has become familiar (it is pronounced Ta-da, in two syllables) to the most illiterate tribal. They probably took a long time to say ITDA but they have learnt to say TADA in a matter of weeks.

Adding to these the hundreds of tribals of Khammam, East Godavari and Visakhapatnam districts, arrested under TADA in recent months for sympathising with, habouring, sheltering, or giving food to Naxalites, the total tally of N.T. Rama Rao, chairman of the National Front which is fighting these elections with the promise of providing a democratic alternative to the authoritarian regime of Rajiv Gandhi, is about 1000 tribals booked under TADA in a matter of one year and a little more. So much then for Indian democracy and the alternatives it offers.

Relevance (or Irrelevance) of Subaltern Studies*

Vinay Bahl

I N THE last thirteen years the Subaltern Studies group has produced a fairly large amount of literature,[1] and its impact has been felt beyond India. Over the years numerous critiques were made of subaltern studies within India, as well as in Britain, Latin America and the US. This essay, while taking into account some of the recent critiques, further evaluates the relevance of subaltern studies to an understanding of working class history and the future of working class emancipation in a world which is dominated by a global capitalist economy.

The impetus for this essay came from my involvement in completing my book, *The making of the Indian working class*,[2] when I realised that the Subaltern Studies group has deviated from the very course which they had set. Their aim after all was to remove from Indian history a top-down approach and replace it with the study of the culture of

*A shorter version of this paper, 'Rethinking Subaltern Studies,' was presented at the Occasional Paper Series of the Centre for Studies on Social Change, New School for Social Research, New York, in December 1995. After the completion of my present essay I was made aware of the article below which in fact in many ways complementary to my discussion above. I am thankful to Rifaat Abou el Haj for this citation as well as for his valuable comments: K. Sivaramakrishnan, 'Situating the subaltern: History and anthropology in the Subaltern Studies project,' *Journal of Historical Sociology*, vol. 8, no. 4, 1995.

the people. In all fairness, we could say that this school got only part of it in the form of value-oriented culture of people and psychoanalysis (as a substitute for social analysis) which is generally based on textual analysis. The emphasis on textual analysis has fortunately created an unprecedented hunt by budding historians for printed materials in various regional languages which are not available in conventional places. It has also generated an interest in discourses of various kinds and in various areas, putting them under historical scrutiny—which is all to the good.

What is missing, however, in their analysis is: how do the social order and social institutions articulate in the formation of the subject (individual); or, how is the link between social and psychic reality to be spelled out, let alone how it should be theorised? In short, subaltern studies left out from their consideration material culture, such as clothes, food, furniture, living and working conditions, housing, technology, and financial system, and failed to show how material culture is produced by human agency in the process of social interaction. Moreover, this material culture is also important in the formation of the value culture of people along with the psychic activity of the brain. Besides leaving out the material aspect of people's culture, the subaltern studies' approach is not even capable of creating any emancipatory politics for the masses in whose name it came into existence. The following remarks of a young Indian student are pertinent in this regard. He said that he found a wonderful way through Gyan Prakash's (once the leader and gatekeeper of the All-India Student Federation at Jawaharlal Nehru University and now a convert to subaltern studies) essay[3] on how to remain non-committal (not to take sides as he put it) and be a leftist radical at the same time. Such remarks coming from a 23-year-old budding historian should be an issue of concern for those who are committed to writing people's (non-élite) history.

Since subaltern studies have been visibly influential amongst the younger generation of scholars, and now among Latin American[4] and US scholars, it is imperative that as an approach it should not be allowed to create a new philosophy just for the sake of having a new one as a passing fad. If we wish to remove the élitist bias from history and empower people, as proponents of subaltern studies claim they wish to do, then my suggestion is that we must rethink it with one goal in mind: to be guided by philosophies that enable us to change our 'miserable' reality as it exists today, rather its promotion. In other words, we need to ascertain what our politics are when we raise certain questions over others, or when we choose certain methods of analysis over others in writing history. These are the concerns which are the core of my discussion.

I should like to start with a telling exchange between a teacher of philosophy and his student.[5]

> Teacher: Si fu, name the basic questions of philosophy.
>
> Si Fu: Are things external to us, self-sufficient, independent of us, or are things in us, dependent on us, non-existent without us?
>
> Teacher: What opinion is the correct one?
>
> Si Fu: There has been no decision about it.
>
> Teacher: Why has the question remained unresolved?
>
> Si Fu: The Congress which was to have made the decision took place two hundred years ago at Mi Sant monastery which lies on the bank of the Yellow River. The question was: Is the Yellow River real or does it exist only in people's head? But during the Congress the snow thawed in the mountains and swept away the Mi Sant monastery with all the participants in the Congress. So the proof that things exist externally to us, self-sufficiently independent of us was not furnished.

We shall come back to the lessons learnt from this exchange, that is 'reality' and where to find it, at the end of the essay.

I

Trained in Western academic institutions, most of the subaltern studies members were clearly influenced by the prevailing trends in historical writings of the 1970s under the impact of social historians such as E.P. Thompson and Eric Hobsbawm. Subaltern studies, in fact, represents the application of these ideas to Indian historiography. Although subaltern studies rejects metanarratives, their own conditions of existence and emergence remain primarily within the metanarrative. Today, the subaltern field heavily depends upon post-modernist ideas (which emerged in the West) and methods for textual analysis while at the same time claiming to 'provincialise Europe and its history.'[6]

Members of the Subaltern Studies group felt that although Marxist historians produced impressive and pioneering studies, their claim to represent the history of the masses remained debatable. Their main thesis is that colonialist, nationalist and Marxist interpretations of Indian history had robbed the common people of their agency. The Subaltern Studies collective thus announced a 'new approach' to restore history to the subordinated in order to rectify the élitist bias characteristic of much academic work in south Asian studies. The subaltern's agency was restored by theorising that the élite in India played a dominant role and not simply a hegemoneous one. Thus, with the logic of this theory the subalterns were made into autonomous historical actors who then seemingly acted on their own since they were not seen to be led by the élites.

At the same time, subaltern studies differed from Western historians' attempts to write 'history from below.' British workers left diaries behind for British historians to find their voices in, but Indian workers and peasants did not leave behind any 'original authentic' voices. Therefore to find Indian subaltern voices, subaltern studies had to use different methods of reading the available documents, that is, read them 'against their grain.' In the process of pursuing this goal, subaltern studies concentrated more and more on how subalternity was constituted rather than finding their voices. It is with this new question that they could critique the West.

Accordingly, the next shift in subaltern studies was to concentrate on the question of how the knowledge of history was produced and how to decolonise such constructed knowledge. While trying to identify the sources which tainted the knowledge of history, subaltern studies scholars realised that they can write history only from a position of subalternity because India herself was a subaltern as a British colony, and after independence was subordinated to the neo-colonialism of the Western world.

It is true of course that in order to write history a non-Western scholar must read and know 'good' Western scholars and historians, whereas a Western scholar does not have to know any non-Western works. For example, Indian economic historians and nationalist leaders in the last quarter of the nineteenth century developed a 'drain theory' showing that the cause of India's poverty was the drain of its resources and wealth by British colonialism. But these theories are rarely discussed or referred to in the dependency theories which came into being after the Second World War. Today people in the West only know about dependency theory as a pioneer idea and the 'drain theory' propounded by Indian economic historians was conveniently made invisible.

In order to find a way out of similar impasse, the Subaltern Studies group wanted to 'provincialise European history' and to 'push history to its limits, and rewrite history from the grounds of ambivalence and contradictions.'[7] In all these efforts, they claim, the subaltern remains the vantage point of their critiques.

With these shifts in goals and ideas subaltern studies changed their approach by borrowing from post-modernist methods, reading texts against the grain using semiotics and literary criticism, and finally reverting to the textual analysis of various sources: novels, biographies, pamphlets or any other available text written by people in regional languages, which in actual effect many times replaced the usual archival work. A prominent subaltern studies spokesperson recently expanded the responsibility of subaltern studies to include 'differences' as a tool for producing possibilities for action. His concern was that by emphasising 'differences' it becomes possible to challenge the 'problem of universality' in history. But interestingly, the same spokesperson does not wish to give up either Marx (let us not forget that initially subaltern studies was critical of Marxist categories and kept a distance from it) nor 'differences' because he finds Marx's category of 'real labour' to be useful in building up the idea of differences.[8] Elaborating his point he clarified that the goal of subaltern studies is not to achieve political democracy or egalitarian distribution of wealth. The most important issue, according to him, is to keep alive the philosophical question of 'differences' because egalitarian concepts are insensitive to this question. Therefore, subaltern studies are not writing the history of how this or that group in Asia, Africa or Latin

America resisted the penetration of colonialism, but instead trying 'to take history to its limits' in order to 'make its unworking visible.'

II

Some Latin American progressive scholars were also in doubt about Marxism and its belief in progress and modernity, a commitment to revolution as forward looking, and linear developmental transformation. They were looking for an alternative approach but were hesitant to embrace the trends offered by post-modernism or post-structuralism. In fact, they questioned the applicability of post-modernism to an area of the world not yet modern and were surprised by the ahistorical claims of this approach. Many of these scholars have doubted the ability of post-modernism to facilitate political engagement and commitment. In such historical circumstances of intellectual doubts and crisis, subaltern studies seemed to Latin American progressive scholars a perfect compromise as it was formulated by a group of intellectuals belonging to the non-Western world. Moreover, these Indian intellectuals seemed anti-colonial and politically radical, yet they were also conversant with the latest in textual analysis and post-modernist methods.

But the problem with the Latin American Subaltern Studies group is that there is only one historian amongst them and the rest of the scholars are literary critics. These literary scholars tend to borrow more from post-modernist methods and techniques (though they initially were suspicious of them), which has reduced subaltern studies to half of its complexity. This simplification of the interpretations made by the literary critiques of the Latin American group led to the creation of a 'poverty of historiography' in their writings. A Latin American historian has pointed out 'the borrowing and application of the original Indian Subaltern group became a "simplified misrepresentation" in the hands of Latin Americans.'[10]

In contrast to Latin American historiography, in African history writings the impact of subaltern studies has not been felt too strongly. Although increasingly subaltern studies are being mentioned in African historiography, as Frederick Cooper[11] points out, only Terence Ranger is using it explicitly. While surveying African historiography Cooper shows that South African historians share some of the 'history from the bottom' concerns with subaltern studies, but generally they do not agree with the concept of subaltern autonomy as is suggested in subaltern studies.

Another difference between Indian subaltern studies and African historians is that both are looking for opposite constructs while reacting to their respective historical situations. Many Indian scholars have been trying to pull apart and examine the idea of an essential 'India' by insisting on differences within communities and identities. But African scholars have felt they had to put together 'Africa' in the face of general perceptions of everlasting and immutable division. Therefore, subaltern studies seem less appealing to African historians.

Moreover, Africanists do not find the ideas propounded by subaltern studies to be new or earthshaking. For example, subaltern studies mainly focuses on the problems of recovering histories while understanding how colonial documents construct their own versions of them. This methodology appears to African historians more as sound practice than a methodological breakthrough. African historians learnt way back in the 1960s that colonial sources distorted history, and they saw the use of oral sources as well as reading colonial documents against the grain as putting themselves on the path of people's history. But in the process of writing people's history, African scholars placed more emphasis on showing that Africans had a history than on asking how Africans' history making is implicated in establishing or contesting power.

Similarly, Africans and Africanists are sympathetic to the subaltern studies critique of the controlling project of a colonial state and the continuation of those projects under the nation-states. But they are also sceptical about the conceivable alternative of autonomous 'communities.' Their scepticism is based on their bitter experience in contemporary Somalia which shows that in the absence of the controlling capabilities of a state and with increasing availability of automatic weapons, 'communities' can also wipe out one another. It seems that African historians who feel the need to construct Africa's history would not find much to borrow from the deconstructionist agenda of subaltern studies.

III

Subaltern studies represented a response to a genuine need for a new methodology, epistemology and paradigms, in order to overcome a crisis of understanding produced by the inability of old categories to account for the world. The old categories, conceived by modernisationists and radicals alike in the decades after the Second World War to understand the structure of the globe, were called into question in the face of the crisis of 'progress' and increased impoverishment of the 'third world.' Mass migration of the people from poor countries to the industrialised world due to the demand for cheap labour has confounded borders and boundaries. It created a flow of cultures which has been at once homogenising and heterogenising in most parts of the world. The infusion and confusion of cultures created a vast identity crisis among the new diasporas. These new global circumstances needed new interpretations and new methodologies to understand people's lives and experiences.

Within this world context the Indian state, which was also following the programmes of capitalist 'development' in fact helped in increasing social and political inequalities among the masses. This growing disparity in society led to the outbreak of powerful social and political movements which challenged the legitimacy of the Indian state. But most of these social movements were crushed with severe repression. Many elements of the old left, instead of challenging the ruling Indian National Congress party (led by Indira Gandhi) strategy, compromised with the authoritarian claims of the Congress. Furthermore, the old left intellectuals accommodated the Congress party's interpretations in their orthodox Marxist Leninist theories in the economist development theory of class struggle. It is in this historical conjunction of new conditions in the world after the Second World War, the increasing crisis of the Indian state, and the emergence of people's movements in India, along with the bankruptcy and hypocrisy of Indian leftist historians and intellectuals, that the Subaltern Studies group emerged.

Most of the members of this group came from a progressive background and insisted in their interpretations on the role of the subordinated and their agency in history. Their concern with the subaltern people means that these historians are committed to the notion of social justice for the oppressed. It is with this concern for the oppressed and subordinated people that I wish to evaluate the role of subaltern studies and therefore raise the following questions:

Does subaltern studies as it has evolved up till now help us in getting closer to the goal of social justice for all? What type of collective action would be possible based on 'differences' as promoted by subaltern studies? With the promotion of 'differences' what type of actions would be taken and against what force/s? Do subaltern studies help in creating an emancipatory politics for the subalterns? Does this historiography help in understanding people's lives, their actions and their histories more meaningfully in terms of developing strategies to make their lives better?

Some of the difficulties we encounter as we seek answers for these questions can be illustrated by the work of Chakrabarty. He suggests that the subjects should be engaged in the formation of their own categories. According to him, this can be done by looking at the primordial values of the people based on the power relations (pre-British hierarchical system) in their day-to-day lives, which have longer historical roots than British rule. Once that is done it would be possible to find the roots of our backwardness in our own culture and there will be no need to find a 'fetishised demon called "colonialism" or imperialism' to be blamed.[12] It is only then, according to Chakrabarty, that we shall be able to break away from master narratives and European influence and thought, which always 'peripheralise non-Western pasts and universalise them.' Chakrabarty challenges Indian historians' debate on 'changes and continuities' in working class history. According to him, 'The more fundamental question seems to be: From what teleological perspective do we even identify and name these "changes?"'[13] Chakrabarty maintains that 'the power relations that made up their (workers) everyday life arose out of a culture that was hierarchical and inegalitarian, subordinating the individual to imagined communities of a distinctly pre-capitalist character.'[14] Therefore

Chakrabarty thinks that 'the issues of consciousness, solidarity, organisation, and protest in that history can be posed within our framework
in terms of a tension between the undemocratic cultural codes of
Indian society and the notion of "equality" that socialist politics both
assume and seek to transcend.'[15] Thus, he tries to resolve the tension
by rejecting 'economistic or narrowly political explanations.' Chakrabarty seems to be saying that by choosing the concepts of 'hierarchy'
and 'inegalitarian relations' to understand Indian working class consciousness, his politics (and those of subalternists in general) is more
radical (emancipatory) because it breaks away from Western bourgeois
culture and master narratives.

Let us examine the issues raised by the subalternists and the claims
made by Chakrabarty to see if their strategy is more radical (emancipatory), valid, or even useful, for rewriting Indian working class
history. The emphasis of Chakrabarty as well as of the subalternists
on 'culture' is fundamental to their writings in their effort to reject
metanarratives. O'Hanlon and Washbrook correctly point out that:

> cultural relativism means that this metanarrative can do no more than
> stand alongside its opposite, that of local cultures' self creation . . . [This]
> brings us close to the classic liberal view that culture represents some realm
> of freedom and choice . . . Thus activity is separated from individuals in
> the name of freedom of choice and thus, the promoters of these views are
> able to ignore the question of class . . . but they see themselves also as
> having to challenge the larger intellectual tradition of historical materi-
> alism that establishes those questions as central, on the grounds that its
> universalist and objectivist pretensions are really no different to those of
> liberal modernisation theory.[16]

Thus Chakrabarty's and the subalternists' re-emphasis of culture
is in keeping with the Western tradition of the old accusation of the
Orientalists and developmentalists, that is, the 'undemocratic culture'
(seen as backward) of India being an obstacle in its development. This
ideology of 'backwardness' based on culture is not new. We can trace
it in Western scholarship since the emergence of classical political
economy.

Let us point out immediately that we are not promoting the idea that culture should not be included in attempting to understand the condition of the working class. Probably it is true that the cultural dimension has been neglected for long in the analysis of labour history, and this should be rectified. But it is one thing to say that culture should be included while analysing working class struggle, and it is quite another thing to say that culture should be the only basis of understanding the workers' struggle. We have no quarrel with the first claim. It is the latter assumption that we are concerned with in this essay.

Since the beginning of classical political economy, references to 'backward countries' were constructed to designate the impact and consequences of European colonial experience on these countries. 'For most political economists, European tutelage through colonialism was the only way to break the "millennial" pattern of stagnation of backward nations and to initiate them on the road to "progress." '[17] Thus, a justification was developed for colonising the 'backward nations,' which was treated as a temporary measure for educating these 'immature' nations in European values and cultures. Marx and Engels also believed in the world mission of European capitalism and showed a similar bias as well. 'The nineteenth-century version of "people without history," stagnant and backward, incapable of any material progress on their own, and unable to present any opposition to the European experience, lingers on in the theory of imperialism.'[18]

The theories of development which emerged after the Second World War within the capitalist world were named modernisation theories. Through these modernisation theories the prejudices which were the concern of the classical political economists were reintroduced. Once again programmes were started to explore and study the institutional arrangements, values and class structures of societies which make development possible. Post-Second World War modernisation theories used 'implicit or explicit reference to a dichotomy between two ideal types: traditional society (which is equal to being "rural" and "undeveloped") and modern society (which is equal to "urban," "developed," and "industrial").'[19] Larrain has pointed out that by using Weber's ideal types one can find for instance the predominance of a traditional type of action (action determined by a well-rooted custom) and a traditional type of authority (whose domination is based on 'the belief in the everyday routine as an inviolable norm of conduct).'[20] Similarly, he maintains that it is possible to construct the ideal type of a modern or rational society.

The crux of development theories was the evaluation of culture, instead of economy or polity, as the basis for measuring the success or failure of various 'backward' societies in being modernised. According to the modernisation perspective, the 'third world' countries represented 'traditional' cultural entities in contrast with West European and North American societies, conceived as modern social entities.[21] Thus the idea that 'cultural processes intervene into the social processes of "modernisation"' gained ground among development theorists (in the West and were applied to the 'third world.' With the increased propagation of 'developmentalism' in the world, polarisation between the West and the third world has increased. Wallerstein has explained this theme in simple terms as follows:

> First of all here is the universalist theme. All states can develop; all states shall develop. Then come the racist themes. If some states have developed earlier and faster than others, it is because they have done something, behaved in some way that is different. They have been more individualist, or more entrepreneurial, or more rational, or in some way more 'modern.' If other states have developed more slowly, it is because there is something in their culture . . . which prevents them or has thus far prevented them from becoming as 'modern' as other states.[22]

Wittfogel also contends that Oriental civilisations, including India, saw no basic change in their social structure even after the advent of the European political, economic and industrial revolutions.[23] The problem is that the majority of writings about India's caste system have undertaken to prove the uniqueness of India and, therefore, its unchanging character. Weber himself started by implying that caste is a peculiarly pan-Indian phenomenon. The well known French theoretician of the caste system, Dumont, has also argued that caste is unique to Indian society and therefore not comparable to other cultures.[24]

Thus, we find that most India specialists have overlooked the ability of the caste system[25] to change drastically in its form, content and meaning in spite of historic changes which took place in the modes of production in south Asia. Interestingly, Chakrabarty agrees that the caste system did change. He writes:

> My stress on the importance of language or religion in the jute workers' consciousness, however, is not intended to situate this working class in a web of immutable, unchanging loyalties that social scientists sometimes classify as 'primordial.' The so-called ties of birth did not carry the same political or social significance in the 1920, and 1930s as they did, say, in the 1800s or before. And for that reason the social meanings of these 'ties' changed. Historians have argued for long—and with considerable justification—that the large-scale eruption of religious or racial violence with which India is often associated today is a phenomenon of 'modern' Indian history . . . Religion or language arose as an issue *within* this context. What is unsatisfactory, however, is the tendency—pervasive in Marxist constructions of working class history—to add up these 'changes' in terms of an overarching notion of 'progress' or 'development' within which the question of 'consciousness' is placed.[26]

Thus, Chakrabarty does not rule out the process of change in society but objects to the 'tendency in Marxist constructions of working class history with an overarching notion of "progress" within which the question of "consciousness" is placed.' By challenging Marx's construct of 'progress' and 'consciousness,' Chakrabarty, while raising an important question, ignores a more fundamental issue, that is, the process through which change takes place in any society and its culture. By ignoring the process of change Chakrabarty wishes to have it both ways with his mastery of rhetoric. When Bagchi raised a similar question about the process of change while reviewing Chakrabarty's book, Chakrabarty replied to his questioning as follows:

> Fundamentally, Bagchi looks for a comforting narrative where all Indians are cast into the role of passive victims of the huge juggernaut of colonialism. No Indians, whether élite or subaltern, take any responsibility for their own histories in this narrative—a far cry from Thompson's point that 'the (English) working class was present at its own making.' We Indians, in contrast, are never present at our own 'unmaking.' This

'unmaking' is something that has been done to us by the British and the fetishised demon called 'colonialism' (a historian's version, I suppose, of what the Indian government, whenever faced with domestic trouble, calls the 'foreign hand'); that is why, for Bagchi, our current 'problem of . . . class, ethnic and linguistic (and gender?) differences' and those created by 'numerous . . . prejudices and superstitions' are all simply inheritances from the colonial period, 'the legacy of colonialism.'

The landlords' authority, even after one fully grants the peculiarities of the colonial context, always had elements—as Ranajit Guha has amply demonstrated in his *Elementary aspects of peasant insurgency in colonial India* (Delhi, 1993), derived from cultural codes that had a history much longer than that of the British in India. To blame everything on colonialism is to present a point of view and not a proven fact; nor is it to give a very precise definition to colonialism itself. But, most of all, it is to write a history that can only be comforting for the modern Indian ruling classes (to which the historian often personally belongs).[27]

In this reply Chakrabarty further tries to evade the question of the process of change and in fact clears the ground for logically exonerating colonialism from the blames of the nationalist historians. This he accomplishes by asking Indians to learn to take responsibility of their own history and not blame colonialism (past or present) for all their 'failures.' These 'sermons' are very familiar in the US where the newly emerging upper-middle-class African-American intelligentsia have started telling poor African-American that they should stop blaming slavery and the white majority rule for their problems and take responsibility for their lives and look into their own cultural values to explain their backwardness. Today these ideas are part of the latest Republican agenda as well. The similarities of such statements in the US and in Chakrabarty's writings cannot be ignored easily.

Furthermore, Chakrabarty's emphasis on the specificity of Indian culture in constructing Indian workers' history with their 'inegalitarian values' brings us back to an old question. Is India unique? If so, then, everything in the world is ultimately unique. As Berreman has rightly said:

Without denying the uniqueness of every culture, every institution, every object and every event, one can extract aspects, elements, principles or relationships which are (or are thought to be) common for purposes of comparison. In fact this is the only way to determine what is specific to one's culture, society or situation and what is common to recurrent processes and historical circumstances. Science, including social sciences, depends upon identifying and comparing common phenomena in the universe of unique elements. Whether and in what ways phenomena are 'the same' must be carefully specified but to require that they be in all respects identical is to deny the possibility of a science of society. In fact unique is scientifically incomprehensible.[28]

There can be no unique Indian society except in a vague geographical sense any more than there are distinctly Indian properties in chemistry or biology. Thus the phenomenon of uniqueness does not necessarily mean anomalous social phenomenon. What is unique in India is the specificity of the social formation in special geographical and ecological conditions. Mukherjee has shown that in southwest India the village community system did not emerge as a dominant institution in society because that region was blessed with two monsoons instead of one and there was therefore no great need for artificial irrigation for the agrarian economy.[29] Every country has its own specific physical and geographical conditions which contribute to the specificity of its history. In that sense, India is not any more unique than, say, China or Egypt. In the words of Berreman,

> The people who comprise the system are depicted as unfeeling, regimented automatons ruled by inexorable social forces, conforming unquestioningly and unerringly to universal values. But like people everywhere, Indian people are also doubters and believers, conformists and nonconformists. They are defiant, compliant, selfish, magnanimous, independent, innovative, tradition bound, fearful, courageous, optimistic, pessimistic. They hope, aspire, despair, subvert, connive, abide, enforce, manipulate and choose among alternatives as they cope with their society and its values.[30]

The arena of culture means the production of forms of consciousness, ideas, feelings, desires, moral preferences, and forms of subjectivity as well as forms of material culture. These forms of consciousness cannot arise in a separate institutional arena of social life from that of material culture. Mentalities and subjectivities are formed and exposed in every sphere of social existence. Therefore the conditions of existence of classes would more profoundly shape class cultures than the specific interests of the castes or caste loyalties. In other words, the development of working class culture cannot be located in the mythologies of kinship network and 'inegalitarian' ideas. It must be located in the understanding of the complex and contradictory forms and conditions within which the working classes live their subordinate lives. The history of working classes is full of narratives to show how they have been struggling to improve their living and working conditions and not always to retain their caste and kinship loyalties.

The dangers of the cultural trap are stronger than we realise. Making 'culture' the basis of historical analyses will only help ruling class interests to justify their actions against oppressed groups in the same social system.[31] Elaborating on this subject Wallerstein wrote,

> It is argued that one group is genetically or 'culturally' . . . inferior to another group in such a way that the group said to be inferior cannot be expected to perform tasks as well as the presumably superior group . . . The Moslems, it is argued, are not culturally capable of recognising the same universal principles of man-woman relations that are said to be accepted in the Western (or Judeo-Christian world) and from this it is said to follow that they are also not capable of many other things . . . the simplest solution was to argue that Western culture is in fact universal culture . . . the Orientalist also suggested that these high Oriental cultures were historically frozen and could not evolve, but only be 'destroyed' from without . . . The West had emerged into modernity; the others had not. Inevitably, therefore, if one wanted to be 'modern' one had in some way to be 'Western' culturally . . . Thus, the universal work ethics justifies all existing inequalities, since the explanation of their origin is in the historically unequal adoption by different groups of this motivation . . . The existence of unequal incomes thus becomes not an instance of racism-sexism but rather of the universal standard of rewarding efficiency. Those who have less have less because they have earned less. . . . Blacks and women are paid less because they work less hard, merit less. And they work less hard because there is something, if not in their biology, at least in the 'culture' which teaches them values that conflict with the universal work ethos.[32]

In order to avoid the 'culture' trap we need to first understand the source through which it is formed. Culture is 'an aggregate of values and traditions which is deeply linked to the everyday life of the people, and in that sense it is a matrix of perception which allows one to appraise the world.'[33] Therefore, as Mukherjee has pointed out, cultures do not change by themselves because by definition culture is not capable of self-revision or self-production. It only registers the world-view. He adds that 'in the ultimate analysis, human beings make their own history but they do so irrespective of individual wills and this means that the process generated to change society may cut across the existent culture.'[34] Giving the example of the English 'nabobs' he writes, 'They emerged from loot and plunder of India after the East India Company came to India and eventually formed a powerful culture there, based on the context of the economy and polity of Victorian England.'[35] Thus, it is the social process which yields cultural products and groups. 'Culture represents what has happened in society in all its manifestations, as recorded at a time point, while social processes indicate what is happening in society—within and across the culture products—over a time period.'[36]

Besides emphasising culture, Chakrabarty rejects the idea that the state or the capitalist classes have any role in putting obstacles in the way of the formation of working class consciousness. He writes, 'Sympathetic observers of the working class often explain the weakness of worker solidarity in terms of the seeds of division deliberately sown among workers by interested people from the ruling classes (naturally including the employers).'[37] For Chakrabarty this 'sounds like a crude theory of manipulation and conspiracy.'[38]

Thus by rejecting the concept of 'subalternity' and related categories, subaltern studies are able to get away from the older frameworks of colonialism and nationalism within which Indian history was studied. Subalternists try to reveal India instead as 'a multiplicity of changing positions which are then treated as effects of power relations.'[39] They are also disparaging of Marxist and social historians' concern with capitalism as a 'system of political economy and coercive instrumentalities.'[40] They do not realise that the role of the colonial state and capitalism in the formation of caste and class identities cannot be easily wished away by denying its existence.[41]

Capital certainly has a stake in the forms of working class culture.

It has a stake in labour availability, willingness of the workers to labour under conditions rational for the production of surplus, and workers having a suitable level of skill and aptitude. Thus working class culture is also the form in which labour is reproduced. These processes require continual management. In order to create the pool of available recruits, capital has to control the social reproduction of the working class. This is the significance of the whole network of social welfare and existence of the welfare state.

Wallerstein's observation is revealing in this regard:

> Indeed, so much were employers of wage-labour unenthusiastic about proletarianisation that, in addition to fostering the gender/age division of labour, they also encouraged, in their employment pattern and through their influence in the political arena, recognition of defined ethnic groups, seeking to link them to specific allocated roles in the labour force, with different levels of real remuneration for their work. Ethnicity created cultural crust which consolidated the patterns of semi-proletarian household structures. That the emergence of such ethnicity also played a political-divisive role for the working classes has been a political bonus for the employers but not, I think, the prime mover in this process.[42]

The above quotation explains that capitalists play upon the existing divisions in the society to their advantage as the divisiveness among the working classes always proves useful to capital in controlling them. Capitalists may not be the prime movers of this divisiveness but they are never neutral in this process. Capital's requirements themselves are frequently undergoing transformation. The process of reproduction is always a contested transformation and many times a weakness of capitalists who, divided by competition, have had to rely on traditional forms of labour management.[43] Elbaum and Wilkinson suggest that workers' organisation in the context of the weakening competitive position of the British steel industries contributed significantly to the survival of archaic structures of production in Britain as compared with the US.[44] The development of industrial capitalism in Britain failed to eliminate all 'traditional' groups. The reason for the perpetuation of 'traditional' groups in British steel industry can be located in the conjunction of the various historical forces at play in that historical time,[45] and not in the culture of the working class as Chakrabarty's approach would suggest.

Working class culture is formed in the struggle between capital's demand for a particular form of labour power and the search for a secure location within this relation of dependency. The outcome of such struggle depends on what ideological and political forces are in play at the particular historical time, as well as on the specific needs of the capitalist. Sometimes capitalists may require a hierarchical division of labour as a mode of management. In the determination of the structure of these hierarchies, formal and informal struggles by strategic groups of workers often play a crucial role, particularly when capitalists are divided by intense competition. Elbaum and Wilkinson explain that mule spinners, who were supposed to have been crushed out of existence by the transition from the common mule to the self-acting mule, remained a strong occupational category. Despite the technical deskilling of the jobs, they continued to perform a crucial supervisory function within the labour process.[46] This continuity, as pointed out by Elbaum *et al.*, cannot be understood solely as resulting from the organised strength of the workers in maintaining their strategic position, but rather as a consequence of the weakness of capitalists who, divided by competition, had to rely on traditional forms of labour management.

Similarly, in the case of India we cannot jump to the conclusion, as Chakrabarty has done, that the workers were holding on to their 'primordial values' (undemocratic) whereas Western workers had 'democratic values' (egalitarian). It seems to us that Chakrabarty's anxiety to illuminate the struggle of the workers is important, but his historical perspective is too narrow. Thompson writes,

> Classes do not exist as separate entities, who look around, find an enemy class and then start to struggle. On the contrary, people find themselves in a society structured in determined ways (crucially, but not exclusively, in productive relations), they experience exploitation (or the need to maintain power over those whom they exploit), they identify points of antagonistic interest, they commence to struggle around these issues and in the process of struggling they discover themselves as classes, and they come to know this discovery as class consciousness. Class and class consciousness are always the last, not the first, stage of the historical process.[47]

The workers of the Western countries did not develop class consciousness based on 'democratic ideas' overnight. Moreover, these
ideas were not there from time 'immemorial' but emerged in the
recent histories of those countries. In India democratic ideas were
introduced later and the reinforcement of 'primordial values' by the
colonial state further delayed the matter. In spite of that, how can one
ignore the changes that took place in workers' consciousness by the
transmission and absorption of ideas whose origins lay outside their
tradition? We cannot treat in isolation the changes in consciousness
that lay behind the struggle from the spread of ideas generated by the
nationalist movement and colonial influence as well as by the needs
of capital. How is it possible to accept that Indian workers remained
untouched in their so-called 'primordial values' in the face of the
strong forces of nationalist movement and capitalism?

Chakrabarty has discussed the jute workers' struggle in terms of
organisation based on 'loyalty,' which was derived from hierarchy and
status:

> It was these culturally given relationships of power that entered the field
> of trade unionism. In terms of their theory, the Bengali trade unionists
> no doubt aspired to build bourgeois-democratic organisations. In reality,
> however, they formed organisations based on 'loyalty,' where authority
> did not flow through a grid of rules and procedures but derived directly
> from hierarchy and status.[48]

Later, on the basis of this hierarchical loyalty he concludes that,
'It is possible, then, to recognise a continuing structure in the nature
of working-class defiance of authority all through the history of the
"political mobilisation' of labour."[49] Thus, Chakrabarty finds jute
workers' defiance of authority within the existing hierarchical cultural
context and not in the labour–capital nexus.

Contrary to Chakrabarty's jute workers' struggle, our study of the
TISCO workers' movement at Jamshedpur[50] shows that in spite of
divisions among the workers based on caste, region, religion and
language, they were able to transcend these and unite against the Tata
management for two long decades. This finding is important because
the unskilled workers in the Tata steel industry came from the same

area as those for the jute industry studied by Chakrabarty. Why did the workers in jute industries coming from the same background remain loyal to their 'primordial values,' whereas during the same time period Tata steel workers were able to transcend these? This question should make us look into different kinds of data. For example, Tata, being both employer and landlord, created conditions which were detrimental to a large extent to united action by steel workers. We find that in spite of the control mechanism of the company to keep workers divided, TISCO workers were able to unite, though at the same time it is true that there were great obstacles in the development of their 'class consciousness.' In spite of having 'primordial values,' TISCO workers became conscious of their poor plight and in fact went in search of a leader in 1920, who could guide them in their struggle against capital. The case of TISCO is similar to that of US Steel and other corporations, where welfarism had been widely implemented but workers 'fought an intense struggle in 1919 for shorter hours of work and relief from oppressive and arbitrary foremen.'[51] In 1920 TISCO workers went on strike demanding relief from the oppressive behaviour of their superiors, foremen and supervisors, along with other basic demands to improve their living and working conditions. Again in 1922 and in 1928 these workers went on strike for the same demands. In all these strikes we find, time and again, that workers were guided in their actions mostly by their day-to-day experiences at the workplace, marketplace and at the place of reproduction (town and housing was owned by TISCO). This shows that workers' consciousness of themselves as a class *vis-à-vis* capital develops in the process of their day-to-day struggle and experiences, and not merely from their 'primordial values,' as Chakrabarty would have us believe.

In our study of TISCO workers' struggles we maintain that historical analysis is guided by the theory of underlying relations among various social and historical forces which can explain the complex processes of actual phenomena of class struggle and emerging forms and expression of workers' consciousness. Division within the labour force can generate radically different outcomes depending on the broader context. In the case of TISCO the colonial context created a division between the 'literate' (mainly Bengali clerks) and pro-Congress workers and 'illiterate' (mainly Punjabis, tribals and unskilled or semi-skilled workers) but militant anti-Congress workers. But these workers' 'class consciousness'[52] was perpetually formed in their daily struggle against the capital (Tatas who were in alliance with the nationalist leaders as well as the colonial state), at both the point of production and reproduction, though it was not in the sense of realising their 'missionary role' in history. Nonetheless, the TISCO workers' struggle against capital and the Congress party hegemony for three decades threatened the process of capital formation, which in turn led to a restructuring of industrial relations in the steel industry. In this struggle TISCO workers' 'primordial values and hierarchical relations' were not the driving force, but workers' consciousness to improve their lot and get better living and working conditions. We should be treating these workers' efforts and actions as heroic rather than as negative forms of resistance and condemning them for not fulfilling their 'missionary role' for our benefit. It is revealing to find that TISCO workers would refuse to listen to any leader (national or charismatic) for two decades if the leader did not promise the redressal of their grievances. The hourly recording of workers' meetings at Jamshedpur, prepared both by the police and TISCO company separately, give us a fairly good idea of workers' mood and consciousness. It may not be a complete story but two different versions of the same meetings (also cross-checked in interviews and newspapers) do help to form some reasonable understanding of the situation.

It is time we stop blaming the 'inegalitarian values' of Indian society, as has been done since the advent of the British in India, and in a real sense start rethinking Indian working class history. 'It is true,' points out Wallerstein, 'that the disillusionment with the efficacy of transforming the world by altering its economic and political forms have led to a new intellectual focus on "culure." '[53] But we should not get into a dangerous trap in the process of finding the alternative. 'Perhaps we should constantly re-evaluate whether in fact what we are doing is deconstructing an inegalitarian system or reinforcing it.'[54]

By asking us to use 'instances of cultural practices with historically evolved structures of semiotics and signification' for understanding labour history, Chakrabarty is sacrificing the politics. 'What kind of resistance can be raised to capitalism's systematic coercion if that resistance apparently denies their existence?'[55] Chakrabarty's view seems to be that 'emancipation becomes a struggle purely internal to the consciousness of those who resist and only representable by them.'[56] It is hard to accept this view because ironically this theory does not leave any scope for collective action by the underclasses.

Subalternists claim that their critiques of other forms of privileged knowledge make it a contestatory act. They maintain that they are trying to 'unlock and release histories, cultures, identities frozen by the essentialisations of the past,'[57] so that the subjects can and do represent themselves on the basis of their own experience. This claim of subalternists suggests that workers' 'resistance' itself would eventually form the knowledge which then would be emancipatory, and would be able to transcend relationships of domination. O'Hanlon and Washbrook point out that,

> There are further difficulties concerning questions of subjectivity and hence of history and agency. The subject-position of the subaltern likewise is an effect, contingent and unstable, which 'resides in difference.' Questions of subjectivity are discussed in terms of discourses which construct it. The difficulty here is that it is hard to see how this approach can have room for any theory about experience as the medium through which resistances emerge and are crystallised or about the conditions under which the subordinate can become active agents of their own emancipation on the basis of this experience. Our present challenge lies precisely in understanding how the underclasses we wish to study are at once constructed in conflictual ways as subjects yet also find the means through struggle to realise themselves in coherent and subjectively centred ways as agents.[58]

Subaltern approaches permit the underclasses to present themselves only as victims of particularistic kinds of gender, racial, and national oppression. This approach is similar to that of the US radical postmodernist in the minorities debate which reinforces the well-known hostility of American political culture to any kind of materialist or class analysis. Thus, by denying the material basis and class analysis the subalternist solutions lead only to a methodological (or mythological) individualism which does not allow any kind of programmatic politics.[59] Obviously such an approach cannot be called radical, subversive, or emancipatory.

We cannot erase the past, and we cannot go back in pre-British time to search for 'indigenous' frozen culture, for the simple reason that how would we decide what is indigenous, and if that indigenous past still exists in its pure form. How can we ever find indigenous culture 'which has longer historical roots than the British rule'[60] without using the concepts we have already imbibed under the British regime? Simply by rejecting Marxist categories do we become 'free' from all the Western influences and thoughts? Do we become free by being 'real' Indian, whatever it may mean? Subalternist historiography does not help in answering these questions and we are left with more confusion.

India, as an entity known to us today, is a modern phenomenon, and India's industrialisation and its working class is a product of modern capitalism. Should we insist on cultural differences only and find our history in cultural context alone, just to establish a distance from European thought and history, but sacrifice our politics of liberation in the process?[61] By doing so, whose interest do we serve? Certainly not working class liberation, as they are condemned for being undemocratic and for being stuck in their cultural mode, where there is no hope for their liberation. By condemning them as 'undemocratic' are we asking them to be like Western working classes? Moreover, the democratic ideas of Western working classes have not created so far any working class consciousness through which they could realise their 'missionary role.' Then the question arises—why should we look for democratic or undemocratic ideas in Indian working class culture and pass judgement on their future role? Why should we use Western concepts of 'class consciousness,' 'missionary role of working class' and 'revolutions' to judge the actions of the Indian working classes?

It seems subalternists are disillusioned with the Indian working classes because they do not fit into the available Western conceptual mould. Therefore they start finding fault with Indian working class culture and inegalitarian ideas, thus convincing themselves that something is wrong with workers' culture which does not allow them to create 'democratic class consciousness.' Subalternists simply refuse to understand that workers do not act or live their lives to prove historians' concepts or hopes. Workers (and poor masses) have to live, struggle and act according to their life situations, needs, and opportunities and their day-to-day experiences at all the levels; at production, reproduction, community, locality, religion, and market, and in fact, all these combined forces and constraints shape their consciousness. Chakrabarty complains that this consciousness of workers is fragile and, therefore leads to the formation of 'community consciousness.' It is surprising that he is judging workers' class consciousness as strong or fragile and not looking at the process of its making as well as the historical and political situation in which it is formed. The problem with Chakrabarty's formulation is that he isolates the process of consciousness making from history and other social, political and economic forces of the time and region, and thus is able to condemn the jute workers of Calcutta as backward, having inegalitarian values and hierarchical relationships, which could generate only 'community consciousness' and not 'class consciousness.'

Interestingly, subalternists challenge metanarratives for studying workers' lives and struggles, but for themselves they do not hesitate to accept the influence of contemporary thinkers. Chakrabarty writes:

> I write at a time when a host of scholars and intellectuals—among them Ranajit Guha, James Clifford, Hayden White, Gayatri Spivak, Richard Rorty, not to mention Foucault and Derrida—have problematised ideas about representation, language, reality and voice/consciousness, in such a way that it is no longer possible for me to be theoretically innocent in these matters . . . Mine was a self-conscious exercise in method, using history to rethink certain ideas in Marxist political philosophy.[62]

This clearly says that his challenge to Marxist categories and master narratives in writing the history of a working class is a product of the historical time and place in which he lives, and that he could not remain innocent to such influences. Surprisingly, he cannot see that the working class also cannot remain innocent of the historical and political time they live in, the place and conditions they live in, and the contemporary wave of different nationalist ideas and movements they absorb in their consciousness along with their 'primordial values.' Why has Chakrabarty used this double standard in judging working class consciousness?

Chakrabarty dismisses any discussion of the living conditions of the workers as irrelevant to the constitution or reproduction of their consciousness as mere 'economism' or 'political economy.'[63] Bagchi correctly points out that

> Most students of society, whether trained in political economy or not, would find it surprising to be told that the experience of living perilously near the margin of subsistence and being exposed to the threats of disease and death, or living away from their nearest family members year in and year out, should somehow not enter into the consciousness of these people [workers].[64]

The responsibility of a social scientist is to look underneath the appearances of social stratification so that he/she does not reinforce an inegalitarian system in the name of dismantling it. If the inegalitarian values of Indian people are the basis of their 'backwardness,' how should one explain the use of the communitarian values of Confucianism by transnational capital? Today Confucianism is found more suitable to a contemporary managerial capitalism than the individualistic values of the entrepreneurial capitalism of an earlier day. What is ironic is that the managers of this new world situation themselves concede that they now have the power to appropriate the local for the global, to admit different cultures into the realm of capital only to break them down and remake them in accordance with the requirements of production and consumption. Capital has the capacity even to constitute subjectivities across national boundaries to create producers and consumers more responsive to the operation of capital. Under such a situation, how can we in our analysis separate the formation of subjectivity from the metanarrative if we are truly concerned with people's history?

IV

The discussion so far shows that subaltern studies are throwing the cover of culture over material relationships in their analysis of subalterns, as if the one had little to do with the other. Such a focus diverts criticism from capitalism to Eurocentricism as a cultural or ideological problem (reducing it as one of ethnocentricism), which blurs the power relationships that energised it. Such an approach fails to explain why this particular ethnocentricism (Eurocentricism) was able to define modern global history and itself as the universal aspiration. The arguments of subaltern studies in actual effect are doing a good job of mystifying the relationship between power and culture and in the process helping the ideology of global capitalism to achieve its goal.

Ironically, the capitalist system and 'democratic' structure of the state seem to go together. But the democratic structure is kept alive by workers who are constantly struggling to improve their wages and living conditions. The capitalist system has to give in a little bit to workers' struggles once in a while to keep social tension at the minimum level and to maintain its own profit margin. For example, in the course of their struggle US workers have compelled capital to restructure itself and share its profits as well. In the US, the welfare system and affirmative action were the result of workers' struggles. Workers in the US did not know how to stop demanding more. After 1945 they wanted automobiles, college education for children, vacations in the sun and adequate health facilities. They bourgeoisified themselves quite extensively. Getting better and better living conditions has become an accepted norm in the US. If democracy has to survive in the US there is no other way but to change the system to give people better material conditions of life. Workers in the US are not in the least interested in overthrowing the system. They merely demand more wages and better living conditions, but today capital cannot give any more due to economic globalisation. In this crisis of the capitalist system the well-proven policy of divide and rule is attractive for those who wish to keep on multiplying their profits in the transnational economic system and with the least amount of social tension directed against them at home where their headquarters are located. It is in this context that the US working masses are being directed to look for their individual solutions for a better life within their communities and ethnic, religion, nationality, race and gender differences.

The above statement is not a figment of my imagination or a theory of conspiracy but based on a clear strategy developed by a think tank in Washington, DC. Realising the grim explosive situation in the US today, it has recommended the improvement of the 'social economy' of the country in which churches, communities and charities are to play an important role in forming individual subjectivity (and individual responsibility). This process will help (hopefully for the capitalists) in controlling the millions who lost their jobs due to the restructuring of the US economy as well as the subsequent social and political tension in the country.[65] Should we help in promoting these differences based on communities, race, nationality and religion and legitimise the efforts of the capitalist world?

Historians should not deprive themselves of the analytical tools necessary to study capitalism and its effects around the world in all their complexity, contingency and limitations. Instead of seeing them simply as metanarrative and modernity, capital and the state should be made the object of an analysis that is more nuanced and interactive. What we really need is to find a method of analysis which does not snatch away the role of agency. At the same time we should not lose sight of the role of the state and the world capitalist system, international historical forces, elite groups, and small merchants and traders; the complicity of the subaltern as well as the oppression of one subaltern group over the other (for example, subaltern men over subaltern women); and the material, social, and spiritual culture of the people, all of which are equally influential in forming agency as well as formed by the actions of agency. We must understand the history of people with all its complexities as well as the complexities of the ruling classes, colonial state and capitalism, which are as much part of people's lives as their own subjectivity.

Three decades before subaltern studies came into existence, such an attempt was made by K. Onwuka Dike[66] to write history from an African perspective. His work is a good example of how not to essentialise agency or resort to metanarrative. Africans do not appear in this text as either resistors or collaborators in the face of European involvement in the delta. Europeans, indeed, appear as actors in the universe of different actors within the region, all trying to work with the opportunities and constraints of overseas trade and regional political structure. Dike was successful in giving an account of African agency intersecting with a European one in a crucial moment of history.

In contrast to Dike's approach, subaltern studies is promoting a very problematic idea of 'differences.'[67] It is problematic because in the world outside the academy, differences show in murderous ethnic conflict and continued inequalities among and within societies, classes and gender. Therefore we should be careful when we define 'differences' among the people and in fact should raise the following questions in this regard:

Are perceptions of differences in a given context enough of a basis for affirming diversity or are they acting more as a mechanism for exclusionary and discriminatory practices? How are different categories of people represented within such discourses? How and why do people themselves construct or represent the specificity of their experiences? Under what circumstances does difference become the basis of asserting a collective identity? What is the process in which the social order articulates with the formation of the subject? How is the link between social and psychic reality to be theorised? What qualities, characteristics and aspects are being compared in deciding the differences? What is the nature of the comparison?

We should be careful that we do not reinvent 'differences' among people based on race, nationality and gender while undermining their commonalities based on material conditions. Differences are not static as an essential culture of people. Therefore there needs to be at once attention paid to the operations of differences (mechanisms through which it is promoted) and an insistence on differences (material differences), but not a simple substitution of multiple for binary differences (such as race, caste, religion and nationality), because simple substitutions will pave the way for pluralism. In fact we should look for more meaningful substitutes for the concept of 'differences' for the simple reason that most of the time people in everyday life do find ways to relate to one another and work together in the same place and environment in spite of apparent 'differences.' Over a period of time these people develop a human bond based on similar experiences at the workplace, which happens more often than we care to admit.

Moreover, identities are never a fixed core.[68] Changing identities do assume specific concrete patterns against particular sets of historical and social circumstances. Our cultural identities are simultaneously our cultures in process, but they acquire specific meanings in each given context. Sometimes, depending upon the context, one ethnic group may legitimise class or caste divisions by proclaiming and stressing only the unity of an otherwise heterogeneous group. They may also take recourse to constructing essentialist differences to save themselves from hegemonic forces of the time. This can be especially problematic for women if the cultural values that the groups in question excavate, recast and reconstruct are those that underscore women's subordination.

Therefore we need to understand the 'differences' within different groups. One needs to understand the subordination of one subaltern group by the other as well. Take the example of women in the most oppressed group in India, called dalits.[69] Recently, many external and certain internal factors have prompted dalit women to organise separately from dalit men because dalit leaders have always subordinated, and at times suppressed, the independent political expression of dalit women. In the cultural field also, dalit women have criticised their male counterparts for dominating the literary scene and not taking serious note of the literary output of dalit women. These women also questioned their exclusion from the top position in dalit literary conferences and institutions.

Since dalit women are not all educated or employed on the same level, it creates another type of exclusion. For example, dalit women from Maharashtra are better educated and employed than their counterparts from Karnataka. Therefore it was Maharashtrian dalit women who represented all Indian dalit women at Beijing.[70] Thus, here too a certain section of dalit women was rendered anonymous.

Most of all, dalit women are dependent on the state to create a space to enable them to challenge dalit male dominance in politics. This dependence on the state complicates the situation for dalit women associations because these associations are also challenging the state and state-mediated dalit patriarchy at the same time. For example, dalit women in Bodh Gaya in Bihar opposed the state's decision to hand over land in the names of dalit men, an act which would further marginalise dalit women. In Maharashtra dalit women under the Bahujan Mahila Aghadi and Shetmajur Shetkari Shramik Aghadi are opposing the process of liberalisation. Most interestingly, dalit women, particularly at the grassroots level in Maharashtra, are exhibiting a spontaneous and strong solidarity across caste and region against the violence let loose by Hindutva forces. They are also parti- cipating in the ongoing struggle regarding pasture land and organising campaigns against Hindutva in Bangalore.[71]

In this example of dalit women we see multiple differences— between women and men, between educated, employed and grassroots- level women, regional and linguistic differences among women— within the same oppressed caste group, as well as their struggle against global forces and demand for modernity (equality), their fight against the primordial values of Hindutva (religion), their capability of trans- cending caste and regional identities, use of the state for their empower- ment, as well as their struggle against the state policies of liberalisation, globalisation and privatisation. Can we understand the complexities of these issues and the struggle of dalit people (men and women across the country) as an ethnic group or 'community' by merely talking of differences between castes or the primordial values of people?

If we wish to keep the concept of 'differences' alive it should be in connection with the overall context, because every individual is part of that context. At the same time the context itself keeps changing as it is conditioned by changes in historical and productive forces. In a highly segregated society, the overall context has a stratified impact on the consciousness of individuals. Therefore, each segregated move- ment in a country responds to other similar movements with its own subjective notions.

Take for example the feminist question, the dalit question, and the tribal question (led by naxalites) in India.[72] All three are the outcomes of an objective condition which subjects them to varying levels of exploitation. Thus, the mass movement born in that context interacts with other mass movements on the plane of diversity. These movements seem to have hostile relations with one another. For example, dalits perceive the naxalite movement as led by upper castes because it did not take the caste question into account. The naxalites called the dalit movement bourgeois because it subverts class politics by raising the question of self-respect and capturing power as the goal, but leaves the land question unanswered. Moreover, dalits have no stand on imperialism nor any economic agenda for the oppressed. A class-based movement also perceives feminist movements largely as movements of the élite and blame them for not having a specific understanding of the problems of women of lower classes, since feminists treat all classes within the same parameter of gender. Feminists, on the other hand, argue that when atrocities are committed on dalits or when police raid villages in search of naxalites, it is the women who suffer the most and are subjected to torture and rape, all of which have their origin not in caste or class but in gender. Thus, we find that each segregated movement perceives other segregated movements more as competitors than as complementary to their goals, more as enemy than friend. In this manner, they in effect work as a check on each other's growth and success. A further vicious circle of hostility sets in when the stagnation of one movement is perceived as the fault of the other mass movement.[73]

The fact is that the agenda of all the three movements, that is, land for naxalites, gender for women, and caste for dalits, are all very real exploitative experiences and not mere hallucinations. But in order for each of them to achieve their goals, all three, while pursuing their separate needs, should also be working with one another in the process of overall emancipation. Since the overall history and the context remains the same for all three movements, it is inconceivable how any one of them can be successful in their goals without all of them achieving their goals at the same time. The net result is that diversity proves more a fetter than a potential transformer.[74]

As I said earlier, the writings of a progressive scholar cannot be devoid of his or her politics. Therefore, we also need to ask what is the politics of subaltern studies? What are they trying to achieve by writing the history of differences? This question is pertinent because subaltern studies came into being when all types of peoples' movements in India were being repressed. Subaltern studies seemed at that time to be the one speaking for the oppressed. Today, that voice has become the voice of 'differences' only, which is leaving no hope for a better future for the oppressed. Poor people are told that to be 'different' (inequality, 'indigenous' culture) is natural and that they should live with it and celebrate it and should have no discussion on how to change it.

But interestingly, subaltern studies do emphasise the issue of resistance, though what is being resisted is not necessarily clear. Resistance is a negative concept and may narrow our understanding of history rather than expand it. Working masses are struggling every day to make ends meet and improve their lives through various available means. Struggling peoples' efforts to survive in extremely difficult circumstances should be treated as heroic rather than as resistance. We are in the habit of making heroes only of those people (generally well off) who go for adventure trips in the mountains or in forests, or of military personnel. But we take for granted the starvation and near-subsistence existence of poor people as natural, or worse, as resistance whenever they are able to survive their plight.

Subalternists ignore that the tensions of colonialism in a capitalist context are equally important to analyse. In their (subaltern studies) analysis colonialism sometimes appears as a force whose nature and implications do not have to be unpacked. Their refusal to consider class as a category within a capitalist context has freed the capitalist society from the stigma of 'classness.' In such a 'classless' (capitalist) society, peoples' resistance can never be directed against capitalist or imperialist forces. In this way subalternists can easily keep both the worlds (capitalism/colonialism and resistance) intact, while at the same time remaining committed to 'peoples' history.'

The above discussion makes it amply clear that subaltern studies do not capture the intricacies of the integration of the world economy in a capitalist system. What is lost in their analysis are the ways the world economy constrains all regions and states to adjust to transnational capital as it infringes sovereignty and limits state 'autonomy' and in fact restructures the nature and role of the state all over the globe. Although globalisation is frequently characterised as a homogenising force, it fuses with local conditions in diverse ways, thereby generating, not eroding, striking differences among social formations. The Subaltern Studies group seems to be promoting those 'differences' which are generated and reinforced by world economic forces. They ignore the fact that their philosophical question of 'differences' will be useful only to right wing ideologues who wish to contain the 'dangerous classes' by appropriating the ideas of individual responsibility and the role of race and community in eradicating poverty. It is not surprising that the US Republican party's slogans and agendas sound very much like the post-modern and subaltern studies ideas.

Subaltern studies do not care to note that transnational linkages are essentially stateless and held together not only by flows of commodities (labour and material) but also by marriage, clans and dialect, for example, in the case of Chinese businesses in Taiwan, Singapore, Malaysia and within the US. Here class is overlaid by ethnic, racial and gender division of labour. With the impetus towards globalisation, cultural responses to the expansion of the market provide intersubjective meanings and intermediate inequalities arising from a changing division of labour in various manifestations. The discussion of this dimension of culture is missing in subaltern studies. Within this world context, some leaders of nation-states may contest the reality of globalisation and try to fan the flames of economic nationalism or build competitive trading blocs. Such resistance inevitably creates social conflict. We can see it happening in India, where the Bharatiya Janata Party is fighting against economic liberalisation and entry of the multinationals in the name of essential India. It is happening in Russia and also in the US (and probably in many more countries) where the main political agenda is either to support corporate America or go back to a protectionist policy in the name of saving American jobs. The social and political conflicts arising in this process cannot be traced to primordial values of people. The fact is that working class identity is one of several mobile identities deriving from changing economic conditions, both international and national, which are enmeshed with the racial, ethnic and sexual division of labour.

Based on the above discussion, we can say that it is not possible to declare a sudden and dramatic deglobalisation of capitalist knowledge as it is deeply entrenched in our day-to-day life. Most of the theoretical conceptions of subaltern studies amount to little more than a hallucination whenever it is brought face to face with the concrete exigencies of society structured in dominance. To denounce hierarchy does not get us anywhere. Instead what must be changed are the conditions that make these hierarchies exist, both in reality and in minds. It is easy to privilege one tradition over the other and retire from the challenge of the contradiction between the two. The original tension in subaltern studies did not go away; instead of addressing that tension the Indian subaltern studies practitioners chose to adopt post-modernist methods.

On the subaltern studies' call to 'provincialise' European history, what we need is to first make a detailed and nuanced engagement with the intricacies of European history. Furthermore, we need to understand that the histories of all societies are also histories of inter-linkages between societies. There is no one permanently rooted static society. Some societies may take long in changing for a period of time but none of them are static. Those which remain static disappear. Change occurs not just due to internal forces or just by external forces. Both interact with one another, and change occurs thereby creating something new at every turn in all societies. In modern times each society is linked to others, interdependent with them or even shaped by the processes of societalisation that cut across them. Obviously this suggested approach would not serve the agenda of those who dwell on 'differences' only. Today all of us, including those of the Western world, experience the pressure of contemporary global circumstances which are affecting every society and bringing changes both intended and unintended, violently and diplomatically, depending upon the specific situations.

From this perspective it seems illogical and unrealistic to interpret and analyse the experiences of people and societies as only a process of internal conditions (therefore, different), thereby creating the dangerous phenomenon of 'differences.' Instead, we should try to understand contemporary hegemonic powers and forces, their ideological and other mechanisms of control.[75] It is then that we can begin to explore how these forces interact with different societies and with different classes and groups within a society and create particular conditions which shape people's lives, culture and consciousness.

We must also find out how people respond to these interactions with new hegemonic forces within and without each society. People do not passively absorb everything as helpless beings but in fact resist these hegemonic influences and develop survival techniques, sometimes as individuals or as a social group, and sometimes as a 'nation.' New situations need new explanations and new strategies for resistance but they need not be devoid of history. To Spivak's rhetorical question 'Can the Subaltern speak?' we may answer in the following way. 'The subaltern can speak in Suheli, Bhojpuri, and so on, if the theoretician has the capability to listen.'

Most of the members of the Subaltern Studies group in India and now a subaltern group in Latin America as well, come from progressive backgrounds. But unfortunately, as Chakrabarty has recently stated clearly, their aim is to keep the idea of 'differences' alive as a philosophical question.[76] He pointed out that having an egalitarian society and political democracy may be laudable thoughts in themselves, but these thoughts are not as important or as sensitive to the philosophical question of differences. Therefore 'better' histories can be written only on a clean slate (removing reality), which is possible by pushing history to its limits.

If we follow this strategy of subaltern studies, we shall not be able to write 'better' histories for a long time to come, or the time may not come at all. Will world historical forces stop functioning and wait for us until we are able to clean the slate? The question is who is benefiting from this strategy? We have no hope of getting political democracy and an egalitarian society since they are, according to subaltern studies, Eurocentric ideas, and cleaning the slate and finding people's history (which is another big IF with all its complexities) would take an unknowable amount of time in the future. What are the poor working masses and subalterns (and agencies) to do in the meantime? What should they hope for while they wait for the slate to be cleaned of colonial constructs? Are we better equipped to answer the main issue concerning subalterns, that is, how to better their lives, by pondering over the philosophical question of 'differences' only?

It is in the light of these questions that we should start rethinking the relevance of subaltern studies so that it can be restored to its original context, that is, creating an emancipatory politics. We should not waste time in finding out if the Yellow River (coming back to our exchange mentioned in the beginning), or reality, exists in our minds or outside autonomously, because the river of historical forces, such as transnational capital would not wait for our answers and all of us would be swept away under its force. If we really believe in the role of agency then we should not allow historical forces to subsume us but truly take charge of our lives and act now in making our own history as we please, before it is too late.

NOTES AND REFERENCES

1. Rañajit Guha and collective (eds), *Subaltern Studies*, nine volumes (Delhi: Oxford University Press, 1982 onwards).

2. Vinay Bahl, *The making of the Indian working class: A case study of Tata Iron and Steel Company 1880–1946* (Delhi: Sage, 1995).

3. Gyan Prakash, 'Writing post-orientalist histories of the third world: Perspectives from Indian historiography,' *Comparative Studies in Society and History*, vol. 32, 1990. Also, Gyan Prakash, 'Can the "Subaltern" ride? A reply to O'Hanlon and Washbrook,' *Comparative Studies in Society and History*, vol. 34, no. 1, 1992.

4. Florencia E. Mallon, 'The promise and dilemma of subaltern studies: Perspectives from Latin American history,' *American Historical Review*, vol. 99, no. 5, 1994. David Knapp in his unpublished essay 'Colonising Eastern Europe and inventing Egypt: Two problematic attempts to rewrite colonial history through the prism of the West,' shows that the Subaltern Studies' approach is also influencing east European and Middle Eastern historiography.

5. B. Brecht, cited in W. Suchting, 'On materialism,' *Radical Philosophy*, no. 31, 1982.

6. Dipesh Chakrabarty, 'Postcoloniality and the artifice of history: Who speaks for the Indian past?,' *Representations*, vol. 37, 1992.

7. Dipesh Chakrabarty, 'Marx after Marxism; A subaltern historian's perspective,' *Economic and Political Weekly*, May 29, 1993. Chakrabarty reinforced his ideas on these issues in his recent presentation, 'The time of history and the times of gods,' at the University of Pennsylvania History Department in November 1995.

8. Ibid.

9. Ibid.

10. The discussion on Latin American subaltern studies is based on Mallon.

11. The discussion on African historiography is based on Frederick Cooper, 'Conflict and connections: Rethinking colonial African history,' *American Historical Review*, vol. 99, no. 5, 1994.

12. Dipesh Chakrabarty, 'Discussion—rethinking working class history,' in *Economic and Political Weekly*, April 27, 1991.

13. Dipesh Chakrabarty, *Rethinking working class history: Bengal 1890–1940* (New Jersey: Princeton University Press, 1989), p. 229.

14. Ibid.

15. Ibid.

16. Rosalind O'Hanlon and David Washbrook, 'After Orientalism: Culture, criticism, and politics in the third world,' *Comparative Studies in Society and History*, vol. 34, no. 1, 1992, 141–67.

17. Jorge Larrain, *Theories of development: Capitalism, colonialism and dependency* (Cambridge: Polity Press, 1989), p. 22.

18. Ibid.

19. Ibid.

20. Larrain, p. 24.

21. Ramkrishna Mukherjee, *Society, culture, development* (Delhi: Sage, 1991), pp. 65–6.

22. Immanuel Wallerstein, *Geopolitics and geoculture: Essays on the changing world-system* (Cambridge: Cambridge University Press, 1991), pp. 177–8.

23. K.A. Wittfogel, *Oriental despotism* (New Haven: Yale University Press, 1957), p. 80.

24. Louis Dumont, *Homo hierarchicus: The caste system and its implications* (London: Paladin, 1972).

25. For my views on the 'caste system,' see Vinay Bahl, 'Class consciousness and primordial values in the making of the Indian working class,' *South Asia Bulletin*, vol. 13, nos 1 and 2, 1993. Also V. Bahl, 'Caste or class,' *International Journal of Contemporary Sociology*, vol. 29, no. 2, 1992.

26. Chakrabarty, *Rethinking*, p. 218.

27. Chakrabarty, 'Discussion.'

28. Gerald D. Berreman, 'The Brahminical view of caste,' *Contributions to Indian Sociology*, vol. 5, 1971.

29. Ramkrishna Mukherjee, *Rise and fall of the East India Company* (Mumbai: Popular Prakashan, 1974), p. 154.

30. Berreman, p. 72.

31. Wallerstein, *Geopolitics*, p. 178.

32. Wallerstein, pp. 172–5.

33. Ramkrishna Mukherjee, 'Social and cultural components of society and appraisal of social reality,' *Economic and Political Weekly*, January 26, 1991, p. PE-21.

34. Ibid.
35. Ibid.
36. Mukherjee, PE-22.
37. Chakrabarty, *Rethinking*, p. 198.
38. Ibid., p. 199.
39. Ibid.
40. Ibid.
41. See for a discussion of the interaction and influences of world historical for-ces, colonial and national forces on the making of the Indian working class, Bahl, *The making*.
42. Immanuel Wallerstein, *Historical capitalism* (London: Verso, 1987), pp. 27–8.
43. B. Elbaum and F. Wilkinson, 'Industrial relations and uneven development: A comparative study of the American and British Steel Industry,' *Cambridge Journal of Economics*, no. 3, 1979, 279–303.
44. Ibid.
45. Ibid. I have further elaborated this point in my detailed study, *The making*, chapter 1.
46. B. Elbaum, William Lazonick, Frank Wilkinson and Jonathan Zeitlin, 'The labour process, market structure and Marxist theory,' *Cambridge Journal of Economics*, no. 3, 1979, 227–30.
47. E.P. Thompson, *The poverty of theory and other essays* (London: Monthly Review Press, 1978), p. 147.
48. Chakrabarty, *Rethinking*, p. 154.
49. Ibid., p. 84.
50. Vinay Bahl, *The making*.
51. R. Edward, *Contested terrain: The transformation of the workplace in the 20th century* (London: Heinemann, 1976), p. 96.
52. Vinay Bahl, *The making*. Also see Bahl, 'Class consciousness.'
53. Wallerstein, *Geopolitics*, p. 229.
54. Ibid.
55. Rosalind O'Hanlon and David Washbrook, 'After Orientalism: Culture, criticism and politics in the third world,' *Comparative Study of Society and History*, vol. 34/1, 1992, 141–67.
56. Ibid.
57. Ibid.
58. Ibid.
59. I mean the type of methodological individualism promoted by J.W.N. Watkins in 'Methodological individualism and social tendencies,' in *Reading in the philosophy of the social sciences*, May Brodbeck (ed.) (New York: MacMillan, 1968), pp. 269–79.

In this type of individualism intentional explanations are seen as primary and intentions remain properties of individuals. Thus, we are left unable to see how social phenomena—most importantly culture and language—interact with and enable subjective capacities.

60. Chakrabarty, 'Discussion.'

61. Lovibond points out in connection with the question of women's emancipation that the ultimate goal of liberation movements is not to invent new 'identities' along the lines laid down by existing structures of domination, but 'to dismantle these structures and so release the energies of each individual for the work of active (as opposed to reactive) self-definition . . . feminists cannot be indifferent to the modernist promise of social reconstruction or the enlightenment promise of an emancipation from traditional ways of life and their arbitrary authority.' For feminists the project of modernity is incomplete . . . How can anyone ask me to say goodbye to 'emancipatory metanarratives; when my own emancipation is still such a patchy hit and miss affair? The post-modernist discovery of the local and customary, the advocacy of pursuit of truth of virtue within local, self-contained discursive communities which should neither be made commensurable nor evaluated from a universal standard: the attraction for legitimation exercises carried out in a self-consciously parochial spirit.

    Sabina Lovibond, 'Feminism and pragmatism: A reply to Richard Rorty,' *New Left Review*, no. 193, 1992, 74.

62. Chakrabarty, 'Discussion.'

63. A.K. Bagchi, review article, 'Working class consciousness,' *Economic and Political Weekly*, July 28, 1990, pp. PE54–PE60.

64. Ibid.

65. For a discussion on the restructuring of the US economy and a strategy for promoting social economy in the US to ease the social tension among the millions of people thrown out of the jobs, see Jeremy Rifkin, *The end of work: The decline of the global labour force and the dawn of the post-market era* (New York: Putnam Books, 1995).

66. K. Onwuka Dike, *Trade and politics in the Niger Delta*, 1956. Quoted and discussed in Cooper, op. cit. Also see Steven Feierman, 'African history and world history,' in *Africa and the disciplines*, Robert H. Bates, V.Y. Mudimbe and Jean O'Barr (eds) (Chicago: Chicago University Press, 1993).

67. Kumkum Sangari wrote the following on the issue of differences and feminist movement:

    The idea of difference seems to be based on an active deferral or denial of commonality . . . A diffuse, overencompassing notion of post-colonial, non-Western modernity combines with the inadequacies of enlightenment rationality to tacitly preclude 'non-Western' women from any other horizon of self-definition but their 'own' culture . . . dismantling a yet incomplete project of modernity for egalitarian, feminist social movements runs the danger of political quietism, parochialism and anti-feminism . . . how the question of rights of women can be posed from within a claim to infinite pluralisation or from outside the parameters of the nation-state . . . Cultural diversity is formed in a complex play of power, resources, geography and political systems. Ideas of 'essential' difference have been a notorious basis of discrimination. So 'differences' produced on the basis of class, caste, race or gender, the products of systemic inequality now need to be preserved as indices of cultural diversity? Can plural practices resulting from the discriminations or exclusions of caste and gender usefully be called diversity and if so is it a desirable diversity? While we cannot afford to politically confuse cultural diversity with social disparity, we have to simultaneously recognise that in our history disparities have indeed produced specific forms of diversity . . . unless cultural diversity is confronted with such questions it runs the danger of becoming a localised replay of the angst of colonial anthropologists or of the bad faith of bourgeois anxiety vacillating between destroying and preserving its 'others.' Kumkum Sangari, 'Politics of diversity: Religious communities and multiple patriarchies,' *Economic and Political Weekly*, December 23 and 30, 1995.

68. Lovibond rejects the idea of pluralism and writes, 'If feminism is not to be mere reformism it must call into question parish boundaries to achieve a thoroughgoing global redistribution of wealth, power and labour' and to 'address the structural causes of existing sexual inequality. This . . . will entail opening a door once again to the enlightenment idea of a total reconstitution of society on rational lines. Otherwise the new pluralism is simply status quoist and there are reactionary implications in the proposed return to customary ethics.' Lovibond, pp. 161, 169.

69. The example is taken from Gopal Guru, 'Dalit women,' *Economic and Political Weekly*, October 14, 1995, 2548–50.

70. Ibid.

71. Ibid.

72. This example is taken from G. Vijay, 'Discussion: Mass movements and Marxist method,' *Economic and Political Weekly*, November 4, 1995.

73. Ibid.

74. Ibid.

75. For a discussion on the transformation of the state in the globalisation era, the emergence of non-state agencies, and the redefinition of citizenship under the new realities of transnational capital, see Saskia Sassen, *On*

governing the global economy: The 1995 Leonard Hastings Schoff Memorial Lectures (New York: Columbia University Press, 1996), forthcoming. Saskia Sassen very kindly allowed me to read the draft of these lectures.

76. Dipesh Chakrabarty, 'Marx after marxism; A subaltern historian's perspective,' *Economic and Political Weekly*, May 29, 1993.

The Decline of the Subaltern
in *Subaltern Studies**

SUMIT SARKAR

M Y TITLE may sound provocative, but at one level it is no more
than description, with no necessarily pejorative implications.
A quick count indicates that all fourteen essays in *Subaltern
Studies I* and *II* had been about underprivileged groups in Indian
society—peasants, tribals, and in one instance workers. The corresponding figure for volumes VII and VIII is, at most, four out of twelve.[1]
Guha's preface and introductory essay in the first volume had been
full of references to 'subaltern classes,' evocations of Gramsci, and the
use of much Marxian terminology. Today, the dominant thrust
within the project—or at least the one that gets most attention—is
focused on critiques of Western-colonial power-knowledge, with
non-Western 'community consciousness' as its valorised alternative.
Also emerging is a tendency to define such communities principally
in terms of religious identities.

Change within a project which is now well over a decade old is entirely understandable and even welcome, though one could have
hoped for some internal analysis of the shifting meanings of the core
term 'subaltern' and why it has been thought necessary to retain it
despite a very different discursive context. What makes the shifts
within *Subaltern Studies* worthy of close attention are their association

*I have benefited greatly from the comments and criticisms of Aijaz Ahmad,
Pradip Kumar Datta, Mahmud Mamdani and Tanika Sarkar.

with changes in academic (and political) moods that have had a virtually global range.

Subaltern Studies emerged in the early 1980s in a dissident-Left milieu, where sharp criticism of orthodox Marxist practice and theory was still combined with the retention of a broad socialist and Marxian horizon. There were obvious affinities with the radical-populist moods of the 1960s and 1970s, and specifically with efforts to write 'histories from below.' The common ground lay in a combination of enthusiastic response to popular, usually peasant, rebellions, with growing disillusionment about organised Left parties, received versions of orthodox Marxist ideology, and the bureaucratic state structures of 'actually existing socialism.' In India, specifically, there were the embers of abortive Maoist armed struggle in the countryside, the spectacle of one of the two major communist parties supporting an authoritarian regime that was close to the Soviet Union, and then the hopes briefly aroused by the post-Emergency electoral rout of Indira Gandhi. Among historiographical influences, that of British Marxian social history was probably the most significant. Hill, Hobsbawm and Thompson were much admired by the younger scholars, and Thompson in particular had a significant impact when he visited India in the winter of 1976–7 and addressed a session of the Indian History Congress.[2] Ranajit Guha seems to have often used 'subaltern' somewhat in the way Thompson deployed the term 'plebeian' in his writings on eighteenth-century England. In the largely pre-capitalist conditions of colonial India, class formation was likely to have remained inchoate. 'Subaltern' would be of help in avoiding the pitfalls of economic reductionism, while at the same time retaining a necessary emphasis on domination and exploitation.[3] The radical, Thompsonian, social history of the 1970s, despite assertions to the contrary which are made sometimes nowadays for polemical purposes, never really became respectable in the eyes of Western academic establishments. It is not surprising, therefore, that the early *Subaltern Studies* volumes, along with Guha's *Elementary aspects of peasant insurgency in colonial India* (1983), were largely ignored in the West, while they attracted widespread interest and debate in Left-leaning intellectual circles in India.[4]

Things have changed much since then, and today a transformed *Subaltern Studies* owes much of its prestige to the acclaim it is receiving from that part of the Western academic post-modernistic counter-establishment which is interested in colonial and post-colonial matters. Its success is fairly obviously related to an ability to move with the times. With the withering of hopes of radical transformation through popular initiative, conceptions of seamless, all-pervasive, virtually irresistible power-knowledge have tended to displace the evocation of moments of resistance central to the histories from below of the 1960s and 1970s. Domination is conceptualised overwhelmingly in cultural, discursive terms, as the power-knowledge of the post-Enlightenment West. If at all seen as embodied concretely in institutions, it tends to get identified uniquely with the modern bureaucratic nation-state: further search for specific socio-economic interconnections is felt to be unnecessarily economistic, redolent of traces of a now finally defeated Marxism, and hence disreputable. 'Enlightenment rationalism' thus becomes the central polemical target, and Marxism stands condemned as one more variety of Eurocentrism. Radical, Left-wing social history, in other words, has been collapsed into cultural studies and critiques of colonial discourse, and we have moved from Thompson to Foucault and, even more, Said.

The evolution has been recently summed up by Dipesh Chakrabarty as a shift from the attempt 'to write "better" Marxist histories' to an understanding that 'a critique of this nature could hardly afford to ignore the problem of universalism/Eurocentrism that was inherent in Marxist (or for that matter liberal) thought itself.' His essay goes on to explain the changes within *Subaltern Studies* primarily in terms of 'the interest that Gayatri Spivak and, following her, Edward Said and others took in the project.'[5] Going against the views of my ex-colleagues in the *Subaltern Studies* editorial team, I intend to argue that the trajectory that has been outlined with considerable precision and frankness by Chakrabarty has been debilitating in both academic and political terms. Explanations in terms of adaptations to changed circumstances or outside intellectual influences alone are, however, never fully adequate. I would like to attempt a less 'external' reading, through a focus on certain conceptual ambiguities and implicit tensions within the project from the beginning.

II

The achievements of the early years of *Subaltern Studies* in terms of widening horizons and concrete historical research need to be rescued, perhaps, from the enormous condescension of recent adherents like Gyan Prakash, who dismisses such work as 'the familiar "history from below" approach.'[6] (It is difficult to resist at this point the retort that post-modernistic moods are today not only 'familiar' but academically respectable and advantageous in ways that would have been inconceivable for radical social historians in the 1970s.) The early essays of Ranajit Guha in *Subaltern Studies* located the origins of the new initiative in an effort to 'rectify the élitist bias,' often accompanied by economistic assumptions, common to much colonialist, 'bourgeois-nationalist' and conventional-Marxist readings of modern Indian history.[7] Thus it was argued with considerable justice by Guha and other contributors that anti-colonial movements had been explained far too often in terms of a combination of economic pressures and mobilisation from the top by leaders portrayed as manipulative in colonial, and as idealistic or charismatic in nationalist, historiography. Studies of peasant and labour movements, similarly, had concentrated on economic conditions and Left organisational and ideological lineages. The new trend would seek to explore the neglected dimension of popular or subaltern autonomy in action, consciousness and culture.

Subaltern Studies from its beginnings was felt by many, with some justice, to be somewhat too dismissive about predecessors and contemporaries working on not entirely dissimilar lines,[8] and the claims of setting up a new 'paradigm' were certainly overflamboyant. Yet a new theoretical—or at least polemical—clarity was added to ongoing efforts at exploring histories from below, along with much empirical work at once solid and exciting. Thus Ranajit Guha's analysis of specific themes and movements—the role of rumour, the interrelationships and distinctions between crime and insurgency, or aspects of the Santal rebellion and the 1857 upheaval, to cite a few stray examples— were appreciated by many who could not accept the overall framework of *Elementary aspects*. The publications of the Subaltern Studies group, within, outside, and in some cases before the constitution of the project, helped to significantly modify the historiography of anti-colonial nationalism through a common initial emphasis on 'pressures from below.' One thinks, for instance, of David Hardiman's pioneering exploration of the peasant nationalists of Gujarat through his meti-culous collection of village-level data, Gyanendra Pandey's argument about an inverse relationship between the strength of local Congress organisation and peasant militancy in Uttar Pradesh, and Shahid Amin's analysis of rumours concerning Gandhi's miracle-working powers as an entry point into the processes of an autonomous popular appropriation of messages from nationalist leaders.[9] Reinterpretations of mainstream nationalism apart, there were also important studies of tribal movements and cults, Dipesh Chakrabarty's stimulating, if controversial, essays on Bengal labour history, and efforts to enter areas more 'difficult' for radical historians such as mass communalism, or peasant submissiveness to landlords.[10]

Once the initial excitement had worn away, however, work of this kind could seem repetitive, conveying an impression of a purely em-piricist adding of details to confirm the fairly simple initial hypothesis about subaltern autonomy in one area or form after another. The attraction felt for the alternative, apparently more theoretical, thrust also present within *Subaltern Studies* from its beginnings is therefore understandable. This had its origins in Guha's attempt to use some of the language and methods of Lévi-Straussian structuralism to unravel what *Elementary aspects* claimed was an underlying structure of peasant insurgent consciousness, extending across more than a cen-tury of colonial rule and over considerable variations of physical and social space. Guha still confined his generalisations to Indian peasants under colonialism, and sought to preserve some linkages with patterns of state–landlord–moneylender exploitation. Partha Chatterjee's first two essays in *Subaltern Studies* introduced a much more general cate-gory of 'peasant communal consciousness,' inaugurating thereby what has subsequently become a crucial shift from 'subaltern' through 'peasant' to 'community.' The essays simultaneously expanded the notion of 'autonomy' into a categorical disjunction between two 'domains' of politics and 'power'—élite and subaltern. Chatterjee claimed that 'when a community acts collectively the fundamental political characteristics are the same everywhere,' and achieved an equally breathtaking, unmediated leap from some very general comments in Marx's *Grundrisse* about community in pre-capitalist social formations to Bengal peasant life in the 1920s.

In the name of theory, then, a tendency emerged towards essentialising the categories of 'subaltern' and 'autonomy,' in the sense of assigning to them more or less absolute, fixed, decontextualised meanings and qualities. That there had been such elements of 'essentialism,' 'teleology' and epistemological naivete in the quest for the subaltern subject has naturally not escaped the notice of recent postmodernistically inclined admirers. They tend, however, to blame such aberrations on Marxist residues which now, happily, have been largely overcome.[12] What is conveniently forgotten is that the problems do not disappear through a simple substitution of 'class' by 'subaltern' or 'community.' Reifying tendencies can be actually strengthened by the associated detachment from socio-economic contexts and determinants out of a mortal fear of economic reductionism. The handling of the new concepts, further, may remain equally naive. The intervention of Gayatri Chakravorty Spivak,[13] we shall see, has not changed things much in this respect for the bulk of later *Subaltern Studies* work, except in purely verbal terms.

The more essentialist aspect of the early *Subaltern Studies* actually indicated moves away from the Marxian worlds of Thompson and Gramsci. Reification of a subaltern or community identity is open to precisely the kind of objections that Thompson had levelled in the famous opening pages of his *Making of the English working class* against much conventional Marxist handling of class: objections that paradoxically continued to the initial *Subaltern Studies* rejection of the rigidities of economistic class analysis. It is true that Thompson's own handling of the notion of community has been critiqued at times for being insufficiently attentive to 'internal' variations;[14] the contrast in this respect with the ultimate trajectory of *Subaltern Studies* still seems undeniable. Through deliberately paradoxical formulations like 'class struggle without class,' Thompson had sought to combine the continued quest for collectivities of protest and transformation with a rejection of fixed, reified identities.[15] He refused to surrender totally the ground of class, and so the rejection of the base–superstructure analogy did not lead him to any 'culturalism.' Thompson, it needs to be emphasised, never gave up the attempt to situate plebeian culture 'within a particular equilibrium of social relations, a working environment of exploitation and resistance to exploitation—its proper material mode.'[16] What he possessed in abundant measure was an uncanny ability to hold together in creative, dialectical tension dimensions that have often flowed apart elsewhere.

It would be relevant in this context to look also.at Gramsci's six-point 'methodological criteria' for the 'history of the subaltern classes,' referred to by Guha with much admiration in the very first page of *Subaltern Studies I* as a model unattainable but worth striving for:

> 1. the objective formation of the subaltern social groups, by the developments and transformations occurring in the sphere of economic production . . . 2. their active or passive affiliation to the dominant political formations, their attempts to influence the programmes of these formations in order to press claims of their own . . . 3. the birth of new parties of the dominant groups, intended to conserve the assent of the subaltern groups and to maintain control over them; 4. the formations which the subaltern groups themselves produce, in order to press claims of a limited and partial character; 5. those new formations which assert the autonomy of the subaltern groups, but within the old framework; 6. those formations which assert the integral autonomy . . . etc.[17]

Subaltern 'social groups' are emphatically not unrelated to 'the sphere of economic production,' it will be noticed—and the indication is clear even in such a brief outline of an enormous range of possible meanings of 'autonomy.' Above all, the emphasis, throughout, is not on distinct domains of politics, but interpenetration, mutual (though obviously unequal) conditioning, and, implicitly, common roots in a specific social formation. Otherwise the subaltern would logically always remain subaltern, except in the unlikely event of a literal inversion which, too, would not really transform society, perspectives that Gramsci the revolutionary could hardly be expected to endorse.

Chatterjee's terminology of distinct élite and subaltern domains was initially felt by many in the *Subaltern Studies* group to be little more than a strong way of asserting the basic need to search for traces of subaltern autonomy. (I notice, for instance, that I had quite inconsistently slipped into the same language even while arguing in my *Subaltern Studies III* essay against overrigid application of binary categories.[18]) The logical, if at first perhaps unnoticed and unintended, consequences have been really far-reaching. The separation of domination and autonomy tended to make absolute and homogenise both within their separate domains, and represented a crucial move away from efforts to develop immanent critiques of structures that have been the strength of Marxian dialectical approaches.[19] Domination construed as irresistible could render autonomy illusory. Alternatively, the latter had to be located in pre-colonial or pre-modern spaces untouched by power, or sought for in fleeting, fragmentary moments alone. Late *Subaltern Studies* in practice has oscillated around precisely these three positions, of 'derivative discourse,' indigenous 'community,' and 'fragments.'

A bifurcation of the worlds of domination and autonomy, I have argued elsewhere, became characteristic of several otherwise unconnected spheres of intellectual enquiry in the political conjuncture of the late 1970s and 1980s: the 'acculturation thesis' about early modern French popular culture, Foucault's studies of modern power-knowledge, Said's critique of Orientalism.[20] Not surprisingly, the similar disjunction that was occasionally made in early *Subaltern Studies*[21] provided the initial point of insertion of Said, through an article, and then a very influential book, by Partha Chatterjee.[22] Said's views regarding the overwhelming nature of post-Enlightenment colonial power-knowledge was applied to the colonised intelligentsia, who were thus virtually robbed of agency and held to have been capable of only 'derivative discourses.' Beyond it lay the domain of community consciousness, still associated, though rather vaguely now, with the peasantry, but embodied somehow in the figure of Gandhi, who was declared to have been uniquely free of the taint of Enlighten-ment rationalism, prior to his partial appropriation by the Nehruvian 'moment of arrival.' Both poles of the power relationship tend to get homogenised in this argument, which has become extremely influential. Colonial cultural domination, stripped of all complexities and vari-ations, faces an indigenous domain eroded of internal tensions and conflicts.[23] The possibility of pre-colonial forms of domination, however modified, persisting through colonialism, helping to mediate colonial authority in vital ways, maybe even functioning autonomously at times—for all of which there is ample evidence—is simply ignored.[24] Colonial rule is assumed to have brought about an absolute rupture: the colonised subject is taken to have been literally constituted by colonialism alone.[25] And so Gandhi's assumed location 'outside the thematic of post-Enlightenment thought' can be described as one 'which could have been adopted by any member of the traditional intelligentsia in India,' and then simultaneously identified as having 'an inherently [*sic*] "peasant-communal" character.' The differences between the 'traditional intelligentsia,' overwhelmingly upper-caste (or élite Muslim) and male, and bound up with structures of landlord and bureaucratic domination, and peasant-communal consciousness, are apparently of no importance whatsoever; caste, class, and gender divides have ceased to matter.[26]

There are elements of a rich paradox in this shift of binaries from élite/subaltern to colonial/indigenous community or Western/Third-World cultural nationalist. A project that had started with a trenchant attack on élite nationalist historiography had now chosen as its hero the principal iconic figure of official Indian nationalism, and its most influential text after *Elementary aspects* was built entirely around the (partial) study of just three indisputably élite figures, Bankimchandra, Gandhi, and Nehru. The passage to near-nationalist positions may have been facilitated, incidentally, by an unnoticed drift implicit even in Guha's initial formulation of the project in *Subaltern Studies I*. The 'historiography of colonial India' somehow slides quickly into that of Indian nationalism: the fundamental lacuna is described as the failure 'to acknowledge the contribution made by the people *on their own* to the making and development of this nationalism,' and the central problematic ultimately becomes '*the historic failure of the nation to come into its own.*'[27]

With *Nationalist thought*, followed in 1987 by the publication in the US of *Selected Subaltern Studies*, with a foreword by Edward Said and an editorial note by Gayatri Chakravorty Spivak, subaltern historiography was launched on a successful international, and more specifically metropolitan and US-academic, career. The intellectual formation of which its currently most prominent practitioners are now part, Aijaz Ahmad argues, has gone through two phases: Third World cultural nationalism, followed by post-modernistic valorisations of 'fragments.'[28] For *Subaltern Studies*, however, located by its subject matter in a country that has been a post-colonial nation-state for more than four decades, an oppositional stance towards existing forms of nationalism has been felt to be necessary from the beginning. The situation was rather different from that facing a member of a Palestinian diaspora still in quest of independent nationhood. This opposition was reconciled with the Saidian framework through the assumption that the post-colonial nation-state was no more than a continuation of the original, Western, Enlightenment project imposed through colonial discourse. The mark of late *Subaltern Studies* therefore became not a succession of phases, but the counterposing of reified notions of 'community' or 'fragment,' alternatively or sometimes in unison, against this highly generalised category of the 'modern' nation-state as the embodiment of Western cultural domination. The original separation of the domains of power and autonomy culminates here in an oscillation between the 'rhetorical absolutism' of structure and the 'fragmented fetishism' of the subject—to apply to it the perceptive comments of Perry Anderson, a decade ago, about the consequences of uncritically applying the linguistic model to historiography.[29]

It might be interesting to take a glance at this point at the glimmerings of an alternative approach that had appeared briefly within *Subaltern Studies* but was soon virtually forgotten. I am thinking, particularly, of Ranajit Guha's seldom-referred-to essay 'Chandra's death'—along with, perhaps, an essay of mine about a very unusual village scandal, and Gyanendra Pandey's exploration of local memory through a small-town gentry chronicle and a diary kept by a weaver.[30] 'Fragment' and 'community' were important for these essays, but in ways utterly different from what has now become the dominant mode within *Subaltern Studies*. Hindsight indicates some affinities, rather, with the kind of micro-history analysed recently by Carlo Ginzburg, marked by an 'insistence on context, exactly the opposite of the isolated contemplation of the fragmentary' advocated by post-modernism. This is a micro-history which has become anti-positivistic in its awareness of the constructed nature of all evidence and categories, but which nevertheless does not plunge into complete scepticism and relativism. 'Chandra's Death' and 'Kalki-Avatar' tried to explore general connections—of caste, patriarchy, class, colonial rule—through 'the small drama and fine detail of social existence' and sought to avoid the appearance of impersonality and abstraction often conveyed by pure macro-history. Their starting point was what Italian historians nowadays call the 'exceptional-normal':[31] a local event that had interrupted the everyday only for a brief moment, but had been unusual enough to leave some traces. And the 'community' that was unravelled, particularly through Guha's moving study of the death (through enforced abortion after an illicit affair) of a low-caste woman, was one of conflict and brutal exploitation, of power relations 'sited at a depth within the indigenous society, well beyond the reach of the disciplinary arm of the colonial state.' These are dimensions that have often been concealed, Guha noted, through a blending of 'indigenous feudal ideology . . . with colonial anthropology.'[32] Not just colonial anthropology but Guha's own brainchild, one is tempted to add, sometimes carries on that good work nowadays, with the result that essays in late *Subaltern Studies* which implicitly take a different stance tend to get relatively little attention.[33]

But there was no theorisation on the basis of such micro-study, nothing of the kind being attempted nowadays by some Italian and German scholars to develop micro-history into a cogent methodological alternative to both positivism and post-modernism. And there was the further fact that this was emphatically not the kind of South Asian history that could win easy acclaim in the West, for its reading demanded, if not prior knowledge, at least the readiness to try to grasp unfamiliar and dense material, thick descriptions which were not at the same time exotic. One does get the strong impression that the majority among even the fairly small section of the Western intelligentsia interested in the Third World prefers its material conveniently packaged nowadays, without too much detail or complexity. (Totally different standards would be expected in mainstream work on any branch, say, of European history.) Packaged, moreover, in a particular way, fitted into the slots of anti-Western cultural nationalism (one recalls Fredric Jameson's assertion that 'all third world texts are necessarily—*national allegories*'[34]) and/or post-structuralist play with fragments. The West, it seems, to borrow from Said, is still engaged in producing its Orient through selective appropriation and essentialist stereotyping: Orientalism flourishes at the heart of today's anti-Orientalist tirade.

Partha Chatterjee's *The nation and its fragments* epitomises the latest phase of *Subaltern Studies* at its most lucid and comprehensive.[35] A new binary has been introduced, 'material'/'spiritual' (or 'world'/ 'home'[36]), probably to take care of the criticism that the earlier 'derivative discourse' thesis had deprived the colonised subject of all autonomy or agency. Through such a bifurcation, we are told, nationalists kept or created as their own an autonomous world of literature, art, education, domesticity, and above all, it appears, religion. They were surrendering in effect to the West, meanwhile, on the 'material' plane: for the efforts to eradicate 'colonial difference' (for example, unequal treatment of Indians in lawcourts, with respect to civil rights, and in politics generally) actually meant progressive absorption into the Western colonial project of building the modern nation-state— a project inevitably left incomplete by colonialism, but realised by Indian nationalists. Here is a paradox indeed, for all commonsensically promising or effective ways of fighting colonial domination (mass political struggle, for instance, or even economic self-help) have become signs of surrender.

Further implications of this suspicion about indigenous ventures into the 'external' or 'material' domain become evident in the principles of selection followed in the chapters about the nation and 'its' women and subordinate castes. For Chatterjee, women's initiative or autonomy in the nationalist era apparently found expression only inside the home, or at best in autobiographies, while evidence for lower-caste protest against Brahmanical hegemony is located solely in the interesting, but extremely marginal, world of heterodox religious sects. He remains silent about the active role of women in virtually every kind of politics, as well as in specific women's associations, from at least the 1920s. Within the home, Chatterjee focuses much more closely on how women preserved pre-colonial modes of being and resistance, echoing standard nationalist concerns. There is not much interest in how women struggled with a patriarchal domination that was, after all, overwhelmingly indigenous in its structures. Even more surprisingly, the book tells the reader nothing about the powerful anti-caste movements associated with Phule, Periyar, or Ambedkar. No book can be expected to cover everything, but silences of this magnitude are dangerous in a work that appears on the surface comprehensive enough to serve as a standard introduction to colonial India for non-specialists and newcomers, particularly abroad.

The new binary elaborated in *The nation* is not just a description of nationalist ideology, in which case it could have had a certain though much exaggerated, relevance. The pattern of stresses and silences indicates a high degree of authorial acceptance. And yet the material/spiritual, West/East divide is of course almost classically Orientalist, much loved in particular by the most conservative elements in Indian society in both colonial and post-colonial times.[37] Chatterjee remains vague about the 'the new idea of womanhood in the era of nationalism,' the 'battle' for which, he tells us, 'unlike the women's movements in nineteenth- and twentieth-century Europe and America,' 'was waged in the home . . . outside the arena of political agitation.'[38] His editorial colleague Dipesh Chakrabarty has recently been much more explicit. Chakrabarty has discovered in nineteenth-century Bengali valorisations of *kula* and *grihalakshmi* (roughly, extended lineage and bounteous wife) 'an irreducible category of "beauty" . . . ways of talking about formations of pleasure, emotions and ideas of good life that associated themselves with models of non-autonomous, non-bourgeois, and non-secular personhood.' All this, despite the admitted 'cruelties of the patriarchal order' entailed by such terms, 'their undeniable phallocentrism.'[39] Beauty, pleasure, the good life . . . *for whom*, it is surely legitimate to ask.

Chatterjee's new book ends on the metahistorical note of a 'struggle between community and capital.' His notion of community, as earlier, is bound up somehow with peasant consciousness, which, we are told, is 'at the opposite pole to a bourgeois consciousness.' (Significantly, this work on what, after all, is now a fairly developed capitalist country by Third World standards, has no space at all for the nation and its capitalists, or workers.) A pattern similar to that just noticed with respect to gender now manifests itself. The Indian peasant community, Chatterjee admits, was never egalitarian, for 'a fifth or more of the population, belonging to the lowest castes, have never had any recognised rights in land.' No matter, however: this profoundly inegalitarian community can still be valorised, for its 'unity . . . nevertheless established by recognising the rights of subsistence of all sections of the population, albeit a differential right entailing differential duties and privileges.' One is almost tempted to recall the standard idealisations of caste as harmonious, even if hierarchical. The Narodniks had tried to read back into the *mir* their own indisputably egalitarian and socialist ideals; Chatterjee's rejection of such 'populist idealisation of the peasantry' has led him back to a Slavophile position.[40]

Late *Subaltern Studies* here comes close to positions of neo-traditionalist anti-modernism, notably advocated with great clarity and vigour for a number of years by Ashis Nandy.[41] A significant section of the intelligentsia has been attracted by such appeals to an earlier, pre-colonial or pre-modern catholicity of inchoate, pluralistic traditions, particularly in the context of the rise in India today of powerful religious-chauvinist forces claiming to represent definitively organised communities with fixed boundaries—trends that culminated in the destruction of the Babri Masjid and the communal carnage of 1992–3. Right-wing Hindutva can then be condemned precisely for being 'modern,' a construct of late- and post-colonial times, the product of Western, colonial power-knowledge and its classificatory strategies like census enumeration.[42] It may be denounced even for being, in some paradoxical way, 'secular,' and the entire argument then gets bound up with condemnations of secular rationalism as the ultimate villain. Secularism, inexorably associated with the interventionist modern state, is inherently intolerant, argued Nandy in 1990. To him, it is as unacceptable as Hindutva, a movement which typifies 'religion-as-ideology,' imbricated in 'non-religious, usually political or socio-economic, interests.' Tolerance, conversely, has to be 'anti-secular,' and must seek to ground itself on pre-modern 'religion-as-faith' . . . which Nandy defines as 'definitionally non-monolithic and operationally plural.'[43]

What regularly happens in such arguments is a simultaneous narrowing and widening of the term secularism, its deliberate use as a wildly free-floating signifier. It becomes a polemical target which is both single and conveniently multivalent. Secularism, in the first place, gets equated with aggressive anti-religious scepticism, virtually atheism, through an unique identification with the Enlightenment (itself vastly simplified and homogenised). Yet in twentieth-century India systematic anti-religious polemic, far less activity, has been extremely rare, even on the part of dedicated leftists and other non-believers. Being secular in the Indian context has meant, primarily and quite often solely, being non- or anti-communal—which is why Mahatma Gandhi had no particular problem with it. 'The Indian version of secularism,' Rajeev Bhargava has recently reminded us, 'was consolidated in the aftermath of Partition, where Hindu–Muslim sectarian violence killed off over half a million people'—sad and strange, really, that such reminders have become necessary.[44] Even in Europe, the roots of secularism go back some 200 years beyond the Enlightenment, for elements of it emerged in the wake of another epoch of 'communal' violence, the religious wars of the Reformation era. The earliest advocates of a 'secular' separation of church from state were not rationalist freethinkers, but sixteenth-century Anabaptists passionately devoted to their own brand of Christianity who believed any kind of compulsory state religion to be contrary to true faith.

The anti-secular position can retain its plausibility only through an enormous widening of the term's meaning, so that secularism can be made to bear the burden of guilt for all the manifold and indisputable misdeeds and crimes of the 'modern nation-state': 'the new forms of man-made violence unleashed by post-seventeenth-century Europe in the name of Enlightenment values . . . the Third Reich, the Gulag, the two world wars, and the threat of nuclear annihilation.'[45] The logical leap here is really quite startling: Hitler and Stalin were no doubt secular, but was secularism, *per se*, the ground for Nazi or Stalinist terror, considering that so many of their victims (notably, in both cases, the communists) were also atheists? Must secularism be held responsible every time a murder is committed by an unbeliever?

A recent article by Partha Chatterjee reiterates Nandy's position, with one very significant difference.[46] The essay is a reminder of the almost inevitably slippery nature of the category of community. Sought to be applied to an immediate, contemporary context, romanticisations of pre-modern 'fuzzy' identities seem to be in some danger of getting displaced by an even more troubling 'realistic' reconciliation or accommodation with the present.[47] Community, in this article, becomes an 'it,' with firm boundaries and putative representative structures: most startlingly, only communities determined by religion appear now to be worthy of consideration. Realism for Chatterjee now suggests that religious tolerance and state non-interference should be allowed to expand into legislative autonomy for distinct religious communities: 'Tolerance here would require one to accept that there will be political contexts where a group could insist on its right not to give reasons for doing things differently provided it explains itself adequately in its own chosen forum. . . . What this will mean in institutional terms are processes through which each religious group will publicly seek and obtain from its members consent for its practices insofar as those practices have regulative power over the members.'[48]

This, to be sure, is in the specific context of the current motivated and majoritarian BJP campaign for imposing an uniform civil code through an unilateral abrogation of Muslim personal law. Chatterjee's argument has a certain superficial similarity with many other positions which express concern today over any imposed uniformity. It remains a world removed, however, from the proposals being put forward by some women's organisations and secular groups for mobilising initially around demands for specific reforms in distinct personal laws. Such mobilisation is definitely not intended to remain confined within discrete community walls, but seeks to highlight unjust gender inequalities within all communities. The Hindutva campaign demanding uniformity in the name of national integration, it has been argued, 'deliberately ignores the crucial aspect of "uniformity" within communities, i.e. between men and women.'[49] Chatterjee's logic, in contrast, unfortunately seems broad enough to be eminently appropriable, say, by the VHP claiming to speak on behalf of all 'Hindus,' or fundamentalists in Bangladesh persecuting a dissenter like Taslima Nasreen. For at its heart lies the assumption that all really dangerous or meaningful forms of power are located uniquely in the modern state, whereas power within communities matters very much less. Despite the deployment of Foucaultian 'governmentality' in the article, this is a position that I find irreconcilable with the major thrust of Foucault's arguments, which have been original and disturbing precisely through their search for multiple locations of power and their insistence that forms of resistance also normally develop into alternative sites of domination.

These, however, cannot but be uncomfortable positions for intellectuals who remain deeply anti-communal and in some sense radical. *Subaltern* historiography in general has faced considerable difficulties in tackling this phenomenon of a communal violence that is both popular and impossible to endorse. There is the further problem that the Hindu Right often attacks the secular, liberal nation-state as a Western importation, precisely the burden of much late *Subaltern* argument: suggesting affinities that are, hopefully, still distasteful, yet difficult to repudiate within the parameters of an anti-Enlightenment discourse grounded in notions of community.[50] In two recent essays by Gyanendra Pandey, communal violence consequently becomes the appropriate site for the unfolding of that other pole of late *Subaltern* thinking, built around the notion of the 'fragment,' and seeking to valorise it against epistemologically uncertain and politically oppressive 'grand narratives.'[51] Epistemological uncertainty becomes the ground for rejecting all efforts at causal explanation, or even contextual analysis. (Such uncertainties, it may be noticed, have never been allowed to obstruct sweeping generalisations about Enlightenment rationalism, derivative discourses, or community consciousness.) The polemical thrust can then be directed once again principally against secular intellectuals who have tried to relate communal riots to socio-economic and political contexts. Such efforts, invariably branded as economistic, allegedly leave 'little room for the emotions of people, for feelings and perceptions' through their emphasis upon 'land and property.'[52] That people can never get emotional about 'land and property' is surely a startling discovery. Even a distinction, drawn in the context of the terrifying riots of 1946–7 and simplistically represented by Pandey as one made between 'good' and 'bad' subaltern violence, is apparently unacceptable.[53] Pandey cannot stop here, for he remains an anti-communal intellectual: but the framework he has adopted leaves space for nothing more than agonised contemplation of 'violence' and 'pain' as 'fragments,' perception of which is implicitly assumed to be direct and certain. But 'fragment,' etymologically, is either part of a bigger whole or a whole by itself: one cannot avoid the dangers of homogenisation that easily. It remains unnoticed, further, that valorisation of the certainty of knowledge of particulars has been a classically positivistic position, well expounded many years ago, for instance, by Karl Popper in his *Poverty of historicism.*[54]

But violence and pain, detached from specificities of context, become in effect abstract universals, 'violence' in general. The essays end with rhetorical questions about how historians can represent pain, how difficult or impossible it is to do so. One is irresistibly reminded of Thompson's devastating comment in his last book about the fatuity of many statements about 'the human condition,' which take us 'only a little way, and a great deal less far than is sometimes knowingly implied. For "the human condition," unless further qualified and disclosed, is nothing but a kind of metaphysical full stop'—or: 'worse—a bundle of solecisms about mortality and defeated aspiration.'[55]

III

Let me try to sum up my disagreements with late *Subaltern Studies,* which flow from a compound of academic and political misgivings.

Two sets of misrecognitions have obscured the presence in *Subaltern Studies* of a high degree of redundancy, the tendency to reiterate the already said. Both follow from a novelty of situation: *Subaltern Studies* does happen to be the first Indian historiographical school whose reputation has come to be evaluated primarily in terms of audience response in the West. For many Indian readers, particularly those getting interested in post-modernist trends for the first time, the sense of being 'with it' strongly conveyed by *Subaltern Studies* appears far more important than any possible insubstantiality of empirical content. Yet some eclectic borrowings or verbal similarities apart, the claim (or ascription) of being post-modern is largely spurious, in whichever sense we might want to deploy that ambiguous and self-consciously polysemic term. Texts are still being read here in a flat and obvious manner, as straightforward indicators of authorial intention. There have been few attempts to juxtapose representations of diverse kinds in unexpected ways, or self-conscious efforts to think out or experiment with new forms of narrativisation. Partha Chatterjee's *Nationalist thought*, to cite one notable instance, reads very much like a conventional history of ideas, based on a succession of great thinkers. One of the thinkers, Bankimchandra, happens to have been the first major Bengali novelist: his imaginative prose, inexplicably, is totally ignored. Again, much of the potential richness of the *Ramakrishna-Kathamrita* explored as a text gets lost, I feel, if it is virtually reduced to a 'source of new strategies of survival and resistance' of a colonised middle class assumed to be living in extreme dread of its foreign rulers—a class moreover conceptualised in excessively homogenised terms.[56] Problems like these are not basically products of lack of authorial competence or quality. They emerge from restrictive analytical frameworks, as *Subaltern Studies* swings from a rather simple emphasis on subaltern autonomy to an even more simplistic thesis of Western colonial cultural domination.[57]

A reiteration of the already said: for it needs to be emphasised that the bulk of the history written by modern Indian historians has been nationalist and anti-colonial in content, at times obsessively so. Criticism of Western cultural domination is likewise nothing particularly novel. The empirical underpinning for the bulk of *Subaltern* cultural criticism has come in fact from work done in Calcutta some twenty years back, which had effectively demolished the excessive adulation of nineteenth-century English-educated intellectuals and reformers through an emphasis upon the limits imposed on them by their colonial context.[58]

Here the second kind of misrecognition comes in, for in the Western context there is a certain, though much exaggerated, novelty and radicalism in the Saidian exposure of the colonial complicity of much European scholarship and literature. Such blindness has been most obvious in the discipline of literary studies, in the West as well as in the ex-colonial world, and it is not surprising that radically inclined intellectuals working in this area have been particularly enthusiastic in their response to late *Subaltern Studies*. There had been some real absences, too, even in the best of Western Marxist or radical historiography, inadequacies that came to be felt more deeply in the new era of vastly intensified globalisation, socialist collapse, resurgent neocolonialism and racism, and the rise to unprecedented prominence of expatriate Third World intellectuals located, or seeking location in, Western universities. Hobsbawm apart, the great masters of British Marxist historiography have admittedly written little on Empire, and the charge of Eurocentrism could appear particularly damaging for a social history the foundation-text of which had deliberately confined itself to the making of the 'English' working class.

Yet the exposure of one instance after another of collusion with colonial power-knowledge can soon become predictable and tedious. Thompson has a quiet but telling aside about this in his *Alien homage*,[59] while his posthumous book on Blake should induce some rethinking about uncritical denunciations of the Enlightenment as a bloc that have been so much in vogue in recent years. With its superb combination of textual close reading and historical analysis, *Witness against the beast* reminds us of the need for socially nuanced and differentiated conceptions of Enlightenment and 'counter-Enlightenment' that go far beyond homogenised praise or rejection. And meanwhile very interesting new work is emerging. Peter Linebaugh, for instance, has recently explored ways of integrating global, colonial dimensions and themes of Foucaultian power-knowledge within a framework that is clearly Thompsonian-Marxian in inspiration, and yet goes considerably beyond the parameters of the social history of the 1960s and 1970s.[60]

In South Asian historiography, however, the inflated reputation of late *Subaltern Studies* has encouraged a virtual folding back of all history into the single problematic of Western colonial cultural domination. This imposes a series of closures and silences, and threatens to simultaneously feed into shallow forms of retrogressive indigenism. An impression has spread among interested non-specialists that there is little worth reading in modern Indian history prior to *Subaltern Studies*, or outside it, today. Not that very considerable and significant new work is not going on along other lines: but this tends to get less attention than it deserves. One could cite major advances in economic history, and pioneering work in environmental studies, for instance, as well as research on law and penal administration that is creatively aware of Foucault but tends to ignore, or go beyond, strict Saidian–Subaltern parameters. Such work does not usually begin with assuming a total or uniform pre-colonial–colonial disjunction.[61] Another example would be the shift in the dominant tone of feminist history. There had been interesting developments in the new field of gender studies in the 1970s and early 1980s, posing important questions about women and nationalism and relating gender to shifting material conditions. The colonial discourse framework threatens to marginalise much of this earlier work. A simple binary of Westernised surrender–indigenist resistance will necessarily have major difficulties in finding space for sensitive studies of movements for women's rights, or of lower caste protest: for quite often such initiatives did try to utilise aspects of colonial administration and ideas as resources.

And finally there are the political implications. The spread of assumptions and values associated with late *Subaltern Studies* can have certain disabling consequences for sections of intellectuals still subjectively radical. This is so particularly because India—unlike many parts of the West, perhaps—is still a country where major political battles are engaged in by large numbers of people: where, in other words, depoliticisation has not yet given a certain limited relevance to theories of sporadic initiative by individuals or small groups glorying in their imposed marginality. The organised, Marxist Left in India remains one of the biggest existing anywhere in the world today, while very recently the forces of predominantly high-caste Hindutva have been halted in some areas by a lower case upthrust drawing on earlier traditions of anti-hierarchical protest. *Subaltern Studies*, symptomatically has ignored histories of the Left and of organised anti-caste movements throughout, and the line between past and present-day neglect can be fairly porous. Movements of a more innovative kind have also emerged in recent years: organisations to defend civil and democratic rights, numerous feminist groups, massive ecological protests like the Narmada Bachao Andolan, and very new and imaginative forms of trade union activity (the Chattisgarh Mukti Morcha arising out of a miners' union, one or two efforts at co-operative workers' control in the context of recession and structural readjustment). A 'social reform' issue like child marriage had been the preserve of highly educated, 'Westernised,' upper-caste male reformers in the nineteenth century; today Bhanwari, a woman of low-caste origin in an obscure Rajasthan village, has been campaigning against that practice in Rajput households, in the face of rape, ostracism, and a gross miscarriage of justice. Any meaningful understanding of or identification with such developments is undercut by two kinds of emphasis quite central to late *Subaltern Studies.* Culturalism rejects the importance of class and class struggle, while notions of civil, democratic, feminist and liberal individual rights—many of them indubitably derived from certain Enlightenment traditions—get delegitimised by a repudiation of the Enlightenment as a bloc.

All such efforts need, and have often obtained, significant inputs from an intelligentsia which still includes many people with radical interests and commitments. This intelligentsia, however, is one constituent of a wider middle-class formation, upwardly mobile sections of which today are being sucked into globalising processes that promise material consumerist dividends at the price of dependency. A binary combination of 'material' advancement and 'spiritual' autonomy through surrogate forms of cultural or religious nationalism is not at all uncommon for such groups. Hindutva, with its notable appeal in recent years among metropolitan élites and non-resident Indians, embodies this combination at its most aggressive. The political inclinations of the *Subaltern* scholars and the bulk of their readership are certainly very different, but some of their work nowadays seems to be unwittingly feeding into softer versions of not entirely dissimilar moods. Words like 'secular,' 'rational,' or 'progressive' have become terms of ridicule, and if 'resistance' (of whatever undifferentiative kind) can still be valorised, movements seeking transformation get suspected of teleology.[62] The decisive shift in critical registers from capitalist and colonial exploitation to Enlightenment rationality, from multinationals to Macaulay, has opened the way for a vague nostalgia that identifies the authentic with the indigenous, and locates both in the pasts of an ever-receding community, or a present that can consist of fragments alone. Through an enshrinement of sentimentality,[63] a subcontinent with its manifold, concrete contradictions and problems becomes a kind of dream of childhood, of a *grihalakshmi* presiding over a home happy and beautiful, by some alchemy, in the midst of all its patriarchy.

Let me end with a last, specific example. There is one chapter in Chatterjee's *Nation* which, for once, deals with an economic theme. This is a critique of the bureaucratic rationalism of Nehruvian planning: not unjustified in parts, though there has been no lack of such critiques, many of them much better informed and more effective. What is significant, however, is Chatterjee's total silence on the wholesale abandonment of that strategy in recent years under Western pressure. There is not a word, in a book published in 1993, about that other rationality of the 'free' market, derived at least as much from the Enlightenment as its socialistic alternatives, which is being imposed worldwide today by the World Bank, the IMF, and multinational firms. The claim, elsewhere in the book, to an 'adversarial' relationship 'to the dominant structures of scholarship and politics' resounds oddly in the midst of this silence.[64]

NOTES AND REFERENCES

1. I am excluding from my count the two chapters in volume VIII about Ranajit Guha and his writings. Out of the four, one is by Terence Ranger about Africa, a second (Saurabh Dube) from outside the editorial group—which leaves us with David Hardiman on the Dangs, and Ranajit Guha himself on nationalist mobilisation/disciplining of subaltern strata through 'social boycott.'

2. The paper he presented at that session was published by the journal of the Indian Council of Historical Research: 'Folklore, anthropology, and social history,' *Indian Historical Review* (1977).

3. Guha's *Elementary aspects of peasant insurgency in colonial India* (Delhi, 1983) frequently cited Thompson with approval, and the references,

significantly were to *Whigs and Hunters* and the essay in *Albion's fatal tree.* In 1985, a defence by Dipesh Chakrabarty of the project against criticism in *Social Scientist,* some of it from orthodox Marxist standpoints, pleaded for greater openness to 'alternative varieties of Marxism' and rejected the base-superstructure metaphor in terms reminiscent of Thompson. 'Invitation to a dialogue,' in Guha (ed.), *Subaltern Studies IV* (Delhi, 1985), pp. 369, 373. See also Partha Chatterjee, 'Modes of power: Some clarifications,' in *Social Scientist,* 141, February 1985.

4. Thus the October 1984 issue of *Social Scientist,* a journal with CPI(M) affiliations, published a collective review essay on *Subaltern Studies II* (written by a group of young scholars of Delhi University. A similar review of volumes III and IV came out in the same journal in March 1988. Guha and his colleagues, in significant contrast, were ignored by *Modern Asian Studies* till Rosalind O'Hanlon's 'Recovering the subject: Subaltern studies and histories of resistance in colonial South Asia' (22, i, 1988), and the footnotes in this article clearly demonstrate that the initial debate around the project had been entirely within South Asia. Western discussion and acclaim has proliferated since then: within India, in contrast, there has been a largely derivative adulation, but nothing remotely resembling the critical engagement of the early years.

5. Dipesh Chakrabarty, 'Marx after marxism: Subaltern histories and the question of difference,' in *Polygraph* 6/7, 1993.

6. Gyan Prakash, 'Writing post-Orientalist histories of the third world: Perspectives from Indian historiography,' *Comparative Studies in Society and History,* 32, 1990.

7. Ranajit Guha, 'Preface,' and 'On some aspects of the historiography of colonial India,' in Guha (ed.), *Subaltern Studies I* (Delhi, 1982). The quoted phrases are from pp. vii and 1. A more explicit critique of orthodox Marxist historiography was made by Guha in the second volume (Delhi, 1983), in his 'The prose of counter-insurgency.'

8. One could think, for instance, of some of the essays in Ravinder Kumar's *Essays on Gandhian politics* (Oxford, 1971) influenced by Rudé, or Majid Siddiqi's *Agrarian unrest in North India: The United Provinces 1918–1922* (New Delhi, 1978). In my *Popular movements and middle-class leadership in late colonial India: Problems and perspectives of a 'history from below'* (Calcutta, 1983), drafted before the publication of the first volume of *Subaltern Studies,* I attempted a catalogue of available research material relevant for such studies (fn. 3, p. 74). And the critique, central to much early *Subaltern Studies,* of nationalist leaders and organisations often restraining militant mass initiatives, had been quite common in some kinds of Marxist writing, most notably in R.P. Dutt's *India today* (Bombay, 1947).

9. David Hardiman, *Peasant nationalists of Gujarat: Kheda district, 1917–1934* (Delhi, 1981); Gyanendra Pandey, *Ascendancy of the Congress in Uttar Pradesh 1926–1934* (Delhi, 1978); Shahid Amin, 'Gandhi as mahatma: Gorakhpur district, eastern UP, 1921–2,' *Subaltern Studies III* (Delhi, 1984). My *Modern India, 1885–1947* (Delhi, 1983), written before I joined the Subaltern Studies group, tried to introduce a 'history from below' perspective while attempting an overall survey.

10. David Arnold, 'Rebellious Hillmen: The Gudem-Rampa risings, 1839–1924,' *Subaltern Studies I* (Delhi, 1982); David Hardiman, 'Adivasi assertion in South Gujarat: The Devi movement of 1922–3,' *Subaltern Studies III* (Delhi, 1984), subsequently enlarged into his fascinating *The coming of the Devi* (Delhi, 1987); Tanika Sarkar, 'Jitu Santal's movement in Malda, 1924–32: A study in tribal protest,' *Subaltern Studies IV* (Delhi, 1985); Dipesh Chakrabarty, 'Conditions for knowledge of working-class conditions: Employers, government and the jute workers of Calcutta, 1890–1940,' *Subaltern Studies II* (Delhi, 1983) and 'Trade unions in a hierarchical culture: The jute workers of Calcutta, 1920–50,' *Subaltern Studies III*; Gyanendra Pandey, 'Rallying round the cow: Sectarian strife in the Bhojpur region, c. 1888–1917,' *Subaltern Studies II*; Gautam Bhadra, 'The mentality of subalternity: Kantanama or Rajdharma,' *Subaltern Studies VI* (Delhi, 1989).

11. Partha Chatterjee, 'Agrarian relations and communalism in Bengal, 1926–35' and 'More on modes of power and the peasantry,' *Subaltern Studies I, II.* My quotation is from the first essay, p. 35.

12. See, particularly, Gyan Prakash, as well as a more nuanced and less dogmatically certain review article by Rosalind O'Hanlon, 'Recovering the subject: Subaltern studies and histories of resistance in colonial South Asia,' *Modern Asian Studies*, 22, 1, 1988.

13. 'Subaltern studies: Deconstructing historiography,' *Subaltern Studies IV* (Delhi, 1985).

14. See, for instance, Suzanne Desan, 'Crowds, community and ritual in the work of E.P. Thompson and Natalie Davis,' in Lynn Hunt (ed.), *The new cultural history* (California, 1989). I owe this reference to Dr Hans Medick.

15. E.P. Thompson, 'Eighteenth-century English society: Class-struggle without class?,' *Social History*, III, May 2, 1978.

16. E.P. Thompson, *Customs in common* (London, 1993), p. 7. It is this methodological imperative to contextualise within specific social relations and material modes that has been progressively eliminated, we shall see, from the dominant strand within late *Subaltern Studies*.

17. Antonio Gramsci, 'Notes on Italian history,' in Hoare and Smith (eds), *Selections from the prison notebooks* (New York, 1971), p. 52.

18. 'The conditions and nature of subaltern militancy: Bengal from swadeshi to non-cooperation, *c.* 1905–22,' in Guha (ed.), *Subaltern Studies III* (Delhi, 1984), pp. 273–6.

19. For a powerful, if also highly 'revisionistic,' exposition of the strength of Marxism as immanent critique, see Moishe Postone, *Time, labour, and social domination: A reinterpretation of Marx's critical theory* (Cambridge, 1993, 1995). The effort, on the other hand, to make resistance totally external to power can attain really curious levels, at times. See, for instance, Gyan Prakash's assertion that 'we cannot thematise Indian history in terms of the development of capitalism and simultaneously contest capitalism's homogenisation of the contemporary world.' 'Post-colonial criticism and Indian historiography,' *Social Text,* 31/32, 1992. How does one contest something, I wonder, without talking about it? The best critique of such positions that I have seen is Arif Dirlik, 'The post-colonial aura,' *Critical Inquiry,* 20 ii, Winter 1994.

20. In studies of early modern French popular culture, notably much early 1970s *Annales* scholarship assumed an autonomous popular level manifested in distinct texts, forms, and practices. With the growing influence of Foucault, and Robert Muchembled's *Culture populaire et culture des élites dans la France moderne* (Paris, 1978), published, significantly perhaps, in the same year as Said, *Orientalism,* there was a shift towards frameworks of successful conquest of once-uncontaminated popular culture through the cumulative impact of Counter-Reformation Church, absolute monarchy, and Enlightenment rationalism. The more fruitful historical works, however, have on the whole operated with a model of multiple appropriations rather than distinct levels: see, particularly, Roger Chartier's critique of Muchembled's acculturation thesis in his *Cultural uses of print in early modern France* (Princeton, 1987), 'Introduction.' I have elaborated these points in my 'Popular culture, community, power: Three studies of modern Indian social history,' *Studies in History,* 8, ii, n.s., 1992, pp. 311–13, and 'Orientalism revisited: Saidian moods in the writing of modern Indian history,' *Oxford Literary Review,* XVI, 1–2, 1994.

21. Ranajit Guha's programmatic essay in *Subaltern Studies I* had also described '*the politics of the people*' as 'parallel to the domain of élite politics—an *autonomous* domain, for it neither originated from élite politics nor did its existence depend on the latter' (p. 4).

22. 'Gandhi and the critique of civil society,' *Subaltern Studies III* (Delhi, 1984), followed by *Nationalist thought in the colonial world: A derivative discourse?* (Delhi, 1986).

23. For a more detailed critique of Chatterjee's *Nationalist thought,* see my 'Orientalism revisited.'

24. For a more extensive discussion, see Chapter 1.

25. For an effective critique of this *tabula rasa* approach, see Aijaz Ahmad, *In theory: Classes, nations, literatures* (London, 1992; Delhi, 1993), Chapters III, V.

26. *Nationalist thought*, p. 100; see also *Subaltern Studies III*, p. 176.

27. Ranajit Guha, 'On some aspects of the historiography of colonial India,' *Subaltern Studies I*, pp. 2–3, 7.

28. Aijaz Ahmad, Chapter V, and *passim*.

29. Perry Anderson, *In the tracks of historical materialism* (London, 1983), p. 55. Very relevant also are his comments about the general trajectory from structuralism to post-structuralism: 'a total initial determinism ends in the reinstatement of absolute final contingency, in mimicry of the duality of *langue* and *parole*.'

30. Ranajit Guha, 'Chandra's death,' *Subaltern Studies V* (Delhi, 1987); Sumit Sarkar, 'The Kalki-Avatar of Bikrampur: A village scandal in early twentieth-century Bengal,' *Subaltern Studies VI* (Delhi, 1989); Gyanendra Pandey, ' "Encounters and calamities": The history of a north Indian qasba in the nineteenth-century,' *Subaltern Studies III* (Delhi, 1984). 'Chandra's death' has been warmly praised by Aijaz Ahmad in *In theory*, but this is unlikely to enhance its reputation with the bulk of present-day admirers of *Subaltern Studies*.

31. Carlo Ginzburg, 'Microhistory: Two or three things that I know about it,' *Critical Inquiry*, 29, Autumn 1993. I have benefited also from Hans Medick's unpublished paper on a similar theme: 'Weaving and surviving at Laichingen 1650–1900: Micro-history as history and as research experience.' I am grateful to Professor Ginzburg and Professor Medick for sending me copies of their papers.

32. The quotations from 'Chandra's death' are from *Subaltern Studies V*, pp. 138, 144, 155.

33. I am thinking particularly about the very substantial and impressive ongoing work of David Hardiman, of which the latest example is *Feeding the baniya: Peasants and usurers in Western India* (Delhi, 1996), which seldom gets due recognition. But even Ranajit Guha's 'Discipline and mobilise,' in Chatterjee and Pandey (eds), *Subaltern Studies VII* (Delhi, 1992), far more critical of Gandhian nationalism than usual nowadays, based on a premise of 'indigenous' as well as 'alien' moments of dominance in colonial India, and emphasising 'the power exercised by the indigenous élite over the subaltern amongst the subject population itself'—seems to have attracted little attention.

34. Frederic Jameson, 'Third world literature in the era of multinational capital,' *Social Text*, Fall 1986. For a powerful critique, see Aijaz Ahmad, *In theory*, Chapter III.

35. Partha Chatterjee, *The nation and its fragments: Colonial and post-colonial histories* (Princeton, 1993; Delhi, 1994).

36. I have no space here to comment on this curious equation of the 'spiritual' with home, domesticity and femininity. How, one wonders, did highly patriarchal religious traditions like Hinduism and Islam manage such an identification?

37. For some data about a near-perfect fit between early-twentieth-century cultural nationalism in Bengal and the current argument, see Chapter 1.

38. Chatterjee, *The nation*, p. 133.

39. Dipesh Chakrabarty, 'The difference-deferral of a colonial modernity: Public debates on domesticity in British Bengal,' in *Subaltern Studies VIII* (Delhi, 1994), pp. 83–5.

40. Ibid., pp. 166–7, 238.

41. See, for instance, the declaration of intent at the beginning of Nandy's *The intimate enemy* (Delhi, 1983) 'to justify and defend the *innocence* [my italics] which confronted Western colonialism' (p. ix).

42. Gyanendra Pandey attempted to apply this Saidian framework to the study of early-twentieth-century communalism in his *The construction of communalism in colonial North India* (Delhi, 1990).

43. Ashis Nandy, 'The politics of secularism and the recovery of religious tolerance,' in Veena Das (ed.), *Mirrors of violence: Communities, riots and survivors in South Asia* (Delhi, 1990).

44. Rajeev Bhargava, 'Giving secularism its due,' *Economic and Political Weekly*, July 9, 1994.

45. Nandy, 'The politics of secularism,' in Das, p. 90.

46. Partha Chatterjee, 'Secularism and toleration,' *Economic and Political Weekly*, July 9, 1994. For a more detailed discussion of both Nandy (1990) and Chatterjee (1994), see my 'The anti-secularist critique of Hindutva: Problem of a shared discursive space,' *Germinal*/Journal of Department of Germanic and Romance Studies (Delhi University, 1994), vol. I.

47. Chatterjee takes over Nandy's secularism/toleration disjunction, but gives it a very 'presentist' twist, explicitly stating in a footnote that he is drawing out the implications of this position in terms of 'political possibilities within the domain of the modern state institutions as they now exist in India.' Ibid., fn. 2, pp. 1776–7.

48. Ibid., p. 1775.

49. Resolution entitled 'Equal rights, equal laws,' adopted by a national convention organised by the All India Democratic Women's Association (New Delhi, December 9–10, 1995).

50. In May 1994, for instance, in the RSS ideologue S. Gurumurti described the Ayodhya movement as 'perhaps the first major symptom of social

assertion over a Westernised and alienated state apparatus' that has imposed secularism and other 'foreign ideologies on the country, provoking a growing feeling of nativeness.' 'State and Society,' in *Seminar 417* (May 1994). An article by Uma Bharati in the same issue entitled 'Social Justice' condemned any labelling of 'Hindutva [as] a Brahmanical and exploitative order' as 'the distorted view that followers of Macaulay hold.'

51. Gyanendra Pandey, 'In defence of the fragment: Writing about Hindu–Muslim riots in India Today,' *Economic and Political Weekly*, Annual Number, 1991, and 'The Prose of Otherness,' *Subaltern Studies VIII*.

52. 'In defence of the fragment,' p. 566.

53. 'The prose of otherness,' *Subaltern Studies VIII*, referring to an old article of mine entitled 'Popular movements, national leadership, and the coming of freedom with partition,' in D.N. Panigrahi (ed.), *Economy, society and politics in modern India* (New Delhi, 1985).

54. Relevant here would be Frederic Jameson's recent caustic comments about 'the latter-day transmogrification of these—quite unphilosophical empirical and anti-systemic positivist attitudes and opinions into heroic forms of resistance to metaphysics and Utopian tyranny.' 'Actually existing Marxism,' *Polygraph 6/7*, p. 184.

55. E.P. Thompson, *Witness against the beast: William Blake and the moral law* (Cambridge, 1993), p. 188.

56. Partha Chatterjee, 'A Religion of urban domesticity: Sri Ramakrishna and the Calcutta middle class,' in Chatterjee and Pandey (eds), *Subaltern Studies VII* (Delhi, 1992), and Chatterjee, *The nation*, Chapter III. The clerical ambience of Ramakrishna's early audience and often of his conversations with them, for instance, has been totally missed. For another kind of effort to explore the *Kathamrita*—one which in its author's opinion tried to go much beyond the mere 'biographical question of Ramakrishna in relation to the middle class Bengal' (*The nation*, p. 36), see my 'Kaliyuga, chakri, and bhakti: Ramakrishna and his times,' *Economic and Political Weekly*, July 18, 1992; reprinted with minor changes as Chapter 8 within this book.

57. Shahid Amin's finely crafted *Event, metaphor, memory: Chauri Chaura 1922–1992* (Delhi, 1995) might be taken to constitute a partial exception, within a basically early-*Subaltern* framework. But the latter often seems too narrow to adequately comprehend the richness of material, while far more has been achieved elsewhere in the innovative handling or representations: as stray examples, one could mention Stephen Greenblatt, *Renaissance self-fashioning: From More to Shakespeare* (Chicago, 1989); Marina Warner, *Joan of Arc* (London, 1981); and Sarah Maza, *Private lives and public affairs: The causes celebres of pre-revolutionary France* (Calcutta, 1993).

58. Partha Chatterjee fully acknowledged this debt, in his 'The fruits of Macaulay's poison-tree,' in Ashok Mitra (ed.), *The truth unites* (Calcutta, 1985). For a sampling of the early-1970s critique of the Bengal Renaissance, see the essays of Asok Sen, Barun De and Sumit Sarkar in V.C. Joshi (eds), *Rammohan Roy and the process of modernization in India* (Delhi, 1975); Asok Sen, *Iswarchandra Vidyasagar and his elusive milestones* (Calcutta, 1977); and Sumit Sarkar, 'The complexities of young Bengal,' a 1973 essay, reprinted in my *Critique of colonial India* (Calcutta, 1985).

59. Commenting on William Radice's statement that the elder Thompson had been 'limited by his missionary and British imperial background,' E.P. Thompson comments: 'These stereotypes are limiting also, and are calculated to élicit predictable responses from a public as confined within the preconceptions of the "contemporary" as that of the 1920s. . . . The limits must be noted . . . but what may merit our attention more may be what lies outside those limits or confounds those expectations.' *Alien homage: Edward Thompson and Rabindranath Tagore* (Delhi, 1993), pp. 2–3.

60. Peter Linebaugh, *The London hanged: Crime and civil society in the eighteenth century* (Harmondsworth: Penguin, 1991, 1993). For an elaboration of my argument with respect to such possibilities, see my 'A Marxian social history beyond the Foucaultian turn: Peter Linebaugh's "The London hanged," ' *Economic and Political Weekly*, 30, July 29, 1995.

61. I am thinking particularly of the ongoing work or Sumit Guha on the Maharashtrian *Longue durèe*, and of Radhika Singha's *Despotism of law* (Delhi, 1997), on legal practices in early colonial India.

62. I am indebted for this resistance/transformation contrast to an illuminating oral presentation in Delhi recently by Madhavan Palat on the relevance of Marxist historiography today. He used these terms to indicate a vital contrast between Marxian and other strands of social history.

63. I owe this phrase to Pradip Kumar Datta. Such a shift in registers, it needs to be added, has become a cardinal feature of much post-colonial theory. See Arif Dirlik's pertinent comments on the dangers of reducing anti-colonial criticism to the elimination of its 'ideological and cultural legacy' alone: '. . . by fixing its gaze on the past it in fact avoids confronting the present.' Dirlik, p. 343.

64. Chatterjee, *The nation*, Chapter 10, and p. 156.

The Contents of
Subaltern Studies I–X

SSI Edited by Ranajit Guha. Delhi: Oxford University Press, 1982, 231pp. (Editorial Team: Shahid Amin, David Arnold, Partha Chatterjee, Ranajit Guha, David Hardiman and Gyan Pandey.)

> Ranajit Guha, 'On some aspects of the historiography of colonial India.'
> Partha Chatterjee, 'Agrarian relations and communalism in Bengal, 1926–35.'
> Shahid Amin, 'Small peasant commodity production and rural indebtedness: The culture of sugarcane in Eastern UP, *c.* 1880–1920.'
> David Arnold, 'Rebellious hillmen: The Gudem-Rampa risings, 1924–39.'
> Gyanendra Pandey, 'Peasant revolt and Indian nationalism: The peasant movement in Awadh, 1919–22'
> David Hardiman, 'The Indian "faction": A political theory examined.'

SSII Edited by Ranajit Guha. Delhi: Oxford University Press, 1983, 358 pp. (Editorial Team: Shahid Amin, David Arnold, Gautam Bhadra, Dipesh Chakrabarty, Partha Chatterjee, Ranajit Guha, David Hardiman and Gyan Pandey.)

> Ranajit Guha, 'The prose of counter-insurgency.'
> Gautam Bhadra, 'Two frontier uprisings in Mughal India.'
> Gyanendra Pandey, 'Rallying round the cow: Sectarian strife in the Bhojpuri region, *c.* 1888–1917.'

Stephen Henningham, 'Quit India in Bihar and the Eastern United Provinces: The dual revolt.'

Arvind N. Das, 'Agrarian change from above and below: Bihar 1947–78.'

N.K. Chandra, 'Agricultural workers in Burdwan.'

Dipesh Chakrabarty, 'Conditions for knowledge of working-class conditions: Employers, government and the jute workers of Calcutta, 1890–1940.'

Partha Chatterjee, 'More on modes of power and peasantry.'

SSIII Edited by Ranajit Guha. Delhi: Oxford University Press, 1984, 327pp. (Editorial Team: Shahid Amin, David Arnold, Gautam Bhadra, Dipesh Chakrabarty, Partha Chatterjee, Ranajit Guha, David Hardiman, Gyan Pandey and Sumit Sarkar.)

Shahid Amin, 'Gandhi as mahatma: Gorakhpur district, Eastern UP, 1921–2.'

David Arnold, 'Famine in peasant consciousness and peasant action: Madras, 1876–8.'

Dipesh Chakrabarty, 'Trade unions in a hierarchical culture: The jute workers of Calcutta, 1920–50.'

Partha Chatterjee, 'Gandhi and the critique of civil society.'

David Hardiman, 'Adivasi assertion in South Gujarat: The Devi Movement of 1922–3.'

Gyanendra Pandey, ' "Encounters and calamities": The history of a North Indian qasba in the nineteenth century.'

Sumit Sarkar, 'The conditions and nature of subaltern militancy: Bengal from Swadeshi to Non-Cooperation, *c.*1905–22.'

SSIV Edited by Ranajit Guha. Delhi: Oxford University Press, 1985. 383pp. (Editorial Team: Shahid Amin, David Arnold, Gautam Bhadra, Dipesh Chakrabarty, Partha Chatterjee, Ranajit Guha, David Hardiman, Gyan Pandey and Sumit Sarkar.)

David Arnold, 'Bureaucratic recruitment and subordination in colonial India: The Madras constabulary, 1859–1947.'

Ramachandra Guha, 'Forestry and social protest in British Kumaun, *c.* 1893–1921.'

Swapan Dasgupta, 'Adivasi politics in Midnapur, *c.* 1760–1924.'

Tanika Sarkar, 'Jitu Santal's movement in Malda, 1924–32: A study in tribal protest.'

David Hardiman, 'From custom to crime: The politics of drinking in colonial South Gujarat.'

Gautam Bhadra, 'Four rebels of eighteen-fifty-seven.'

Bernard S. Cohn, 'The command of language and the language of command.'

Gayatri Chakravorty Spivak, 'Subaltern Studies: Deconstructing historiography.'

Dipesh Chakrabarty, 'Invitation to a dialogue.'

SSV Edited by Ranajit Guha. Delhi: Oxford University Press, 1987, 296pp. (Editorial Team: Shahid Amin, David Arnold, Gautam Bhadra, Dipesh Chakrabarty, Partha Chatterjee, Ranajit Guha, David Hardiman, Gyan Pandey and Sumit Sarkar.)

David Hardiman, 'The Bhils and Shahukars of Eastern Gujarat.'

David Arnold, 'Touching the body: Perspectives on the Indian plague, 1896–1900.'

Gayatri Chakravorty Spivak, 'A literary representation of the subaltern: Mahasweta Devi's "Stanadayini." '

Ranajit Guha, 'Chandra's death.'

Shahid Amin, 'Approver's testimony, judicial discourse: The case of Chauri Chaura.'

Asok Sen, 'Subaltern Studies: Capital, class and community.'

Ajit K. Chaudhury, 'In search of a subaltern Lenin.'

Appendix A: 'Breast-giver' by Mahasweta Devi, translated by Gayatri Chakravorty Spivak.

Appendix B: The testimony of Shikari, the approver, in the court of sessions judge H.E. Holmes.

SSVI Edited by Ranajit Guha. Delhi: Oxford University Press, 1989, 335pp. (Editorial Team: Shahid Amin, David Arnold, Gautam Bhadra, Dipesh Chakrabarty, Partha Chatterjee, Ranajit Guha, David Hardiman, Gyan Pandey and Sumit Sarkar.)

Sumit Sarkar, 'The Kalki-Avatar of Bikrampur: A village scandal in early twentieth-century Bengal.'

Gautam Bhadra, 'The mentality of subalternity: Kantanama or raj-dharma.'

Julie Stephens, 'Feminist fictions: A critique of the category "non-Western woman" in feminist writings on India.'

Susie Tharu, 'Response to Julie Stephens.'

Gyanendra Pandey, 'The colonial construction of "communalism": British writings on Banaras in the nineteenth century.'

Partha Chatterjee, 'Caste and subaltern consciousness.'

Ranajit Guha, 'Dominance without hegemony and its historio-graphy.'

Veena Das, 'Subaltern as perspective.'

SSVII Edited by Partha Chatterjee and Gyanendra Pandey. Delhi: Oxford University Press, 1993, 272pp. (Editorial Team: Shahid Amin, David Arnold, Gautam Bhadra, Dipesh Chakrabarty, Partha Chatterjee, Ranajit Guha, David Hardiman, Gyan Pandey and Sumit Sarkar.)

Sudipta Kaviraj, 'The imaginary institution of India.'

Partha Chatterjee, 'A religion of urban domesticity: Sri Ramakrishna and the Calcutta middle class.'

Ranajit Guha, 'Discipline and mobilize.'

Saurabh Dube, 'Myths, symbols and community: Satnampanth of Chhattisgarh.'

Amitav Ghosh, 'The slave of MS. H.6.'

Terence Ranger, 'Power, religion and community: The Matobo case'

Upendra Baxi, 'The state's emissary: The place of law in Subaltern Studies.'

SSVIII Edited by David Arnold and David Hardiman. Delhi: Oxford University Press, 1994, 240pp.

Partha Chatterjee, 'Claims on the past: The genealogy of modern historiography in Bengal.'

Dipesh Chakrabarty, 'The difference-deferral of a colonial modernity: Public debates on domesticity in British India.'

David Hardiman, 'Power in the forests: The Dangs, 1820–1940.'

David Arnold, 'The colonial prison: Power, knowledge and penology in nineteenth-century India.'

Gyanendra Pandey, 'The prose of otherness.'

Shahid Amin and Gautam Bhadra, 'Ranajit Guha: A biographical sketch.'

Gautam Bhadra, 'A bibliography of Ranajit Guha's writings.'

SSIX Edited by Shahid Amin and Dipesh Chakrabarty. Delhi: Oxford University Press, 1996, 248pp.

Ranajit Guha, 'The small voice of history.'

Ajay Skaria, 'Writing, orality and power in the Dangs, Western India, 1800s–1920s.'

Gyan Prakash, 'Science between the lines.'

Kamala Visweswaran, 'Small speeches, subaltern gender: Nationalist ideology and its historiography.'

Shail Mayaram, 'Speech, silence and the making of partition violence in Mewat.'

Kancha Illaih, 'Productive labour, consciousness and history: The Dalitbahujan alternative.'

Vivek Dhareshwar and R. Srivatsan, ' "Rowdy-sheeters": An essay on subalternity and politics.'

Susie Tharu and Tejaswini Niranjana, 'Problems for a contemporary theory of gender.'

David Lloyd, 'Outside history: Irish new histories and the "subalternity effect." '

SSX Edited by Gautam Bhadra, Gyan Prakash, and Susie Tharu. Delhi, Oxford University Press, 1999, 252pp.

Sudesh Mishra, 'Diaspora and the difficult art of dying.'

Kaushik Ghosh, 'A market for aboriginality: Primitivism and race classification in the indentured labour market of colonial India.'

Indrani Chatterjee, 'Colouring subalternity: Slaves, concubines and social orphans in early colonial India.'

Ishita Banerjee Dube, 'Taming traditions: Legalities and histories in twentieth-century Orissa.'

Sunda Kaali, 'Spatializing History: Subaltern carnivalizations of space in Tiruppuvanan, Tamil Nadu.'

Vijay Prasad, 'Untouchable freedom: A critique of the bourgeois-landlord Indian state.'

Christopher Pinney, 'Indian magical realism: Notes on popular visual culture.'

Rosemary Sayigh, 'Gendering the "nationalist subject": Palestinian camp women's life stories.'

Additional Bibliography*

Alam, S.M. Shamsul,1993, 'When will the subaltern speak?: Central issues in historical sociology of South Asia,' *Asian Profile*, 21, 5, October, 431–47.

Apffel-Marglin, Frederique, and Purna Chandra Mishra, 1995, 'Gender and the unitary self: Looking for the subaltern in coastal Orissa,' *South Asia Research*, 15, 1, 78–130.

Arnold, David, 1984, 'Gramsci and peasant subalternity in India,' *Journal of Peasant Studies*, 11, 4, 155–77.

————, 1993, *Colonizing the body: State medicine and epidemic disease in nineteenth-century India*, Berkeley: University of California Press.

————, 1996, *The problem of nature: Environment, culture and European expansion*, Oxford: Basil Blackwell.

Bagchi, Alakananda, 1996, 'Conflicting nationalisms: The voice of the subaltern in Mahasweta Devi's Bashai Tudu,' *Tulsa Studies in Women's Literature*, 15, 1, 41–50.

Barkan, Elazar,1994, 'Post-anti-colonial histories: Representing the other in Imperial Britain,' *Journal of British Studies*, 33, 2, 180–204.

Bayly, C.A., 1988, 'Rallying around the subaltern,' *Journal of Peasant Studies*, 16, 1, 110–20.

Bhabha, Homi K., 1994, 'The postcolonial and postmodern: The question of agency,' in *The location of culture*, London: Routledge, 1994. pp. 171–97.

————, 1997, 'The voice of the Dom,' *The Times Literary Supplement*, 4923, August 8, 14–15.

Bhattacharya, Nandini, 1996, 'Behind the veil: The many masks of

*Compiled from http://www.lib.virginia.edu/area-studies/subaltern/ssallau. htm with additions by Lauren Nauta.

subaltern sexuality,' *Women's Studies International Forum*, 19, May/
June, 277–92.

Bose, Brinda, 1997, 'Contemporary problems routed through history,'
The Book Review, 21, June 6, 5–7.

Brass, Tom, 1991, 'Moral economists, subalterns, new social movements, and the (re-)emergence of a (post-)modernised (middle) peasant,' *Journal of Peasant Studies*, 18, 2, 173–205.

Brennan, Lance, 1984, Book Review, *Pacific Affairs*, 57, 3, 509–11.

Chakrabarty, Dipesh, 1992a, 'The death of history,' *Public Culture*, 4,
2, 47–65.

———, 1992b, 'Trafficking in history and theory,' in *Beyond the disciplines: The new humanities*, K.K. Ruthven, ed., Canberra.

———, 1993a, 'Marx after marxism: A subaltern historian's perspective,' *Economic and Political Weekly*, 28, May 22, 29, 1094–6.

———, 1993b, 'Marx after marxism: Subaltern histories and the question of difference,' *Polygraph*, 6/7, 10–16. [An earlier, shorter version
of 1993c.]

———, 1993c, 'Marx after marxism: History, subalternity and difference,' *Meanjin*, 52 Spring, 421–34; also in *Positions: East Asia cultures critique*, 2, 2, Fall, 446–63 (another version is in *Marxism beyond marxism*. Edited by Saree Makdisi, Cesare Casarino, and Rebecca
E. Karl, New York: Routledge, 1996, pp. 55–69).

———, 1995, 'Radical histories and question of enlightenment rationalism: Some recent critiques of Subaltern Studies,' *Economic and
Political Weekly*, 30, April 8, 751–9.

———, 1997, 'The time of history and the times of gods,' in *The politics
of culture in the shadow of captial*, edited by Lisa Lowe and David
Lloyd, Durham and London: Duke University Press, pp. 35–60.

———, 1998, 'Minority histories, subaltern pasts,' *Economic and Political Weekly*, 33, 9, February 28, 473–9.

Chatterjee, Partha, 1983, 'Peasant, politics and historiography: A response,' *Social Scientist*, 11, May 5, 58–65.

———, 1994, 'Was there a hegemonic project of the colonial state?' in
Contesting colonial hegemony: State and society in Africa and India,
edited by Dagmar Engels and Shula Marks, London: British Academic Press, pp. 79–84.

———, 1995, *The nation and its fragments: Colonial and postcolonial
histories*, Delhi: Oxford University Press.

————, 1997a, *A possible India: Essays in political criticism*, Delhi: Oxford University Press.

————, 1997b, *The present history of West Bengal: Essays in political criticism*, Delhi: Oxford University Press.

Chaudhary, R.B., 1986, 'Fruits of anti-colonial struggle denied to the masses,' *Indian Historical Review*, 12, July 1985–January 1986, 378–82.

Chaudhuri, B.B., 1986, 'History of peasant movements in British India: Some new perspectives,' *Indian Historical Review*, 12, July 1985–January 1986, 115–32.

Chopra, Suneet, 1982, 'Missing correct perspective' (Review of *SSI*) *Social Scientist*, 10, 8, 55–63.

Copland, Ian, 1983, 'Subalternative history: Reflections on the conference on the subaltern in South Asian history and society, Canberra, November 26–28, 1982,' *Australia South Asian Studies Association Review* (Canberra) 6, 3, April, 10–17.

Currie, Kate, 1995, 'The challenge to orientalist, elitist, and Western historiography: Notes on the "Subaltern Project", 1982–9,' *Dialectical Anthropology*, 20, 2, 217–46.

Dhanagare, D.N., 1988, 'Subaltern consciousness and populism: Two approaches in the study of social movements in India,' *Social Scientist*, 16, 11, 18–35.

Das Gupta, Ranajit, 1996, 'Indian working class and some recent historiographical issues,' *Economic and Political Weekly*, 31,8, February 24, L27–31.

Dienst, Richard, 1987, 'Imperialism, subalternity, autonomy: Modes of third world historiography,' *Polygraph*, 1, 67–80.

Freitag, Sandria, 1984, Book Review, *Journal of Asian Studies*, 43, 4, 779–80.

Guha, Ramachandra, 1991, Book Review, *Indian Economic and Social History Review*, 28, 1, 116–18.

————, 1995, 'Subaltern and bhadralok studies,' *Economic and Political Weekly*, 30, August 19, 2056–8.

Gupta, Dipankar, 1985, 'On altering the ego in peasant history: Paradoxes of the ethnic option,' *Peasant Studies*, 13, 1, Fall, 5–24.

Hardiman, David,1986, ' "Subaltern Studies" at Crossroads,' *Economic and Political Weekly*, 21, February 15, 288–90.

————, 1996, *Feeding the baniya: Peasants and usurers in Western India*, Delhi: Oxford University Press.

Hauser, Walter, 1991, Book Review, *American Historical Review*, 96, 1, February, 241–3.

————, 1991, Book Review, *Journal of Asian Studies*, 50, November, 968–9.

Heidrich, Petra, 1988, 'Subaltern Studies—eine neue richtung in der Indien-historiographie,' *Asien, Afrika, Lateinamerika* (Berlin) 16, 2, 251–63.

Jalal, Ayesha, 1996, 'Secularists, subalterns and the stigma of "communalism": Partition historiography revisited,' *Modern Asian Studies*, 30, July, 681–9.

Kaviraj, Sudipta, 1994, 'On the construction of colonial power: Structure, discourse, hegemony,' in *Contesting colonial hegemony: State and society in Africa and India*, edited by Dagmar Engels and Shula Marks, London: British Academic Press, pp. 19–54.

————, 1995a, 'The reversal of orientalism: Bhudev Mukhopadhyay and the project of an indigenist social theory,' in *Representing Hinduism*, edited by Vasudha Dalmia and H. von Stietencron, New Delhi: Sage Publications, pp. 253–79.

————, 1995b, *The unhappy consciousness: Bankimchandra Chattopadhyay and the formation of nationalist discourse in India*, Delhi: Oxford University Press.

————, 1997, 'A critique of the passive revolution,' in *State and politics in India*, edited by Partha Chatterjee, Delhi: Oxford University Press, pp. 45–87.

Kopf, David, 1996, Book Review, *Journal of the American Oriental Society*, 116, October–December, 754–5.

Latin America Subaltern Studies Group, 1993, 'Founding statement,' *Boundary*, 2, 20, Fall, 110–21.

Lochan, Rajiv, 1987, 'A medley for subalterns—review article,' *Contributions to Indian Sociology* (Delhi) 21, 1, January–June, 225–37.

Mallon, Florencia E., 1994, 'The promise and dilemma of Subaltern Studies: Perspectives from Latin American history,' *American Historical Review*, 99, December, 1491–1515.

Mayaram, Shail, 1997, *Resisting regimes: Myth, memory and the shaping of a Muslim identity*, Delhi: Oxford University Press.

McGuire, John, 1986, 'The making of a new history for India: Subaltern Studies [review article],' *Australian South Asia Studies Association Review* (Canberra) 10, 1, July, 115–22.

Mishra, Girish, 1983, 'Elite–People dichotomy: An exaggerated view,' *Indian Historical Review*, 12, 1–2, 133–8.

Mukherjee, Mridula, 1988, 'Peasant resistance and peasant consciousness in colonial India: "Subalterns" and Beyond,' *Economic and Political Weekly*, 23, 41, October 8, 2109–20; and 23, 42, October 15, 2174–85.

Nag, Sajal, 1984, 'Peasant and the Raj: Study of a subaltern movement in Assam (1893–94),' *North-East Quarterly*, Dibrugarh: Assam, India, 2, July 1, 24–36.

O'Hanlon, Rosalind, and David Washbrook, 1992, 'After Orientalism: Culture, criticism, and politics in the third world,' *Comparative Studies in Society and History*, 34, 1, 141–67.

Pandian, M.S.S., 1992, *The image trap: M.G. Ramachandran in film and politics*, New Delhi: Sage Publications.

Pandey, Gyanendra, 1992, 'In defence of the fragment: Writing about Hindu–Muslim riots in India today,' *Representations*, 37, Winter, 27–55

———, 1995, 'Voices from the edge: The struggle to write subaltern histories,' *Ethnos*, 60, 3–4, 223–42.

Patnaik, Arun K., 1988, 'Gramsci's concept of common sense: Towards a theory of subaltern consciousness in hegemony processes,' *Economic and Political Weekly*, 23, 5, January 30, PE2–10.

Perusek, Darshan, 1992, 'Subaltern consciousness and the historiography of the Indian revolution of 1857,' *Novel*, 25, 3, Spring, 286–302. [Reprinted in *Economic and Political Weekly*, 28, 37, September 11, 1993, 1931–6.]

Prakash, Gyan. 1990a, *Bonded histories: Genealogies of labour servitude in colonial India*, Cambridge: Cambridge University Press.

———, 1990b, 'Writing post-Orientalist histories in the third world: Perspectives from Indian historiography,' *Comparative Studies in Society and History*, 32, April 2, 383–408.

———, 1992a, 'Postcolonial criticism and Indian historiography,' *Social Text*, 31/32, 8–19.

———, 1992b, 'Can the subaltern ride?" A reply to O'Hanlon and

Washbrook,' *Comparative Studies in Society and History*, 34, 1, January, 168–84.

————, 1994, 'Subaltern studies as postcolonial criticism,' *American Historical Review*, 99, December, 1475–90.

————, 1995a, editor, *After colonialism: Imperial histories and postcolonial displacements*, Princeton: Princeton University Press.

————, 1995b, 'Orientalism now,' *History and Theory*, 34, 3, 199–211.

————, 1997, 'The modern nation's return in the archaic,' *Critical inquiry*, 23, 33, Spring, 536–55.

————, 1999, *Another reason: Science and the imagination of modern India*, Princeton: Princeton University Press.

Rai, A.S., 1997, ' "Thus spake the subaltern . . .": Postcolonial criticism and the scene of desire,' *Discourse: Berkeley Journal for Theoretical Studies in Media and Culture*, 19, 2, 163.

Sarkar, Sumit, 1993, 'The fascism of the Sangha Parivar,' *Economic and Political Weekly*, 27, 5, January 20, 163–7.

————, 1994, 'Orientalism revisited: Saidian frameworks in the writing of modern Indian history,' *Oxford Literary Review*, 16, 1–2, 205–24.

————, 1997, *Writing social history*, Delhi: Oxford University Press.

Sathyamurthy, T.V., 1990, 'Indian peasant historiography: A critical perspective on Ranajit Guha's work,' *Journal of Peasant Studies*, 18, 1, 93–141.

Scott, David, 1995, 'A note on the demand of criticism,' *Public Culture*, 8, 41–50.

Siddiqi, Majid, 1985, Book Review, *Indian Economic and Social History Review*, 22, 1, 94.

Singh, Lata, 1995, 'Subaltern historiographic critique of colonialist and national discourses,' *Indian Historical Review*, 21, 1–2, July 1994–January 1995, 99–112.

Spivak, Gayatri Chakravorty, 1988, 'Can the subaltern speak?' *In marxism and the interpretation of culture*, edited by Cary Nelson and Lawrence Grossberg, London: Macmillan, pp. 271–313.

Stein, Burton, 1990, 'A decade of historical efflorescence,' *South Asia Research*, 10, 2, 125–38.

Usuda, Masayuki, 1997, '*Subaltern Studies IX*: Writings on South Asian History and Society,' *Biblio*, 2, 6, 15–17.

Yadav, Yogendra, 1989, 'Whither Subaltern Studies?' *New Quest*, 76, July–August, 245–50.

Yang, Anand, 1985, Book Review, *Journal of Asian Studies*, 45, 1, November, 178.

Zinkin, Taya, 1989, Book Review, *Asian Affairs*, February 20, 86.